A Dictionary of the Old West

A DICTIONARY

OF THE

OLD WEST

1850-1900

BY PETER WATTS

Alfred A. Knopf ○ New York ○ 1977

**This Is a Borzoi Book
Published by Alfred A. Knopf, Inc.**

Copyright © 1977 by Peter Watts

All rights reserved under International and Pan-American Copyright
Conventions. Published in the United States by Alfred A. Knopf, Inc.,
New York, and simultaneously in Canada by Random House of Canada
Limited, Toronto. Distributed by Random House, Inc., New York.

Because this page cannot legibly accommodate all acknowledgments,
permissions to reproduce art can be found on page 401.

Library of Congress Cataloging in Publication Data

Watts, Peter Christopher.
A dictionary of the Old West, 1850–1900.

Bibliography: p.
1. Americanisms.
2. English language—Provincialisms—The West.
3. The West—Social life and customs.
4. English language—19th century.
I. Title.
PE2970.W4W3   1976   427'.9'78   76-13724

Manufactured in the United States of America

First Edition

This book is dedicated with respect
to
the memory of

J. Frank Dobie

whose love and knowledge of brasada
words first made me want to write it.

Special Acknowledgments

Grateful acknowledgment is made by the compiler of this dictionary to those authors and editors responsible for the authoritative works which have been cited in confirmation of the authenticity of terms; especially—

Andy Adams: *The Log of a Cowboy* 1909

Ramon Adams: *Western Words* 1944

Jules Verne Allen: *Cowboy Lore* 1933

Albert Barrère and Charles G. Leland: *A Dictionary of Slang, Jargon and Cant* 1897

John Russell Bartlett: *Dictionary of Americanisms* 1877

Lester V. Berrey and Melvin van den Bark: *The American Thesaurus of Slang* 1942

Hank Wieand Bowman: *Antique Guns* 1953

E. Gould Buffum: *An Account of Six Months in the Gold Mines* 1850

Robert R. Dykstra: *The Cattle Towns* 1971

Duncan Emrich: *It's an Old Wild West Custom* 1951

John S. Farmer: *Americanisms Old and New* 1889

William Foster-Harris: *The Look of the Old West* 1955

Wayne Gard: *The Chisholm Trail* 1954

John A. Hawgood: *The American West* 1967

F. W. Hodge: *Handbook of the American Indians North of Mexico* 1907–10

Stan Hoig: *The Humor of the American Cowboy* 1960

Robert West Howard (ed.): *This Is the West* 1957

William Dale Jennings: *The Cowboys* 1971

Charles Lee Karr, Jr., and Caroll Robbins Karr: *Remington Handguns* 1960

Nelson Klose: *A Concise Study Guide to the American Frontier* 1964

David Lavender: *The Penguin Book of the American West* 1969

William Christie MacLeod: *The American Indian Frontier* 1928 and "Police and Punishment among the Native Americans of the Plains" 1937–38

Mitford M. Mathews (ed.): *A Dictionary of Americanisms on Historical Principles* 1951

Don McCarthy (ed.): *The Language of the Mosshorn* 1936

Tom McHugh: *The Time of the Buffalo* 1972

D'Arcy McNickle: *The Indian Tribes of the United States* 1962

H. L. Mencken: *The American Language III* 1948

Jo Mora: *Trail Dust and Saddle Leather* 1950

Lewis W. Newton and Herbert P. Gambrell: *Texas Yesterday and Today* 1949

Escott North: *The Saga of the Cowboy* 1942

Ernest Staples Osgood: *The Day of the Cattleman* 1929

Morley Roberts: *The Western Avernus* 1924

Paul A. Rossi and David C. Hunt: *The Art of the Old West* 1971

Carl P. Russell: *Firearms, Traps and Tools of the Mountain Men* 1967

George Frederick Ruxton: *Life in the Far West* 1849

Mari Sandoz: *The Buffalo Hunters* 1954 and *The Cattlemen* 1958

Walter Prescott Webb: *The Great Plains* 1931

Paul I. Wellman: *The Trampling Herd* 1939

Harold Wentworth: *American Dialect Dictionary* 1944

Maurice H. Weseen: *A Dictionary of American Slang* 1934

George F. Willison: *Here They Dug the Gold* 1952

and, finally, to all the works of J. Frank Dobie.

Introduction

This dictionary has two purposes: first, to be a guide to the Old West for readers of books covering the period 1850–1900; second, to record certain words and phrases belonging to the Old West.

It is a dangerous subject and period to cover, mainly because a number of terms whose origins are now attributed to the Old West have actually been brought into use in the present century. The media of television, movies, and fiction have greatly influenced a vast audience, so that many people have a mental picture of a period and place that never existed. So when I faced the task of collecting the contents of this book, I had a list of words which originated partly in the Old West itself and partly in the imagination of twentieth-century pulp-fiction and script writers. That is not to say, however, that many novelists in the 1920s, for example, did not collect words directly from men who had been alive during the period we cover here.

What can be done to separate the two has been done, but it is often difficult to find the dividing line between the authentic and the phony. An added difficulty is that many authentic words were not recorded until the twentieth century, and often writers in the Old West itself are not to be entirely relied upon to give us the truth, or at least the whole truth. There were many pulp-writers about in the last quarter of the nineteenth century who consistently gave a false picture of the frontier.

Still another difficulty is that a number of men who left records of certain times and places, who were eye-witnesses of historical events, show a dismaying tendency toward mishearing and obviously misrecording words. For example, in accounts by soldiers, the names of those present in battles are often so varied in spelling that the reader is hard put to know if he is reading of one or two men. In general, the spelling of men on the frontier seems to have had the delightful but confusing freedom of the letter-writers of the sixteenth and seventeenth centuries. At times it has the wild abandon of Clark of exploring fame. Just to see what the ears, tongues, and pens of men have done with the words *caballada* and *cabrie* makes the point.

The reader cannot fail to notice that little guidance to pronunciation is given here. This has been generally omitted for the simple reason that in many cases there is no sure way of knowing exactly, and often even roughly, how the Old Westerner did pronounce his words. Certainly, many of the terms contained in this volume are used today, but I would hesitate to vouch for the fact that the old-timer employed the same pronunciation. It must be remembered that, particularly during the early period, the men using these words were not necessarily Westerners in the modern meaning of the word. Many of them spoke words that they had never seen written down. They caught a sound, sometimes incorrectly, and frequently proceeded to mangle it with their tongues—and, as often as not, with a delightful result. So, when you see a word which to you is plainly Spanish, you can be sure that an old-timer could make two or six different sounds of it. Take the word *jáquima,* for example—his imaginative tongue could make *hakima, hakeema, hackymore, hackamore,* or *hackmore* out of it. *Adobe* (ah-doh-bay) could be *adobee, adoab, aydoab, 'dobie,* and heaven knows what else. So I have generally steered clear of pronunciation, and I doubt very much if anybody will blame me for it. Just remember, if you see a Spanish letter *j,* it is pronounced like a guttural *h* (the Irish *gh* or Scottish and North German *ch*). The Spanish treat their *g* at times in much the same way. The Mexicans never sounded an *h,* so the word *hombre* was said *om-bray.* Also the Mexican *d* was soft, rather like *dh* or the thick *th* in the English word *they.* Hence, *remuda* was pronounced *ray-moo-dha*—though the average cowboy no doubt made it into *ray-moo-der, remudy,* et cetera. On the other hand, if he were a Texan raised with Mexicans, he might have acquired a nice Mexican accent.

So far as the language of the cattle-range is concerned, we must not forget that, in certain areas, quite a substantial part of cow-crews was made up of Negroes. Little work has been done on the influence of their language on the speech of the range, and probably it is now too late to assess it.

In the period of, say, 1850–1880, the proportion of true Westerners to intruders was very small indeed. Cattlemen, corrupting and anglicizing Spanish from Old Texas, from Arizona and New Mexico, were first- (or possibly) second-generation Texans who worked cheek-by-jowl with Tejanos. Some of these Anglo-Saxons brought English and Celtic words from the British Isles via the U.S. Eastern Seaboard and the South (where some must have come under the influence of the French and Negroes). In Texas, they added pure and bastard Spanish to their vocabulary. When these men moved on to other parts of the West, their tongues and ears picked up sounds from Californios, gold-seekers from the slums of Europe, Welsh and Cornish miners, Dutchmen, French and métis from Canada, and Indians speaking a score of tongues. In the army one moment and deserting the next were men of many nationalities: homesteaders—Dutch, Swedes, Swiss, and the rest; Yankee and Jewish traders; Irish railroad workers; squawmen, trappers, lumberjacks, gamblers, whores, and preachers. They all contributed cloth and color to the tapestry, a small portion of which I have attempted to record here.

Cattle-range vocabulary was mostly provided by the Mexicans and the Anglo-Saxons: the latter supplied a wry, slangy humor that gave the language an individual tang and pithy richness that is a delight; the former gave the sonorous, apt words to describe the gear of the stockman and the details of the country. The American cowboy took those dignified Spanish words and cut them to waggish shapes, created phrases which have become a part of the English language wherever it is spoken, and produced a nicety of meaning that no amount of university education could have succeeded in doing. Powerful, healthy language always starts in the so-called lower strata of society. When the educated man controls language, it loses its rich taste, its contact with the earth, its very means of renewal. I like to think that some of the earthiness of Western speech, some of the irony of its humor, was provided by the Negro cowboy and the Negro cook, who so often dominated a crew. The conclusion cannot be proven, but it seems logical.

There is no room here to enumerate the peoples who contributed to the speech of the West. However, if I delayed the reader a moment longer without mentioning the influence of the Indian, an injustice would have been done. A culture gains more unconsciously than consciously, and the presence of the Indians made a profound impression on the whites which, possibly without their being aware of it, stayed with them. Indian skills crept into the behavior of the frontiersman, and Indian words settled forever into the language. Words of Indian origin are now embedded in the English language far beyond the boundaries of the United States.

No one is more aware than I that my study is incomplete, and it would be foolish to pretend otherwise. And no doubt even more terms will come to light in time. However, some sort of start has been made, and it is possible that enthusiastic and helpful readers, inspired or infuriated by the interpretations they see here, will provide fresh information, quoting, I hope, chapter and verse to substantiate their claims. You will note in the pages that follow just how much authorities may disagree on the meaning of a word.

Great use has been made of the works of more profound scholars than myself. Without the works of such respected and delightful writers as J. Frank Dobie, Andy Adams, Ramon Adams, and Jo Mora, no start could have been made. Also used have been a number of dictionaries of Americanisms, slang, jargon, cant, and English dialect, to which must be added the reading of fictional works, which, one suspects, should be numbered in thousands. Owen Wister, Ned Buntline, Zane Grey, Jack Schaeffer, Frank O'Rourke, Luke Short, Louis L'Amour, Ernest Haycox, Will Henry, Wayne D. Overholser, Dudley Dean, Les Savage, Steve Frazee, Norman Fox—one could go on forever, it seems. All of which goes to show that while the market for Western stories is not proportionately large, it is never-dying. Which is just as well, because quite a number of us make our living from them.

· · ·

Any literary work is a solitary task, but beyond the isolation of the work-room a writer invariably has allies without whom the work could not be done. This dictionary is no exception. My wife, Sonia, has borne patiently with me for fifteen years, listening to rambling monologues and hunting for references. My friend and colleague Newland Hunt untiringly read and re-read drafts and proofs. Emmie Mygatt, of Western Writers of America, found time in a very busy life to send me invaluable material. Mrs. Marjorie Read, a friend and neighbor, undertook the typing of the first drafts. The man essential to the production of a book such as this is, of course, the editor—and professional writers know at the outset whether he is an ogre or a friend. From the moment that Angus Cameron of Alfred A. Knopf saw a fragment of the first draft, he offered me encouragement, advice from his store of knowledge and experience, and, above all, a boundless en-thusiasm for the subject. In addition, I would like to thank his assistants and colleagues at Knopf—Bill Reynolds, Bobbie Bristol, Virginia Tan, Martha Kaplan, and Neal T. Jones—for their help. Last, my thanks to Paul A. Rossi, without whose sharp eye and background knowledge of the Old West there would be many gaps in the text.

A Dictionary of the Old West

Cross-references appear in *bold, italic type.*
A cross-reference is made when it elaborates on a point under discussion (an entry may not be cross-referenced each time it appears) or clarifies a term that may be unfamiliar to the reader.

Variants appear in **bold, roman type.**

Abbreviations used:

Fr = French   NW = Northwest
Mex-Sp = Mexican-Spanish   SW = Southwest
Sp = Spanish   w = western

abergoin
Also **abrogans**. Supposed to be a corruption of *aborigine,* applied to the Indians and used fairly frequently in nineteenth-century literature. Hodge 1907–10 quotes **aberginian** as a collective term used by the early settlers in the East for the Indian tribes to the north. "The word may be a corruption of Abnaki [an Algonkian confederacy of tribes], or a misspelling for 'aborigine.' " He quotes variants—**abarginy, abergeny, aberieney, aborginny**—and goes back as early as 1628 to find them. (Farmer 1889; Bartlett 1877; Chisholm 1966)

aboard
To **get aboard** meant to fork (mount) a horse.

about East
About right. In the rough days of the Western settlements, the word *East* meant "good," "proper," "civilized," and is met in a number of terms. (Farmer 1889)

above my bend
Out of my power, beyond my capabilities. Also **above my huckleberry.** (Farmer 1889)

above snakes
Above ground. (Bartlett 1877)

abra
(Mex-Sp; SW, especially Texas). A narrow pass between hills, a narrow valley. (Mathews 1951)

ace in the hole
A man's secret advantage—with reference to the game of stud poker, in which the first card, dealt face down, is the "hole card": if an ace, it gives the player an advantage over his opponents. It makes sense that in the latter days of the Old West this expression came to mean the concealed gun in shoulder-holster, sleeve, boot-top, or anywhere else a man could hide one. (Ramon Adams 1944)

acequia
(Sp; SW). An irrigation canal. Dunn 1886: "All through this country are the ruins of immense *acequias* (irrigation canals—sometimes written **zequias**) some of which can be traced through lengths of fifty miles or more." Mathews 1951: **acequia madre:** a main irrigation ditch. (Dobie 1930)

acion
(Mex-Sp *ación*; extreme SW, border country, and California). A *stirrup-leather.* (Ramon Adams 1944)

acorn calf
A runt calf. (Weseen 1934; Ramon Adams 1944)

across lots
By short-cuts, in the quickest manner. Cited by Bartlett 1877 from an 1857 speech by Brigham Young.

act up
To misbehave. (Andy Adams 1909)

adios
(Sp *adiós*). Good-bye. A Southwesternism that became general among Anglos in the West. Meaning literally, "to God," a convenience for *vaya con Dios* ("go with God"). (Dobie 1930; Ramon Adams 1944)

adobe
(Sp).
(1) Brick made of clay, straw, and water, formed in a mold and hardened in the sun. *Adobe* designated both the material (Ramon Adams 1944) and a building constructed of the material (Ramon Adams 1944). This method of construction came from Mexico, but such buildings were to be found in the early days as far north as Wyoming and Montana. Often shortened to **'dobe;** Farmer 1889 spelled it **adobe, adobie, 'dobie.**
(2) Anything inferior: a Mexican dollar was called a **'dobe dollar, 'dobie dollar,** or simply a **'dobie.** (Webster's Third New International Dictionary 1909; Ramon Adams 1944; Mathews 1951)

afoot
Said of a man who had lost or sold his horse. In a world of horsemen this word contained a world of meaning. To be afoot in cattle-country could mean danger, which varied according to time and place. In a big country, a man afoot was in danger from thirst and starvation, from wild beasts, Indians, and the elements, and from cattle—which had no fear of a dismounted man, whose journey home might be greatly increased by the need to avoid the animals. (Ramon Adams 1944)

agarita
(Mex-Sp; SW). Also *agrito.* Wild currant. As quoted from Dobie 1929: "every leaf an armada of spines."

agregado
(Mex-Sp; SW). A farmhand or a man allowed to work for himself on part of the landowner's soil. (Mathews 1951)

agrito
(Mex-Sp; Texas). A term applied to a great many species of thornbrush—among them, the wild barberry, genus *Berberidaceae.* Dobie 1941: "The leaves of the agrito are themselves thorns, each with three to seven lobes; its currant-like fruit makes a jelly with a sting of the wild in its taste and wine-ruby light in its color that no other jelly can equal."

aguardiente
(Sp corruption of *agua ardiente:* fiery water). Originally brandy, but its meaning widened and its progress is hard to trace. Certainly it was extended to cover whiskey, then was used for spirits distilled from Mexican red wine. Later it covered rum as well as whiskey and brandy and was re-spelled in various forms: **aquardiente, aquedent, aquediente,** etc. (Farmer 1889)

aguatamote
See *batamote.*

agur-forty
Aqua fortis (nitric acid) used medicinally. (Farmer 1889)

aim
To intend: "I aim to saddle up and go." Possibly of Tennesseean origin, it was used throughout the West. (Wentworth 1944)

airtights
Canned food. Of limited variety during our period, but canned peaches and tomatoes were the great refreshers. Milk in cans was also a wonderful

asset when the only way to acquire the stuff was by roping a long-horned cow and persuading the reluctant lady to part with her dairy produce. Some harebrains did attempt this, but it was not a practice to be recommended. Gail Borden, of course, canned beef—**meat biscuit** (Wellman 1939), **beef biscuit**—in the early 1850s and later and made a fortune with condensed milk. (Ramon Adams 1944; Rossi 1975)

alameda
(Mex-Sp: poplar grove, public walk—from *álamo:* cottonwood tree, poplar; S and W). A road or trail bordered by trees; possibly a boulevard. (Mathews 1951)

alamo
(Sp *álamo:* cottonwood tree, poplar; Texas and SW). *Populus monilifera.* This simple Spanish word for poplar is surely the most evocative in the American language, for it gave its name to the old Spanish mission fort built in 1756 within sight of San Antonio de Bexar. Here, against a powerful Mexican army, the original Texans (with a number of adventurous spirits who became Texans overnight) made a stand which they all knew was to the death—one that will stay in the history books for as long as the story of the Greeks at Thermopylae. See also *cottonwood.*

albino
A pigmentless or near-pigmentless horse "color." A white to pale-cream horse with bluish eyes. (Ramon Adams 1944)

alcalde
(Sp; SW). Also **alcade, alcaide.** A title applied to a mayor or sometimes to a judge in the Southwest. Among totally Mexican populations, the alcalde appears to have been mayor, judge, and chief of police all rolled into one. (Lamar 1966)

alfilaria
(Sp *alfilerillo*). Also **alfilena, alfilerilia.** *Erodium cicutarium.* The pin grass of the plains. (Mathews 1951)

alforja
(Mex-Sp). A saddlebag, a bag, a bag to hang on either side of a pack-saddle. Anglicized as **alforche, alforge, alforka, alforki,** with *alforje* as a respectable Mexican variant. (Ruxton 1847; Ramon Adams 1944)

algarroba
(Mex-Sp; SW). Also **algaroba.** *Prosopis juliflora.* A variety of low-growing *mesquite.* Sometimes called **honey mesquite.** (Dobie 1929; Mathews 1951)

algodon
(Sp *algodón*). In the Southwest this word for cotton was sometimes applied to the *cottonwood* tree. (Mathews 1951)

alkali
(1) Country badly affected by alkali. (Mathews 1951). Also **alkali-land.**
(2) An inhabitant of alkali country. (Weseen 1934)

alkalied
(1) Said of a man who had drunk and become sick on water impregnated with alkali, or of a stream or soil affected by alkali. (Beadle 1870)
(2) Said of a man who was a veteran of the big dry country (Weseen 1934), much as in the desert fighting of World War II one would remark that a man had sand behind his ears.

alkali-flat
A flat stretch of country ruined by alkali. Certainly used before 1850. (Mathews 1951)

alkali grass
Possibly also **alkaline grass** (Mathews 1951), referring to grass growing in alkaline soil in the Rocky Mountain region. Sometimes applied to *wheat grass.*

alla
(Sp *allá;* SW). Yonder. (Dobie 1930)

all-a-settin'
In good condition. Applied to stock, for example, after good grazing. (Farmer 1889)

all-day
Good, strong, capable of working a whole day; hence, an **all-day horse.** I recall a wonderful movie seen as a child starring Chic Sale and called, if I remember rightly, *The Star Witness,* in which Chic referred, in that never-forgotten voice, to an **all-day sucker,** meaning a long-lasting candy. (Berrey and van den Bark 1942; Mathews 1951)

all hands and the cook
A cattle-range phrase meaning everybody—the whole outfit, even the ornery cook. (Ramon Adams 1944)

allow
(1) To declare, assert.
(2) To think, suppose. (Wentworth 1944)

all-thorn
Koeberlinia spinosa. Thorny brush found in Southwest desert country. (Hornady 1908). See also *jonco.*

amansador
(Sp; SW and California). A horse-tamer. (Mora 1950)

amble
To go, to walk, indicating an unhurried pace. Suggests a horseman's dislike of walking. (Ramon Adams 1944)

amigo
(Sp). Friend. Generally used by Western men in its Spanish sense. (Ramon Adams 1944; Berrey and van den Bark 1942)

amole
(Mex-Sp from Nahuatl; SW). Also **ammole, amolli.** A variety of plants from which soap can be made. (Waters 1950)

angle
To move at an angle from a given point. Andy Adams 1909: "He angled across the street." Wentworth 1944 mentions a modern Texan definition: to enter.

angle iron
The triangular instrument that hung outside a cookhouse on the range. The cook rattled a striker around inside the triangle to produce a deafening row, which he augmented with such persuasive phrases as "Come an' git it or I throw it away." (Rossi 1975)

► **Anglo**
(SW). A person not of Mexican or Indian origin. Found generally throughout Western fiction, and a good deal of factual Western literature. Its meaning, under some circumstances, could be taken to further exclude Italians, Greeks, et al. and, in fact, to include only "true" Anglo-Saxons, whoever they may be—for Scots, Irish, and Welsh were counted as Anglos. (Mathews 1951)

angoras
Also **woolies.** Chaps made from goathide,

with the hair retained and worn on the outside. (Ramon Adams 1944; Foster-Harris 1955)

animal
A bull. Just as a Westerner would avoid any inference of sex in female company by saying *cow* for *bull,* he might also say *animal* for *bull.* (Mencken 1948; Weseen 1934; Wentworth 1944; Ramon Adams 1944)

anquera
(Sp). A wide piece of leather found at the base of a Western saddle lacking a rear jockey. (Ramon Adams 1944). Used for riding double, the anquera served as a pad for the second rider while protecting his clothing from the horse's sweat. Farrow 1881 says that the Mexicans and Californians used it as part of their regular saddle equipment, but Rossi 1975 notes that it was sometimes used "simply for looks." Rossi identifies the anquera as a flanker fastened back of the saddle and adds that though some were small, others, highly decorated, extended over the horse's rump and reached almost to the ground.

ante
Also **ante-up.** To risk. In ordinary American: to bet; but in the West it came to mean "to pay up," "to hand over." (Bartlett 1877; Farmer 1889)

antelope
Antilocapra americana. The antelope of the West that was not an antelope at all. A *pronghorn* or prongbuck found on the High Plains, but not in wooded country or the mountains. (Parkman 1872; Stansbury 1852)

antelope brush
Purshia tridentata. A common brush growing in dry country. (Mathews 1951)

antelope goat
Oreamnos americanus. The **Rocky Mountain goat.** (Mathews 1951). See *mountain goat.*

antelope jack rabbit
Lepus alleni. A species of hare living in desert country. (Mathews 1951). See also *jack rabbit.*

antelope range
Open country frequented by the *pronghorn.* (Mathews 1951)

anti-godlin'
Going sideways. Ramon Adams 1944 says: "to go . . . in a round about way." Wentworth 1944 uses **anti-goslin'**, meaning "crooked" in any sense: for example, a hat not on straight. (Allen 1933; Berrey and van den Bark 1942)

antigua
(Sp: ancient; SW). A term for an old-timer. (Dobie 1930)

anxious seat
A front seat at a revivalist meeting, indicating that the occupant was anxious to be saved. William Dale Jennings uses the term in his novel *The Cowboys* (1971). Berrey and van den Bark 1942 and Mathews 1951 quote the term, but not as a Westernism.

Apache plume
Fallucia paradoxa. A shrub of the Southwest, said to be so called because of its reddish seed cluster resembling a feathered Indian head-dress. (Dobie 1956)

aparejo
(Sp). Also **aparayho; Mexican pack-saddle.** An old and simple form of pack-saddle, of padded leather or canvas, though sometimes made of quilted cloth. Literature mentions Indians, particularly the Apache and Navaho, using this kind of saddle for riding. Gregg 1844 writes: "a large pad consisting of a leather case stuffed with hay, which covers the back of the mule and extends halfway down on both sides, this is secured with a wide sea-grass banda, with which the poor brute is so tightly laced as to reduce the middle of the body to half its natural size." (Berrey and van den Bark 1942; Ramon Adams 1944; Chisholm 1966)

apishamore
An arrangement of rugs or blankets to lie on; a bed; a saddle-blanket made of buffalo-calf skins. (Ruxton 1849; Bartlett 1877)

Appaloosa
Also **Apaloochy, Palouse.** A strain of horse whose spots, of varying size and color, can be felt with the fingertips. The word is said to originate from the fact that such horses were bred by the Nez Percé Indians in the Palouse River country of eastern Washington and central Idaho. Among the Indians, Appaloosas were considered good war-horses and were said to have great stamina. Lewis and Clark also noted the excellence of the animals. The type is certainly a very ancient one, and paintings of it appear in the Neolithic caves of Europe. (Dobie 1952; Ramon Adams 1944; Chisholm 1966; Glyn 1971)

apple

A saddlehorn. A real disgrace to *grab the apple* or *pull leather* when trying to stay on a wild one. (Weseen 1934; Ramon Adams 1944; Mora 1950)

apple-horn

A type of saddle, the horn of which suggested the shape of an apple. Ramon Adams 1944 says it was a term given to the saddles of the 1880s which replaced those with broad horns. Rossi 1975 notes interestingly that the horn was more like an apple cut in half—usually of wood and screwed down into the metal plate or base and covered with leather—and that it was actually not too small, but often measured three to four inches at the base. He adds that it was developed in the early 1860s and was common on cattle-drives out of Texas in the post–Civil War period.

appola

(thought to be American Indian, from French-Canadian). Frémont used the term as early as 1843, referring to sticks on which small pieces of meat were roasted over an open fire. (Mathews 1951)

apron

The skirt of a saddle. Possibly not solely a Westernism. (Mathews 1951)

apron-faced

Said of a horse with a white forehead and face. (Ramon Adams 1944; Berrey and van den Bark 1942 quote it, but not as a Westernism)

apron-straps

Also **apron-strings**. Straps attached to the leather skirt of a saddle, for securing bedroll, slicker, and all manner of things to a saddle. (Dobie 1941)

aquardiente, aquedent, aquediente

See *aguardiente.*

arancel

(Mex-Sp; Texas and SW). Also **aransel**. A legal charge, an import tax.

arapaho

A corruption of *aparejo.* Somebody sometime must have confused the term with the Arapaho Indians.

Arbuckle

(1) A generic term for coffee, taken by cattlemen from the trade-name

paramount throughout the West. (Ramon Adams 1944; Foster-Harris 1955). Also **Arbuckle's.**

(2) A greenhorn cowhand said to have been obtained by the boss in exchange for premium stamps given away with cans of coffee. (Weseen 1934; Ramon Adams 1944)

arciones
(Mex-Sp). Stirrup-leathers. (Mora 1950)

argolla del entreatador
(Mex-Sp; SW and California). Part of saddle equipment: the ring of the rigging straps.

▶ **Arizona nightingale**
A burro, a donkey. (Ramon Adams 1944)

Arizona strawberries
Also **Arkansas strawberries; Mexican straw-berries; prairie strawberries.** Dried beans, pink in color. Only a man who made his living on the back of a horse that pitched the kinks out of its back when mounted could live on a straight diet of the things. It has been suggested that the only way these beans could be properly digested *was* for the consumer to break wild horses. Beans were also called **strawberries** by lumberjacks and by lodgers. (Weseen 1934; Berrey and van den Bark 1942)

Arizona tenor
A man suffering from tuberculosis. The dry desert air was considered beneficial for such sufferers. (Berrey and van den Bark 1942; Ramon Adams 1944; Mathews 1951)

Arkansas toothpick
Bartlett 1877 says: "a bowie-knife of a peculiar kind, the blade of which shuts into the handle." Farmer 1889 adds: "a grimly facetious name for a folding bowie-knife of large dimensions." Mathews 1951 agrees. It is interesting to note that a number of writers in the last century referred to any large knife as a bowie knife (with a small *b*). However, in spite of the examples above, *Arkansas toothpick* is generally accepted as referring to a knife with a long and sharply tapering blade. (Weseen 1934; Foster-Harris 1955). Weseen called it "a large sheath knife; a bowie knife; a dagger." But Ramon Adams 1944 knew better. He described it as "a large sheath knife; a dagger," showing that he did not accept *bowie* as a generic term covering this kind of sticker. See also *Bowie knife.*

armas
(Mex-Sp). A forerunner of chaps which were little more than two large flaps

of hide fastened to the saddle and protecting a rider's legs against brush and thorns. (Foster-Harris 1955). Not to be confused with armitas (see *chinks*), which were worn by the rider, not the horse.

armitas
See *chinks.*

army model
When applied to revolvers the term indicated
U.S. army specifications, which required a larger caliber and longer barrel than that of the *navy model.* (Foster-Harris 1955; Karr and Karr 1960)

arrastra
(Mex-Sp; SW). Also **arrastre, rastra.** A millstone used in a primitive fashion for crushing gold or silver ore on a stone bed. Literature makes several mentions of such from the 1830s into the present century. (Dunn 1886)

arriero
(Mex-Sp). A muleteer, usually a Mexican. A *packer.* (Gregg 1844; Ramon Adams 1944)

arroba
(Mex-Sp; Texas and SW). A measurement of weight, equal to about 25 pounds. One finds Longhorns measured by this unit. Sometimes used in Old Texas even among the Anglos. (Wellman 1939; Mathews 1951)

arroyo
(Mex-Sp; SW). Also **arroya** (Wentworth 1944). A deep-sided watercourse, usually cut in a soft surface, with or without water in it. In Arizona, for much of the year they were dry, when they were referred to as **arroyos secos.** (Weseen 1934; Chisholm 1966)

artillery
Hand-guns generally. (Dobie 1930; Ramon Adams 1944)

ast
A variant of *ask,* still found in Eastern and Southern U.S. dialect and in British dialect. Also **ax,** which is still heard in parts of southeastern England.

as they ran
(Texas). If you bought or sold cattle as they ran, you did so without counting them and took a chance on gain or loss. That was in the days when men lived on their reputations. (Dobie 1941)

a-tall
(Texas). At all. (Wentworth 1944)

atole
(Mex-Sp from Nahuatl; SW). Corn meal, or porridge made from corn. (Ober 1885)

augur
(1) To talk. (Ramon Adams 1944)
(2) See *big augur.*

ax
See *ast.*

babiche
Of Canadian-Indian origin, meaning either a rawhide thong or mesh made of such thongs. The term reached the Canadian border states and the Far West in the early days of our period. Perhaps not truly a Westernism in the terms of this book. (Hodge 1907–10)

bach
Also **batch.** Said of a man or men keeping house without the aid of a woman; in fact: **to bachelor.**

back down
(1) To give way, to give in to pressure or threat.
(2) To back up, to support.

back East
In the Eastern states. The opposite of the Easterner's **out West.** (Wentworth 1944)

backfire
A method of fire-fighting on grassland: a counter-fire was deliberately lit ahead, and when the original fire reached the burned land, it would die out. (Ramon Adams 1944)

back jockey
See *rear jockey.*

back out
To leave a situation with your face to the enemy, particularly if he held a gun and was threatening you. If you wisely decided that a situation was

dangerous in a crowded place—even if you held the gun—you also backed out, in case your unprotected rear tempted an enemy.

back-track
To go along a set of tracks or *sign* against the direction traveled by the man or beasts that made them. (Mathews 1951)

back trail
(1) The trail just traveled by a man.
(2) To go back the way one has come.
(3) To follow the tracks or *sign* of another, man or animal, back to the point from which he came. (Ramon Adams 1944)

back up
Much the same meaning as **back down.** To go out of a situation without turning your back; to retreat morally. Odd to remember that this also means to support someone, to back his play.

badger
Taxidea taxus. Also known as a **taxel.** The Western species was often called the **Mexican badger.** Smaller and more carnivorous than its European relative, it was lethal to most other rodents and ferocious if cornered, capable of holding off a dog. Silvery black above and with a lighter yellowish color along its belly, it had a broad white stripe along the length of its dark head and face. Found in open country—where its holes were a nuisance and often a real danger to horsemen, particularly after dark—the badger made a long burrow that led to a grass-lined nest. The Navahos used the skins for making caps.

badlander
An inhabitant of the *badlands* of the Dakotas and Nebraska. (Berrey and van den Bark 1942)

badlands
(1) Literally, land that was bad from the cattleman and farmer's point of view—usually savagely eroded, forming buttes and mesas. Said by some writers to possess little grass or water, or to be entirely treeless; others record the presence of grass in breaks.
(2) The brothel district of a town. (Ramon Adams 1944)

badman
Also **bad man, bad-man.** Delightful entry in Barrère and Leland's *A Dictionary of Slang, Jargon and Cant* (1897): "BAD MAN (American). This has a special meaning in the West, where it indicates a heartless cruel

murderer. Rowdies and bullies in their boasting often describe themselves as 'hard *bad men* from Bitter Creek.' "

The word *badman* could have any number of meanings read into it.
It was used with both admiration and distaste: decent men had "misunder-
standings," killed a man, moved ahead of the law through the years, and
bore the title; so did men who had their own way simply through ruthlessness or skill with a gun.

A number of reasons can be found for the flourishing of the breed in
the West. Where there is little law-enforcement, the worst elements will act
without restraint. Coupled with this was the God-given right to bear arms
and the powerful folk-tradition of the "snapping turtle"—"chock full of
brag and fight"—and the "ring-tailed roarer." The war-like virtues of an
earlier period survived into an era which could have done with a little less
of them. Further, the economic failures in the land of opportunity, which
was almost free of the restraint of law, saw their betters making use of
public land as their own and holding it against all comers, often creating
their own rules for the game. Everybody knew that many a wealthy cattleman (now respectable and imposing his own law on the range) had started
with a very wide loop and some other man's calves.

There was scarcely a badman of any notoriety worth having who did
not leave people behind to weep for him. We have documentary evidence
that shows however bad a man might have been, however many innocent
bystanders he might have injured in his brawls, he always had admirers,
even among members of the press. In folk-song and -tale many such were
given virtues they never possessed in the flesh: it was ever thus with the
cut-throat, the highwayman, and the lawless. Billy the Kid (who could be
recklessly brave) killed an old friend without warning and refused to draw
on an ex-pard who might have proved a shade faster, yet he was described as a freehearted, generous boy who was always courteous to
women. Jesse James, on whose career of slaughter I have no wish to dwell,
always paid his financial debts. Wyatt Earp and Doc Holliday have both
been practically canonized in this century—not bad for two recorded con
men and bunko-steerers. Wyatt, of course (to my knowledge), was never
called a badman in his lifetime, because he collected peace-keeping
offices. About the only so-called badman I find myself liking is good old
Sam Bass.

The list of renowned badmen is a long one and can be divided
roughly into two groups: the more or less lone killers and the leaders of
organized crime. Probably the first of the latter was Joaquin Murieta, who,
when he went from New Mexico into the goldfields of California in the
early 1850s, didn't find much gold in "them thar hills," and so looked
elsewhere. He found, as did others, that it was easier to kill a man for gold
than to dig for it. In later writings, this earned him the reputation of a Robin
Hood, but literature of the period does not agree. He was a ferocious killer
with an organization and intelligence service that was excelled only by the

notorious Henry Plummer. This gentleman started in the goldfields of Idaho and Montana, held office as sheriff, and was considered by the ladies to be urbane and charming. Nobody moved gold out of the fields without his knowledge. There is no knowing how many were victims of his cut-throats. Finally, with admirable efficiency, the local vigilantes caught and hanged him and a number of accomplices. (See Ernest Haycox's 1942 novel, *No Law and Order,* for the classic story on the subject; see also *vigilance committees*.)

There is a group of characters whom Western buffs will argue over. Are they "goodies" or "baddies"? The argument should last as long as such buffs exist. These characters, like Plummer and the notorious Bill Longley, were both lawmen and killers and included Wild Bill Hickok, Wyatt Earp (along with Doc Holliday), and Ben Thompson: men who killed on their own account at one period and for the law during another. Hickok announced his presence among pistoleers with his murder of Dave Mc-Canles. A man of hair-trigger nerves, Hickok served the Union army well and lived out his post-war years as both gambler and fearless and fearsome lawman (deputy U.S. marshal and elected county sheriff in Kansas). The climax of his career came when he reacted too quickly with his edgy nerves in a shadowy street and killed a friend. This was capped by his being shot in the back at a game of cards. Wyatt Earp and Doc Holliday also killed their men legally and otherwise, as did Ben Thompson—a violent, generous, impetuous, gun-happy Texan. All three of these gentry were said to be fast and accurate with a gun—probably truly, with the exception of Holliday (see Jahns 1961).

John Wesley Hardin (who could be a normal, pleasant-enough fellow when he wanted) was probably one of the deadliest death-dealers in the West. Extremely fast and apparently reckless, he first made his name, so the story goes, by killing Negro Union soldiers in Texas—which put him down as a Texas patriot. The tale has it that Thompson, who knew Hickok's penchant for shooting Texans, tried to persuade Hardin to kill Hickok. But Hardin, impressed by Hickok's rep, wasn't having any. Which showed he might be reckless, but was no fool.

Of those who ran in gangs (mostly cowboys gone wrong), none were more notorious than the Wild Bunch and the Hole in the Wall Gang—though some discredit should be given to Black Jack Ketchum's outfit of the Southwest. These gangs were loosely knit, and some men, in the course of their careers, belonged to more than one of them: Bob Lee, his cousin Harvey, and Loney Logan; Longabaugh (the Sundance Kid); George Curry—the name Curry was also used by other owl-hoots (see *owl hoot [2]*); Ben Kilpatrick (the Tall Texan); and Will Carver. Not to forget Butch Cassidy (real name George Parker). These boys were late-comers to the game and saw the nineteenth century out.

Even with all the strong tradition of two fast guns meeting and drawing on Main Street, a badman didn't need to risk his life against an armed man:

instead, he could shoot Indians, Negroes, and Chinese without the law noticing too much. Mexicans didn't really count either. I suspect that much of the badman spleen was used up on these unfortunates.

I expect I've missed out some of your favorites. My apologies. I don't like any of them much. Except, as I said, old Sam Bass.
(Will Brown 1960; Cunningham 1934; Watson n.d.; Hamlin 1959; Jahns 1961; Waters 1962; Dobie 1930)

bad medicine
A term used by whites and Indians, sometimes with quite different meanings. To fully understand these two words, one must first understand the meaning of an Indian's *medicine.* The nearest one can get to it is the New Zealand Maori's *mana,* which was a man's spiritual aura, his total being, body and soul; his character, his reputation, and his potential; the result of his spirits working for or against him. An Indian's medicine depended on his dreams, his protecting spirits, and his relationship to them. If a man had continual bad luck, his medicine must have been bad, maybe through a mistake in his ritual which had caused his spirits to guide him wrongly. If his medicine was good, he was successful, he was being true to his spirits. Indians often broke off a fight because they thought their medicine had soured on them.

In the world of the whiteman, bad medicine eventually came to have two meanings:
(1) A man who was bad medicine was dangerous, he was a killer: he was **real bad medicine.**
(2) Bad news. (Ramon Adams 1944)

baho, bahoo
See *paho.*

baile
(Sp). A dance, a ball—especially of a Mexican nature. Used particularly in New Mexico and Arizona. (Ramon Adams 1944)

bait
Food for horse or man. Direct from England, where it is still used to mean fodder for a horse. (Weseen 1934; Ramon Adams 1944)

bajada
(Sp). A downward slope in the land. (Mathews 1951)

bake
To ride a horse until it was overheated. (Ramon Adams 1944)

bald-faced
(possibly from the Celtic *bal:* a white mark on an animal's forehead).
(1) Applied to a cow with a white face. Ramon Adams 1944 states that the white must extend to include one or both eyes.
(2) Said of a man wearing a starched or *boiled shirt* (Ramon Adams 1944). **Bald-faced shirt**. (Farmer 1889)
See also *Hereford (2)*.

balling up
Referred to bunching up by cattle—at a river-crossing or entrance to a corral, for example. It was usual for a large herd to be broken up into smaller bunches to prevent this from happening. (Rossi 1975; Ramon Adams 1944)

bamoose
See *vamose.*

banco
(Sp; SW). A sandbank in a watercourse. (Mathews 1951)

band
A bunch of horses, either wild or in remuda. While the word usually referred to horses, it was sometimes applied to other animals and to men. Also, as a verb: **to band,** to herd together. Andy Adams 1909: "It only remained to sod over and dirt the bridge thoroughly. With only three spades the work was slow, but we cut sods with axes, and after several hours' work had it finished. The two yoke of oxen were driven across and back for test, and the bridge stood it nobly. Slaughter then brought up his *remuda,* and while the work of dirting the bridge was still going on, crossed and recrossed his band of saddle horses twenty times." (MacEwan 1969). Ramon Adams 1944 applies it to horses only.

bandana
(from the Hindi *bandhnu,* via Eastern United States). Also **bandanna**. The neckerchief of the cowman. Folded in a triangle to tie at the front or back, according to taste. Often of cotton but preferably of silk, which was cool in summer and warm in winter; bright colors and spots were favored. It served endless uses: it covered the neck above an often collarless shirt, masked mouth and nostrils against dust, filtered foul water, and tied down hat brims over the ears during cold weather. If you wanted to rob a bank or hold up a stage without being recognized, it could serve as a mask. Those who know have questioned whether the word was much used by cow-country men.

bandera
(Sp; SW). A flag. (Dobie 1930)

bandido
(Sp). Used in the Southwest usually to mean a bandit of Mexican origin.
(Dobie 1930; Ramon Adams 1944)

band wagon
Truly an Eastern U.S. expression in the first place (a highly decorated wagon used for advertising), but sometimes the term was applied in the West to a traveling salesman's wagon of sale-goods. (Ramon Adams 1944)

bangtail
A term that has always puzzled me. The word implies a horse with a tail cut short or plucked—hence, a *range horse,* one that might run free for only part of the year and thus not become completely wild. I have also seen the word applied in fiction to branded range horses. But Ramon Adams 1944, along with others of less renown, vouches for it as meaning a *mustang,* or feral horse, usually, as opposed to a range horse. In Eastern states it became slang for a race-horse.

banter
(possibly of Georgian origin; S and W). To challenge, to defy. Possibly to challenge to a race, a shooting match, etc. (Bartlett 1877). Closely connected with the true meaning of *banter,* which implies light talk or mockery. (Wentworth 1944)

baquero
See *vaquero.*

bar
(1) A straight horizontal line in the design of a cow or horse brand.
(2) A variant of *bear,* the animal. Fiction puts such pronunciations in the mouths of Mountain Men and old-timers. There is some justification for this, judging by the writing of such men as Ruxton 1849.

barbed brand
A cattle or horse brand decorated with a short protuberant line or spur.
(Ramon Adams 1944)

barbed mesquite
(w Texas). Genus *Bouteloua.* **Mesquite grass.** Mentioned by Bartlett 1877 as **barbed mesquit.** (Mathews 1951)

barberry
Also *agarita,* **berberry**; sometimes mistakenly called **bearberry.** Species

berberis or *barbaris* of the genus *Berberidaceae*. The wild barberry is called **agrito** by the Tejanos. (Dobie 1952)

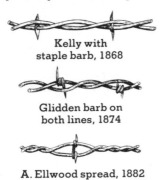

bar-bit
A straight or nearly straight bit for a horse's mouth, at either end of which is a ring for the bridle and reins. (Mora 1950; Ramon Adams 1944)

barboquejo
(Mex-Sp). Also **barbiquejo**. The chin strap of a hat. It had to be strong and durable, for, as Dobie 1929 says, the hat was liable "to be torn off a vaquero's head in the tenacious brush." (Ramon Adams 1944). Rossi 1975 advises: "It should never be too strong or the vaquero's head might go with it. It should be strong enough to withstand light stuff, but break if hung up on anything too heavy. A similar idea is a single **whang** tying the belt or center of chaps today—heavy enough to do the job, but one that would break immediately if a rider got hung up on his saddlehorn." I have seen this term used only in the brush-country of southwest Texas, but it was possibly more widely used.

barbwire
Kelly with staple barb, 1868

Glidden barb on both lines, 1874

A. Ellwood spread, 1882

Two inventions brought about the end of different eras in the West. One was the repeating firearm, the effect of which was dramatic enough; the other was barbwire, the effect of which was not only dramatic but traumatic. It was simply fence wire with barbs on it, the commonest designs consisting of two wires twisted together with the barbs themselves twisted a number of times and in various ways around the wire. Within a decade of its introduction in the 1860s, it changed the character of the wide-open ranges of the West. Its effect upon the economics and upon the social and workaday habits and customs of Western folk was abrupt and final: with it, the old days went. What the term *Old West* fully stood for was gone.

The story and facts of this wicked-looking wire are impressive and astonishing; the variety of types and the tonnage produced to meet the insatiable demand are staggering. Osgood 1929, for example, quotes impressive production figures starting at five tons in 1874 and mounting steadily year by year to 200,000 tons annually in 1900, the last year of our period. In 1884 Charles Goodnight and friends ran a fence from Indian Territory across the Panhandle and thirty-five miles into New Mexico. The numbers of patents issued on an extraordinary variety of designs are equally astonishing: starting modestly with 11 patents in the years 1868–73, the figures climb steadily to 94 in the years 1881–85, and make a total of 306 patents in 17 years.

All you could want to know on this subject is to be found in Glover

1972. (Mr. Glover publishes his authoritative material from what I consider to be the most colorfully named press in the world — the Cow Puddle Press of Sunset, Texas.) He writes: "The beginning of the need for barbed wire was seen in the year 1867 as a few men applied, that year, for patents pertaining to restraining wire with sharp points to turn and hold livestock." Most of the early manufacturers were established in Iowa, Illinois, and areas near enough to the Great Plains to be aware of stock and range problems that had not been solved by the smooth wire produced as early as 1853 (the Meriwether type, patented at New Braunfels, Texas). A good many men patented designs of "thorny fence" before the famous Joseph Glidden, who, with good organization, plant, and franchises, rose to be the chief manufacturer by 1885.

Barbwire was the answer to all those who wished to keep their range from outsiders on the treeless plains where there was little timber for fencing. Ranchers used it to stop cattle from drifting (and lived to regret it bitterly when the animals died by the thousands when prevented from escaping the worst effects of winter during the great die-ups—see *die-up [1]*); they planted wire to stop other men from using precious water sources; some strung wire to block trails; farmers fenced crops in and cattle out. In fact, whole towns were cut off by cattlemen hastily encircling ranges.

Many powerful ranchers were passionate open-rangers, but when the mighty *XIT* outfit of the Texas Panhandle went in for the stuff in a big way, most of them were convinced that the old days had gone. Shorthorn cows were coming in and they could not walk twenty miles to water as could the old Longhorns. Also, they were more valuable. Barbwire had become an economic necessity, and the cowboy was downgraded from the historic herdsman on horseback to a laborer whose spade, pick, hammer, and pliers were now as important as his rope, gun, and branding iron. (Osgood 1929; Glover 1972)

bar-dog
A barman, a bartender, a barkeep. (Ramon Adams 1944)

barefooted
Said of a horse that was unshod. Indians rode such horses, though they also shod horses with rawhide. The mustangs of the hills developed hard feet and could run on rock and hard ground without injury to them. (Ramon Adams 1944; Dobie 1952)

barking squirrel
Early-nineteenth-century reference to the prairie dog, and a pretty good description too. (Mathews 1951)

barking wolf
The coyote. Not in common use. (Dobie 1950; Mathews 1951)

bark off squirrels
Bartlett 1877 cites Audubon's *Ornithology:* "A common way of killing
squirrels among those who are expert with the rifle in the Western States,
is to strike with the ball the bark of the tree immediately beneath the
squirrel, the concussion produced by which kills the animal instantly without mutilating it." This obviously applies to the West *then.* (Bowman 1953)

Barlow knife
Variously seen as **barlow knife, Russell Barlow knife, barlow pocket knife,
barlow pen knife.** Mathews 1951 quotes the term as early as 1819. Usually a single-bladed pocketknife with a blade that folded into the handle,
it came in a number of different sizes and was named for the original
maker. Carl Russell 1967, the authority on such implements, states that its
distinguishing feature is its extra-long bolster. It was widely in use in the
West from the earliest days when it was carried by the Mountain Men.

barnyard stock
Also **pilgrims, States cattle.** Eastern cattle, stock that could be raised in a
farmer's yard. (Osgood 1929)

barranca
(Mex-Sp; New Mexico and Texas). A steep-sided ravine; often, a watercourse created by heavy rains. (Mora 1950; Dobie 1956)

barrel
(1) The chap guard of a spur. (Mora 1950)
(2) The torso of a horse. (Dobie 1952)

bar shoe
A horse-shoe with a strengthening bar across the heel. (Ramon Adams
1944)

basto
(Mex-Sp; SW). The skirt of a saddle (Weseen 1934). A later development
in the Western saddle. Ramon Adams 1944 also describes it as "a pad,
the skirt of a saddle." But the word was sometimes used in reference to a
saddle-lining (Farrow 1881); and Berrey and van den Bark 1942 quote it
as being a pack-saddle. Not in common use.

batamote
(Mex-Sp; SW). *Baccharia glutinosa.* A seep-willow tree. The Anglos did

not pronounce the final *e* as did the Spanish. Also written as **aguatamote** and used as **guatamote** by Anglos. Mathews 1951 says that it is now corrupted to **water wally,** which sounds rather nice to me.

batch
See *bach.*

batch of crumbs
Bugs a man might find in his blankets. (Siberts 1954)

batea
(Mex-Sp; SW and California). Originally, I think, this referred to a wooden bowl, but later also applied to a small receptacle used in *panning* gold. (Lavender 1969)

bat wing chaps
Also **bat wings** (Ramon Adams 1944), **Texas wing chaps,** *winged chaps.* Chaps with wide wings, so wide that they were easy to put on and pull off when the wearer was booted and spurred. (Mora 1950)

bay
(1) A horse color—in full color, a deep rich chestnut red-brown. Such animals had black mane, tail, and possibly points (extremities). The Mexican word *bayo* became applied to duns (see *dun*), which were really faded bays. (Dobie 1952; Ramon Adams 1944)
(2) An open prairie surrounded usually by trees, but sometimes by rock. Rather rarely used. (Colton 1850)

bayeta
(Sp: baize; SW). Also **bayjeta, vayeta.** A wool-fiber yarn, extremely hard-wearing, apparently spun by the Pueblo Indians; also, the cloth made from it. The word could also be applied to the material from which the Navaho made blankets, some of which were known as **bayeta blankets.** (Waters 1950)

bayo
(Mex-Sp; SW). In Mexican-Spanish, the word came to mean a *dun* rather than a *bay* horse. It was in fact a faded bay. While some varieties had other markings, most had black points (such as ears, muzzle, and lower legs). In his charming book *The Mustangs* (1952), J. Frank Dobie gives the Mexican terms for the varieties of bays and duns. *Bayo azafranado:* a horse of a saffron color, between dun and *sorrel. Bayo blanco:* a horse of a pale dun color. *Bayo cebruno:* a horse of a dun color that faded into a smoky tone. *Bayo coyote:* a horse of a dun color with a black dorsal stripe; known to the Anglos also as a **coyote dun.** *Bayo naranjado:* a dun horse of an

orange hue. *Bayo tigre:* a dun horse with stripes around the legs and along the shoulders; also called **gateado** and much the same as the *zebra dun.*

bead
The foresight of a firearm. Hence, to **draw a bead** on a man: to aim your gun at him. Not in itself necessarily a Westernism, but frequently used in Western fiction and probably in the Old West itself. (Bartlett 1877; Croy 1956)

bean-eater
A Mexican. (Weseen 1934; Ramon Adams 1944)

bean-master
The cook. (Ramon Adams 1944)

bear
(1) To **tie on the bear:** to get drunk.
(2) To be **loaded for bear:** to be fully armed, prepared for trouble, spoiling for a fight whether armed or not.

bearberry
See *barberry.*

bear grass
Coarse, tough grass growing high from Montana to Oregon; its buds were lavender in color, its bloom lilac. Bartlett 1877 says that it was *Yucca filamentosa* and adds that it was sometimes called **silk grass,** from the fibers on the edges of the leaves, but it really wasn't grass at all. The Shorter Oxford English Dictionary 1973 writes it **bear-grass,** the genus of grasses *Polygon.* Mathews 1951 says the term covers various yuccas and other plants. See also *sacaguista.*

bear sign
A cattle-range word for doughnuts. The cook who could make good ones was much sought after and worth his weight in gold. (Ramon Adams 1944)

bear trap
A severe horse bit. The term **bear trap saddle** was given to a saddle developed in the first quarter of the twentieth century (outside our period) which had a small seat and cantle close to the fork, making it a major achievement to fall out of it. Shame on the man who used one. (Rossi 1975)

beaver
(1) *Castor canadensis.* Since the pursuit and trapping of this small industrious animal led to the discovery and exploration of much of the Old West,

it deserves a substantial mention. Not to be confused in literature with the much smaller so-called **mountain beaver** or sewellel (see *boomer [2]*), *Aplodontia rufa,* which, in spite of its name, is not closely related to our beaver. The real beaver, because of fashion in the United States and Europe in the first half of the nineteenth century, took lone trappers and fur-brigades into the Rockies—which, to a great extent, gave rise to that incredible breed, the Mountain Men. In fact, to tell the beaver's story in full would need the full story of the Mountain Men and the whole history of the thrust of adventurers into the unknown territory

beyond the *Great American Desert.* On the trapping of this animal lay the fortunes of the Hudson's Bay Company and the American Fur Company. The beaver did not, of course, provide all the peltry for the fur-trade; but, if in the 1830s the beaver-hat fashion had not been replaced by that of the silk-hat, the beaver would have become extinct, even though it is estimated that there were thousands of millions of them originally.

The beaver's fast-growing sharp teeth demand constant use and he obliges by biting through the boles of fair-sized trees. In spite of legend he does this to obtain the leaves, twigs, and bark for gnawing. He sometimes, in the case of small trees, utilizes the trunks for dam-building and forming the pool that protects the entrance to his home from intruders. His powerful flat tail is used for swimming and gives warning signals by slapping the surface of the water. (This tail the Mountain Men thought a pretty tasty dish, by the way.) Guard hairs cover a thick, softer fur—a treasure for which men risked their lives. The beaver was also caught for his musk (castoreum), thought to possess medicinal properties. This castor was also used to bait beaver-traps (or -sets), which weighed around five pounds each and must have been a great encumbrance to men often moving through hostile Indian country. These traps were attached to stakes driven into stream-beds, which made beaver-catching a wet and unenviable job. The animal was usually drowned in the trap. Skinning was usually done immediately after the beaver was taken from the trap. The skins were stretched and dried on a circular willow frame and stored in a cool place. (Carl Russell 1967; Grzimek 1974)

(2) Used as a term of familiarity by one man to or about another, mostly among Mountain Men, much as **hoss** and **coon** were. (Ruxton 1849)

(3) In all the English-speaking world, of course, a beaver was a man with a beard.

bedding down

The act of cattle-drovers bringing the herd to rest, a process that had to be carried out with skill and precision if the semi-wild Longhorns were to pass a peaceful night. (Dobie 1941; Ramon Adams 1944)

bed-ground
Also **bedding-ground**. Area selected for bedding-down cattle at night on a trail-drive. This might be chosen by the trail-boss or by the cook, who usually went ahead of the slow-moving herd to find a good camp-site and to prepare the evening meal. (Andy Adams 1909; Ramon Adams 1944)

bed-rock
(1) Rock met by miners when they had dug through softer strata.
(2) To **get down to bed-rock**—in conversation, to get to the crux of the matter. (Mathews 1951; Berrey and van den Bark 1942)

bed-roll
Also **bedding roll**. A cowhand's bed, usually consisting of a tarp (tarpaulin) and blankets. In the later days, the tarp was sometimes called a **paulin**. Later too the bed-roll might contain a sougan, a quilted cover. This roll contained most of the cowboy's possessions. (Andy Adams 1909; Ramon Adams 1944)

bed-wagon
Also *hoodlum,* hoodlum **wagon**. A wagon that carried the bed-rolls and other equipment on the trail. A later development and only used by the larger outfits on long drives. Generally such tackle was carried on the chuck wagon. (Ramon Adams 1944; Gard 1954)

beef
In the old days, this meant especially a *steer,* an ox. Bartlett 1877 agrees with this. Later its use was restricted to steers over four years old. (Ramon Adams 1944; Mora 1950)

beef biscuit
See *airtights.*

beef book
The tally book, the beef account book of the ranch. (Berrey and van den Bark 1942; Ramon Adams 1944)

beef-cut
Animals cut out from the herd to be sent to market. (North 1942; Ramon Adams 1944)

beef-issue
The allotment of free beef in the form of live cattle to an Indian reservation. (Osgood 1929; Ramon Adams 1944). It was often short, and many Indian agents made their private deals and cuts, so that treaty obligations for certain amounts of beef were frequently not met. On occasion, the cause

of serious "Indian trouble." Indian agents issued **beef tickets,** against which an Indian could claim his rations. Unscrupulous whitemen would buy these up cheaply when possible.

beef round-up
Usually the *cutting-out* of cattle for market in the fall of the year; the fall round-up. (Ramon Adams 1944; Berrey and van den Bark 1942)

beef tea
Shallow water fouled by cattle. (Ramon Adams 1944)

beef treaties
Treaties made between the U.S. authorities and Indian tribes in which a free *beef-issue* was part of the agreement. (Hawgood 1967)

belduque
(Mex-Sp; SW and Texas). A large knife with a formidable blade. Found spelled variously as **berduque, velduque, verduque.** Mathews 1951 gives numerous references.

belinka
(Navaho). An Anglo, an American.

bell-mare
A mare with a bell or bells suspended from her neck to keep a bunch of mules together. Rossi 1975 adds that mules will follow a mare with or without bells. White mares were often used, as they were easier to spot if they wandered with their wards while grazing. They were also sometimes used to keep horses together.

bell-mule
The lead mule of a *pack-train* that wore the guiding bell. (Mathews 1951)

bellwether
Properly, a castrated ram that wore a bell, the sound of which kept the flock together. However, in the West the term was often used loosely to denote any animal wearing a bell, at the sound of which associated animals would follow: for a bunch or string of horses or mules the bellwether might be a mare or a mule.

belly cheater
A cook. (Ramon Adams 1944; Berrey and van den Bark 1942)

bench
A flat elevated stretch of land, above a river or a plain and usually on the edge of hills. (Weseen 1934; Ramon Adams 1944; Mathews 1951)

bench brand
A brand consisting of a horizontal bar with two downward strokes, making the design look like a bench. (Berrey and van den Bark 1942; Ramon Adams 1944)

berberry
See *barberry*.

between a rock and a hard place
Financially broke. (Berrey and van den Bark 1942)

between hay and grass
Between boyhood and manhood. I had never come on this beautiful phrase before I read William Dale Jennings's 1971 novel, *The Cowboys*. The glossary of Western words the author gives at the back of this book is of great interest and most reliable. He rightly dedicates his book to Ramon Adams.

bible
A cowhand's cigarette papers. (Ramon Adams 1944)

Bible-puncher
Usually a preacher, ordained or not, but also a religious man who quoted the holy text.

Bible Two
The second Bible of the Texas Rangers, which provided them each year with a list of wanted men and was therefore read by them more avidly than Bible One. (Ramon Adams 1944)

big antelope
A man might so refer to a cow when he had killed it for food knowing that it belonged to another man. There was a saying that only a fool ate his own beef. (Ramon Adams 1944)

big augur
Also **augur**. The boss of a ranch, an important man. (Berrey and van den Bark 1942; Ramon Adams 1944)

big ditch
The main ditch of an irrigation system. See also *acequia*. (Mathews 1951)

Big Fifty
The ultimate in buffalo guns (see *buffalo gun*). The 1875 *Sharps* .50–90, of which McHugh 1972 says: "(sometimes referred to as the .50–100 or .50–110 . . .). When the old buffalo hunters themselves spoke of the 'Big Fifty,' this was the load they were describing, although succeeding generations of Western writers have mistakenly used this famous name to refer to another model, the .50–140–700. This last load, most assuredly the 'biggest' Fifty, was a special-order caliber that did not come along until about 1880, when the great herds had been exterminated from all but the northern plains." I don't know about you, but for me that settles the debate about what a Big Fifty is.

big horn
Properly, the **big horn sheep.** Two distinct species: the true big horn (the **Rocky Mountain sheep** or **mountain sheep:** *Ovis canadensis*) and Dall's sheep (*Ovis dalli*). Between them they range from Alaska (Dall's) into Mexico and divide into numerous local races which have developed through isolated inbreeding, with the southern races larger than the northern. Extremely hardy, active, and footsure, they are recorded as having been seen running down perpendicular cliffs—a fact which, I am sure, has to be seen to be believed. Their massive horns curve back, then downward and sideways. The rams may go up to 300 pounds in weight and 6 feet in length. Colors range from white in the far north to darker shades and almost black on the moist Pacific slopes; the darker, *Ovis canadensis,* have a pale circular patch on the rump. If you've heard the old tale about them jumping from great heights and using their horns as landing gear and believe it, you'll believe anything. They were the targets of Mountain Men, California-bound wagon-trains, and European sportsmen alike. There is certainly no need to add that their numbers have since been greatly reduced.

big house
The home of the ranch's owner. (Ramon Adams 1944)

big jaw
A cattle disease found among the Longhorns. (Dobie 1941)

big loop
Also **wide loop.** The loop of a cow-thief's lasso, said to be so big that, when thrown, it landed on other men's cattle.

bilberry
A berry not confined to the West, of course, but one mentioned much in Western literature. It covered various species of the whortleberry (*Gaylussacia*).

bilk
According to Bartlett 1877, as a noun it was applied to a man who failed to pay his dues. (Barrère and Leland 1897)

billet
A strap on the *off-side* of a saddle for the cinch-buckle. (Ramon Adams 1944)

billy
A small club, a blackjack, a "life preserver." Not a Westernism, but a word found not infrequently in Western literature. (Bartlett 1877)

birchbark
(1) A canoe made from the bark of a birch tree.
(2) The word could also be applied to other items which could be made from the bark: **birchbark basket, birchbark lodge, birchbark wigwam,** etc. (Mathews 1951)

biscuit
The saddlehorn. (Ramon Adams 1944; Berrey and van den Bark 1942)

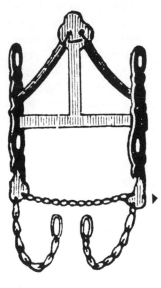

biscuit-roller
A cook. (Berrey and van den Bark 1942; Ramon Adams 1944)

biscuit-shooter
(1) A cook. (Berrey and van den Bark 1942; Ramon Adams 1944)
(2) A waitress in a restaurant. (Ramon Adams 1944)

bit
(1) The metal part of a bridle inserted in the horse's mouth. Some Indians used rawhide bits.
(2) A type of cattle *ear-mark:* a triangular nick in the ear. (Mora 1950)

bitch
(1) A primitive form of lamp made by filling a mug, tin cup, or can with grease and using a wick made of rag or any other handy material. (Foster-Harris 1955)
(2) The cradle (or cooney) of rawhide under a wagon. (Ramon Adams 1944). See *caboose.*

bite the dust
To fall on your face; to come off a horse, either knocked down by fist or club or simply shot out of the saddle by a bullet. Popular phrase in early dime novels in which more Indians bit the dust than there were abergoins (see *abergoin*) living on the American continent. (Mencken 1948)

bit house
A saloon or store where everything sold cost a bit (12½ cents). Mathews 1951 records the term as a Westernism as early as 1839. Rossi 1975 informs me that odd change, if made at all, was made with a U.S. dime, or **short bit**.

blab
Also **blab board**. A board attached to a calf's nose to prevent it from suckling while being weaned. (Berrey and van den Bark 1942; Ramon Adams 1944; Aldridge 1884)

black cattle
The cattle of early Texas, not to be confused with the Longhorns, but nevertheless possessing long horns which they well knew how to use. In the brush-country, they were referred to as *cimarrones* (wild ones), as were the Longhorns. They were usually black (these were also known as *mustang cattle*), but not always, for they could be marked by a light dorsal stripe. Such line-backed cattle, according to Dobie 1941, were also called *zorrillas* (polecats); Ramon Adams 1944 uses the same name for them.

black chaparral
A kind of live-oak brush of the brasada country of southwest Texas, called by the Tejanos **chaparro prieto**. (Dobie 1929)

black-eyed susan
A revolver. Rare. (Ramon Adams 1944; Mathews 1951)

black jack
(1) *Quercus nigra.* The barren or scrub oak. Mathews 1951 refers to it as *Quercus marilandica,* which possibly indicates that the term varies in meaning according to locality.
(2) Rum and molasses, with or without water. (Barrère and Leland 1897). Not solely a Western drink.
(3) After mentioning the two meanings above, Bartlett 1877 quotes a third: a face blackened from difficulty with breathing, such as while being hanged by the neck.
(4) A miner's word for ore or zinc. (Bartlett 1877)
The term also has a number of other meanings in other areas of the Anglo-American language.

blackleg
A certain disease in cattle, the sign of which was swollen legs. It was fatal to the upgraded stock of the later years, particularly to young stock, and a vaccine was developed to combat it. It was also the old Missourian name for scurvy. (Sandoz 1958)

black prairie
Prairie land, the soil of which was black. (Mathews 1951)

black sage
A variety of sage found in the Southwest and California. (Mathews 1951)

black snake
(1) A name given to a number of varieties of snake, most of them non-poisonous.
(2) A heavy whip, usually of cowhide, but possibly of snakeskin.

black strap
Molasses. Also a mixture of rum and molasses, though Ramon Adams 1944 limits its use to just molasses. Not necessarily a Westernism.

blacktail deer
Odocoileus hemionus columbianus. A sub-species of the *mule deer*, found in great numbers during the mid-nineteenth century from Alaska to below the Mexican border, both in high mountains and on the plains. There are various local races which vary in size and color, but most have a tail with a black tip. (Grzimek 1974)

blanket coat
A coat made from a blanket.

blanket Indians
Some writers have used this term to indicate Indians who took to the blanket as clothing and were therefore no longer in the wild state. However, its original use was as Bartlett 1877 points out: "A wild Indian, whose principal article of dress is the blanket." Farmer 1889 substantiates this: "A Western term for an Indian who still remains in the wild state." Mathews 1951 defines the expression as applying to an Indian who had not adopted the clothing of the whites. To accuse anyone of having **worn the blanket** was to say they were of mixed white and Indian descent. Naturally, this was used in a derogatory sense. Such values, of course, have gone full circle and there are now many Americans who boast of their Indian blood.

blankets
Blankets of inferior quality, either of cotton or wool, were traded or given

to the Indians. The Indians themselves traditionally made blankets in a number of ways in a basketry process, with wool, hair, fur, feathers, down, bark, cotton, etc. The blankets served a variety of functions: as clothes, bed-covers, partitions in lodges; women dried fruit on them and carried babies in them. Hudson's Bay blankets found their way from Canada directly to the Northwest tribes and indirectly to the Plains Indians in trading with the Canadian tribes. They were, on the whole, of good quality. In the Southwest, the Navaho learned the art of weaving from the Spaniards and became famous for their seemingly indestructible, almost waterproof blankets that they wove from the wool of their sheep. (Hodge 1907–10)

blattin' cart, blattin' wagon
See *calf-wagon.*

blaze
(1) To mark a trail. Originally a blaze was usually an axe mark made on a tree so that a man could retrace his own steps or indicate a trail for others to follow. This came to mean the making of a trail that could be followed. (2) A white mark on a horse's forehead. (Ramon Adams 1944; Dobie 1952)

blazer
A lie, a deception. (Mathews 1951)

blazing star
A plant said by Bartlett 1877 to be *Aletria farinosa,* the root of which was used by Indians and Westerners as a medicine. Also called **devil's bit**. Both names were also applied to other kinds of plants.

blind
Also **blinder**. Anything used to cover a fractious horse's eyes, possibly while the breaker mounted or the horse was led. Blinds were also used on pack-mules to make packing easier and were useful when an animal was being shod. (Ramon Adams 1944; Mora 1950)

blind trail
Generally this has been used in literature in three senses:
(1) A lost trail: one taken, used, and then concealed; thus, a hunted man would leave a blind trail.
(2) A trail, the marks of which are either indistinct or misleading.
(3) A completely false trail laid to mislead pursuers.

blind trap

A hidden trap, in the form of a corral, for catching cattle or wild horses. (Ramon Adams 1944). Long wings of poles, camouflaged by or composed of tree branches or brush, to hide the presence of the corral, formed an ever-narrowing lane down which the animals ran into the pen. (Rossi 1975)

Blocker loop

A lasso loop named for John Blocker, a man of good renown among Texas cattlemen and greatly skilled with a rope. Besides being salty and a cow-man to his bones, Blocker was noted for the large size of the noose he cast (and by that I don't necessarily mean in the vernacular sense which implies that the loop was large enough to encompass other men's cows); he developed his famous throw with a loop-size that lesser men could not have handled. While a small, accurately cast noose was an object of admiration, Blocker's performance with a big loop was recognized as pure magic. Thrown from behind a running cow, the noose seemed to hang stiff in the air, pass over the shoulders of the quarry, and catch both forefeet. Ramon Adams 1944 describes it: "The cast is made when the loop is behind the right shoulder, the right arm being whipped straight forward across the circle it has been describing. At the same time the hand and wrist give the loop a twist toward the left. The loop goes out in front of the roper, appears to stop, stand up, then roll to the left, showing the **honda** to be on the side of the loop opposite its position when the throw was started." Which sounds to me about equal to playing a Beethoven piano concerto left-hand only. However, Rossi 1975 assures me that this throw would be a piece of apple pie to a good vaquero. He adds that Blocker undoubtedly learned his roping from Mexican vaqueros. Further, he says that the loop probably passed over the cow's right shoulder, then around the forefeet—a **hoolihan**-style throw. Maybe it should be mentioned that Wellman 1939 claims this loop for John's brother, Ab. Dobie 1929, like Ramon Adams 1944, gives the honors to John. Possibly they both used it, for Ab was one of the best cattlemen going. Weseen 1934 says: "The longest possible loop in a lariat; used for **forefooting**."

blot a brand

To deface a brand so that it is unrecognizable. (Berrey and van den Bark 1942; Ramon Adams 1944)

blotched brand

A defaced brand. (Berrey and van den Bark 1942)

blow
After a steep climb or a hard run, a rider would stop to rest his horse and let it **blow**.

blow a stirrup
To lose a stirrup-iron while riding in a rodeo bucking contest. I suspect the term developed in the 1890s. (Allen 1933; Weseen 1934; Ramon Adams 1944)

blow in
(1) To arrive.
(2) To spend; to blow in your pay; to spend it all. (Weseen 1934; Ramon Adams 1944)

blow out
(1) A gaseous explosion in a mine.
(2) A good feed, a celebration.
(Weseen 1934; Ramon Adams 1944)

blue backs
Paper money of the Confederacy. When depreciated, they became known as **shucks,** probably because they had no more value than corn-shucks, which were used as brief-burning torches. (Mathews 1951)

blue belly
A soldier, on account of his blue uniform. After the Civil War started, this term was naturally applied to Northerners generally. (Mathews 1951)

bluegrass
A name that covered scores of varieties of grasses, genus *Poa.* Among the most common in the West are *Poa ampla* (big bluegrass), *Poa arachnifera* (Texas bluegrass), and *Poa secunda* (Sandberg bluegrass), a northern bluegrass. Always thought, with probable justification, to be superior feed for horses. On this, the small Texas horses, when moved to the North, were said to have increased in height and weight with remarkable speed. (United States Department of Agriculture 1948; Mathews 1951)

blue stem
Andropogon furcatus or *Agropyron smithi.* A

Texas bluegrass

little blue stem

kind of grass, of blue-greenish color, found on the Great Plains. Sometimes called **gumbo grass**. (Foster-Harris 1955). Chase 1919 calls *galleta* (genus *Hilaria*) by this name.

blue wood
Also *brazil. Condalia obovata.* A variety of bush found in the Southwest. (Mathews 1951)

boar's nest
A cattle-ranch's *line camp.* Probably so called on account of the maleness of the occupants and the manner in which they kept house. (Berrey and van den Bark 1942; Ramon Adams 1944)

bobble
A mistake, a mishap. Dobie 1941 writes: "A breeze suddenly springing up after dark carried the odor of a Negro cooking for another outfit to a herd of steers that had been driven for three months by a Mexican crew without a bobble. They ran as if to make up for lost opportunities." (Berrey and van den Bark 1942; Mathews 1951)

Bob Rulys
(Fr: burnt woods). The Bois Brulés Indians, of Western or Teton Sioux, west of the Missouri River. Divided into Upper and Lower Brulé.

bob-tail guard
The first guard of the night on a trail-drive. (Berrey and van den Bark 1942; Ramon Adams 1944)

bob war, bob wire
See *barbwire.*

bodega
(Mex-Sp: grocery store; SW). A liquor store. (Wentworth and Flexner 1960)

bodewash
See *bois de vache.*

bog camp
A camp set up in waterlogged country so that cowhands could quickly extract bogged cattle. (Weseen 1934; Ramon Adams 1944)

bogged his head
A horse did this when he put his head down between his legs before pitching. (Ramon Adams 1944; Dobie 1964)

bogin' in
To push in. On the trail, yearlings boging into the herd at night sometimes stampeded them. (Dobie 1941; Mathews 1951). Possibly derived from *to bogue:* to push or sail in, to wander aimlessly.

bog rider
A cowhand detailed to haul cattle from bogs and marshes. (Berrey and van den Bark 1942; Ramon Adams 1944)

boiled shirt
Also **fried shirt** (Weseen 1934; Berrey and van den Bark 1942; Ramon Adams 1944). A white shirt. (Bartlett 1877). This came to mean a stiff-fronted shirt and its accompanying snobbishness. Although this meaning was in use in the nineteenth century, a boiled shirt was also a "city shirt": one that needed boiling and ironing to attain sartorial elegance. Hence, a man who was a boiled shirt was a soft-living, starchy man (even "soft" shirts were slightly starched), stiff and snobbish—not a range man. See also *bald-faced (2); Hereford (2)*.

boiling
The **hull kit an' bilin'** (the whole kit and boiling); the whole lot, completely. Not necessarily a Westernism.

bois d'arc
Maclura pomifera. The **Osage orange** of Missouri and Arkansas. (Bartlett 1877). Marcy 1853: "The bows [of the Comanche] are made of the tough and elastic wood of the *bois d'arc* or Osage orange, strengthened and reinforced with the sinews of the deer wrapped firmly around them."

bois de vache
(Fr: wood of the cow). The métis name (see *mestee*) for cow-droppings. The buffalo chips when dry were used as fire-fuel on the treeless plains. The great Parkman (1872), writing in *The Oregon Trail* (which should be read by all interested in the West): "Stopping near its bank, we gathered *bois de vache*, and made a meal of buffalo meat." Anglo variants included **bushwa** (Wentworth 1944), **bodewash**, **booshwa**, **bushwah**. Male Westerners probably referred to it as "buffalo shit."

bonanza
(Sp: prosperity, success). As originally used in English, the term meant much the same as in the Spanish. By the time it came into wide use in the West, it meant a lucky find of precious metals and, hence, any successful strike, whether in business generally or in mining. (Ramon Adams 1944). Weseen 1934 adds: "A hole in the ground owned by a champion liar."

bone orchard
A cemetery; boothill. (Weseen 1934; Ramon Adams 1944)

bonnet strings
The thongs of a man's hat, which were either tied under his chin or put through a toggle or ring and pulled tight to the chin. (Weseen 1934; Berrey and van den Bark 1942; Ramon Adams 1944)

bonsal
See *bozal.*

booger
To scare; sometimes, to be scared. Not necessarily a Westernism. (Berrey and van den Bark 1942; Wentworth 1944)

boogers
Cattle which were inclined to spook and run. (Dobie 1941)

boomer
(1) A sooner. A man who started on a landrush sooner than he should ought to. (Klose 1964). Rossi 1975 adds that the expression came into use just prior to the run on the Cherokee Strip in 1889.
(2) The little sewellel (sometimes seen as **showt'l**), known also as the **mountain beaver** (*Aplodontia rufa*) but only distantly related to the true *beaver (1).* A tiny mountain animal, burrowing extensively near water, it has no tail and is about rabbit-size. So called because of its cry. (Wentworth 1944)

booshwa
See *bois de vache.*

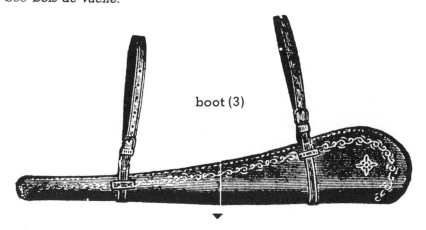

boot (3)

boot
(1) Originally a folding cover of leather or canvas on a gig or buggy, extending from the dashboard to the faces of passenger and driver, protecting them from rain and mud. The term also referred to the tarp or leather curtain used at the rear of a stagecoach to protect and retain

baggage, and to the actual space for baggage and valuables in the front and rear of the coach.

(2) A horse-shoe with toe and heel calked to make it more solid. (Berrey and van den Bark 1942)

(3) The scabbard or covering of a *saddle-gun* (rifle or carbine—more usually, the latter). Made of leather and carried on the saddle in a number of ways: it could be fastened under the girth and under the rider's leg, usually to the right; or it could hang by a loop from the saddlehorn, or by a single strap at the rear of the saddle.

boothill

Also known as the **boot graveyard**. The cemetery of a cow-town. The arguments over why it is so named will no doubt go on for some years yet. Certainly it is connected with a man's wish to die with his boots on. I don't doubt that at times men were bundled into their graves with their boots on, because it isn't easy to get a pair of boots off a stiff without damaging them. Also, many rough crosses over graves were decorated with the boots of the occupants.

boots

High boots were worn at the beginning of our period by males generally and were necessities for miners and cattlemen, though the footgear of the farmers was often shoes. As the fifty years we cover progressed, so the difference in styles increased. At the outset, boots were fairly heavy, came almost knee-high, and were straight across at the top. They were pulled on by canvas loops which were worn inside the boot-top or by leather mule-ears which could be worn inside or outside, according to taste. The miner's boot remained heavy and strong and long in the leg; the cowman's grew lighter, more supple, more highly decorated and generally shorter in the leg, with the heel becoming more underslung and delicate. The early part of our period, however, saw men in and out of the cattle-trade wearing pantlegs tucked into the boots; some of these were of heavy cowhide and all had to be generous in the leg to contain the heavy cloth of the pants. Many drovers, however, wore *half-breed leggings* instead of boots. Once fancier calfskin boots were available, they never lost their popularity. The pantlegs fitted snugly inside them, and often the upper part of the boot-leg was of a different color, either red or blue, frequently with a decorative motif on it. Not *every* cowman wore high heels: some of the old-timers stuck to the broad flat heel and plain leg to the end of the century.

border draw
A method of drawing a revolver with the weapon on the hip opposite the drawing hand, butt forward. Probably not the fastest way of drawing a gun, but many men favored it, especially when wearing a coat; also, for some, it was the best manner in which to wear and draw a gun on horseback. Though a cross- or side-draw would probably not have taken any longer than a regular draw with the earlier heavy, long-barreled guns of 1850–70, this was not the case with more modern revolvers and holsters designed for increasingly rapid removal of iron from leather. (Cunningham 1934; Ramon Adams 1944)

border shift
The passing of a gun from one hand to the other during a gun-fight. Some men were said to be adept at this and could apparently do it without any break in their firing. If a man were right-handed and wounded in the right arm, he might pass his gun to his left hand; or, more rarely, he might be a two-gun man and, with both guns drawn, empty his right-hand gun and pass his left-hand gun into his right hand. When "Long-haired" Jim Courtright, gun in hand, was shot in the gun-hand thumb by that little gamecock Luke Short, it is said that Jim tried the border shift—one of those tales that can never be proved, for before he could catch the gun in his right hand Luke had killed him. (Cunningham 1934; Ramon Adams 1944). Rossi 1975 shares my skepticism: "Seen more in Hollywood and Western fiction than in real life. If Courtright tried the trick in this serious predicament, he deserved to get shot. Folks said he tried the border shift and the story grew."

borrowed
Stolen. (Dobie 1930; Ramon Adams 1944). There is no certainty that this is a true Westernism, for it has long been common in British-English.

bosal
The most common Anglo form of *bozal.* Also seen as **bosaal, bonsal.**

bosal brand
A branded line around an animal's nose. (Berrey and van den Bark 1942; Ramon Adams 1944). See also *bozal.*

boscage
Land covered with clumps of trees. A word already in British-English, but in the West, I suspect it came from the Spanish *bosque* (forest). There were a number of nice variants, **bosky** being the most common. A genuine meeting of the two languages, with much the same meaning.

bosque
(Sp). A wood. See also *boscage.*

boss
(1) The Eastern word for an employer, a foreman; used extensively in the West.
(2) As **Boss,** a term for the buffalo, used in the early days. (Bartlett 1877). Possibly from the Latin *bos,* the generic name for cattle.
(3) **Boss of the Plains** shortened to **Boss,** which John B. Stetson first called the famous hat he designed for the cattleman. The name did not catch on and the hat survived to be called the **John B. Stetson,** the *Stetson,* or simply the **JB** or the **John B.** (Chilton 1961)

bottom
(1) Low-lying land, particularly that with water lying on it or flowing through it. Also **bottom lands.**
(2) The stamina or staying power of a horse. A horse with it was said to have **plenty of bottom.**

boudin
(Fr). Also **boudins.**
(1) Tender buffalo meat made into a sausage, possibly also using the entrails, and baked over a fire. It could also be cooked in the bladder to make a kind of haggis, as the Hidatsa Indians were said to do.
(2) In French *boudin* is the equivalent of the English and Scottish black pudding. Favored by the Mountain Men, who also made a white pudding in much the same way, using, I think, more fat and some flour. (Ruxton 1849; Stansbury 1852)

boughten
Also **store-boughten** (Mora 1950), **broughten, store-broughten.** Store-bought, brought from outside, not home-made. New England dialect carried West. (Wentworth 1944)

bounty hunter
A man who temporarily or permanently occupied himself with the catching or killing of animals or humans for a bounty placed on them. Wolves in cattle-country were the common target; gophers also when they became troublesome. Pulp-fiction has concentrated on the ruthless pursuer of men on the run from the law. However, history often makes the bounty hunter a Mexican claiming rewards for Apache scalps, including those of women and children. Often innocent victims of other Indian nations were also killed for the bounty, for who could tell one Indian scalp from another? There were, on more than one occasion, horrible massacres of Indians by whites for the sake of the bounties. Which is not to underplay the presence in the West of the professional Anglo who hunted "wanted" men for the reward on their heads, dead or alive. This allowed men with the killer instinct to enjoy it legally to the full. (Gregg 1844). It is interesting to note that while Mathews 1951 makes no mention of bounty *hunters,* he does

state that bounties covered Indians and vermin. I suspect, though some will disagree with me, that the term, applied to whitemen hunting white criminals, came to be used more commonly in the twentieth century than in the nineteenth.

bourgeois
(Fr: person of the middle class, citizen). Also **bourgeway** (Ruxton 1849), **bushway** (Lavender 1969). This word came down from Canada with the French fur-hunters during the fur-trade days in the second half of the eighteenth century and referred to an owner or partner in a fur-trading company or fur-hunting expedition. See *A Bourgeois, Joseph Redford Walker, and His Squaw,* a painting by Alfred Jacob Miller (Northern Natural Gas Company Collection, Omaha, Nebraska). Parkman 1872 writes: "Papin was the *bourgeois* or 'boss' of Fort Laramie."

bow
(1) A weapon composed of haft and string, for propelling arrows; used by Indians and such Mexicans as the ciboleros (see *cibolero*).
(2) One of the wooden arch supports of a wagon canvas: wagon bow.

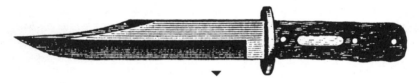

Bowie knife
As **bowie knife,** a name given carelessly to many kinds of heavy knife. The genuine article had a long blade that broadened along the spine toward the tip before suddenly tapering to a point. The main part of the blade was single-edged, but the tip was double-edged. The blade shape brought the weight to the tip, thus making it possible to throw the weapon to some effect. Some of the tougher old Texas hands preferred to settle their differences with this knife rather than with their fists, feet, or guns. Claims have been made for several men as the original makers of this famous weapon. It seems most likely that the title goes to Rezin Bowie (pronounced *boowie*), but the knife was made famous by his brother Jim (Colonel James Bowie), who died in the Alamo and was greatly skilled with this formidable instrument. However, several theories have been advanced that others than Rezin invented it: some claim it for the "notorious" Jim; some for others of similar name. In my humble opinion this type of knife had been in use for some time before either Rezin or Jim had a superlative model made to his own design by a smith. Lavender 1969 and Dobie 1955 both think that it was made for Jim. Bartlett 1877 notes that the name could be used as a verb: to **bowie-knife** somebody.

box brand
A cattle-brand contained within or containing a box shape. (Ramon Adams 1944)

box canyon
A blind canyon, one with an entry and no other way of exiting. (Ramon Adams 1944)

bozal
(Mex-Sp: muzzle). Also **bonsal** (North 1942), **bosaal, bosal,** etc. A strap of leather or rawhide which went around a horse's face immediately above its mouth, used in place of a bit, usually when breaking or riding an unruly horse. Dobie 1930 describes it as a "nose hitch." (Bartlett 1877; Ramon Adams 1944). An essential part of a hackamore (see *bridles [3]*).

brace
(1) To challenge.
(2) To fix a gambling game. Hence, a **brace game.** Not necessarily a Westernism. (Mathews 1951)

Brahma cattle
Also **Brahman cattle, zebu.** The Longhorns did not carry enough beef in Texas. When they were crossed with Durhams and Herefords, the off-spring put on the beef, but were not immune, like the Longhorn, to *Texas fever.* Descend-ants of the Asian-Indian Brahma stock, which had been introduced into South Carolina in 1849, were experimented with on the great King Ranch. They came into Texas in the early 1880s to be retained "in breed," but also to cross with Longhorns and Longhorn–short-horn crosses. Though they were better able to survive Texas fever than were the shorthorns, they did not have the hardiness associated with the Longhorns.

brand artist
An invaluable man in the cow-stealing business. A man who could skillfully change brands, probably with a *running-iron.* (Ramon Adams 1944)

brand blotter
Also **brand blocher** (Berrey and van den Bark 1942), **brand blotcher** (Weseen 1934). A man who blotted out brands with further burning to destroy the identity of the cattle, with a view to stealing them. (Weseen 1934; Ramon Adams 1944; Mora 1950)

brand book
The use of brand books varied according to time and place, but, for example, in Montana and Wyoming in the 1880s a legal brand was obtained from and recorded by the county clerk and the list of brands was open to public inspection. Plainly, in the later days of the West the whole branding system was tightened up. In the earlier days, in Texas, the situation was freer, though brand records did exist. (Osgood 1929; Ramon Adams 1944)

brand bunch
A small herd of cattle, presumably wearing the same brand.

brander
The man who, at branding time, actually applied the hot iron to the hide of the animal. (North 1942; Ramon Adams 1944)

branding
While branding was carried out on individual ranges using a single brand, the branding described here covers that undertaken on round-up or before a trail-drive, in both of which a number of different brands were involved. On round-up, the reps would consult if there was any disagreement over which brand should be used on any particular animal. If a calf was in question, it would bear the brand of its mother, of course. If a fully grown steer, the men would have to come to agreement, basing their judgment on where the animal had been gathered and on whose range it had been found. In the case of **road** or **trail branding,** the bunches of cattle concerned might belong to several owners who either had sold them to the trail-driver or were employing him to take the cattle up the trail. There would, therefore, be a number of brands among the animals; the road brand, usually only a hair brand, was to show that they all belonged to the same trail-herd. (See also *hair branding; round-up [1]; trail-drives.)*

The process of branding cattle obviously varied from place to place and at different times in history, but basically there were two methods. In **chute branding,** the one often used for quick trail or road branding, the animals were run through a branding chute, a narrow passage usually formed of stakes and poles. Cattle could be halted by a removable cross-piece, as necessary, so that they could be branded standing, without being thrown. Instances of this method have been found from the old days, when there were not enough men to carry out the throwing and hog-tying. Though calves were branded faster by roping and holding in the normal way, some cattlemen had a general preference for the chute method, since it could save considerable sweat and labor. (Dobie 1929; Ramon Adams 1944; North 1942)

As good a description of road branding as any appears in Gard 1954: "As these bunches bore different brands, the men gave them a common trail brand at the point of departure. After gathering the cattle, the trail hands drove them through a chute and imprinted a road brand with a hot iron. The usual brand was a light slash or bar. In early days, it might be burned on the shoulder, side, or rump. Later it was required to be on the left side behind the shoulder." Texas had a law in 1866 that a road brand should be a large plain mark on the left side of the cow behind the shoulder. (Harger 1892)

The second method was to catch up and throw the animals, holding them down while burning the owner's mark on their hide. Although the number of men involved varied, the branding crew usually consisted of a roper (see *roping*), a bulldogger (see *bulldogging*), a brander, a flanker (see *flanker [1]*), a *butcher,* and a *tallyman.* In the early days, branding was carried out in the brush and on the open prairie, but in later days, branding pens were almost always used for big brandings. The general system was for a number of animals to be close-herded or penned within working distance of the branding fire. As necessary, a rider cut out a calf and roped it as he choused it to the branding team (see *chouse*). If he cast for the hind legs (as almost always, in the case of a big calf), the roper himself would drag it nearer to the fire, where it was seized upon by the bulldogger and either thrown and held or hog-tied. Alternatively, the roper could catch the calf's neck with the noose, and the bulldogger would throw it. Mora 1950 says: "In a general way, [the bulldogger] reaches over the calf's back, takes a double handful of loose hide, lifts the calf up on his knees like he would a bale of hay, and then gets out from under." If the calf was big and difficult it also might be thrown by the tail; though there were a number of ways to do this, it was not easy and took experience.

Having probably called out the name of the brand (in a general round-up), the roper would then cast off his rope. In the tying and holding of the calf, the bulldogger would probably be assisted by a second man, the flanker. The methods of holding the calves down varied slightly. A common one took two men. The first placed a knee on the calf's neck, took hold of the upper part of a front leg, bent the lower back acutely, and held it. The flanker, sitting on the ground at the animal's tail, hooked one foot just above the joint of the hock of the groundside leg, pushed it forward, took the upper part of the leg in his hands, and forced it back. Said to be a perfect hold in which a calf gave no trouble.

Meanwhile, the man at the fire (who might or might not be the actual brander) had found the brand worn by the calf's mother. Before or after the brand was burned in the hide (the iron was not *too* hot), the ears were marked with a sharp knife and, if flesh was actually cut away, the piece was either slipped into the marker's pocket as a tally or passed to the tallyman nearby. If the calf was male he was usually castrated and the fries thrown in a pile. These might be cooked and enjoyed later. Often a man was detailed solely to attend the fire and irons while another man carried out the actual branding. Then would be heard the time-honored cry of

"Hot iron." In the later years, there might be yet another man, who disinfected the castrated calves.

The work was exhausting for all concerned, particularly the bulldoggers and the cutting horses, the latter being changed constantly.

branding corral
Also **branding pen.** A small pen in which the branding of cattle could be carried out. (Sandoz 1958)

branding crew
Men of a cow-outfit detailed for the job of cutting out, roping, throwing, and branding cattle.

branding fire
A fire in which branding irons were heated. (North 1942)

branding season
The time of year set aside for branding cattle. Calf branding, of course, took place in the spring. (North 1942)

brand inspector
An inspector of brands hired by cattlemen's associations to check cow-stealing and the sale of stolen cattle. (Osgood 1929; Ramon Adams 1944)

brand owner
The owner of a particular brand. Some owners used more than one brand. (Osgood 1929)

brand reader
A man specially skilled in the reading of brands.

brands
A brand was one method of marking an animal for identification of ownership, the others being the *ear-mark* and such cuts as the *dewlap.* A brand on a cow was most often burned by a hot iron on the animal's left hip but might be found on the ribs, jaw, neck, or leg. In the early days, when the *running-iron* was in general use, a brand might cover the whole side of an animal, even both sides. (Horse brands were generally much smaller, possibly to make them less unsightly.) The positioning of a brand on the animal was noted in the county *brand book* and, along with the ear-mark, was as important as the brand itself. If there were two outfits with similar brands in fairly close proximity, the position naturally became extra important.

But not even a brand was a sure deterrent against thieves who could (if they knew their business) alter one, especially in the days of the running-iron. This style of branding was so open to abuse and the brands so open

Screw Plate   Bell   Hashknife   Flying O   Slash T

E Lazy Y   Tumbling K Lazy K   E2 Connected   Triangle Crazy A   Rafter K

Heart   Bar B   Diamond Cross   Running W   Stirrup

Lazy Ladder   Sombrero   Turkey Track   Open A Swinging A   7NL

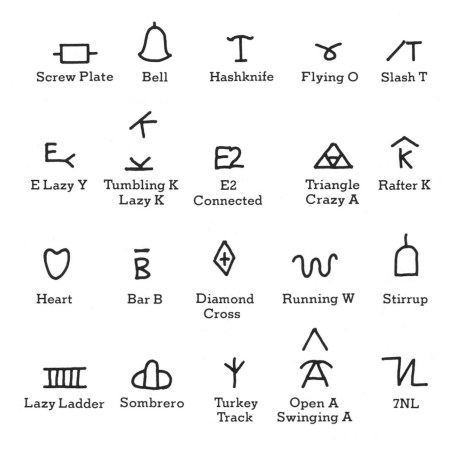

Cattleman's brand book with the name of the owner,
his brand, and ear-marks

to being changed that many states and territories legislated against the use of such a tool. A **brand artist** could create an effective imitation of an established brand with a cinch-ring heated in a fire and held with the tips of two sticks, or he could deftly alter an existing brand to one more to his own liking: a camp cook's pot-hook was used on more than one occasion. In the states in which a man could be arrested for carrying a running-iron tied to his saddle, the brand blotter merely resorted to carrying a short one in his boot-top, slicker, or maybe his **warbag.**

A man learned to read brands much as an expert read heraldic devices in Europe during the Middle Ages. There were a number of basic and universally recognized symbols—box, circle, rafter, diamond, etc.— and there could be half and quarter symbols, such as half-circle, quarter-circle, half-diamond. A figure or a letter lying down was "lazy"; thus, you could have the Lazy S. If a letter was tilted forward it was "tumbling"; if it sat on a quarter-circle it was "rocking"; if it had a half-circle resting on its head it was "swinging." It could be "barbed," "flying," "walking," "reversed," or "inverted."

As a brand was often made up of more than one letter, digit, or geometrical shape, there had to be a generally accepted method of reading it: this was from left to right, top to bottom, and from the outside inward. Thus the Circle A brand was a circle enclosing an A. The Box or Boxed 7 was a square enclosing a seven. The Rafter 2 was the figure two with an inverted V over it. If two letters were touching each other, such as MC, the brand was known as the MC Connected. If the two letters were connected by a small horizontal stroke (generally like a hyphen), the brand would be the M Bar C. The figure ¼ would be 1 Bar 4. Many brands were made up of the initials, nickname, or abbreviation of the name of the owner. Some made words: for example, STORY, the brand of L. J. Story of Caldwell County, Texas, 1869 (Allen 1933). Typical names of brands were such ones as 76 Bar, Circle R, Rafter K, Bar Key, the Hashknife, XIT, and The Thistles. A cow-outfit often went by the name of its brand and a whole range was referred to by the brand of the cattle it supported. (Osgood 1929; Mora 1950; Dobie 1941)

brasada
(Sp *brasada:* armful, armful of firewood; from *brazo:* branch or arm). Brush-country, a land of deep thickets, found typically in southwest Texas, the land of the brush-poppers. (see **brush-popper**). (Dobie 1929; Ramon Adams 1944; Mathews 1951)

brasada measure
The stretch of a man's arm along a *reata* held taut in both hands. (Dobie 1929)

brasaderos
Men and cattle of the brush-country. (Mora 1950)

brassero
(Mex-Sp *brasero;* SW). A brick oven used by Mexicans and Pueblo Indians. (Waters 1950)

brave
An Indian warrior. Bartlett 1877 says that it was a term borrowed from the French of Canada, and this is not to be doubted. Early dime novels use *brave* frequently as white heroes kill warriors by the score and prove them anything but brave.

brave-maker
Whiskey. (Ramon Adams 1944)

bravo
(Mex-Sp; SW).
(1) Fierce, brave. (Dobie 1930)
(2) A nickname for the Rio Grande.

brazil
Also **brasil, blue wood.** *Condalia obovata.* An evergreen growth that formed some of the impenetrable thickets of the brasada of southwest Texas.

brea
(Sp). Pitch, tar. Used for roofing in California and the Southwest. Also used domestically by certain Indian peoples in those areas.

breachy
Said of a cow with the habit of breaking through fences to freedom. (Weseen 1934; Ramon Adams 1944)

breadroot
See *camas (1).*

break
(1) In the West, this word commonly implied riding a wild horse until it became tame, though a horse could also be broken in other ways. Many horses in remudas in early times were scarcely even half-broken, and every time a hand called for a fresh mount he could be in for a fight. More rarely the word was used to imply the opposite of gentling a horse (see *gentle*). As Dobie 1952 points out, the conventional breaking of a mustang could indeed often break its spirit completely and thus ruin it. Also **bust.**
(2) To **make a break** (for freedom). Said of a cow or horse trying to leave the herd or bunch, or of a captive man attempting escape.

break down timber
See *timber (1)*.

breaking age
An age at which a horse is ready for breaking, generally from three to four years old during our period. (Ramon Adams 1944)

breaking brush
Brush-popping, working brush-country. (Ramon Adams 1944). See also *brush-popper.*

breaking pen
A small pen in which horses may be broken. Usually without ninety-degree corners, to lessen the chance of accidents. (Ramon Adams 1944)

break in two
I have always thought that this term applied to a horse erupting under a rider, figuratively breaking in two. Ramon Adams 1944 substantiates this: "Said when a horse starts bucking." The explanation of Weseen 1934 ("When a bronco finally submits he is said to break in two") may be accepted as a localism, but not as a generality.

breastwork
Not a Westernism, but frequently met with when a fight between whites and Indians is described. A defense-work of logs, earth, brush, rocks, etc., thrown up breast-high. (Beal 1963)

breechclout
Breechcloth, loincloth: a flap of cloth that usually passed over a belt, back and front, and between the legs; worn (often with hide leggings) by male Indians to cover their private parts. It is said that when Apaches appropriated whitemen's pants, they cut out the seat and wore the legs of the trousers with a breechclout.

breed
An abbreviation of *halfbreed.*

bridle chain
A short chain attaching the reins to the bit of a horse's bridle. (Ramon Adams 1944)

bridle ring
A ring at each end of the horse's bit to which the reins or bridle chains are fastened. (Ramon Adams 1944)

bridles

In the main, there are three types, with slight variations on all three.
(1) The **split-ear bridle,** which is the simple affair we see so often on the movie and TV screens. A leather strap goes over the animal's head, down the cheeks, and is attached to the bit. Over the top of the head, the strap is split, so that one part is behind the ears and the other in front, the strip in front being the narrower of the two. As with most of such gear, it could be improvised in an emergency from any right-sized strip of leather or rawhide. (See also *ear head*.)

(2) The **California bridle** was a more elabo-
rate affair (as we would expect from the color-
ful Californios). It could be made of leather and
was composed of a strip that hung down from
the horse's crown, behind the ears, and was
held in place by a band across the forehead.
It was sometimes made of horsehair of varied
colors, skillfully and attractively woven.

(3) The **hackamore.** (Mex-Sp *jáquima*). The
conventional Anglo variant of the Mexican
word. A horse's halter without a bit. It was com-
posed of a braided rawhide noseband (see *bozal*) "with two strips of *latigo* whang [see *whang*] interlaced to either side to act as cheek-plates and tie at the poll to hold it in place. . . . Buckles are seldom used. Some may have a browband of the same narrow whang, or a throat latch." (Mora 1950). The reins were made of light-weight hair rope (*mecate,* or McCarty), and a blind (*tapajos*) could also be added. The hacka- more could be properly constructed or extemporized from rope, and its importance to Western horsemen cannot be over-emphasized: in the hands of the right man it was a subtle and vital tool, one reason why the old Californios rode well-mannered, sweet-mouthed horses. As Mora adds, all they needed was a hackamore and plenty of time and patience. Hackamore training could last for six months to a year, and a horse trained with a reined hackamore was sometimes referred to as a **hackamore colt.**

bridle-wise

A horse expertly trained to the bridle. (Weseen 1934). Ramon Adams 1944 stresses that a horse, to be bridle-wise, must be disciplined to neck-reining (see *neck-reiner*).

brindle

(1) To go.
(2) Not a Westernism, but found frequently in Western literature to describe a coloring of cattle. Also *brockled.*

brockled

Applied to cows, implying a patchy coloring; brindled; blotched with a number of shades and colors. (Ramon Adams 1944; Jennings 1971). The only other mention of this word I can find in dialects is in sixteenth-century England, when it was applied to a cow given to breaking out of its pasture. I wonder if it is connected with *brock,* a badger.

bronc

Originally an unbroken horse, but came to mean *cow horse.* (Allen 1933)

broncho

(Sp *bronco:* uncouth, rough, rude). Also **bronco.** This could be used in reference to any animal or man who had gone wild, but normally it was used as a common Anglo form of the Spanish word—much used in literature written during the latter half of the nineteenth century—and referred to a Western horse, presumably a mustang or one of mustang descent. Later commonly cut to **bronc,** really meaning an unbroken horse, but also used in reference to any native horse—a cowpony. Bartlett 1877 says: "a native Californian horse." Allen 1933 uses the word as "mean."

bronco buster

Also **buster** (Weseen 1934; Ramon Adams 1944), **bronc breaker, bronc peeler, bronc twister,** etc. A breaker of wild or unbroken horses. Now commonly **bronc buster.**

broomie

Also **broomtail.** A wild horse, a mustang. Sometimes applied to a *range horse* that had not been brought in for breaking (as opposed to a *shave-tail*). Ramon Adams 1944 says: "*broom-tail*—range mare, a horse with a long bushy tail. Usually shortened to *broomie.*" Weseen 1934 says: "ponies with short bushy tails." (McMechen 1967)

broughten

See *boughten.*

broughtens up

Upbringing, bringing-up, education. No doubt a Northeastern provincialism that crept into the West via New England from Old England. Both Farmer 1889 and Bartlett 1877 mention the term.

brujo

(Sp; SW). A wizard. (Dobie 1930). A witch, of course, was a **bruja.**

brush-hand

Also **brush-buster** (Ramon Adams 1944), *brush-popper.* A cowhand accustomed to working cattle in the brush-country of southwest Texas and elsewhere. The work was difficult, dangerous, and arduous; skill at it was the result of hard experience. (Dobie 1929; Ramon Adams 1944; Berrey and van den Bark 1942)

brush-popper
Applied to both men and horses that popped or drove Longhorns from the dense thickets of the Texas *brasada*. (Dobie 1930; Weseen 1934; Ramon Adams 1944)

buchario
I suspect an Eastern contemporary version of *buckaroo*. (Henry Nash Smith 1950)

buck
(1) The whiteman's name for an Indian male, thus putting him on the same level as an animal.
(2) A horse's pitch, which term was in more common use on the Southern and Texas ranges. (de Quille 1876)

buckaroo
(Sp *vaquero*). Also **bucaroo** (Mora 1950), **buccaro** (Remington in Harby 1890), **buckara** (Barrère and Leland 1897; Berrey and van den Bark 1942), **jackeroo** (Wentworth 1944). A word that was no doubt popular in pulp-literature because of its suggestion of a rider on a bucking horse. Buckaroo was a form commonly associated with the range country in the Northwest. (Wentworth 1944). Weseen 1934 has **buckaree** as a Southwestern variant.

buckboard
Also **buck wagon**. A light, four-wheeled vehicle drawn by one or two horses and made to carry two to four people.
The floor was of springboard, which provided the bucking effect that gave the vehicle its name and which slightly lessened the violent jolting on bad trails and in rough country. The vehicle was not usually springless, however,  for the seat or seats were individually sprung. (Ramon Adams 1944; Mathews 1951; Foster-Harris 1955)

buckbrush
Any one of a number of bushes on which deer grazed. Weseen 1934 thought it a bush on which sheep grazed.

bucking roll
A blanket or coat rolled and tied in front of the rider to give him a tight

seat on a bucking horse. (Weseen 1934; Berrey and van den Bark 1942; Ramon Adams 1944). Rossi 1975 informs me that they were also manufactured for many years in the twentieth century (the Clark bucking roll) for use with the *slick-fork* saddle, prior to the introduction of the *swell-fork.*

bucking straight away
Describes a horse bucking in long jumps straight ahead. Really a rodeo term which probably did not come into use until the end of the nineteenth or early twentieth century. (Ramon Adams 1944; Rossi 1975)

bucking strap
(1) Weseen 1934 writes: "A strap attached to a saddle to be held on to in an emergency."
(2) Rossi 1975: "Rigging around the flank of a rodeo horse, a touchy part of the anatomy . . . it somewhat urges the horse to buck harder and longer. Also used on bulls in bull-riding events." It was probably in use toward the end of the nineteenth century. Also **flank rigging** (Ramon Adams 1944). See also *bull rigging.*

buck jumping
The pitching or bucking antics of a horse. (Weseen 1934)

buck nun
(1) A bachelor. As short and sweet a Westernism as ever I heard. (Berrey and van den Bark 1942)
(2) A recluse. (Ramon Adams 1944)

buckshot
The Shorter Oxford English Dictionary 1973 states that it is shot used for shooting game. Any Western buff could augment that statement. It was and is the small balls which constitute the load of a shot-gun, formed in the past by dropping molten metal from a shot-tower. Useful ammunition for the shot that needs a scattering fire, causing terrible devastation at close range. A useful load for lawmen and stage-guards. The individual balls of buckshot ranged from .24 of an inch (No. 1 Buck) to .33 of an inch, the famous Double O (OO) Buck. The latter was usually loaded with nine pellets in the 12-gauge shot-gun. Not a Westernism.

buckskin
(1) The skin of a buck antelope or deer, used in the early days by the Indians and some whitemen for shirts and leggings.
(2) A horse the color of buckskin, with black tail and mane. (Wentworth 1944; Ramon Adams 1944)

buckstrap
Ramon Adams 1944 says: "A narrow strap rivetted to the leather housing of the saddle just below and on the *off-side* of the base of the horn. Top riders have nothing but contempt for this hand hold, and of course it is barred at contests." Not to be confused with *bucking strap (1)*.

buck the saddle
Said of an unbroken horse bucking against an empty saddle on its back. The horse is rope-held until it becomes accustomed to the new weight on its back. (Ramon Adams 1944)

bucky horse
An unbroken horse. (Berrey and van den Bark 1942)

buff
Buffalo hunters' slang for the buffalo. (Rossi 1975)

buffalo
As with other animal names in the Old West—for example, *antelope* and mountain lion (see *cougar*)—the buffalo was not a buffalo at all, but a bison. But to the men of the Old West he was  —and to Western buffs he is and ever shall be —a buffalo. They came in two sub-species: the **plains buffalo** (*Bison bison bison*) and the **woods buffalo** (*Bison bison athabascae*), the latter known to early frontiersmen as **mountain buffalo,** because they wintered in the Rockies. The plains buffalo is the one we read so much about, but, in fact, in the early days both were pretty widely dispersed, although the plains type spread much farther south. The woods buffalo were bigger and darker than the plains, with bulls up to 2,500 pounds and cows up to 1,600 pounds.

The animal was first recorded about 1530 by Nuñez Cabeza de Vaca on the plains of Texas. At that time it probably ranged from the Rio Grande up into Canada and from the eastern Rocky Mountains into western Maryland and down into northern Mississippi and Louisiana.

So closely was the buffalo integrated with the Plains Indians' mode of life that these Indians were really a part of a buffalo culture. The animal provided tents and clothing; its meat was jerked; its horns were made into spoons and utensils; and its hair was woven into ropes, belts, and ornaments. Not surprisingly, the buffalo became an essential part of Indian religion. Charms, totems, and ritual were centered about the buffalo in order to make the herds come and provide the Indian with his necessities.

Once the Indians had the horse, they used the technique of running the buffalo, shooting them with arrows or guns or lancing them from horseback. In earlier days, they took advantage of the buffalos' tendency to panic and stampeded them over cliffs or into log traps. Surrounds were also formed, in which a large number of tribesmen encircled a bunch of animals and then rushed among them on foot, shooting them with arrows. In the horse-period, the summer hunt occupied the whole tribe; discipline was strict, and any man killing buffalo on his own was severely punished, sometimes by death. June, July, and August were the official hunting months. The animals were butchered by the men, divided, and the meat was taken by the women. Small organized parties carried out the winter hunts.

To look at, the animal was cumbersome, with massive forequarters covered with long hair, its shoulders humped, and its head carried low and bearing formidable horns. In spite of his appearance, Boss (see *boss [2]*) could move and then some, clocking up to 35 to 40 miles per hour over a quarter mile and holding speed over a long distance—which meant that if a hunter was running buffalo and didn't make a hit in the first few hundred yards, the quarry could outrun him for a clear 10 miles. Immediate acceleration was gained from standing position by a characteristic four-footed bound.

By the time the white hunters were out on the plains, there were three main herds: the northern, the Republican (or central), and the southern. Originally, on the plains, it was the whiteman's custom to hunt the animal from horseback, to come alongside the buffalo and shoot it on the run. However, when hide-hunting became an industry, hunters worked in teams and shot from afoot. (See also *stand*.) By the 1880s the buffalo were as good as finished, and an industry had sprung up collecting bones for phosphorous fertilizer from the slaughter-ground where the hunters had killed wastefully for hides alone, leaving the meat to rot. One collector gathered the bones of about 100,000 animals. Dodge 1877 reckoned that, between the years 1872 and 1874, nearly 4½ million buffalo were killed and nearly 32½ million pounds of bones were shipped out on the railroad. Senior soldiers and civilians vigorously expressed the opinion that the only way to clear the frontier for settlement was to wipe out the buffalo and so finish the Indian. Simple ecological logistics, if you'll pardon the phrase. In all fairness, it should be recorded that there were soldiers and civilians who added their protests against the slaughter to those of the Indians. Encouraging to know that the nation and dedicated men have saved this fine animal, which, having nearly disappeared from earth, now numbers something like 30,000 in the United States.

For justice to be done to the subject a volume is needed—and has been written by Tom McHugh: *The Time of the Buffalo.* (Sandoz 1954; Hawgood 1967; McHugh 1972; Grzimek 1974)

buffalo berry
Also **bull-berry**. Genus *Shepherdia*. The fruit of the *buffalo bush;* the scarlet berries were eaten by Indians.

buffalo bush
Bartlett 1877 says this was a small tree or bush growing in thickets on the banks of streams in the Rocky Mountains near the Humboldt River. Its fruit was called the bull-berry and the buffalo berry. (Mathews 1951)

buffalo chips
The dung of the buffalo, which, when dried in the wind and sun, provided fuel for fires. (Weseen 1934; Berrey and van den Bark 1942). Possibly a polite version of "buffalo shit." Literary references to it are many.

buffalo clover
A species of clover found in the West: *Trifolium reflexum stoloniferum*. The term also referred to the Texas bluebonnet (*Lupinus texensis*).

buffaloed
(1) Confused. Wentworth 1944 also quotes the term as **buffaloo**. (Ramon Adams 1944)
(2) Said of a man struck over the head with a gun before he had the chance to draw his own weapon. (Lake 1931)

buffalo gnat
A small gnat found on the plains, of various species of the genus *Simulium*, the famous "black fly." Its bite could cause painful swelling in humans. (Mathews 1951)

buffalo grass
The coarse grass of the Great Plains on which the buffalo fed. There were various kinds. Dodge 1877: "The buffalo grass of the high plains and the gramma grass are identical, though entirely different in growth and appearance." (See also *grama grass*.) Farmer 1889 adds interestingly: "The BUFFALO GRASS is uninviting to the eye, being so very short that an inexperienced man in search of pasture for animals would pass it without consideration. It makes up in thickness what it lacks in length and horses and cattle not only eat it greedily, but fill themselves much quicker than would seem possible. The Arkansas Valley at Fort Lyon is covered with tall, fine-looking grass, which the large herds of domestic cattle will scarcely touch, preferring to go eight or ten miles from the river, to feed upon the BUFFALO GRASS of the high plain."

buffalo gun

Any make of rifle which had the range, velocity, and penetrating power (which had to be considerable) to drop a buffalo. The Spencer and the Henry, which were the popular repeating rifles at the start of the large-scale buffalo kills, did not have this power in the cartridges for which they were chambered, nor did the early average single-shot rifle. Indeed, the early hunters using .44 guns from Remington, Springfield, Bullard, Sharps, Maynard, etc., demanded more lethal weapons. When buffalo hunting became a serious industry, many of the first hunters out of Fort Hays, Kansas (according to McHugh), used the U.S. government .50-70, a size made available by Springfield and later by other manufacturers. But the hunters demanded even a heavier load, and in 1875 Sharps came up with the .50–90. This was the *Big Fifty* in hide-hunter parlance, although Sharps brought out in 1880 a more powerful .50-caliber cartridge, a "Bigger Fifty" as it were, the .50–140–700. An efficient gun was, of course, the most essential tool of the hunter, and this meant that he must be able to kill the biggest bull with one shot, if a vital part were hit. (Ramon Adams 1944; McHugh 1972)

buffalo mange

Lice. Probably because buffalo hunters, stinking and unwashed, were good breeding grounds for same. (Ramon Adams 1944)

buffalo-nut

Bartlett 1877: "(*Pyrularis oleifera*). Oil nut. Western." Mathews 1951 says: "the rabbitwood, *Pyrulia pubera.*"

buffalo-range

Country on which bison grazed. Weseen 1934 defines it as wide-open empty spaces. (Berrey and van den Bark 1942; Ramon Adams 1944)

buffalo-robe

The hide of a buffalo prepared for use—preferably that of a cow because of its comparative softness. The Indian method of dressing the hide was for a woman to first remove all scraps of flesh left by the skinner, then to scrape the inner surface clean and to an even thickness. Hides for robes were worked only on the flesh side. (For other purposes, the hair was removed.) The skin was then dressed with a mixture of cooked brains, liver, and fat, after which it was dried in the sun and later soaked in water. The next step was to wring out the surplus water, stretch the hide on a frame, and work it with a tool until it was almost dry. Then it was grained with a piece of stone or bone to smooth it. After another drying period, the robe was hung over a suspended line and worked backward and forward, creating heat and bringing about the final softening that made it ready for use. (If the skin was to be used for garments, yet another process was needed: it was smoked thoroughly so that it would not dry stiff after being soaked by rain.)

Buffalo-robes (as well as buffalo leather) became extremely popular in the United States and Europe during the 1870s, and millions of raw-hides went to Eastern U.S. and European tanneries to be dressed in the conventional manner. (Hodge 1907–10; McHugh 1972)

buffalo runner
See *hide-hunter.*

buffalo skinner
See *skinner (1).*

buffalo soldiers
Originally the Indian name for Negro soldiers, who reminded the Indians of the buffalo (probably because of their short curly black hair), the term came into general use on the frontier. John Prebble, one of those rare Englishmen who can write well of the West, wrote a fine novel titled *The Buffalo Soldiers* (1959). (Ramon Adams 1944)

buffalo-tea
The water left in a wallow after a buffalo (or range cow) wallowed in it. (Foster-Harris 1955)

buffalo wallow
It was the habit of the buffalo to wallow in natural dips in the prairie. After the dust had been wallowed in for possibly centuries, the dips often became saucer-shaped and of considerable size. In times of rain, water could be found in them, and on occasion they provided cover for white-men under attack from Indians. The buffalo's desire to wallow is closely associated with its rubbing habits. It is recorded that one poor fellow had his solitary cabin quite destroyed by the giant animals rubbing themselves into an ecstasy against it. They probably resorted to rubbing themselves on the ground when there was an absence of trees (or settlers' cabins) against which to titillate themselves. (Ramon Adams 1944; McHugh 1972)

bugger
To show sudden fright; to spook, to booger. Dobie 1941: "If the boys could get the stampeders to milling, Old Blue's bawl had a powerful effect on quietening them. At the head of a herd, he never 'buggered' when a jackrabbit suddenly jumped up under a sagebrush at his nose. . . . "

buggy boss
An absentee ranch-owner who presumably did not trust himself on the back of a horse and visited his property in a buggy. (Ramon Adams 1944; Berrey and van den Bark 1942; Sandoz 1958)

bug juice
Alcohol, whiskey. (Ramon Adams 1944; Emrich 1951)

build a loop
To prepare the noose of a lasso for a throw, to shake it out. (Ramon Adams 1944)

build a smoke
To roll a cigarette.

bulger
Something uncommonly large. (Bartlett 1877)

bull-berry
See *buffalo berry; buffalo bush.*

bull briar
Also **bull brier.** Mathews 1951 says that the term covers two species of *Smilax.* Bartlett 1877 says: "Bamboo briar in the alluvial bottoms of the South-West, the root of which contains a farinaceous substance from which the Indians make bread."

bulldogger
A cowboy employed in *bulldogging.* Also **dogger** (Weseen 1934; Ramon Adams 1944), which, I think, has a connection with *dogal.* (North 1942; Berrey and van den Bark 1942; Ramon Adams 1944)

bulldogging
The act of throwing a cow by hand. Now an important part of rodeo competition, it originated with the throwing of calves by the bulldoggers at branding time. The bulldogging of steers is best described by Ramon Adams 1944, who writes: "To throw one's right arm over a steer's neck, the right hand gripping the loose, bottom skin at the base of the right horn or the brute's nose, while the left hand seizes the tip of the brute's left horn. The dogger rises clear of the ground and, by lunging his body downward against his own elbow, so twists the neck of the animal that the latter loses his balance and falls. The first bulldogger was a Negro named Bill Pickett,

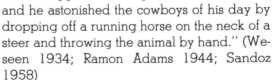

and he astonished the cowboys of his day by dropping off a running horse on the neck of a steer and throwing the animal by hand." (Weseen 1934; Ramon Adams 1944; Sandoz 1958)

▶ ## Bull Durham
The cowhand's brand of smoking tobacco—both rolled into cigarettes and smoked in a

pipe, I suspect. It came in a muslin sack on which was the famous label showing the bull. Good example of early advertising psychology. (Foster-Harris 1955)

bullet mold
A hinged mold for making bullets. Even after brass cartridges were introduced, isolated or thrifty men molded their own bullets.

bullets
In addition to its common meaning, it also referred to pockets or pieces of gold.

bull-hides
(1) The hides of bulls; according to time and place, "bull" could refer to the hides of buffalo or cow-critters.
(2) Chaps made from bull-hide.

bull prick
A miner's word for the steel drill he drove into the rock-face with a single-jack (one-headed) hammer. (Evans 1959)

bull-puncher
A man employed to keep steers on their feet in railroad cattle-cars going to market. He was armed with a long, spiked pole with which to prod the animals to their feet when they lay or fell down in the crowded cars. (Roberts 1924). I think that **cow-puncher** and **cowpoke** were first used in the same sense and only at quite a later date came to be applied to the cowboy of the range. See also *jobbing*.

bull rigging
In rodeo bull-riding, the rigging around a bull's body just back of the hump, which provided a handhold for the rider. Usually a bell was attached underneath to increase the bull's action; a flank strap was also used. Probably a comparatively modern Westernism. (Rossi 1975). See also *bucking strap (2)*.

bull-running
A sport practiced by the rancheros of California and the Southwest in the early nineteenth century. A bull was played with lances in an arena or corral from horseback, then let out onto the plain, where it was chased, caught, and tailed (see *tailing*). (Towne and Wentworth 1955)

bull-train
Also **grass-train** (Ramon Adams 1944; Rossi and Hunt 1971). Most of the heavy freighting of the Old West was carried out by such trains,

though the animals involved were not bulls but oxen, which could live well on the grass at the side of the trail on the long hauls and, being slower than horses, were less likely to be run off successfully by Indians. Although in places bull-trains were succeeded by the railroad, they survived in parts of the West until the 1890s. There was much argument between freighters over the superiority of oxen or mules, since oxen could not survive so well in hard country. (Vestal 1939; Rossi and Hunt 1971). Also called a **bull outfit** (Mathews 1951) when a number of teams were involved. See also *corn freight.*

bullwhacker

A driver of a *bull-train,* the team of which was made up of oxen. Bullwhackers usually walked beside their teams, and a delightful picture of such men is left to us by R. B. Cunningham Graham in "Hegira," one of his *Thirteen Stories* (1900): "Great teams of wagons driven by Texans creaked through the streets, the driver dressed in a 'defroque' of his old town clothes, often a worn frock-coat and rusty trousers stuffed into cowboy boots, the whole crowned with an ignominiously battered hat, and looking, as the Mexicans observed, like 'pantomimas, que salen las fiestas.' " (Howard and others 1960; Weseen 1934; Ramon Adams 1944)

bull whip

A whip, the stock of which was short and often weighted with lead; used by bullwhackers, whose skill with it, both as a tool and a weapon, was phenomenal. The older whips had a separate wooden stock about two feet long with the whip attached to the end; the stock was often held in both hands. Normally, the lash was 15 to 25 feet long, of braided rawhide, and tapering to the end. (Rossi 1975). Ramon Adams 1944 defines the whip as "a heavy cow whip, sometimes the knotted end of a rope." Mathews 1951 quotes it as a non-Westernism.

bunch

A group or gathering of anything living in the West was a bunch: a bunch of cows; a bunch of horses; the Wild Bunch (a collection of badmen renowned in fact and legend). The word was even applied to trees. It could also be used as a verb meaning "to gather together," "to corral." (Bartlett 1877). See also *wild bunch.*

bunch grass

Western grasses that grew in bunches, belonging to any number of species. Mentioned frequently in fiction for a touch of local color.

bunch grassers
(1) Inhabitants of the foothills. (Weseen 1934; Ramon Adams 1944)
(2) A *range horse* living on such grass. (Ramon Adams 1944; Berrey and van den Bark 1942)

bunch-quitter
A horse or cow that had the habit of breaking free of its bunch or herd. By extension it could be applied to a man who deserted his group. Ramon Adams 1944 applies the term to horses only, as do Berrey and van den Bark 1942.

bunk
Bartlett 1877 says it is from the Anglo-Saxon *benc:* a bench or form.
(1) A box bed with shallow wooden sides, found in cowhands' bunk-houses or in cabins generally. Not exclusively a Westernism in this sense.
(2) To sleep, to share a bed with another. (Weseen 1934; Ramon Adams 1944)

bunk-house
The bachelor living-quarters of ranch-hands. So named for the bunks in which the men slept. They were sometimes two-tiered. (Weseen 1934; Ramon Adams 1944)

bunkie
Also **bunky**. In a trail-driving camp, cowboys (often partners) were paired off, and the two men would sometimes share the same tarp over their blankets—or the blankets themselves—for warmth. These men were called bunkies. (Andy Adams 1909). Also common among U.S. army enlisted men in the 1880s and 1890s. (Rossi 1975). See also *partner (1)*.

bunko
Also **bunco**. A game of chance played with a board of 43 squares and either cards or dice; the name possibly came from a Spanish card game. A favorite of the con man, in which the sucker was allowed to win at first only to lose heavily later. The decoy, who steered the suckers to the game or to a gambling house generally, was called the **bunko-steerer** (also seen as **bunco-steer**). The notorious Doc Holliday is said to have been a **bunko-artist** (Jahns 1961), but Soapy Smith was the acknowledged master of the game.

buñuelo
(Mex-Sp; New Mexico). Also **sopapilla**. Biscuit fried in fat.

burn the breeze
To ride fast. (Weseen 1934; Ramon Adams 1944)

burro
(Sp). A donkey. In the early days, large herds of these animals ran wild in Texas, particularly in the region between the Rio Grande and the ▶ Nueces River. Until the 1920s, they were a great pest in many parts. (Dobie 1952). Southwestern Texas used to export them in droves to the mines of Colorado.

burrowing owl
Also **squinch owl** (Rossi 1975). *Speotyto cuniculania hypogaea.* The small prairie owl, which takes over the burrow of a prairie dog for its home. Although the prairie dog does not seem to resent him overly, the owl repays this hospitality by sometimes consuming the young of its host. It also eats mice and small vermin. It appears to have become almost earth-bound at times, for when danger approaches it may conceal itself rather than take to flight. (Dobie 1965)

buscadero
(Sp *buscador:* seeker, searcher). Used originally for a lawman, but latterly applied to any gunman. (Ramon Adams 1944; Cunningham 1934)

bushed
Worn down, tired. Applied to man, horse, or cow.

bushwa, bushwah
See *bois de vache.*

bushway
See *bourgeois.*

bushwhack
To ambush. Sometimes to shoot from behind. At all events, to attack in surprise from cover. Thought to be derived from the days when the riverboatmen moved their boats by gripping overhead branches of the trees at the bow and then walking to the stern. Later, during the Civil War, the term was applied to guerrillas who made their raids in the woods. Also, **bush-whacker.** Not a true Westernism. (Ramon Adams 1944)

bust
(1) To throw an animal violently.
(2) To break a horse. (Berrey and van den Bark 1942; Weseen 1934; Ramon Adams 1944)

buster
See *bronco buster.*

butcher
Also **marker** (Chilton 1961). A later development of the branding team: the man who did the knife work, cutting animals' ear-marks (see *ear-mark*), etc. (Ramon Adams 1944)

butt
(1) The handle of a gun, rifle, quirt, etc.
(2) The smoked end of a cigarette. The Englishman's "dog-end."
(3) A man's posterior. Short for buttocks. Found much in Western fiction. (Bartlett 1877)
(4) To oppose. (Bartlett 1877)

butte
(Fr). A hill, a sudden rise in the land. Ramon Adams 1944 defines it neatly as "a conspicuous hill or mountain left standing in an area reduced by erosion." Dunn 1886 writes that, in the Northwest, it was used as the equivalent of the Southwesterner's hill.

butternuts
Bartlett 1877: "A term applied to the Confederate soldiers during the late civil war, so called from the color of their clothes, a cinnamon color from the skins of the butternut." Not a Westernism, of course, but a term that appears fairly frequently in literature about the Civil War period.

button
(1) A small boy. Not exclusive to the West, but appearing often in Western fiction. (Jennings 1971)
(2) The small nub of a calf's horn. (Rossi 1975)

buzzard bait
A poor horse, fit only to be food for the buzzards. Unkindly or in humor, the term could be applied to a man. (Weseen 1934; Ramon Adams 1944)

caballada
See *cavallard.*

caberos
(Sp *cabestro:* halter). Originally a soft halter of hair rope, this came to mean a hair rope itself. The original word **cabestro** was also retained, and in many areas it was used to distinguish a hair-rope halter (see *hair lariat*) from one made of rawhide or leather (Dobie 1930; Ramon Adams 1944), though it was sometimes applied to a form of *reata,* which properly was made of hide. Cabestro was also seen as **cabestra, cabras,** and **cavraces.** (Mathews 1951)

cabeza del fuste
(Sp: head of the saddle). The Mexican term for the head of the saddle-tree. Texans called this the *fuste* or **fusty.** (Mora 1950)

caboodle
A word common in all states and territories north of the Mexican border. The whole bunch, everything, everybody—that is, the **whole kit and caboodle.** Bartlett 1877 claims it for the whole United States; Ramon Adams 1944 claims it as Western; and Wentworth 1944 quotes it from Cape Cod in 1850 and also gives the variant **camboodle.**

caboose
(probably from the Middle Dutch *kabuys* or *kabanhuys*).
(1) While it referred, on the railroad, to the brakeman's car, in the West it was a dried cowhide slung under the chuck wagon on the cattle trail to carry wood and other fuel (such as cowchips or buffalo chips), stake pins

for horses (see *picket pin*), etc. Also **bitch, cooney, cradle, 'possum belly.**
(Fletcher 1968)
(2) When one wagon was towed by another, as was so often the case on
freight-lines, the rear one was called the caboose or **tail-wagon.** (Foster-
Harris 1955)

cabrie
Also **cabree, cabri, cabril,** etc. *Antilocapra americana.* The **pronghorn**
antelope. "When Alexander Henry came upon the Cheyenne, in 1806,
south of the Missouri River during a gala season, he saw their horses as
'most spirited animals, some were masked in a very singular manner, to
imitate the head of a buffalo, red deer, or cabrie with horns, the mouth and
nostrils—even the eyes—trimmed with red cloth.' " (Dobie 1941)

cabron
(Sp *cabrón:* he-goat). Extending from the old meaning of a man who allows
his wife to commit adultery and who "wears the horns," it came to mean
in the Southwest an outlaw of the lowest order. (Ramon Adams 1944)

cache
(Fr *cacher:* to hide; it came into the United States via Canada).
(1) To hide something, to store it. (Weseen 1934)
(2) A hiding place or store. (Dunn 1886; Ramon Adams 1944)

cacique
(Sp). Also **casick, casique.** A village headman. Usually applied to settled
Indians, but occasionally to Mexicans. (Stansbury 1852)

cactus
Apart from meaning a desert succulent, the
word was applied to the desert country itself.
(Weseen 1934; Ramon Adams 1944)

cactus boomers
(1) Wild brush cattle. (Ramon Adams 1944)
(2) Cattle from sparsely grazed desert country.
(Mora 1950)

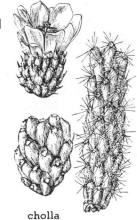

cholla

cafecito
(Mex-Sp). A cup of coffee. (Dobie 1930)

cahoots
Partnership. Used thus: "He was in cahoots with a fellow." Possibly, but
not very convincingly, from the French *cahute* (cabin), implying that two
men lived in the same house. Probably from the French *cahorte* (a gang).

Bartlett 1877 says there was a verb form, **to cahoot:** to act in partnership. (Ramon Adams 1944; Wentworth 1944)

calaboose
(Sp *calabozo,* Fr *calabouse;* SW). Jail. Dunn 1886 notes the Anglo corruption from the Spanish. Bartlett 1877 also gives **to calaboose:** to incarcerate.

calf branding
The branding of the *calf-crop* in the spring of the year. The sooner the owner's brand was on them the better.

calf-crop
The aggregate of the calves born in herd during the season. (Ramon Adams 1944)

calf-rope
To surrender, acknowledge defeat. (Weseen 1934)

calf 'round
Also **calf around.** To loaf, to idle. (Weseen 1934; Berrey and van der Bark 1942; Ramon Adams 1944)

calf round-up
The spring gather, when calves were branded. (North 1942)

calf-time
The spring; the time of the buffalo calving in Mountain-Man speech. (Ruxton 1849)

calf-wagon
Also **blattin' cart** (Ramon Adams 1944; Gard 1954), **blattin' wagon.** A wagon used on latter-day trail-drives in which calves born on the trail were carried. Such calves might be sold or given to farmers who lived by the trail and who would raise them by hand, but as late as 1875, it is recorded that calves were killed because they couldn't keep up with the mature cattle. Dobie 1941 writes: " 'That year, 1875,' he said, 'we were taking up a mixed herd to Wichita, Kansas . . . we didn't have room for hauling the calves, and "calf wagons" hadn't then come into use.' " Not surprisingly, some drovers preferred not to make mixed drives in which there were steers, cows, and calves; like-aged steers drove best of all. But it must be stated that there were men who liked to have a few cows and young along, believing that it steadied the rest of the herd.

calico
(1) A horse color. Some say a dappled animal, but in the West it was applied mostly to a pinto. (Weseen 1934; Ramon Adams 1944)

(2) A woman—from the calico dress she wore. (Berrey and van den Bark 1942; Ramon Adams 1944)
(3) As a verb, to pay court to a woman.

california
To bring an animal down by tripping it. (Weseen 1934; Ramon Adams 1944)

California banknote
A cowhide; used as currency in California before the goldrush of 1849. (Mora 1950)

California bridle
See *bridles (2)*.

California moccasins
Sacks tied around the feet as protection against extreme cold. You can imagine this being practiced on the old California Trail in the High Sierras. (Weseen 1934; Ramon Adams 1944)

California pants
Striped or checked pants of heavy wool, hard-wearing and favored for use on the range; this in spite of the current belief that all cattlemen wore Levi's. (Weseen 1934; Ramon Adams 1944)

California rig
See *center-fire rig.*

California sorrel
An older term for palomino. (Rossi 1975)

calumet
(Old Norman *chalumeau:* reed, pipe). A long-stemmed pipe used by Indians for smoking tobacco. A term that probably entered the United States from Canada. (Hodge 1907–10)

calzoneras
(Mex-Sp; SW and California). The Mexican-Spanish pants, split on the outside of the leg from just at or below the knee downward, usually to reveal the white linen or cotton of the underwear. The edges of this split were decorated with braid and silver *conchas.* (Gregg 1844)

camas
(1) *Camassia esculenta.* A staple food of the Indians of the Northwest and Canada. The early white settlers in Oregon also found it was valuable food and were said to be referred to as **camas eaters** because of this. Also

breadroot (Beal 1963), **camass, chamas, commas,** *kamas root,* **kamus, prairie turnip, quamash.** Sometimes confused by fiction writers with *cowish.*

(2) *Camas* may also be used to refer to the field, prairie, or ground where it is found. Beal 1963 quite frequently uses the term **camas prairie.**

camboodle
See *caboodle.*

camino real
(Sp: royal road; SW). The public highway. (Dobie 1930)

camp
Could be applied to the ranch-house itself as a leftover word from the early days when a ranch was first settled in camp form. Or it might refer to a line camp, one or more cabins from which men guarded the boundaries of a spread. It could also mean the temporary bivouac of a traveler or a trail-crew's resting place near the wagon.

camp cart
A two-wheeled cart, usually pulled by a pair of steers; it later gave way to the four-wheeled wagon. Mora 1950 notes that the term was used in 1857 by "Austin Jack" Thatcher in reference to the vehicle used on the then not well-established cattle trail from Texas to Hannibal, Missouri.

camp robber
Also **camp robin.** The jay, which was a great stealer of provisions from camps. Lone prospectors were said to be superstitious about them and would offer them no harm. (Emrich 1951; Mathews 1951)

camps
The old-time Texan would usually say "in camps" rather than "in camp." (Dobie 1929)

camp staller
A horse that was reluctant to leave camp in the morning. (Ramon Adams 1944)

camp wagon
The forerunner of the chuck wagon. Certainly a term in use before 1860. A wagon that carried supplies on the pre-war trail-drives, such as those from Texas through Louisiana to New Orleans. In fact, they were not generally wagons but two-wheeled ox-carts, hooped and tarpaulined, carrying a water-barrel and pulled by two yoke of oxen. (Mora 1950)

can
(1) To can a cow was to tie a tin can to its neck to stop it from fence-breaking. (Weseen 1934; Ramon Adams 1944)
(2) Ramon Adams 1944 gives the further meaning of firing an employee.

cañada
(Sp). A narrow valley or canyon. (Bartlett 1877)

canebreak splitters
Cattle brought into Texas from western Louisiana. They were probably of Spanish origin, and they undoubtedly interbred with the *black cattle,* the Longhorns, and possibly the Cherokee cattle. (Dobie 1941)

canelo
(Sp). Usually applied to a horse of cinnamon color and of California or Spanish stock. According to Dobie 1952, it was a red roan. Quote from *Real Academia Española Diccionario de la Lengua Española* 1956: *"Canelo, la, de color de canelo aplica especialmente a los perros y caballos"*—which informs us that this is the color of cinnamon, applied particularly to dogs and horses. Frémont performed his famous ride to deliver the message to García using two horses of this type, which were renowned for their stamina in Old California. The fiction writer Matt Chisholm 1973 mounts his hero McAllister on one.

cantina
(Mex-Sp).
(1) A saloon or wine-shop, Mexican style. (*Harper's Monthly Magazine* 1875)
(2) A pocket of a *mochila.* (Bradley 1913)
(3) A saddlebag; even a container that was hung from and lashed to a pack-saddle. (Gregg 1844). Ramon Adams 1944 refers to *saddle pockets* as **cantinesses,** which sounds like a fair variant. See also *pommel bags.*
(4) North 1942 uses it in another sense, which I have seen nowhere else: "the aroma of the coffee from the *cantina* on the glowing embers of the fire." He seems to be referring to a coffee-pot or cooking container of some kind, reminiscent of the word *canteen,* used by some English-speaking people for the container-cum-plate of soldiers.

cantle
The raised rear part of a saddle. (Ramon Adams 1944)

canyon
(Sp *cañón*). A steep-sided cut or valley in mountains or plain. (Ramon Adams 1944). A simple Anglo variant of the Spanish word.

cap-and-ball gun

Usually this referred to a single-shot pistol or revolver loaded with ball and loose powder and fired by a percussion cap placed on the nipple of the chamber in the case of the revolver. Cap-and-ball rifles survived into the later years of the nineteenth century, and, in spite of what many fiction writers maintain, the cap-and-ball revolver was used in the West for many years after the Civil War. Metal cartridges were expensive, and a man could be fairly self-sufficient with his own makings. The trouble was that a cap could fall from a nipple and cause failure to fire at a crucial moment in a fight. It is said that some noted gun-fighters kept spare ready-loaded cylinders in their pockets, handy for a fairly rapid reloading. As metal cartridges became cheaper and more readily available, so many Western-ers had their old cap-and-ball guns converted to cartridge. (Karr and Karr 1960). But the picture of an 1860s cowhand draped with shell-loaded belt is mostly erroneous. He would have carried his *hog-leg* high on his hip, with a powder flask, balls, and caps in pouches.

Both conical bullets and round balls of soft lead were molded for use in these weapons, but the latter were easier to mold and load and were quite satisfactory in performance. Men learned to load quickly under stress, but it was better done slowly and carefully. The wise man first cleared the nipples; this could be done extravagantly by firing a cap on each, but most men did not have caps to waste in this way. Then the hammer was half cocked so that the cylinder could turn. Next, the powder went in from the powder flask; it was of the old black variety, which made a man want to escape from his own smoke in a fight. The ball was so molded that, if the rammer was used properly to seat it, it would fit so snugly in the chamber that a patch to hold it in place would have been more of a detriment than a help to good shooting. The introduction of paper and linen cartridges did away with the tedious business of pouring loose powder into the chambers. These contained powder and ball, but percussion caps, of course, were still separate.

caponera

(Sp: coop). A bunch of geldings, horses that had been castrated (a *capón* in Spanish being a gelded animal). (Ramon Adams 1944)

caporal

(Sp: chief, boss, foreman; SW). Also **corporal**. A term used in northern Mexico to denote a foreman of cowhands. In Texas, it was usually applied to a foreman who was a Mexican—which was not uncommon in southwest Texas and the Southwest generally, where the crew on a cattle-ranch might be wholly or partly Mexican. (Andy Adams 1909). Sometimes it was used to indicate an under-foreman (Weseen 1934) or a Mexican trail-boss (Dobie 1964). Ramon Adams 1944 says: "The boss, the manager or assistant manager of a ranch." Dobie 1930 simply says "boss."

caps
Percussion caps, used as a source of ignition on cap-and-ball firearms (see *cap-and-ball gun*). (Bowman 1953)

captain
Leader of a wagon-train or the boss of a cattle-drive.

carabina
(Sp; SW). A carbine or rifle. (Dobie 1930)

carajo!
(Sp; SW). An expletive like *caramba!* Dobie 1930 writes: "an exclamation much used by mule-drivers, vaqueros, and other outdoor workers." Also seen in the verb form **carajoing.**

carbon
(Sp *carbón;* SW). Charcoal. (Dobie 1930)

carne asada
See *jerky.*

carreta
(Sp; Texas and SW). A large Mexican cart with two solid wooden wheels and drawn by oxen. (Dobie 1930; Stewart White 1933)

carretela
(Sp; SW). A horse-drawn carriage. (Mathews 1951)

carts
On the whole, Anglo-Americans used four-wheeled wagons, while the French and Mexicans favored two-wheeled carts—which seemed ideal for the rough surface of the plains. (Parkman 1872 substantiates this). The Texans, though, sometimes used carts (see *camp cart; camp wagon*).

cartucho
(Sp; SW). Cartridge shell. (Dobie 1930)

cartwheel
(1) A spur with a large rowel. (Mora 1951)
(2) A silver dollar. (Ramon Adams 1944; Mathews 1951)

carver, carving horse
See *cutting horse.*

cascabel
(Sp: jingle bell, jingle bob, the rattle of a rattlesnake). The enlarge-

ment at the loose end of a reata, which, after the *dally* around the sad-dlehorn was made, could be caught under the right leg of the roper. (Mora 1950)

cased wolf
In the fur-trade, a term for the coyote, because the pelt was "cased"—that is, peeled from the body without being split—then dried over a frame. (Dobie 1950)

casick, casique
See *cacique.*

castration
With cattle, a bull-calf's stones might be taken to make him easier to handle, to stop him from breeding, to put fat on him, or because a draft ox was wanted. Sometimes grown bulls were castrated—they were called *stags* and had slightly shorter horns than the early castrated steers (see *steer*). The operation made a shorthorn more tractable, but it didn't always work with Longhorns; there are some hair-raising tales of warlike perform-ances put on by steers when some poor *thirty-and-found* Texas boy tried to dab a rope on them. Wholesale bull-gelding took place in Texas when the Longhorns were brush-popped (see *brush-popper*) for the trail north. Many men believed that a herd of steers with no bulls and cows along was easiest to handle; on the trail a steer did not suffer from inflammation of the testicle-bag, as a bull might on long, hot marches. The great Charlie Goodnight found a way of preventing this distress without depriving the bovine Lord of the Brush of his glory, for which see *goodnighting.* The castration of calves was simple: the branding iron singed the little fellow's hide and the butcher cut short his breeding potential.

On the whole, the Westerner preferred his horseflesh gelded. The cowman regarded the bringing of ungelded horses to a round-up as a grossly unsocial act. Certainly, gelding made a horse more manageable, and a stallion (kept mainly for breeding purposes) could be a dangerous nuisance to gelded animals or mares. Indians, for hunting and war, pre-ferred stallions, which they considered to possess more stamina than gelded horses. (Dobie 1952)

cat
(1) A lynx. (Inman 1897)
(2) Short for catamount (see *cougar*). (Ramon Adams 1944)

catamount
See *cougar.*

catawampously
Or even **catawamptiously**. Take your pick of these two incredible words.

They meant "fiercely," "eagerly." Two of those delicious monstrosities created orally in a West that liked size in words as much as in anything else. (Bartlett 1877)

catawba
(1) A Sioux Indian.
(2) A kind of grape and the wine made therefrom.

catch dogs
See *dogs.*

catch on a snag
To meet one's superior, to be defeated or given one's comeuppance. Apparently confined to the Northwest. (Barrère and Leland 1897).

catch rope
A rope with a running noose with which to catch animals—mostly horses and cattle, but one song records the Devil being lassooed. It also had a hundred other uses. A lasso, lassoo, lariat, reata, etc. Weseen 1934, Berrey and van den Bark 1942, Ramon Adams 1944, and Wentworth 1944 all cite **ketch rope,** one of the best terms for this ubiquitous Western tool.

catch up
To catch up was merely to catch; to rope a horse ready for saddling, etc. Bartlett 1877 says: "Among travellers across the great prairie, the phrase means, to prepare horses and mules for the march"—thus extending the catching to include the saddling.

cattalo
The result of crossing Longhorns or fully domestic cattle with buffalo. A Spaniard first suggested the idea in 1598. The colonists tried it about 1750, and the mixed breed is recorded as having been quite common. A few men attempted it in the nineteenth century (notably "Buffalo" Jones, who originated the name), but the meat proved inferior to beef, and cattalo were found to be difficult as draft animals. Rossi 1975 notes that, though the females are able to produce their own kind, the males are said to have a high percentage of sterility. McHugh, who should know, says the breed may yet prove useful. (Ramon Adams 1944; McHugh 1972)

cattle baron
A man who, by fair means or foul, became the proprietor (if not the legal owner) of a vast acreage of range-land and had his brands on a large number of cattle. A number of men of high reputation were referred to by this term, mainly in literature and the press: Christopher Columbus Slaughter, Charles Goodnight, Dudley H. Snyder, John Wesley Iliff, Conrad

Kohrs, John B. Kendrick, and others. (Osgood 1929; Haley 1936; Gressley 1966)

cattle-drives
See *trail-drives*.

cattle-thief
Cow-thief. The weight of the term varied with time and place, often depending on from whom a man stole and the manner in which he did it. While there is a large pulp-literature that rests upon the cowboy's code of honor, it was not unknown for a rancher's crew to build up a herd on the side by slapping on their own brands instead of the boss's; maybe this was the way in which the boss had máde *his* start. There were few other ways a rider on low pay could build a stake. Some bosses allowed their men to run animals of their own in the main herd; these could be quietly supplemented with calves from the ranch. Strays, too, were a temptation. There were also many men (such as the Clantons of Arizona and the Hole in the Wall boys) who lived by rustling—stealing from one man and selling to another, no questions asked—on a fairly wide scale. Billy the Kid, it's said, stole from John Chisum because he owed money to the Kid and wouldn't pay. Some homesteaders, who had no reason to love a cattleman, were not too particular from where their supply of fresh beef came. On the Texas-Mexico border cattle-stealing ran wild, and in Arizona, New Mexico, and Texas men robbed on one side of the border and sold on the other, moving hundreds of cattle at a time. The ways and means of stealing cows were many and varied and there is not space here to tell the whole rich story. One should end, however, with the old range-land saying that only a fool ate his own beef. (Osgood 1929; Lamar 1966; Sandoz 1958; Webb 1931)

cattle-town
See *cow-town; trail-town*.

cattle trail
A path or road beaten out by cattle. While this term could cover any local trail along which cows were driven, history will always turn memory to the great Texas–Kansas cattle trails and those that thrust on north into Wyoming, Montana, and Nebraska. The most famous historically was the Chisholm Trail, said to have been first marked out by the wagon-wheels of Jesse Chisholm, the Cherokee mixed-blood. It was also known in the early days as the Abilene Cattle Trail or the Great Texas Cattle Trail, but finally the name Chisholm stuck. Originally, one should remember, the Chisholm Trail proper was not on Texas soil at all: its predecessor was the Shawnee Trail farther east. Its successor, the Western Cattle Trail, extended north into Wyoming and the Dakota territory. Farther west was the famous Goodnight–Loving Trail that crossed the Pecos and drove up

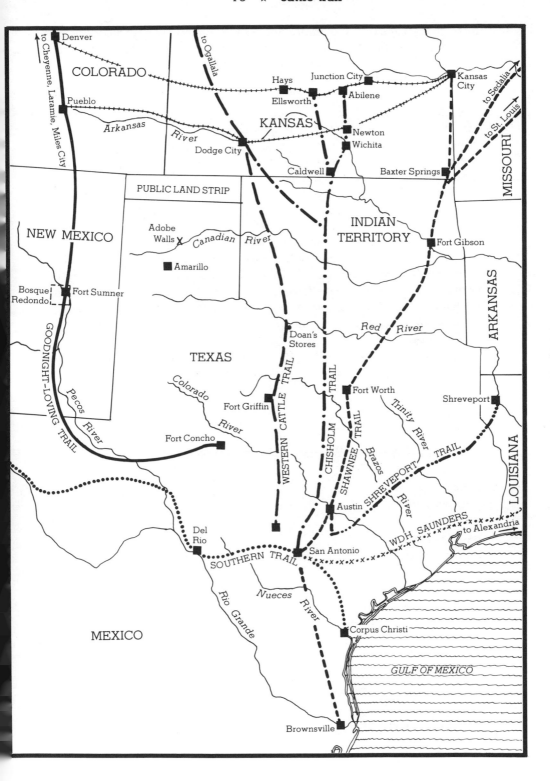

through New Mexico, Colorado, and into Wyoming. Nor must one forget the hazardous Southern Trail, blazed by Baylis John Fletcher through southern New Mexico and Arizona to California. (Osgood 1929; Gard 1954; Dykstra 1971). See also *trail-town.*

cavallard

(Sp *caballada*). Also **cavoy** and **cavvieyah** (Hough 1897), **cavallada, caviada, caviarde, cavvie, cavvyard,** etc. The original Spanish word simply meant a band of horses; while most authorities agree that it denoted a band of saddle-horses, literature has insisted on applying it to a band of wild horses. It was corrupted by the Mexicans into *cavaya* or thereabouts, with many Anglo variants. (Dobie 1930; Ramon Adams 1944)

Of cavallard, Bartlett 1877 says: "(Span. *caballada,* pron. cav-vy-yard). A term used in Louisiana and Texas, by the caravans which cross the prairie, to denote a band of horses or mules." Modern authorities cite **cavvieyard** as meaning a band of saddle-horses, but in the nineteenth century, this word and cavallard, like *caballada,* were used on occasion to denote a band of wild horses. However, certainly on the Santa Fe Trail, the *remuda* and a band of draft horses were referred to thus. **Cavvy** was probably the most common variant and was in general use on the northern ranges, while remuda was the term found in Texas and the Southwest (Berrey and van den Bark 1942; Ramon Adams 1944). Later, the word **cavieyah** mostly appeared on the northern ranges and remuda on the southern.

cavallo

(Sp *caballo*). A horse. (Weseen 1934; Berrey and van den Bark 1942)

caverango

See *wrangler.*

cavraces

See *caberos.*

cavvy-broke

If a horse had not been broken to saddle, but was tame enough to run with the remuda, he was cavvy-broke. (Ramon Adams 1944)

cavvy-man

The hand looking after the saddle-horses; the horse rustler, the horse-wrangler, the remudero.

cayote, cayute

See *coyote.*

cayuse
Also *kiuse.* Originally a word for the wild horse of the Northwest and named for the Cayuse Indians; it soon became a general term among the cowmen of the northern ranges for a cow horse of mustang descent. Weseen 1934 says: "An Indian pony." Ramon Adams 1944 adds that in later years the word was applied contemptuously to *scrub*-horses. (Dunn 1886; Berrey and van den Bark 1942)

celerity wagon
See *mud wagon.*

cenizo
(Sp: ash-colored). Also **chamiso, chamizo.** *Atriplex canescens.* A brush-country shrub, thornless, with lavender-colored blossoms after rain. (Dobie 1941)

center-fire rig
Or simply **center-fire;** also **California rig, single-fire rig, single-fire saddle.** A saddle with a single cinch-ring in a central position directly below and on either side of the saddle-tree. Also called **single-barreled, single-rigged.** (Weseen 1934; Berrey and van den Bark 1942; Ramon Adams 1944; Mora 1950)

cerro
(Mex-Sp; SW). A hill. (Dobie 1930)

chamas
See *camas.*

chamisal
Also **chamise, chemisal, chemise brush, chimisal, greasewood.** A thicket of chamisos (see *cenizo*): the California *Adenostoma fasciculatum.* Mathews 1951 says it is also *Atriplex canescens* of New Mexico.

champ
See *chaw.*

chaparajos, chaparejos.
See *chaps.*

chaparral
(Mex-Sp *chaparro:* evergreen scrub oak; SW). Also **chapparo, chapparal.** Literally, a place abounding in scrub oak. The thickets of chaparral were sometimes of vast extent and almost impenetrable; the wild Longhorns took shelter in them during the day and came out to graze at night. It

became a word covering all deeply brushed country. Bartlett's quote of 1877 is of interest: "In Spain, a *chaparral* is a bush of a species of oak. The termination *al* signifies *a place abounding in:* as, *chaparral* a place abounding in oak bushes. . . . This word . . . has been introduced into the language since our acquisition of Texas and New Mexico, where these bushes abound. It is a series of thickets, of various sizes, from one hundred yards to a mile through, with bushes and briars, all covered with thorns, and so closely entwined together as almost to prevent the passage of anything larger than a wolf or hare." And this, remember, was the kind of country worked by the brush-poppers. No wonder **chaparejos** were used (see *chaps*).

chaparral bird, chaparral cock
See *road runner.*

chaparro
(Mex-Sp; SW).
(1) Brush. (Dobie 1930)
(2) An evergreen oak. (Ramon Adams 1944)

chaparro prieto
See *black chaparral.*

chap guard
A small protuberance (a knob or hook) on the shank of a spur to prevent the chaps from catching on the rowel. (Mora 1950)

chapote
(Mex-Sp from Nahuatl). *Diospyros virginiana.* A kind of brush (black persimmon, Mexican or mustang persimmon) growing to 20 or 30 feet. Used by the Mexicans for making dye. (Dobie 1930; Mathews 1951). Interestingly, the word *persimmon* is an Algonkian Indian word of the Northeast.

chapping
The beating of a man with *leggins.* This could be a serious punishment for a transgression by a member of a cow-crew or it could be carried out mildly in fun. (Ramon Adams 1944)

chaps
(Mex-Sp *chaparreras*). Also **chaparajos, chaparejos.** Pronounced *shaps,* of course. A leg covering from the hide of any convenient animal, which prevented horsemen from having their legs injured by thorns of brush or cactus. The Texans copied them from the Mexicans, and they came in various forms; in the early days, they seem to have been made of goatskin or calfskin. Interestingly, here was the meeting of two forms of clothing:

one might say that somewhere north of the Mexican border the chaps of the Spaniards met the leggings of the Indians as adapted by the plainsmen. A pair of *shotgun chaps* were pretty much like a pair of Mountain Man's leggings. Mexican vaqueros are recorded as having worn close-fitting leggings which they might well have adapted from the garb of the wild Indians. (Weseen 1934; Ramon Adams 1944; Berrey and van den Bark 1942; Mora 1950). See also *leggins.*

chaqueta
(Sp). A heavy jacket, either of cloth or leather, worn by cattlemen in the Texas–Mexican border country. (Mathews 1951)

Charlie Taylor
A makeshift butter made of molasses and fat. (Weseen 1934; Berrey and van den Bark 1942; Ramon Adams 1944)

chaw
(1) To chew. To **feel like chawin'**: to be hungry. To **git all chawed up**: to be beaten, damaged; to get the worst of a situation. **Chawin' the fat**: talking, exchanging gossip. Also **champ, chomp**—the latter common in the nineteenth century both in England and New England.
(2) A cut of plug tobacco for chewing. Not a native Westernism.

cheek
To cheek a horse was to force its head around toward its neck by holding on to the left cheek-strap of the bridle; usually done for the purpose of holding a fractious animal while a rider mounted. The strap was released as the rider's right foot came off the ground. As this movement was used only on tricky horses, the rider had to execute the rest of the movement with speed and was usually slammed into or out of the saddle as the animal made its first jump forward. Alternatively, he could twist its ear. There were even more savage methods, which I will not go into here. (Berrey and van den Bark 1942; Ramon Adams 1944; Mora 1950)

chemisal, chemise brush
See *chamisal.*

che-muck
(NW). The miner's term for food. A word apparently borrowed from the Indians; current among miners in the 1890s, but possibly first heard much earlier. (Mathews 1951)

chew the cud
To talk, discuss. Not necessarily a Westernism. (Ramon Adams 1944)

Cheyenne
See *dog soldiers.*

Cheyenne leg
Also **Cheyenne cut** (Ramon Adams 1944). A modification of the *winged chaps* developed in Wyoming. It was cut away on the under part of the thigh and lacked fastening below the knee. (Foster-Harris 1955)

Cheyenne roll
Ramon Adams 1944 defines this as a saddle "with a leather flange extending, over, to the rear, of the cantle-board. . . . " The saddle with such a roll was referred to as a **Cheyenne** or **Cheyenne saddle** and was originated by Frank Meanea, a saddlemaker from that town, and one of the greatest makers of Western saddles.

chicken fixings
Bartlett 1877: "In the Western States, a chicken fricasse."

chief
As it applied to Indians, this title has been used as loosely by fiction writers as it was by eye-witness reporters of actual events in the Old West—just as even earlier writers had misunderstood the title among the tribes of the Eastern Seaboard. The republican and sometimes anarchical organization of Indian society was seldom realized; neither was the variation from tribe to tribe of the authority of chiefs, nor the limitations of their powers and rights. This total misunderstanding was one of the factors in the tragic consequences of so many Indian treaties with the whites in instances when the latter made agreements with individual Indians without realizing that the whole tribe was not thereby committed. (Hodge 1907–10; MacLeod 1928; McNickle 1962)

chigaderos
See *chinks.*

chihuahua
(SW). The Mexican place-name used as an exclamation. (Dobie 1930)

Chihuahua cart
A heavy cart with solid wooden wheels, used by the Mexicans in the Southwest. (Dobie 1930)

chilchipin
(Mex-Sp from Nahuatl; SW). *Capsicum frutescens baccatum.* A plant and

its berry employed in making very hot Tabasco sauce. Castetter and Bell 1942 refer to it as **chiltepiquin,** which by sound links this term with *chilipiquines;* the Mexicans call it *chiltipiquín.*

child
This child. Ruxton 1849 wrote: "This child has felt like going West for many a month, being half froze for buffalo meat and mountain doin's." Similarly, **this hoss,** also meaning oneself.

chileno
(Mex-Sp; SW and California). A ring bit. (Mora 1950)

chili
Derisive title for a Mexican. (Mencken 1948)

chili colorado
Cayenne pepper. Bartlett 1877: "(Span.) Red pepper. In California and Texas and the States bordering on Mexico, the Spanish term is universally used. It is used as liquid and in great quantities."

chili-eater
An insulting nickname for a Mexican. (Weseen 1934; Ramon Adams 1944)

chilipiquines
Small red peppers that could be found growing wild in the brush of southwest Texas.

chimisal
See *chamisal.*

chinch-bug
This originally referred to a small bug that was destructive to corn, but in the West it applied to a bed-bug. (Mathews 1951)

chink
To daub; to fill the spaces between the logs of a cabin with clay or any other handy wet soil available. Sometimes used as **chink and daub.** (Bartlett 1877)

chinks
Also **armitas** (Foster-Harris 1955). Rather like half-chaps or riding apron coming just below the tops of the old high boots and fastened around the legs with thongs. Sometimes made of buckskin and often fringed. Mora 1950 says they were worn "quite a bit" on some coast ranges and in Nevada and adds: "Personally, I like them immensely for light brush and

very hot weather." Ramon Adams 1944 cites **chinkaderos** as a play on *chinks;* properly, **chigaderos.**

Chinook
(1) A broad term covering members of Indian tribes living along the Columbia River.
(2) A *lingua franca* of English and Indian words used between traders and Indians in the Columbia River region. (The Shorter Oxford English Dictionary 1973)
(3) A warm, moist wind blowing in from the southwest Oregon coast. Extremely important to the Western cattleman, particularly in the north, for it could melt the snow that so beleaguered the cattle industry in winter. A good Chinook could make the difference between success and ruin by allowing the cattle to reach grass. (Rossi 1975)

chip box
Also **chip pile.** Where the buffalo- or cowchip fuel was kept at a ranch or in camp. (Berrey and van den Bark 1942; Ramon Adams 1944)

chipper
Lively. (Bartlett 1877)

chisel
Bartlett 1877: "To cheat, to swindle. Comp. to *gouge.* A Western word."

chiv
Short for *chivalry,* used as a noun to cover any Southerner. Bartlett 1877 indicates that he thought it confined to California, but it came into occasional Western use and has been employed by a few fiction writers.

chivarras
(Mex-Sp; SW). Chaps, leggings. (Dobie 1930)

cholla
(Mex-Sp). Also **deer brush** (Dobie 1930). A common cactus, covering several species, which bristles with spines and has quite colorful blooms. Also known as **jumping cholla,** not because it jumps, but because it has an uncanny way of adhering to humans and animals. Horses, dogs, and other animals, however, soon become desert-wise and learn to run through cholla country safely. (Rossi 1975)

chomp
See *chaw.*

chongo
(Mex-Sp). A steer with a drooping horn. Probably usually confined to

Mexicans of Texas and Mexico itself. Dobie 1941 writes: "This steer was what the Mexicans call a *chongo*—a steer with a drooped horn. A horn drooped over the steer's eye may not make him any wilder, but it makes him look wilder."

chop
To separate chosen animals from the herd; to cut. See also *cut (2)*.

chopper
(1) A *cutting horse*. A term that was certainly in use by the end of our period. (Mathews 1951). Also **chopping horse** (Weseen 1934; Ramon Adams 1944)
(2) A man who cut out cattle from the herd (see *cut [2]*). (Ramon Adams 1944)

chouse
Also **chowse**. Used frequently in Western fiction to cover the act of driving cattle or horses, but truly it meant to drive them boisterously or roughly, to hurry them along, just as cow-thieves might who wanted space between themselves and the cows' home range. (Dobie 1930; Weseen 1934; Ramon Adams 1944)

chow
Food; cooked food. (Weseen 1934; Mathews 1951)

chuck
Food, grub, chow. (Weseen 1934; Ramon Adams 1944; Wentworth 1944)

chuck-a-luck
Bartlett 1877 describes it as a Western game of chance played with a die. It appears in literature as early as 1820, sometimes as **chuckaluck**. My limited research suggests that during our period the term actually covered a variety of systems of rolling dice: for example, a table-throw, a bird-cage-type dice box, a turning wheel. (Weseen 1934)

chuck away
Meal-time, the cook's summons for men to eat. (Weseen 1934)

chuck box
The cook's hold-all box at the rear of the chuck wagon. It did not appear in the very early days of trail-driving—and certainly not on the early Texas cowhunts, when not even chuck wagons were used—but developed in

design as the northern drives became commonplace. A later refinement was that the door of the box was also the tail-gate of the wagon and was let down to become the cook's work-table, revealing drawers and shelves in and on which he kept his utensils and stores. Jennings's useful little glossary at the end of his 1971 novel, *The Cowboys,* says that the table had only one leg. He may be correct, but I have seen two legs mentioned, and I possess a drawing from the period of such a box with two legs. The first chuck box was said to have been built into an ex-army wagon by Charles Goodnight of the Texas Rangers and the famous Goodnight–Loving Trail—one of the greatest cowmen of them all. (Haley 1936; Weseen 1934; Ramon Adams 1944)

chuck house
The cookhouse of a ranch or mining camp. (Ramon Adams 1944; in the latter sense, Weseen 1934)

chuck-line rider
Also **grub-line rider.** A man, out of work or just plain idle, who rode from ranch to ranch for free chuck or grub. (Weseen 1934; Ramon Adams 1944). Andy Adams 1909 uses the phrase **riding the chuckline,** which is also seen as **riding the grub-line.** Weseen 1934 cites **ride the chuck-line.**

chuck tender
A cook in a mining camp. (Mathews 1951)

chuck wagon
The wagon that was a cookhouse on wheels for trail-drives and round-ups. Not employed during the early cowhunts in Texas, when every man was expected to carry his own grub, the chuck wagon was no more than an ordinary ranch-wagon, usually pulled by a pair of mules (or, in the early days, by a span of oxen), and with a box full of drawers and shelves at the tail-end. The men's personal gear might be carried in the bed of the wagon, and underneath would be slung the *cooney,* or cradle, for carrying various items, including wood or cowchips for fuel. The chuck wagon was the social center of the round-up and the meeting-place for any riders scattered on the trail-drive. Here the cook reigned supreme, and it was not only bad manners but imprudent either to raise dust near the cook's area or to help yourself to anything from his stores. As will be seen from the *chuck box* entry, Charles Goodnight was the first to make a purpose-built chuck wagon, by modifying an ex-army wagon that had iron instead of wooden axles. (Weseen 1934; Ramon Adams 1944; Gard 1954)

chunk
Bartlett 1877 says that to chunk was "to throw sticks or chips at one. Southern and Western." Sounds to me very much like the British-English *chuck*. (Wentworth 1944)

chunked
"Any person who is impudent and bold, at the South-west is said to be *chunked*," says Barlett 1877.

churn-twister
A farmer, according to a cowboy. (North 1942)

churro
(Mex-Sp). The unimpressive type of sheep which the Spaniards introduced into New Mexico and thus to the Pueblo and Navaho Indians. They were thin-legged, with straight, almost greaseless wool that did not have to be washed before it was woven. The animals were extremely hardy.

chute
A narrow lane, generally formed by fencing, down which cattle could be driven for dipping (see *dip [1]*) or *branding*. A stopping bar was inserted through the rails in front of and behind an animal to render it immobile under treatment. Chutes were also employed for driving cattle from one corral to another or loading them on railroad cars. (Ramon Adams 1944)

chute branding
See *branding*.

cibola
(Mex-Sp *cíbola;* SW). Buffalo, the bison.

cibolero
A Mexican halfbreed or *mestizo* who in the early days hunted the buffalo on the plains with bow and arrow and lance. Unlike the whiteman who hunted there later, he did not kill for the hides alone, but for the meat, which he jerked and sold to the villagers. It is pretty certain that he lived mostly at peace with the Indians and was the prototype of the trader who later bore the hated title of Comanchero (see *Comancheros*).

cienaga
(Sp *ciénaga;* SW). A marsh. (Dobie 1930)

cigarito
(Sp *cigarrito;* SW). A small cigarette or cigar. (Mathews 1951)

cimarrones
(Sp: wild ones). The wild black cattle of Texas. Often, however, the name was applied to intractable Longhorns. (Dobie 1941; Gard 1954). Ramon Adams 1944 says the term applied to intractable cattle or men who stayed apart from the rest of their kind.

cinch
(Sp *cincha*). Also **sinch**.
(1) Saddle girth. The Mexican type was made of separate strands of  braided hair, the American of cotton, mohair, hair, canvas, or leather. Also **cincha, cincho**. (Weseen 1934; Ramon Adams 1944; Mora 1950)
(2) To girth tightly. Also, to **cinch up**. (Weseen 1934; Ramon Adams 1944)
(3) A certainty; a matter that had been tightened up, tied neatly and tidily.

cinch binder
A bucking horse which reared and fell backward. (Ramon Adams 1944; Rossi 1975)

circle
(1) To ride in a circle around a bunch of cows.
(2) To drive cattle in a circle; to mill them so that they circled tighter and tighter until they could mill no more. (North 1942). See also *milling.*
(3) Used on round-up as **go on circle**: when the riders would scatter to all points of the compass to work the cattle generally toward the center. (Rossi 1975)

city shirt
See *boiled shirt.*

claim
The legal right by which a person held mining, farming, or grazing land. The size and condition of holdings varied according to time and place. (Mathews 1951)

claim-jumper
A man who illegally took possession of another man's land-claim or mining-claim. (Ramon Adams 1944). In both the fiction and history of the West, mention is made of open murder to appropriate mining-claims during the gold and silver rushes. The claim-jumping of grazing and agricultural land was done by settlers when the landowner was absent, and by powerful cattle organizations which did not tolerate settlers on the public domain (see *public land*) they claimed for themselves.

clawhammer coat
A swallowtail coat; a dresscoat with tails. Not confined to the West and, according to some fiction, when seen there, often a point of fun. Reaction to such garb depended on time and place. (Foster-Harris 1955)

claybank
A horse of a yellowish-brown color. (Ramon Adams 1944; Dobie 1952)

clean his plow
A common and pithy Westernism which may now be considered a part of general American-English, meaning "to whip or defeat a man." (Weseen 1934; Ramon Adams 1944)

clear-footed
Said of a horse whose gait was clean and sure. Dobie 1941 writes: "Near each sleeping man stood a horse—his night horse, the clearest-footed and surest-sighted of his mount—saddled and tied." (Ramon Adams 1944)

Clipped Ears
See *Sydney Birds.*

coachwhip snakes
(S and Texas). A name given to a number of harmless snakes that resembled coach whips.

coal-oil
Bartlett 1877 says that it was oil extracted from a certain coal; petroleum. Others called it kerosene or paraffin. On the range it was a luxury not to be wasted. Used for lamps and lanterns and, in fiction, to burn down the houses and barns of enemies. Not a Westernism, but a term used frequently in Western fiction of the mid-twentieth century. (Wentworth 1944; Foster-Harris 1955)

coasters
Also **sea-lions.** Longhorns that ran on the coastal ranges and off-shore islands of Texas. (Dobie 1941; Ramon Adams 1944; Mora 1950)

cocinero
(Sp; SW). Also **coosie, coosy, cosi, cusi, cusie,** etc. Ranch or trail-drive cook. (Dobie 1930; Weseen 1934; Ramon Adams 1944). Andy Adams 1909 uses **cusie.**

cock of the desert
See *road runner.*

cock of the plains
See *sage cock.*

cocktail guard
Also **cocktail relief.** The last guard of the night on a trail-drive. (Mathews 1951, who records it as early as 1891)

coffee mill
See *pepperbox.*

cold-blooded stock
Also **cold-bloods.** Originally in Europe this term was applied to horses of northern descent, as opposed to Arabs and Barbs. In the West it meant cows or horses lacking good blood or breeding. (Weseen 1934; Ramon Adams 1944). See also *hot-blood.*

cold-jawed
Said of a horse with an insensitive mouth. (Weseen 1934; Ramon Adams 1944). A matter of indifference to those cowhands who, though they could stay on a horse's back, did not necessarily possess a good understanding of the animal and rode the lines, or reins, instead of the horse. The condition of the mouth may well have been caused in the first place by such a rider. J. Frank Dobie wrote of such men with feeling more than once, as did Jo Mora.

colear
To throw an animal by the tail while the thrower was a-horseback; to tail. Anglos also used **to colear.** In Mexican-Spanish this means to throw a bull by the tail or, literally, to wag the tail. Gregg 1844 refers to the sport as **el coleo** (the *tailing*). Mora 1950 uses **coleo.**

collops
Claimed to have been applied by the Mexicans to strips of sun-dried game. I have met this only in the quotation below and have not been able to verify it further. It may well be an example of a word being heard wrongly and recorded in the same way—a not uncommon occurrence in the West. "Upon his return, with scarcely a word of greeting, the game was flung down before her; she proceeded to unsaddle, and lariat in hand again to hobble and 'turn him out.' Then the game must be dressed and cooled and cut into long thin strips and flung over the large frames to dry. Thus dried, the Mexicans call it 'Collops.' . . . " (Captain Richard G. Carter, *On the Border with Mackenzie; or Winning West Texas from the Comanches,* quoted in Rifkin 1967)

colonel
Bartlett 1877: "A title of courtesy. There is a great fondness in the West

and South for the higher military titles, but particularly for that of Colonel. New England, too, may be charged with the same weakness."

color
Prospector speech, meaning a trace of color, a sign of the presence of gold. (Wentworth 1944; Lavender 1969)

Colorado Ranger
A type of spotted horse, similar in appearance to an *Appaloosa*.

colt
(1) A young horse, especially male, from its weaning until about the age of four.
(2) As **Colt,** in Western literature the name has become almost synonymous with revolver, a state of affairs brought about to some extent by the vigorous advertising of Sam Colt, said to be the inventor of the modern revolver as we know it. The Colt, in its various forms, was an excellent gun, and no denying it; but there were other makes which were also very popular with the old-time Westerner—Remington,  Smith and Wesson, and Starr, to mention only a few. Colt himself was a living example of American commercial vigor and enterprise, and one would have thought that his invention was one the authorities would have jumped at, bringing its young maker fame and fortune. But Colt had a hard time from the start, in spite of his initial success with the old simply constructed Paterson Colt—an historically famous model, the merits of which were at once recognized by the Texas Rangers, who used them with great success against the Comanches in 1844. These guns were also employed successfully in the Seminole and Mexican wars. However, Colt was forced into liquidation in 1843, though he had created a prototype upon which the revolver in the United States was to be based for many years to come. In 1847, with Eli Whitney as his works manager and with the unwieldy Walker-Whitneyville as his ware, he once more entered the market. From this gun developed the various Dragoon models, and these, through the army, became Western guns. Though one cannot see very fast draws being made with them, with all their clumsiness they were good, useful guns for the period and, in spite of what has been written about them in this century, could in the hands of the right men do effective damage up to and beyond 50 yards. With the famous Model 1860, Colt stayed with his basic design, ignoring the top-strap above the revolving chamber that strengthened the Remington rival, and produced a wonderful streamlined gun as good or better than any cap-and-ball in the world (see *cap-and-ball gun*). For so big and so long-barreled a weapon, the balance was remarkable. But Colt was yet to produce his finest revolver—the Model 1873, a cartridge hand-gun, perfect in balance and "feel," which, with slight variations and with vari-ous names such as Colt Frontier and Peacemaker,

continued in production into the 1940s, when it ceased to be manufactured for some years (it was later continued). This was the handy gun that gave rise to the fast draws for which Western gun-handlers became legendary. Colt varied his calibers to suit the needs of his customers: the so-called Baby Dragoons (pocket-pistols) came in .31, and the Walker-Whitneyville and its like that followed were .44; but a number, such as the Model 1851, were available in the popular caliber of .36. Around the time of the Peacemaker the average big caliber had settled down to the .44–40 or .45, and the later years saw Colt turn to .38 as his lighter caliber.

Comanche moon
The September moon under which these Indians were said to ride out on their raids, especially in the direction of western Texas and Mexico. As Dobie 1952 says: "Every fall, for a third of a century, beginning about 1830, the Comanches rode down the established trails to despoil ranges and huddle inhabitants into ruin and terror hundreds of miles below the Rio Bravo."

Comancheros
Men, usually of Mexican-Indian hybrid origin, who might be called the go-betweens for the Comanche Indians and the whites. They were the trading link between the two peoples and were a natural development from the ciboleros (see *cibolero*). The Comanches would plunder in Old Mexico and sell through the Comancheros to the whites, and vice versa. Mostly by tacit consent, the Comancheros were neutral, because one party might gain and the other at least recoup losses by their existence. The Comancheros were also used in the release of white captives from the Indians, and, needless to say, were neither admired nor loved by the Texans. Dobie 1950 says: "traders with Comanches." (Chisholm 1966)

Comanche Trail
The trail from the Staked Plain (see *staked plain*) down into Old Mexico which the Comanches took on their raids into that country.

Comanche yell
A high-pitched, blood-chilling cry said to have been made by those Indians when attacking. See also *Texas yell*.

comb
To rake a horse's back with spurs to make it pitch. (Weseen 1934; Berrey and van den Bark 1942; Ramon Adams 1944)

come
Applied to the bringing down of game or an enemy by rifle-fire: **to come,**

to make come. (Bartlett 1877; Ruxton 1849). Bartlett 1877 adds "*To make drunk come* means to produce intoxication."

commas
See *camas*.

committees of vigilance
See *vigilance committees*.

common doings
Indicating something plain, as opposed to special—particularly food, but it could be applied to people, actions, and things. (Bartlett 1877)

community loop
An extra large lasso noose. (Allen 1933)

compadre
(Sp; SW). Among the Mexicans of the Southwest this referred to godfathers of the same child or to a close friend. (Dobie 1930). Cowboys used it in the Southwest in much the same way as **pardner**. (Ramon Adams 1944)

compañero
(Sp; SW). Also **companyero** (Ruxton 1849). Partner, companion. (Farmer 1889; Dobie 1930; Berrey and van den Bark 1942). See also **pardner.**

complected
Complexioned. **Dark complected:** of a dark face. Brought to the West mostly by the dialect speakers of New England. (Wentworth 1944)

compliment
(SW). A present. (Bartlett 1877)

conchas
(Sp *concha:* shell). Knobs of silver or other material used to decorate spur straps, horse gear, chaps, vests, etc. Ramon Adams 1944 nicely refers to a concha as "a shell-like ornament of metal." Dobie 1930 gives precisely the same definition, but writes *silver* for *metal*. Rossi 1975 writes that conchas could be of leather (single or doubled), silver, or brass and were not so much shell-like as merely concave, similar to a dished disc.

Concord
Practically the generic name for a stagecoach. These vehicles were named for the New Hampshire town where the best coaches were said to be made. The most famous maker was Abbott, Downing and Co., who made what was for the period a stagecoach de luxe, with the body suspended

on leather thoroughbraces and the driver's seat attached to the body—which meant that the driver had the same suspension and comfort as the passengers. The woodwork was hickory, the metalwork steel and brass, the exterior gaily painted and scrolled. Inside were three lines of three seats each, two facing forward and one back; the roof could take three more passengers. Under the driver's seat was a small compartment for a strongbox or some such; under that, a boot for baggage; to the rear was another and larger boot, canvas-covered. The driver sat on the off (right-hand) side, where there was a brake-handle, with the shotgun messenger or guard to his left. The team could be made up of four or six animals, but, for difficult country, this could be increased to eight. In the West, the windows of the coach were usually without glass and were protected by canvas curtains.

conducta
(SW). A guard of a party of travelers or of a convoy. (Dobie 1930)

Conestoga
Conestogas, a type of large wagon, are said to have been developed by an Englishman named Richard Carter in Conestoga Valley, Pennsylvania, from an ordinary English road-wagon. The first models were supposed to have been made by the Dutch farmers of Conestoga Creek, Pennsylvania, for the English general Edward Braddock. Later the same type became popular for heavy hauls on the Great Plains. It had a boat-shaped body, deeper in the middle than at either end, and a hooped canvas covering. Bartlett 1877 says that, in Pennsylvania and New York, before the advent of the railroad, Conestogas were pulled by noble Conestoga horses, which were thought to be a cross between a Flemish cart-horse and an English breed. Studebaker made wagons of the same type, but slightly lighter for the plains crossing, as did the Lagans. (Stewart 1964). See also *wagons.*

contract buster
A horse-breaker who contracted to break so many horses for an agreed price. (Weseen 1934; Ramon Adams 1944)

contraries
Members of an Indian society, especially among the Sioux, who were the clowns and jesters of the tribe. Their speciality was to do anything backward: dress backward, walk backward, etc. They were greatly valued and treated with respect.

cooks
Though there was nothing romantic about a cook, and though he might be looked down on by the elevated horseman, he was respected, valued, and often feared. He was one of the unsung heroes of the West, and on him rested much of the morale of the outfit. A bad cook invariably spoiled

a good crew and made an indifferent one bad. Fortunately for Western buffs, one or two excellent writers have given due credit and color to the breed who produced hot meals after hail-storms, stampedes, and day-long drives; who medicked the sick; and who, on more than one occasion, shot to death a man who broke the rule that nobody approached the chuck wagon without the cook's permission. Many were self-willed tyrants with the temperament of a prima donna; many were the reason why good cowmen hired out to the brand that employed them. Some of the cook's saga is told in Ramon Adams 1952 and Dobie 1964; and there's a good description of the breed and its equipment in Gard 1954. For variants, see *cocinero.*

cooley, coolly
See *coulee.*

cooney
Also **coonie.** A dry cowhide slung under a chuck wagon to hold equipment and fuel such as wood and buffalo chips. From the Spanish *cuna* (cradle); the Spanish word itself was sometimes employed. (Ramon Adams 1944; Dobie 1929). Also called **bitch, caboose, cradle, 'possum belly.** (Dobie 1941; Ramon Adams 1944)

coosie, coosy
See *cocinero.*

Copperhead
A Northerner who sympathized with the Southern cause during the Civil War. Not a Westernism, but a word found fairly frequently in Western literature.

corn-dodger
Also **dodger.** Bread made from corn and water or milk, and baked on a skillet. Bartlett 1877 describes it as a kind of cake made from Indian corn and claims it, along with fried bacon, as the universal food of the people of Texas: "A hard-baked cake or biscuit. *Dead* and *garred,* i.e. thoroughly done. Dead gar. . . . " Wentworth 1944 shows that the term was not of Western origin.

corn freight
Freight carried on wagons hauled by mules, as opposed to that pulled by oxen (which was termed *grass freight*). Oxen were slower but cheaper. You weighed the pros and cons and argued like hell with other freighters which was the best. (Ramon Adams 1944). See also *bull-train.*

corona
(Sp: crown). A saddle-pad, usually shaped to the lines of the saddle and

open at the top to permit ventilation between saddle and horse. (Berrey and van den Bark 1942; Mora 1950)

corporal
See *caporal.*

corral
(Sp). A pen or enclosure to confine horses or cattle. Commonly in Western literature it was composed of posts and poles, but there were many varie-ties, including temporary corrals of rope; in the Southwest they were frequently made of high adobe walls to keep out marauding Indians. Bartlett 1877 notes that the word was used in Texas and New Mexico especially in reference to wagons being laagered (formed in a circle) at night on the trail. It could also be used as a verb. This Spanish word had many (some unbelievable) Anglo variants (**coral, corel, corrale,** etc.). (We-seen 1934; Ramon Adams 1944)

corrida
(Mex-Sp; SW). A cattle-crew. Interestingly, corrida—from the verb *correr* (to run)—is connected with hunting, the chase, the beating up of game, and was extended to those who ran or hunted animals. It could also mean a bullfight and was used to cover the bullfighter's retinue and, parallel to this meaning, a cattle-crew—rightly, for the earliest cowboys in Texas and the Southwest were indeed cattle-hunters, running cattle which were as wild as animals hunted in the chase.

cosi
See *cocinero.*

coteau
(Fr: hill). Dunn 1886 says it is the Northwesterner's equivalent of the Southwest divide or watershed.

cottonwood

Several varieties of North American poplar, so called from the cotton-like surroundings of the seeds. The tree was a silent and omnipresent character throughout American history and folklore, for almost everywhere man wandered across the continent, except in the most barren places, he found the cottonwood. The Spaniards planted avenues of them and had a word for such in **alameda.** Ranchers saw that their houses stood so that a cottonwood could provide shade over a sun-roasted yard. It was even turned into a verb: to **get the cottonwood over on somebody** was to have the advantage of them. In the Southwest the tree was called *alamo*, as recorded by Bartlett 1877.

cougar

In the West, *Panthera concolor* was known by many names, among them cougar, from the French *couguar;* **catamount,** from the Spanish *gato montés;* and **puma** (also applied to *Felix concolor*), from the Guarani word for this big cat. It was also called a **mountain lion,** no doubt because it looked much like a small maneless lion. All referred to a large American feline carnivore, of tawny or brownish-yellow color and without spots or stripes. Found from Canada to Cape Horn, it could survive in a variety of habitats and was a predator: deer, horses, sheep, calves, and fowl were common victims. In spite of tales of its ferocity, it was an elusive animal that survived by escaping danger, often by climbing trees. Dogs were used in its hunting—and it was hunted vigorously: by the end of the nineteenth century it had been cleared from much of its former habitat. It was also called **panther** and, an old variant, **painter.**

coulee

(Fr *couler:* to flow; mainly NW). Also **cooley, coolly.** A steep-sided ravine, gully, or valley. Dunn 1886 equates **coulie** with the Southwestern arroyo. (Berrey and van den Bark 1942; Ramon Adams 1944; Wentworth 1944)

count-corral

A corral used for the counting of cattle. (Mathews 1951)

counter-brand

When a branded cow was sold, the brand of the new owner was placed on the other side of the animal, superseding the first (Bartlett 1877), through which a cancellation bar was put. Or if an original brand was placed incorrectly it could be canceled and a counter-brand positioned correctly. (Ramon Adams 1944). There were various complications to counter-branding, and the rules changed with the years; but it always meant the changing of one brand for another and was done in such a way that it should not be construed as illegal. See also *brands; cross-brand.*

county attorney
See *son-of-a-bitch stew.*

couse, cowas
See *cowish.*

Cousin Jack
Applied to Cornishmen, many of whom were miners in the West. Said to be used because all Cornishmen seemed to be related. Berrey and van den Bark 1942 go further to say it meant a Welshman, and **Cousin Anne** a Welsh miner's wife.

cowboy
Westerners with a knowledge of the old days have claimed that the word was seldom used within the cow-community except when applied to juveniles who herded or hunted cattle. However, it is certain that the term was applied freely by others, at an early date, to men herding cows. By the 1870s, the term seems to have been pretty generally used for any man tending cattle. Although pulp-fiction at the end of the last century glorified the cowboy, he was often held in disfavor by the general population as a rough, uncouth, and possibly lawless man. In fact, certain criminal fraternities of horse- and cattle-thieves were called the Cowboys, typically the Clanton faction during the Tombstone troubles between the Cowboys and the Earps in the 1880s. (Frantz and Choate 1955; Henry Nash Smith 1950; Horgan 1954)

cowcamp
It could mean a relatively permanent settlement in cattle-country; if a man built himself a shack or a *soddy (1)* and corral, that was a cowcamp. The term could also be applied to a temporary camp of cowhunters (in Texas) or to a camp of trail-drivers. (Siberts 1954)

cowchips
Dry cattle-droppings which could be used as fire-fuel. (Weseen 1934; Ramon Adams 1944; Dobie 1930)

cow-critter
Also **cow-crittur,** *critter,* crittur. Weseen 1934 says: "Anything that can be turned into beef"—and who can do better than that? Both in the West and in New England this term was used to denote any individual bull, cow, steer, etc. *Cow* was preferred in the nineteenth century because *bull* was considered indelicate, especially in the presence of ladies. (Bartlett 1877; Wentworth 1944; Ramon Adams 1944)

cow crowd
(1) Those engaged in a *cowhunt* in the early Texas days. (Foster-Harris 1955)
(2) A crew of cowboys. (Ramon Adams 1944)

cow driver
(Texas). One who drove cows on the trail north from Texas or who trailed them west into Colorado and California; essentially, a man who drove cattle on a long trail. I can't resist quoting from Baylis John Fletcher's 1968 *Up the Trail in '79:*

> Astonished, the boy rode in silence for several minutes. Then, giving Mr. Snyder a furtive glance, he asked: "Mister, is you a Christian?"
> "I hope so," was the reply.
> "And a cowdriver?"
> "Yes, why not?" said Mr. Snyder.
> "That's awful damned strange," shouted the boy as he put both spurs to his horse and galloped away as if the *heel-flies* were after him.

cow-fever
The powerful desire to follow the cows, to become a cowboy (exemplified by the famous Ike Pryor in Dobie's *Cow People* [1964]).

cowhand
A man hired to play nursemaid to cows, commonly also called a *cowboy.* As the century progressed he picked up other titles such as *cowpoke,* **cow-puncher,** etc. (McCarthy 1936; Ramon Adams 1944)

cowhide
The skin of a cow-creature. Applied also to a whip of plaited rawhide. Bartlett 1877 states that the word could also be used as a verb: **to cowhide,** to beat with such a whip. It could also be used to mean the act of beating a man with cowhide as punishment in a cattle-camp. Cowmen found almost as many uses for a cowhide as the Indians did for a buffalo hide. Not necessarily a Westernism. (Dobie 1941)

cow horse
A horse trained to work cattle. (Ramon Adams 1944; Foster-Harris 1955)

cowhunt
The cattle round-ups of the early days in Texas were given this name. In fact, they were "hunts" because the activity was the equivalent of hunting down wild animals, particularly in the brush-country. (Osgood 1929; Gard 1954; Ramon Adams 1944; Dobie 1929). See also *round-up.*

cowish
Also **couse, cowas, cows.** (From the Nez Percé *kowish*). *Cogswellia cous.* An herb growing in Oregon, the root of which was eaten by the Indians. Sometimes confused by fiction writers with *camas* or **quamash.** (Beal 1963)

cowjuice
Milk. (Berrey and van den Bark 1942)

▶ cowman
"One who raises cattle," says Ramon Adams 1944. Rossi 1975 adds that cowmen are very particular about this—a cowman owns cattle.

cowpaper
When money was scarce in early Texas, cows and calves were the medium of exchange, and they could be represented by a promissory note or maybe an oral promise; the note was called a cowpaper.

cow-pease
About which Bartlett said in 1877: "A small black bean growing luxuriously in Texas. They are eaten alike by cattle and their owners."

cowpen herd
A small herd owned by a *shirt-tail outfit.* (Ramon Adams 1944; Berrey and van den Bark 1942)

cowpen Spanish
Bad Spanish such as that picked up by cowhands in the Southwest from Mexican vaqueros. (Dobie 1930)

cowpoke
Originally—say, from the late 1860s through the 1880s, at a guess—it meant those men who were employed on the cattle-trains carrying live cattle to the East and who kept the cows on their feet during the journey by the use of a long goad. In later years, it was applied to a cowhand. (Weseen 1934; Wentworth 1944; Ramon Adams 1944). See also *bull-puncher.*

cowpony

Bartlett 1877 gives an incredible explanation which must be quoted: "A young and unbroken mustang." Which goes to show how the authorities of the period could be mistaken. A cowpony was, of course, a pony trained to work cows. A "pony" because the animal probably originated in Texas, where the horses were pony-size. As Ramon Adams 1944 points out, this is really an Easterner's term for a Western critter.

cowprod

A cowboy. The term obviously originated from **cow-puncher** and *cowpoke.* (Ramon Adams 1944; Berrey and van den Bark 1942)

cow-puncher

See *bull-puncher.*

cows

See *cowish.*

cow sense

A man, a horse, or a dog could have cow sense, but it was applied particularly to a good *cutting horse:* many of them had legendary stories told of their skills. The term implied that they understood cows and possibly anticipated their moves. (Andy Adams 1909). Wentworth 1944 explains the term tersely and delightfully as "horse sense."

cowskin

The skin of a cow, which could serve many purposes. The term was used as commonly in the early days as *cowhide.* (Andy Adams 1909)

cow-thief

See *cattle-thief.*

cow-town

Also **cattle-town.** One of those terms that added up to very different things at different historical times. It was probably first used in reference to towns that sprang up along the northing trails into Kansas from Texas and those towns which were shipping points for the Texas cattle. (For this interpretation see *trail-town*). Later in the nineteenth century this term came to mean the supply center of cattle-country, which came alive a little more than somewhat on Saturday night, when the cowboys were paid and came in to blow their pay on whiskey, women, and cards. Here the rancher and farmer bought supplies, banked and borrowed, and brought in their families for social contacts. Here was the church and the preacher, if the place had yet reached that state of civilization. And here the cattleman might find new hands drifting through the country. The settlement might be the county seat, with a magistrate in residence and a lawman voted into office

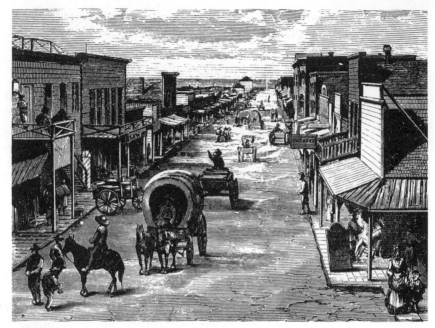

Wichita, Kansas, *circa* 1875

by the few inhabitants of the county. If the county was predominantly given over to cattle, that made the place a cow-town. I never heard of a sheep-town—nor, I suspect, has anyone else.

cow-waddy
See *waddy.*

cow-wood
Cowchips used as fuel. (Ramon Adams 1944)

coyote
(Mex-Sp from Nahuatl *coyotl*). Also **cayute** (Ruxton 1849; Berrey and van den Bark 1942), **cayote, kiote.** *Canis latrans* (barking dog). The little wolf of the prairies and hills, known also as the **prairie wolf** or the **barking wolf** and, to fur-hunters, as the *cased wolf.* The coyote lived on carrion—on rabbits, mice, ground squirrels, and poultry—when he could, and on berries when he had to. In times of need he was known to kill sheep and lambs. A cat would need a great many more than nine lives with a coyote in the vicinity. It is conceivable that a cattleman could be found who liked coyotes; a sheepman—never. The Westerner's attitude toward this animal was much the same as the present-day Australian's toward the rabbit, and among whitemen the name *coyote* came to stand for treachery. (Dobie's *The Voice of the Coyote* [1950] shows a different side to the little animal

and should be read by every lover of the
West.) Most Indian peoples told admiring tales
of his intelligence and ingenuity; often he appears in them as a fellow a mite too smart for
his own good.

coyote diggings
Small diggings made by miners, so called
because of their close similarity to the holes
dug by coyotes. Also found as a verb: **coyoting**— the act of making such
diggings.

coyote dun
See *bayo.*

crackerboxes
Bronc saddles, so called by rodeo riders; a comparatively modern term.
Frank O'Rourke uses this term in his 1958 novel, *The Last Ride*—probably
the most authentic and compelling by this writer.

cradle
(1) A *rocker* or rocking box used in washing gold from dirt and gravel.
(Billington 1956)
(2) See *cooney.*

craw
The crop of a bird. Hence, a man might be said to have **sand in his craw,**
meaning that he had courage. Or a man might say that another man's
words or actions **stuck in his craw,** meaning that they choked him. Not
confined to the West, but the word has become closely associated with it
in fiction.

crawfish
According to Bartlett 1877, **to crawfish** was "to back out of a position once
taken; particularly applied to politicians, evidently from the mode of
progress of the animal. Western." When applied to horses, it meant to
pitch or buck backward. (Weseen 1934; Ramon Adams 1944)

crawl his hump
Ramon Adams 1944 says it was to start a bodily attack; Weseen 1934
states that it was to kill a man, especially by stealth; Berrey and van den
Bark 1942 say it meant "to kill."

creasing
Really, parting another's hair with a bullet; dealing the skull a glancing
blow with a bullet. Which gives the following:

(1) Bringing down wild horses by shooting them through the upper part of the neck. This was supposed to stun them. It usually killed them. (Dobie 1952)

(2) The act of stunning a man by the glancing blow of a bullet; or, latterly, stunning a man in any way.

creosote
Also **hediondilla.** *Larrea mexicana.* A tree or bush of the Southwestern states that grew with sagebrush and greasewood and gave off a resinous liquid which, according to Bartlett 1877, could be applied to relieve rheumatism. Apparently, animals would not eat it. See also *greasebrush, greasebush, greasewood.*

cricksand
Quicksand. (Weseen 1934; Wentworth 1944). A beautiful Western transference of sounds.

cristianos
(Sp; SW). Christians; "civilized" white-people, as opposed to Indian "barbarians." (Dobie 1930)

critter
Also *cow-critter,* **cow-crittur, crittur.** A Mountain Man might mean *creature,* but a cattleman meant a cow of any age, sex, or size. (Weseen 1934; Ramon Adams 1944)

crony
Pal or chum. Seventeenth-century English. Could also be a verb. Andy Adams 1909: "Down at another gambling house, The Rebel met Ben Thompson, a faro dealer not on duty and an old cavalry comrade, and the two cronied around for over an hour, pledging anew their friendship over several social glasses in which I was always included."

crop
A cattle *ear-mark* which took off the top half of the ear. (Ramon Adams 1944; Foster-Harris 1955)

cross-brand
The seller of a cow re-branded the animal to show that his brand was vented, or canceled. (Mathews 1951). See also *counter-brand.*

cross-brander
A cow-thief who altered brands. (Mathews 1951)

cross-buck saddle
The conventional pack-saddle, double-cinched and consisting of two flat

pieces of wood with a wooden cross-piece at either end. (Rollins 1922; Ramon Adams 1944)

cross-cut
To take a short-cut on a journey. (Andy Adams 1909)

cross hobble
Ramon Adams 1944 defines this as "to hobble one front foot to the hind one on the opposite side"—which, as he points out, may throw and injure a nervous horse.

crowbait
A decrepit beast, usually a horse. (Dobie 1930; Ramon Adams 1944)

crowding pen
An enclosure into which cattle were put tightly for branding. (Allen 1933; Weseen 1934; Ramon Adams 1944)

crow hop
The short, stiff-legged jump performed by a horse in a mild form of bucking. (Weseen 1934; Berrey and van den Bark 1942; Ramon Adams 1944)

crown fire
Fire that swept through the tops of trees. (Mathews 1951)

cuff
A leather cuff worn by cowboys to guard their wrists against rope-burns, etc., often used with gloves. They existed certainly in the latter half of the nineteenth century. Rossi 1975 writes: "Never a practical piece of equipment; often seen on dude ranches. Popular in 1920s."

cull
A worthless animal, one to be culled. (Ramon Adams 1944)

cuna
(Sp: cradle). See *cooney.*

curandero
(Mex-Sp: quack, healer; SW). One who cured. Usually a Mexican who might be called an unqualified doctor, probably an herbalist with something of the medicine man about him. (Dobie 1930)

curb-strap
A strap passing under the lower jaw of a horse and attached to the upper parts of the bit. Useful in the control of a difficult animal.

cure
To **take the cure**: to get divorced.

Curly Bill spin
See *road agent's spin*.

curly mesquite
(SW). *Hilaria belangeri.* A variety of pasture grass. (Mathews 1951 records the term from 1877)

curly wolf
One of those old-time bragging terms that belongs with "wild and woolly" and the earlier "snapping turtle." A formidable hombre. (Ramon Adams 1944; Mathews 1951)

curry comb
An implement in common use by horsemen and livery-stable men for the care of horses' coats, it consisted of iron plates fastened to a metal back and notched at the other end with teeth; the back was fitted with a handle or a strap through which the user could slip a hand. Really a scraper and not a comb and should not generally be used for currying or cleaning a horse. Occasionally used on a thick or matted coat, but more often to clean the bristle brush every few strokes. Not a Westernism.

cusi, cusie
See *cocinero*.

cut
(1) To **cut a man down**: to shoot him.
(2) To **cut a herd**: to select and take out certain animals from a herd. One might also **cut out** an individual animal. The noun *cut* covered the actual animals cut from a herd. (Weseen 1934; Ramon Adams 1944)
(3) To **cut the dust**: to take a drink, preferably alcoholic.
(4) To **cut a rusty**: to do your best, to outdo yourself. (Weseen 1934; Ramon Adams 1944, who adds: to court a girl; Berrey and van den Bark 1942)
(5) To **cut a shine**: as Weseen 1934 and Ramon Adams 1944 put it, "to perform an antic."
(6) To **cut your wolf loose**: to go on a bender, to raise some hell while stimulated by strong drink. (Ramon Adams 1944)
(7) To **cut for sign**: to examine ground for tracks; rather indicative of cutting across the line of tracks. See also *sign*.

cut-back
An animal culled on round-up. (Ramon Adams 1944)

cut-herd
A herd of selected cows cut out from the main herd. (Berrey and van den Bark 1942)

cut-off
A branch-trail; sometimes a short-cut.

cutter
(1) A gun.
(2) A *cutting horse.*
(3) The man doing the ear-marking, etc., at branding time. (Ramon Adams 1944). See also *ear-mark.*

cutting horse
Also **carving horse** and **carver** (Ramon Adams 1944; Weseen 1934; Mathews 1951), **chopper**. A horse trained to select and remove cattle from a herd. (Berrey and van den Bark 1942; Ramon Adams 1944). See also *cut (2).*

cutting-out
The act of selecting and removing cows from a herd. (North 1942)

Cyprian
A prostitute. More properly a Cypriot—referring to Cyprus, where once worship of her flourished. (Emrich 1951)

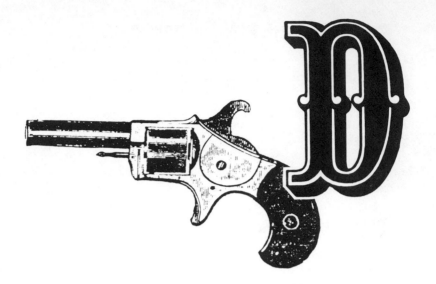

dally

Also **dolly welter** (Allen 1933; Weseen 1934), **dally welta, dally welter, dolly.** Wellman 1939 says that the word was derived from the Spanish *da la vuelta* (give the turn), Mora 1950 has a slightly different version and gives the imperative, *dale vuelta* (give it a turn), and Dobie 1930 gives the infinitive, *dar la vuelta.* To take a turn around the saddlehorn with a lasso after the throw had been made—as opposed to the hard-and-fast method in which the rope-end was permanently fastened to the horn. The dally

man could, if necessary, ease off the rope to relieve the immense strain on it, essential sometimes with the rawhide reata, which could snap. Mexicans were dally men almost to a man. (Dobie 1930; Weseen 1934; Berrey and van den Bark 1942; Ramon Adams 1944; Mathews 1951). See also *cascabel; roping.*

dally man

A man who threw a loose rope and turned it around the saddlehorn after he had caught his animal; as opposed to a man who threw a fixed rope. It was said that if a man had a thumb missing, that was sure proof he was a dally man—which illustrates that if you weren't good at the art, you'd best not employ it at all, because you paid dearly for a mistake. (Weseen 1934; Ramon Adams 1944; Mora 1950)

dancing devil

A dust devil, a whirlwind dust column. (Weseen 1934)

datil

(Sp *dátil:* date). Used in the Southwest for **Spanish bayonet**—several varieties of yucca cactus, particularly *Yucca baccata* and *Yucca aliofolia;* possibly also refers to *Spanish dagger.* (Dobie 1941; Mathews 1951)

daunsy
Moody, depressed. A dialect word from the Eastern Seaboard. (Weseen 1934; Ramon Adams 1944; Wentworth 1944)

day wrangler
The remudero, or hand in charge of the remuda (horse-herd) by day as opposed to the night wrangler, or night-hawk, who had charge of it by night. (Weseen 1934)

deadfall
(1) A drinking den; a shady gambling establishment. Sometimes both. (*Harper's Monthly Magazine* 1875; Ramon Adams 1944)
(2) A dead, fallen tree.
(3) A primitive form of trap employed mostly by Indians, but also used at times by white trappers. A heavy object was caused to fall on the prey in order to stun, cripple, or kill it. See also *trap (1)*.

dead man's hand
The poker hand said to have been held by Wild Bill Hickok when he failed to stick to his habit of sitting with his back to the wall and was killed by Jack McCall. Whether this term came from this incident or not, I wouldn't like to swear. The hand? Every Western buff knows it: aces and eights. (Ramon Adams 1944)

deadmen
Rocks or boulders sunk in the ground to anchor fences and attached to them by wires. (Forbis 1973)

deadshot
(1) A powerful liquor.
(2) An accurate marksman.

deadwood
To have the advantage over someone, to have the drop on them. A term thought to have been derived from the shooting of Wild Bill Hickok in the back of the head by Jack McCall in Deadwood, South Dakota. (Weseen 1934; Ramon Adams 1944)

deal from the bottom
To cheat. (Weseen 1934; Ramon Adams 1944)

Dearborn
A light four-wheeled carriage, horse-drawn; named for its inventor. Not truly a Westernism, but found occasionally in Western literature; may be strange to a modern reader. (Vestal 1939; Foster-Harris 1955)

death camass
Zygadenus venenosus. A variety of poisonous plant, fatal to cattle and horses. (Mathews 1951)

deer brush
See *cholla.*

dehorn
A quarrelsome hard-drinker. (Weseen 1934; Ramon Adams 1944)

dehorning
Sometimes a cow was dehorned (usually in the case of Longhorns) if it was a troublemaker and the owner had no wish to kill it. A pretty horrible business it could be, too. In early days, the horns were simply sawn off or jerked off with a lariat; later, dehorning clippers were used. Either way, the animal could bleed to death, though sometimes cauterization was employed to stop the bleeding. Calves could be discouraged from growing horns if the sprouts were rubbed with caustic potash when sighted in the first week of life. (Foster-Harris 1955; Forbis 1973; Rossi 1975)

democrat
Also **democrat wagon, democratic wagon.** A light wagon, usually two-seated; popular in cow-country. Not necessarily a Westernism. (Ramon Adams 1944)

democrat pasture
A grazing area, formed by enclosing a natural gap in rock, such as the mouth of a canyon. (Ramon Adams 1944)

derringer
Also sometimes spelled **deringer.** A small pocket-pistol with a short barrel and a large bore, to be used only at short range. It could be concealed in vest pockets, sleeves, boot-tops, and even hats and was much  favored by gamblers and convenient for ladies. Usually a single-shot, but also made with two barrels, which were placed one above the other; such a weapon was called an **over-and-under.** Originally applied to a gun named for its inventor (who spelled his name Deringer), the word later became the generic name for all such small firearms. Like most nouns in the West, this one could be turned into a verb to indicate the use of such a weapon. Deringer also manufactured rifles of good repute.

derrotero
(Sp: ship's course, course of life; SW). A chart; a described direction; a diary. (Dobie 1930)

desert rat
(1) An inhabitant of the desert. (Berrey and van den Bark 1942)
(2) A wandering prospector for gold, etc. (Weseen 1934; Ramon Adams 1944)

devil's bit
See *blazing star.*

Devil's Head
See *nopal.*

devils lane
Referring to *barb wire,* Glover 1972 writes: "Many a man has been killed over a fence line. . . . Some land owners dropped back from the survey line and each built his own fence and maintained it, leaving a 10 or 15 foot lane between them. These lanes were referred to as 'devils lanes.' "

dewlap
A fold of loose flesh hanging from the front of the neck of cattle, sometimes cut to hang like a pendulum as a mark of identification. When cut it still bore the name *dewlap* to denote the cut—which is a little confusing when written of, but clear enough in Western speech. (Ramon Adams 1944)

dew wrangler
The man who herded horses in the morning. (Ramon Adams 1944)

dicho
(Sp; SW). A saying, a proverb; in the old days of the West, this had the same meaning among the Anglos in the Southwest as among the Mexicans from whom it originated. (Dobie in numerous works)

dicker
To barter, to negotiate. Also, goods received in barter.

die-up
(1) The death of cattle on a large scale. Hence:
(2) A dead cow. "Before the rush developed into such a stampede, the skinning of dead cows, 'die-ups,' was looked forward to as perfectly natural and called the skinning season on the low coast ranges." (Dobie 1929)

difficulty
A quarrel resulting in trouble; a brush with the law that might make a man wish to be in distant parts. (Dobie 1930)

dig
To cheat. (Weseen 1934)

digger
(1) A miner, a man engaged in digging for gold or silver. (Willison 1952)
(2) A spur. (Ramon Adams 1944)

diggings
(1) An area, usually along the banks of a creek, which was being dug by gold- or silver-seekers. (Buffum 1850)
(2) Living quarters, home. (Weseen 1934)

dig out
To depart.

dimes
Bartlett 1877: "Common in the West and South for money. 'She's got the dimes,' i.e. she is an heiress."

dinero
(Sp). Money. (Dobie 1930; Weseen 1934; Ramon Adams 1944)

dip
(1) A powerful antiseptic to rid cattle and sheep of ticks, lice, scabs, etc. (Ramon Adams 1944). Old-timers defended the Texas Longhorn on the grounds that he needed little of such treatment. The operation could be carried out on individual animals or by placing a tank of antiseptic in a *chute* and driving animals through it, a universal and time-honored method.
(2) Range word for a pudding sauce. (Berrey and van den Bark 1942; Ramon Adams 1944)

district attorney
See *son-of-a-bitch stew.*

ditties
Odds and ends, in range language; bits and pieces. Obviously related to the American nautical ditty box, in which a sailor keeps his odds and ends. Allen 1933 gives another and rather nice version: "a new tool or contrivance or practically anything unfamiliar to the cowboy." Many dialects have equivalent words. I like the one from Yorkshire, England: bibs and bobs. (Weseen 1934; Berrey and van den Bark 1942; Ramon Adams 1944)

dive
The bunk-house of a ranch. Possibly a twentieth-century development. (Ramon Adams 1944)

divide
Bartlett 1877 writes: "The name applied by Western hunters and guides to a ridge of land which divides waters running in different directions; a dividing ridge." Farmer 1889 writes similarly. A further quote, from Webb 1931: "For example, if the first ranchman occupied both sides of the stream, then his recognized range extended backward on both sides to all the land drained by the stream within the limits of his frontage; if he held but one side, his range (for thus it was called) extended back only on that side. In the range country 'divides' became of much importance, marking the boundary between the ranchman of one stream-valley and those of another." To **cross the divide** was to die.

'dobe
Also **'dobie**. See *adobe (1)*.

'dobe dollar
Also **'dobie dollar**. See *adobe (2)*.

'dobe wall
If a man was **'dobe walled,** he was put up against one and shot. This expression probably came into being during the border troubles between Mexico and Texas in the 1870s, when to be put up against a wall and shot was the fate of Texans (that is, if the Mexicans could catch them) who went across the border to lift cattle and to avenge themselves on Mexicans for doing the same to them. (Ramon Adams 1944)

'dobie
See *adobe (1)* and *(2)*.

Doc
(1) A medical practitioner. A general American colloquialism.
(2) A pianist in a saloon.
(3) Any learned male.
I feel that there was a mixture of respect and slight derision in this ab-breviated title, such as an uneducated man feels for another with skills beyond his understanding and capacity.

dodger
See *corn-dodger; flier*.

dog
God. Used in polite society or by a man who did not like blasphemy. For *god-damned,* he might say: "Well, I'll be **doggoned**." Also, in Texas: "Dog my cats!" (Farmer 1889; Hoig 1960)

dogal
(Mex-Sp: noose, halter). To tie by the neck. Usually applied to cattle.

dog-fall
In wrestling, a term describing a fall in which both fighters hit the ground together. In the Old West it meant the attempt of a cowhand to throw an animal and, failing to lay it on its side with all four feet off the ground, to land it with one or more feet on the ground. (Allen 1933; Weseen 1934; Ramon Adams 1944)

dogger
See *bulldogger.*

doggery
Bartlett 1877: "A low drinking house. W. and S." (Mathews 1951)

doggoned
See *dog.*

dog house
(1) The bunk-house of a ranch. (Ramon Adams 1944)
(2) The mound of earth left by a prairie dog after burrowing. (Ruxton 1849)

dog-house stirrup
An old-fashioned wooden stirrup. (Charles Russell 1927; Mora 1950)

dogie
Also **doge, dogey.** A motherless calf; often a runt. Origin unknown. Also seen as **doughies.** (Weseen 1934; Ramon Adams 1944). Weseen 1934 spells it **dogy.**

dogie-man
A cattle-raiser (possibly a farmer) who took in calves to raise to cattle. For example, a Kansas farmer might fatten calves abandoned on the trail by Texas trail-drivers. (Ramon Adams 1944)

dog run
See *dog trot.*

dogs
Many dogs in the West were used for sport—coursing hounds were fashionable in the 1870s and 1880s; Custer was frequently out with his hounds and away from his command when he should have been with it; "Hound

Dog" Kelly (or simply "Dog" Kelly), mayor of Dodge City, ran his own pack of hounds. But many were also used to hunt and corner wild cattle or other wild animals. These were called **catch dogs** (Ramon Adams 1944 cites the variant **ketch dogs**). They were trained to great skills and were very courageous, holding the wildest of cattle by the nose, perhaps, or nipping at or holding on to their heels. They could also corner a cow until a roper dropped a loop over it or even throw it themselves for tying. Hunters also used them: when the hounds had cornered the quarry, say a lynx or a bobcat, the catch dog would go in, literally to catch it. Although they were used fairly extensively for cowhunting, particularly in the early days of the Texas cattle industry, there is not much detailed literary evidence of this practice, and their existence has been practically ignored in popular fiction; nor have I been able to find detailed descriptions of the breeds employed.

Dobie 1941 writes of the Blockers' famous hound: "Day or night Hell Bitch never caught anything but slick-ears. She would unerringly pick the one maverick out of any bunch of cattle, grab it by a long ear, drop between its front legs, throw it and keep it stretched out until a man came to her assistance." Fletcher 1968 writes: "Big roundups did not pay now, as the range was depleted of the particular brand we sought and what remained were so scattered, that it was advisable to divide our forces into small squads of four men each and to substitute pack-horses for the grub wagon which had followed the big roundup. A guide familiar with the country was sent with each detachment. The river bottoms were dense and in some places it was necessary to use trained dogs to run the cattle out of the thickets. Some of the wild ones would fight furiously when surrounded by horsemen or held at bay by the dogs. The wildest we roped. . . ." For a light but interesting description of dogs on the frontier, see Ross Phares's 1954 *Texas Tradition.*

dog soldiers
A term used with extreme laxity by writers of Western fiction. Almost every Cheyenne warrior to appear in pulp-fiction is called a dog soldier. In fact, they were members of a warrior society, among the Cheyenne and other tribes, who had certain privileges and duties, often those of policing ceremonies, hunts, and raids. It is sometimes said that the use of the term in French gave rise to the name *Cheyenne* (because of the similarity to *chien,* the French word for dog), but this is not so: *Cheyenne* is a corruption of the Sioux word *Sha-hi'yena* or *Shai-ena* (indicating that these were a people speaking a strange language) and is also seen as Chiyenne, Chyane, Chyene, etc. (MacLeod 1937–38)

dog town
A settlement of prairie dogs. (Dobie 1965)

dog town grass
A variety of prairie grass which was bad graze, especially for sheep. Mathews 1951, quoting W. C. Barnes's *Western Grazing Grounds* (1913), gives it the Latin name of *Aristida*.

dog trot
Also **dog run**. The covered space between two parts of a double cabin or house. This style of building was called a *Texas house* or **saddlebag house**. (Foster-Harris 1955; Chilton 1961; Rossi 1975)

dogy
See *dogie*.

doings
Cooked food, victuals. Much the same as *fixins*. (Bartlett 1877)

dolly, dolly welter
See *dally*.

doofunnies
Weseen 1934 defines the term as "knives and trinkets carried in pockets." Wentworth 1944 says the term is also to be found in Eastern U.S. dialects.

door rock
The door-stone or doorstep of a house. (Bartlett 1877)

dornick
(Irish Gaelic *dornog:* a small stone). Bartlett 1877: "Donock. A stone; a term peculiar to Arkansas, though used more or less throughout the South. In the West it is *Dornick*."

doted
(W and S). Bartlett 1877: "Changed or half-rotten; as 'doted wood.' " (Mathews 1951)

double cabin
See *Texas house*.

▶ **double rig**
A saddle with two cinch rings on either side—one below the front skirt of the saddle, the other below the cantle—thus enabling the rider to have two saddle girths. One such was the Texas rig. (Mora 1950)

double-shuffle
The change in the pace and rhythm of a pitching horse. (Weseen 1934; Ramon Adams 1944)

double-tree
The cross-piece of a wagon to which was attached the *single-tree* (on which the teams were hitched). (Mathews 1951)

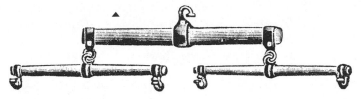

dough-gods
Also **dough-goods**. Biscuits. (Weseen 1934; Ramon Adams 1944)

doughies
See *dogie.*

dough-roller
A cook. There were almost as many terms for cooks in the old West as there were terms covering the act of hurried departure. (Weseen 1934; Ramon Adams 1944)

dove
Past tense of the word *dive,* as opposed to the British-English *dived. Dove* is regarded disapprovingly by the purists, which includes Bartlett 1877, who considers it a horrible Americanism. It was, however, to be found in old English dialects and seems perfectly harmless, sensible, and charming to me.

drag
(1) The rear part of a driven herd of cattle, usually watched over by junior cowhands. An unenviable position, because there a rider swallowed dust and had to contend with animals that could not keep up—sick animals and calves. A day in that position and a man was ready for his blankets at night. To ride drag was sometimes a punishment for bad behavior on the part of a drover. A drag was also a single animal that lagged behind. (Weseen 1934; Ramon Adams 1944)
(2) The spoor or path made by a snake. (Dobie 1965)

Dragoon
The popular name for an early revolver by Colt which, over the years, came in various shapes and sizes, though conforming to the same basic pattern. Its forerunner was really the Walker-Whitneyville Model 1847, an

unwieldy weapon that took some strength to carry and more to fire. The Dragoon Army Model 1848, a single-action .44, was somewhat handier. All the models were designed for use by cavalry or dragoons—hence the name. One version was capable of being used with a detachable skeleton rifle-stock. (Peterson 1963; Bowman 1953)

draw
(1) Gully; the offshoot of a canyon. Ramon Adams 1944 says: "A shallow drain for rainfall." (Weseen 1934; Wentworth 1944, who also places it in some Eastern U.S. dialects)
(2) The act of pulling a pistol from a holster. Also **draw iron.** (Weseen 1934)
(3) To **draw a bead.** Bartlett 1877: "To take aim with a rifle, by raising the front sight called a *bead,* to a level with the hind sight."

drift
(1) Used to describe the act of cattle moving ahead of bad weather; or to move almost aimlessly in one direction.
(2) As an extension of this meaning, when a cowboy moved a body of cows easily and without unduly disturbing them, he was said to drift them. Webb 1931 writes: "In many cases, however, it was the practice of cowboys to throw the neighboring cattle across the divide, or to 'drift' them back to their own range." This implies that the cattle were started in one direction and then allowed to travel free. (North 1942; Ramon Adams 1944)
(3) Further extended, the term referred to the movement of a man, meaning simply "to go"—for example, "I reckon I'll drift up Cheyenne way." (Rossi 1975)

drift fence
A fence to stop cattle from drifting, usually on the outskirts of a range. (Ramon Adams 1944). In the early days, before there was full fencing of range, drift fences might be erected across areas through which cattle easily drifted from their home range. Also, if bad weather came consistently from one direction, a rancher might erect a drift fence to stop his animals from moving ahead of it. There were times, of course, when these fences actually caused the death of thousands of cattle: in a big freeze, when animals naturally headed for a warmer clime to survive, many were caught on these fences and died from starvation and cold.

drive
In the later days of the Old West, this mostly meant the main trailing of Longhorns from Texas into Kansas and farther afield. But the word was also employed, especially in the early years, to cover work on gathers (see *gather*). In Bartlett 1877, we find: "In Texas, the annual gathering of herds for branding. This is provided by law in California." In Olmsted 1857 we

find: "When a regular *drive* is made, a dozen neighbours from twenty or so miles about, assemble at a place agreed upon, each man bringing two or three extra horses. These are driven before the company, and form a nucleus of the cattle herd collected. They first drive the outer part of the circuit, within which their cattle are supposed to range, the radius of which is about forty miles. All cattle having their marks, and all calves following their cows, are herded and driven to pens which have been prepared. They are absent from two to three weeks upon the first *drive*, usually contriving to arrive at night at a pen in which the stock are enclosed, otherwise guarding them in the open prairie. When the vicinity of a house is reached, the cattle are divided, the calves branded, and all are turned loose again." See also *trail-drives.*

driving the nail
A sport mentioned by Farmer 1889 which consisted of attempts to drive a nail into a post with rifle- or pistol-fire.

drop
To **get the drop on** anybody: to have a gun in your hand while someone else did not have one in his. (Farmer 1889)

drovers
The Kansas cattle-town folk and Eastern writers referred to the Texas cattle-trail drivers by this name.

drunk water
Apparently a term among the Sioux Indians for whiskey or strong spirits in general. "Then another of the Indian orators got up, and began to talk about the white people sending whiskey into their villages, and cheating them of their beaver-skins, and the mink and otter and muskrats, and buffalo robes, and how the Indians were getting fewer and poorer all the time from the 'drunk water' which the white men sent out." (Captain Eugene F. Ware, *The Indian War of 1874,* quoted in Rifkin 1967)

dry diggings
Mine diggings some distance from water; as opposed to wet diggings, those near water, where the gold was washed from the dirt. (Buffum 1850)

dry drive
A cattle-drive or part of a cattle-drive across waterless country.

dry-gulch
(1) To ambush; to make a surprise and treacherous attack when the victim was in camp.
(2) A shot from cover at an unsuspecting person. (Cunningham 1934). See also *gulch.*

dry-lander
A farmer in arid country who irrigated his land. (Weseen 1934; Ramon Adams 1944)

dry stuff
Steers. (Weseen 1934). Compare *wet stuff.*

dry-wash
An *arroyo;* a dry watercourse or channel left by flood water.

ducking
Stout cotton cloth. (Wentworth 1944)

dude
An Easterner; a man dressed in store clothes, as opposed to one dressed in range clothes. A somewhat deprecatory term. Farmer 1889 thinks the word derived probably from the Lowland Scots *duds* (clothes). In British-English the word during the same period meant a fop, derived from the German *dudendop, dudenkop* (a lazy fellow).

dude horse
Rossi 1975 writes succinctly: "a plumb gentle horse that will allow kids to crawl up its legs or dudes to sit on it."

dude wrangler
See *rough neck.*

dueño
(Sp; SW). An owner, usually in reference to such property as a store or land. (Dobie 1930)

dug-out
(1) A cabin made by digging into a hill or ridge, the front possibly faced with logs or turfs. The name *soddy* could be applied to it, but not all soddies were dug-outs. (Mathews 1951)
(2) A canoe made from a single tree trunk. Mentioned by both Bartlett 1877 and Farmer 1889.

dun
(from Saxon *dun:* chestnut-brown). A horse color. Some writers describe the color as a dull grayish-brown, and there are various interpretations of this word among the horsemen of different countries. But in the Old West, a dun was, as Dobie 1952 states, a bay of a faded, dull-brown shade. The

mane, tail, and points (other extremities) were black, and other markings, such as a dorsal stripe, were numerous. Their reputation among Westerners and Indians was one of hardiness and endurance. The Mexicans had a term for each variety, and these, as noted by Dobie, may be found under *bayo.*

Durham

A breed of cattle originally from County Durham, England. Also referred to in the West as shorthorns. The breed was commonly imported into the West to interbreed with and up-grade the Longhorns and northern range cattle. (See Ernest Osgood's 1929 *The Day of the Cattleman*, an authoritative and fascinating book—the best of its kind.)
Several Durham stock farms were established in Kansas in the early 1870s, and five bulls went to Montana in the same year. Stock from the Crane herd in Marion County and the Grant herd in Ellis County, Kansas, were used to improve range herds. In the 1880s, Herefords started to replace Durhams for breeding.

dust

(1) To **get up and dust.** Attributed by Farmer 1889 to Texas. He assigns to it the meaning "to move about quickly." I would add that it also suggests "to depart, to raise dust." To **dust out of,** also in use in the Eastern states, was used widely in Western fiction to mean "to depart."
(2) **To dust:** to throw dust in the eyes of a charging cow. (Ramon Adams 1944)
(3) Gold dust, money, etc. (Weseen 1934)

dusting pan

A pan, used in placer mines (see *placer mining*), in which gold dust was removed from a stream.

dust the trail

To travel.

Dutchman

Commonly, all Germans and Dutchmen were covered in the West by this term, but so were other Europeans not of Latin blood whose mother tongue was not English.

Dutch oven

Also **Dutch bake oven.** A heavy cast-iron pot usually with three feet and a heavy tight lid which allowed the pot not only to be placed on the fire but to have hot coals placed on its lid so that the food could brown all around. (Weseen 1934; Ramon Adams 1944; Foster-Harris 1955)

eagle bills
Tapaderos with long sides and a down-tapered snout resembling an eagle's bill. (Rossi 1975)

ear down
To prevent a horse from rearing or fighting by holding it by (or twisting) the ears, usually while another man mounted. (Weseen 1934; Berrey and van den Bark 1942; Ramon Adams 1944; Mora 1950). Also, a man's teeth could be sunk in a horse's ear to take the animal's mind off what was going on. (Rossi 1975)

ear head
Usually a single or double split-ear bridle (see ***bridles [1]***) with no noseband, browband, or throat latch. Popular in the Southwest for use on well-broken, trained horses. (Rossi 1975)

ear-mark
A cut in a cow's ear made in addition to a brand and used to identify an animal when a brand was hidden or obscured. It made a thief's rebranding of a cow more difficult. There were numerous cuts, all of which had individual names, such as ***over-slope, under-bit, over-halfcrop, swallow fork,*** etc. (Weseen 1934; Ramon Adams 1944)

easy on the trigger
Quick-tempered, always temperamentally at half-cock. (Weseen 1934; Ramon Adams 1944)

eat gravel
Also **eat grass.** To be thrown by a horse or cow; nice alternatives to "***bite***

the dust.'' (Weseen 1934; Berrey and van den Bark 1941; Ramon Adams 1944)

eating drag dust
(1) To ride behind a herd (an inferior and uncomfortable position).
(2) To be humiliated. (Weseen 1934; Ramon Adams 1944)

eight bits
Spanish colonial dollars, called ''pieces of eight'' by Southwestern Americans. They broke down into 8 reales (8 bits, each of which was worth 12½ cents). (Rossi 1975)

eight up
A wagon team composed of eight horses or mules. (Rossi 1975)

elephant
To **see the elephant:** to go to town, maybe for the first time; to see the world and gain experience of its sin and glitter, generally at some cost to the investigator. I always connect it with seeing an elephant for the first time at the circus. Bartlett 1877 comes up with one of his wonderful explanations: ''doubtless originated from some occurrence at a menagerie.''

◄ Ear-marks

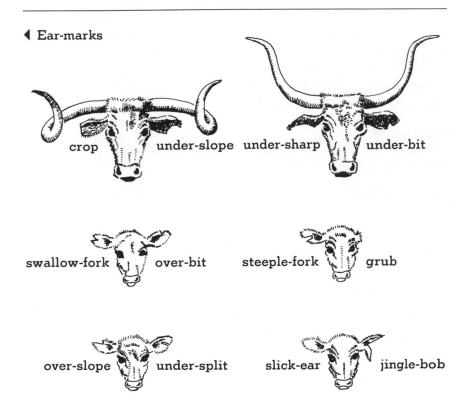

crop   under-slope   under-sharp   under-bit

swallow-fork   over-bit   steeple-fork   grub

over-slope   under-split   slick-ear   jingle-bob

elk
A little confusion here. Europeans call the American *moose* by this name.

The Americans gave the name to the wapiti (a Shawnee word meaning "white rump"), a large relative of the European red deer. The American *Cervus canadensis* stands 5½ feet at the shoulder and carries impressive antlers. Elks were slaughtered for meat and hide on a large scale and also hunted purely for sport; by the end of the nineteenth century they had been mostly wiped out from their extensive habitat, and the breed retreated mainly into the north-central Rockies. (Rossi and Hunt 1971; Grzimek 1974)

encina
(Sp; SW). Also **encino**. Live oak, covering a number of evergreen varieties of oak tree. (Dobie 1965)

engagé
(French-Canadian: an engaged man). A man employed as a trapper and hunter by a fur company, as opposed to the free trapper who worked on his own account. However, the engagé was not prevented from taking a limited amount of trade goods on a trip to do a little private trading. (Reginald Stuart 1957)

enramada
(Sp). A bower, a shady grove. (Mora 1950)

equalizer
A revolver. From the expression: "a Colt makes all men equal." (Ramon Adams 1944; Rossi 1975)

essence pedlar
See *polecat (1)*.

estray
A stray animal. R. B. Cunningham Graham in "A Hegira," one of his *Thirteen Stories* (1900), writes: "He told me that he 'had a right smart of an Indian trouble here yesterday about afternoon. Me and my vaquerys were around looking for an estray horse, just about six of us. . . . ' " It could be used both as a noun and an adjective.

estribo
(Mex-Sp). *Stirrup-iron*.

estufa
(Sp: stove, heated room).
(1) Farmer 1889: "A stove. Of Spanish origin, a part of the common speech of the Rocky Mountain States in which the Spanish element prevails." (Waters 1950; Mathews 1951)
(2) Among Pueblo Indians, an underground room in which a sacred fire burned.

euchered
To be outwitted, defeated, suckered. Based on the card game of euchre, in which, if a player does not gain a recognized number of tricks, he is said to be "euchred" or "euchered." Not strictly a Westernism, but a word used in Western fiction.

ewe-neck
The neck of a thin horse, which was bowed concavely like that of a ewe. Many Indian ponies showed this characteristic, which was not necessarily a sign of inferiority. Not a Westernism; common in British-English. (Rossi 1975)

exalted
To be uplifted by a rope drawn tightly around the neck—in short: hanged. A nice touch of macabre Western humor. (Weseen 1934; Berrey and van den Bark 1942; Ramon Adams 1944)

excuse me, ma'am
A bump in the road. (Weseen 1934; Berrey and van den Bark 1942; Ramon Adams 1944)

eyeballer
A nosy man; one who showed undue interest in the affairs of others; a meddler. (Allen 1933; Weseen 1934; Berrey and van den Bark 1942; Ramon Adams 1944)

fag, fagg
See *fogging.*

fallen hide
The hide of a dead cow found on the range. In the early days, it was legitimate for any finder to take the hide regardless of brand, just as anyone had the right to brand a maverick. (Mora 1950)

fall round-up
The round-up of beef cattle which took place in the last months of the year. (North 1942; Ramon Adams 1944)

fan
(1) To hasten; to **fan the breeze.**
(2) To **fan a gun**: a method of firing a revolver—not always accurate and

not recommended for anything but a short range. The trigger-finger kept the pressure on the trigger of a single-action hand-gun while the hammer was knocked back with the free hand, thus allowing extremely rapid fire. Another method was to file off the trigger so that the weapon could be fired only by fanning the hammer.

(3) To fan a horse or steer with a hat so as to liven it up. (Weseen 1934; Berrey and van den Bark 1942; Ramon Adams 1944)

fandango
(Sp; SW). A lively dance, with castanets and in triple measure. Also used

to describe a party or celebration. (Dobie 1930; Berrey and van den Bark 1942)

The fandango

faro
In the eighteenth century, the word was *faroon* (said to be from the French word *pharaon,* meaning pharaoh, which stood for the king of hearts in a pack of playing cards). A game, popular in the gambling halls of the West, in which the players bet on the order that cards would be drawn from a box. Traditionally there was a tiger painted on this box, hence the expressions to *buck* or *fight the tiger*. Not a Westernism.

Far West
Until quite late in the nineteenth century this applied to the country west of the Mississippi. Farmer 1889 uses it as late as that year.

feeder
(1) A man who fattened cattle, either his own or someone else's. In the 1860s, for example, Kansas farmers were acting as feeders when they bought cattle from the herds coming north from Texas, which they fattened on their own grass and hay. Right up to the 1880s, Middlewest stock growers were buying Texas beef steers for fattening; at times this also happened on the northern ranges of Montana and Wyoming. (Weseen 1934)
(2) The cattle thus fattened.
(Osgood 1929; Berrey and van den Bark 1942; Ramon Adams 1944)

feed lot
A small enclosure in which cattle were fed. (Berrey and van den Bark 1942; Ramon Adams 1944)

fence-crawlers
Cattle or horses which could not be contained in an enclosure; fence-breakers and -jumpers. (Berrey and van den Bark 1942; Ramon Adams 1944)

fence cutting wars
Usually local trouble, in which farmers and small cattle-outfits fought against the enclosure of public lands by large cattle companies and ranchers. It could also be the other way around—cattlemen could object to a settler fencing off good grassland or a watercourse. Wholesale fence cutting usually marked the start of the troubles. Dates of these wars varied according to locality. (Ramon Adams 1944; Sandoz 1958)

fence lifter
Also **goose drownder, gully washer.** A heavy rain. (Dobie 1930; Berrey and van den Bark 1942; Ramon Adams 1944)

fence rider
(1) A fence-sitting spectator at a horse-breaking. (Weseen 1934; Berrey and van den Bark 1942)
(2) See *line riders.*

fences
Their names and kinds were many. We find board fence; various kinds of rail fence, including the worm- or *snake-fence; Osage orange hedge* and other hedges; leaning fence; and the two boarded fences, shanghai and bloomer, where an extra-strong structure was necessary to protect fields against the intrusion of powerful animals such as Longhorns. Certainly most types were in use in Iowa around 1870, with fewer examples of them in the less developed Kansas. Some farmers on northern prairies, such as those of Nebraska, used earth or mud fences. (Osgood 1929; Mathews 1951)

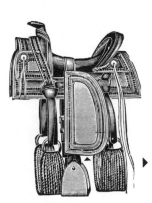

fence worming
A horse buck which gave the animal a zigzagging motion. The horse brought its feet to the ground first on one side and then the other. The term probably originated because the pattern of movement made was a zigzag like a *snake-fence.* (Berrey and van den Bark 1942; Ramon Adams 1944)

▶ **fenders**
Also *rosaderos, sudaderos.* Part of a saddle: wide leather shields under or over (and al-

most as long as) the stirrup-leathers. They hang below the middle skirts, between the rider's legs and the horse. (Ramon Adams 1944; Mora 1950)

fiador
(Sp: guarantor, Mex-Sp: chin-strap). Also **fiadore;** sometimes corrupted to **theodore**—as nice a Westernism as you'll ever find. For a definition we can do no better than to go to Mora 1950, who says: "a small-diameter hair rope, or one of rawhide, or of white cotton sash cord . . . it acts as a throat-latch and converts the hackamore [see *bridles (3)*] into a strong halter, as it goes around the neck and leads down under the jaw to tie into the bosal [see *bozal*] at the heel knot. The cord leads double all around, and the knots used in the ties are very tricky and smart looking." (Mora 1950; Ramon Adams 1944; Berrey and van den Bark 1942)

fiddle
"**Not enough to dust a fiddle**" meant that there was not much of something. (Weseen 1934)

Fifty-niners
Those who took part in the rush when gold was found near Denver, Colorado, in 1859. (Klose 1964). See also *Forty-niners.*

fill
A depression or dip in the land that was filled in with earth. (Berrey and van den Bark 1942)

fill a blanket
To roll a cigarette. (Berrey and van den Bark 1942; Ramon Adams 1944)

filly
(1) A young female horse.
(2) A young woman. (Ramon Adams 1944)

fireguard
Double furrows plowed in the soil about 100 or 200 feet apart. The grass between was burned, thus protecting grassland beyond the burned area from advancing fire. The intentional burning was done with great care, and, if possible, water was kept handy to suppress any flames that threatened to cross the furrows to the protected grass. (Ramon Adams 1944)

firewater
Whiskey. A term said to have originated with English-speaking Indians, it became a general Western term. (Dobie 1930)

fish
Also **slicker** (Weseen 1934; Berrey and van den Bark 1942). A yellow

oilskin raincoat (called fish because of the design in the trade-mark of a manufacturer of such articles) which a cowboy rolled and tied behind the cantle of his saddle. As with city-dwellers and their raincoats, the cowboys found that when it rained they didn't have their fish with them, and when it didn't, they did. Like so many articles of Western clothing, it served many purposes: While it was no protection against cold, a bed-roll, called a **slicker-roll** (Mathews 1951), could be made in its cover, and it could also be used to cover packs against rain and during river-crossings. Tied behind the saddle, with both ends hanging low against the legs of a horse, it just might stop an animal in the habit of bucking. Sometimes it was also slapped in the faces of running cattle to turn them. (Berrey and van den Bark 1942; Ramon Adams 1944)

fit
Past tense of the infinitive *to fight.* (Lamar 1966)

five-eighths rig
An uncommon saddle-rig with the cinch between the center-fire and three-quarters position. (Ramon Adams 1944; Mora 1950). See also *center-fire rig; three-quarter rig.*

five-shooter
A revolver capable of holding five loads, either of cartridge or cap-and-ball (see *cap-and-ball gun*).

fixing for high-riding
Preparing to depart in a hurry, indicating that the speaker had bought himself some trouble. It is fascinating to contemplate how many Western terms there were to cover a hurried departure. (Ramon Adams 1944)

fixins
Also **fixings.** As nice a term as was ever conceived and one which calls for an essay to cover all its ramifications. It was probably well-used by the time the Mountain Men embroidered upon it. One of those utility words that could mean anything you wanted it to mean—the equipment with which something was made or simply the thing that was made. A hunter's fixins might be his knife, powder-horn, and gun. It might mean trimmings, frills, and frivolous extras in reference to food or clothes. Without embarrassment it could turn itself into a verb; for example, a man planning to depart could say: "I'm fixin' to raise the dust." Perhaps its most common use was in reference to tobacco and paper for the rolling of cigarettes.

fizzy
See *fuzztail.*

flag your kite
Yet another term for a hurried departure. (Ramon Adams 1944)

flank
An action sometimes used to throw a calf by a pull on the rope with one hand and a slap on the flank with the other, at the same time making an upward movement with the knees against the animal's side. (Weseen 1934; Berrey and van den Bark 1942; Ramon Adams 1944)

flanker
(1) In branding, a cowhand who received and threw a calf so that the brander could apply the hot iron.
(2) A term sometimes applied to *flank riders.* (Ramon Adams 1944; Berrey and van den Bark 1942)

flank girth
The rear girth of a *Texas rig.* (Ramon Adams 1944)

flank riders
Trail riders who guard a trail-herd behind the swing riders, who were behind the point riders; at the rear came the drag. (Foster-Harris 1955)

flank rigging, flank strap
See *bucking strap (2).*

flannel mouth
An overly talkative man, a boaster. (Weseen 1934; Ramon Adams 1944). An expression not confined to the West.

flat-footed
Farmer 1889 says that it denoted a man standing firmly, thereby exhibiting honesty and resolution. However, Western fiction frequently uses the term to describe a man caught unawares, unprepared.

flea-bag
Sleeping bag. (Berrey and van den Bark 1942; Ramon Adams 1944)

flea-bitten
Said of a white horse with brownish-yellow spots. (Ramon Adams 1944; Berrey and van den Bark 1942)

flea-trap
A bed-roll. (Berrey and van den Bark 1942; Ramon Adams 1944)

flier
A poster or handbill (a **dodger**) advertising a man wanted by the law. I'm puzzled how they ever caught anybody before the printing of photographs.

flint hides
Hides that had dried and become hard without being scraped. Dobie 1941 and Sandoz 1958 use the term for cattle hides; Sandoz 1954 uses it in reference to buffalo hides.

float gold
Fine gold of dust and small nuggets washed down from the hills. (Willison 1952)

fly
A waterproof sheet used as a lean-to shelter, particularly at the rear of a chuck wagon as a protection for the cook. (Ramon Adams 1944)

flying brand
One bearing wings or a protuberance that might be interpreted as a wing. (Berrey and van den Bark 1942; Ramon Adams 1944)

fofarraw
Fancy or highly decorated dress; sometimes used in reference to the decorations on dress. Originated by the Mountain Men. (Ruxton 1849; Mathews 1951)

fogging
To travel rapidly, particularly a-horseback. It is possible that this is a corruption of the American expression **frogging on,** which had the same meaning and was common at the end of the nineteenth century. (Barrère and Leland 1897; Ramon Adams 1944). Weseen 1934 and Berrey and van den Bark 1942 cite **fag** and **fagg.**

following the tongue
In order to set his course for the following day, a trail-boss might point the tongue of his wagon at the polestar during the night. (Ramon Adams 1944; Dobie 1941; Gard 1954)

fonda
(Sp; SW only). An inn. (Mathews 1951)

▶ **fool brand**
One so complicated in its design or so difficult to read that it defied description. (Ramon Adams 1944)

footermans
To be afoot. (Jennings 1971)

forefooting
The roping of a horse or cow by its forelegs. (Weseen 1934; Ramon Adams 1944). See also *mangana.*

foreman
A man hired to boss the daily working of a ranch.

forging
The striking of a horse's front shoes by its hind ones. (Berrey and van den Bark 1942; Ramon Adams 1944)

fork
(1) To mount a horse. (Weseen 1934; Ramon Adams 1944)
(2) The front part of a *saddle-tree.* (Wentworth 1944; Ramon Adams 1944; Mencken 1948)

forked brand
A brand with two prongs protruding from any part of it. (Berrey and van den Bark 1942; Ramon Adams 1944)

fort up
To prepare for battle in a defensive position—perhaps from a house, a *buffalo wallow,* rocks, or any other form of protection. (Ramon Adams 1944)

Forty-niners
Participants in the California goldrush in 1849. (Hawgood 1967). See also *Fifty-niners.*

forty rod lightning
Also simply **forty rod.** Barrère and Leland 1897 say: "one of the innumerable names given to whiskey, like a rifle that will kill at forty yards." I yield to them: it is impossible to do better than that. Used also in the Eastern states. (Emrich 1951)

fourflusher
A deceiver, a sham, a bluffer.

fox-fire
See *St. Elmo's fire.*

fox-trot
A horse pace said to be extremely comfortable for the rider. Not all authorities agree on what it is or was. Commonly, the term refers to a pace in which the animal's front legs walk while the hind legs trot; a lively but gentle gait. (Eaton 1953)

fraggle
Farmer 1889 says that this was a Texan word meaning "to rob."

'fraid hole
A cellar or cave used as a storm shelter: "afraid hole." (Weseen 1934; Berrey and van den Bark 1942; Ramon Adams 1944)

free grass
Also **free range.** Open range that was public domain, the fencing of some of which by the big cattle companies led to *fence cutting wars.* In the days before fencing there was also friction, brought about by cattle barons and powerful cattle companies hogging public grass and excluding small outfits and farmers. (Ramon Adams 1944)

free ranger
A man opposed to the fencing of open range; usually a cattleman objecting to fencing by other cattlemen and farmers. (Ramon Adams 1944). See also *public land.*

freeze
To become suddenly still when in danger, after the manner of a wild animal. Thus a man holding a gun on another man would order: "Freeze."

freeze onto
To hold tight to something.

freno
(Sp). Usually referred to a horse's bit, but could also mean the whole bridle. (Weseen 1934 says it was the bridle only; Ramon Adams 1944 gives our explanation; Berrey and van den Bark 1942 agree with Weseen)

fried shirt
See *boiled shirt.*

frijoles
Dried Mexican beans; staple cow-country diet, also of the Mexicans of the

Southwest. (Ober 1885; *Harper's Monthly Magazine* 1875; Weseen 1934; Ramon Adams 1944). Wentworth 1944 quotes the spelling **freeho-lies** from the 1930s, but it is too good to miss; I'll bet some smart fellow used it before 1900 and brought it within the orbit of this book. (Berrey and van den Bark 1942)

frog-sticker
Knife. (Dobie 1941)

frog walk
Describes the movement of a horse making short, easy hops. (Berrey and van den Bark 1942; Ramon Adams 1944)

front jockey
The front part of a saddle, of leather and fitting around the horn. (Ramon Adams 1944; Mora 1950)

fryin' size
A small young fellow; an allusion to a fish that was small enough to nicely fit a skillet. (Weseen 1934; Ramon Adams 1944; Gard 1954; Jennings 1971)

fuke
A sawed-off shot-gun often loaded with a single large ball instead of shot, and lethal to buffalo at close range—if aimed at the right spot. It was sometimes used by early buffalo hunters, who ran buffalo (shot them from the saddle of a running horse), and originally applied to a fowling-piece. (Schultz 1935)

full-ear
See *slick-ear (1)*.

full of prunes
Spirited. (Weseen 1934; Berrey and van den Bark 1942)

full-rigged
A saddle completely covered by leather; not always the case in the early days. (Ramon Adams 1944)

fumadiddle
Fancy dress. (Ramon Adams 1944)

furrow fence
A furrow that marked the boundaries of claimed land. (Ramon Adams 1944)

fuste
(Mex-Sp). A Mexican saddle. Sometimes referred only to the Mexican wooden saddle-tree, over which a cloth was thrown. The horn was usually flattish and broad at the base. Farmer 1889 gives the word as **fusty** and says: "In California a raw hide and wood saddle-tree." (Ramon Adams 1944)

fuzztail
Also **fizzy** (Berrey and van den Bark 1942; Ramon Adams 1944), **fuzzy** **(fuzzies)**. The old disagreement here (see *bangtail*). Ramon Adams 1944 says "range horse"; Weseen 1934 says "wild horse"; North 1942 uses the term for wild horses, mustangs. I think the explanation is that, properly, the word should be applied to range horses (that is, horses which have an owner but which are running free on the range), but usage has been loose and the term has indeed been applied often to mustangs. Hence, we have **fuzztail running**: running mustangs; hunting and catching wild horses. (Weseen 1934). Berrey and van den Bark 1942 seem to treat mustangs and range horses alike. I think that, again, this is part of the confusion: a number of writers have interpreted the term *range horse* as "wild horse."

gaboon

Also **goboon**. A spitoon or cuspidor usually found in a saloon, often consisting of a box filled with sawdust. (Ramon Adams 1944). Not a true Westernism.

Gachupin

(Nahuatl *cac-chopina:* prickly shoes—referring to the fact that Spaniards wore spurs; SW). A Spaniard. Ruxton 1849 writes: "At this moment there issued from the door of the Mission Don Antonio Velez Trueba, a Gachupin—that is, a native of Old Spain—a wizeened old hidalgo refugee. . . . " Dobie 1930 defines the word as "upper class Spaniard." (Ober 1885)

gad

(1) Normally, a wooden haft with a metal point for goading cattle; a goad.
(2) A spur. (Ramon Adams 1944)
(3) A usually Eastern word for a cow's *ear-mark,* a term that goes back to the seventeenth century. (Mathews 1951)

gaff

To spur a horse. (Weseen 1934; Berrey and van den Bark 1942; Ramon Adams 1944)

gain

In mining, the amount of gold or silver obtained. (Mathews 1951)

gala

Festive, high-spirited. Andy Adams 1909 writes: "McCann had been frozen out during Roundtree's yarn, and had joined the crowd of storytellers on the other side of the fire. Forrest was feeling quite gala, and took a special delight in taunting the vanquished as they dropped out."

gallery
The porch of a house. (Dobie 1930; Weseen 1934)

galleta
(Sp: hardtack). Also **galleta grass**. Genus *Hilaria*. A variety of range grass that made good hay and graze. Chase 1919 refers to it as *blue stem*. (Mathews 1951)

gallin'
Also **galling**. Courting; visiting with a girl. Used in other parts of the States than the West. (Weseen 1934; Ramon Adams 1944)

gallito
(Sp: little cockerel). A name covering several varieties of violets in the Southwest. (Mathews 1951)

galloping fence
A zigzag rail fence; used elsewhere in the States besides the West.

galoot
Originally this was an Eastern slang word meaning an awkward, simple fellow; but it became a word associated with the West and was used mostly for a man not present—maybe in a mildly derogatory way, but not necessarily so. It entered the Western vocabulary late in the nineteenth century and was almost synonymous with *hombre.*

galvanized Yankee
A Confederate soldier captured by the North and given his freedom on condition that he joined the Union army, usually for the purpose of fighting Indians. Or, after the War Between the States, a Confederate ex-soldier who joined the Union army usually for the same purpose. Not strictly a Western term, but one met in Western literature. (Vestal 1939)

gama grass
Possibly a variation of *grama grass.* It grew on the plains to a great height and was a good cattle graze. (Mathews 1951)

gambusino
(Mex-Sp). A gold prospector; one who hunts gold in a small way; possibly a gold-thief. The origin of the term is unknown. (Mathews 1951)

gander pulling
A sport in which a captive gander had its head and neck greased, after

which horsemen tried to grab and take the head from the neck on the gallop; men with whips ensured that the horsemen moved fast. Farmer 1889 states that this sport was enjoyed in Texas; certainly there was a similar sport in Mexico, where they employed a chicken and called the game *carrera del gallo*. No doubt it was the Mexicans who passed the sport on to the Navahos. (Wentworth 1944; Rossi 1975)

ganted
Also **ganted down, gaunted**. Grown thin through lack of food or water. Usually applied to horses and cows, it could also be applied to humans. Wentworth 1944 notes it in New England in the nineteenth century. (Berrey and van den Bark 1942)

gateado
Another name for **bayo tigre** (see *bayo*).

gate horse
A rider posted at a gate for any duty, such as controlling cattle going in or out, tallying, etc. (Berrey and van den Bark 1942; Ramon Adams 1944)

gather
The cattle collected from a round-up. Hence, to **gather up**: to round up. (Berrey and van den Bark 1942; Ramon Adams 1944)

gee
The cry of the *bullwhacker* when he wanted his team to swing right; if he wanted them to turn left, it was "Haw."

gentle
When applied to horses, this term could mean different things to different men, just as *break* did (see **break [1]**). Applied loosely, it could simply mean that a horse was broken in the conventional way, by being ridden into submission and then worked on until it was thoroughly pacified. The term could also indicate a lengthy and subtle process of training which did not include riding a horse against its will. Anglos, Mexicans, and Indians all had knowledge of such methods, but they were not applied to cowponies, which had to be broken or half-broken quickly and cheaply. (Dobie 1952)

gerga
(Mex-Sp; SW). Also **xerga** (Ramon Adams 1944), **zerga**. A coarse cloth worn by poor Mexicans and used at times for saddle-cloths; hence, the word was used as a term for such a saddle-cloth.

get there with both feet
Barrère and Leland 1897 write: "(Western Americanism), to be very suc-

cessful." Francis 1887 says: "He said he'd been gambling, and was two hundred dollars ahead of the town. He got there with both feet at the starting, and was eight hundred ahead once, but he played it off at monte." (see *monte[2]*).

ghost cord
A string tied tightly around the animal's lower jaw over the tongue, with the free end used as a rein—somewhat after the manner employed by Indian horsemen. The use of this cord could make breaking a horse into a torture—for the horse. (Berrey and van den Bark 1942; Ramon Adams 1944)

ghost town
I have not been able to find evidence of the use of this term during the nineteenth century. It probably came into use toward the end of the first quarter of the twentieth century, but it refers to towns which certainly existed during the period covered by this dictionary: towns deserted of people, towns that emptied overnight as the inhabitants heard rumors of gold and rushed to get it. Such an incident is wonderfully described in what must be one of the most amusing Westerns in print: *Dead Warrior* by John Myers Myers (1957). The dedication of this book is worth quoting: "To Ernest Jerome Hopkins, who has not only seen but ridden the *elephant.*" This book came to me as fresh as ever after the sixth reading.

gig
(1) To swindle. (Weseen 1934; Ramon Adams 1944)
(2) To spur an animal. (Berrey and van den Bark 1942; Ramon Adams 1944)

gimlet
To ride a horse so that its back became sore. (Ramon Adams 1944). Hence, the term **gimleted** to describe the horse that has been ridden in this way. (Berrey and van den Bark 1942)

gin
To disturb, move, or chase cattle here and there. Dobie 1929 writes: "Now ten men were a small crew to handle a herd of 4,500 cattle, especially when the cattle are hungry, thirsty, and feverish from having been ginned about. . . . " Osgood 1929 quotes a letter of T. H. Durbin's from the Laramie Stock Growers Association's *Letters of Old Friends and Members:* "But so many outfits had come in and rounded up the stock, and ginned them over so much, they could never get fat." Ramon Adams 1944 uses the phrase **to gin around** in the same sense.

girls of the line
Also **ladies of the line.** Prostitutes. So called because the women plied

their trade in shacks and tents drawn up in lines on the outskirts of cow-towns, mining camps, and railroad end-of-track camps. (Emrich 1951)

girt
A variant of saddle *girth.* A reasonable one, for *girth* was pronounced *girt* in Texas. (Weseen 1934; Berrey and van den Bark 1942). See also *cinch (1).*

girth
The cinch of a saddle. Of Texas origin (pronounced *girt,* of course). (Ramon Adams 1944)

git
(1) Bartlett 1877 describes this word rather haughtily as "a favorite West-ern vulgarism for 'go,' or 'go ahead,' 'leave quickly,' equivalent to 'got it,' of which it may be a contraction." I confess this does not convince me. It seems to be merely a variant of *get,* with a meaning stronger than "go." In the imperative, it has the feel of the later slang word *scram*—or even at times *git the hell outa here.* Others have been of the same opinion. We find also to **git to go.** Also **git up an' dust,** which was known in Kentucky in the mid-nineteenth century. Not a true Westernism, but a small word that will always be associated with the West.
(2) To kill; to catch up with and punish. (Weseen 1934)

goat
(1) Ramon Adams 1944 describes the term as "half-hearted pitching." Berrey and van den Bark 1942 say it describes a horse pitching with stiff legs and arched back. Weseen 1934 says short, stiff-legged jumps, like a *crow hop.*
(2) A sheepherder. (Berrey and van den Bark 1942)

goat antelope
See *mountain goat.*

goboon
See *gaboon.*

goddam
(1) A general Indian term for a whiteman, mostly belonging to the South-west. The Indians were quick to notice that the Anglos larded their speech liberally with "God-damn," both as a straightforward oath and as an adjective. The French had the same name for the English in the Middle Ages.
(2) An Indian term for a whiteman's wagon. (Foster-Harris 1955)
(3) A variant of God-damn, used frequently in Western fiction. There were a number of polite euphemisms for the expression, such as goldarned.

go-devil
Ramon Adams 1944 and Weseen 1934 both note this as a Westernism, which indeed it is, in the context they employ. Also a term in general use throughout the United States, usually in reference to various mechanical devices. (Mathews 1951)
(1) A wire stretched from the top of a bank to an anchor in the middle of a stream, up which a bucket was pulled for easy conveyance of water. (Ramon Adams 1944)
(2) A hayrake (Weseen 1934). A horse-drawn mechanical hayrake. (Mathews 1951)
(3) A sled used in farming to cover seed sown in deep furrows. (Mathews 1951)
(4) In general American English the term has been used to cover a widely diverse variety of objects—a common sled, a sled for clearing roads of snow, a logging sled; an axe or wedge for splitting logs; a small tractor; a dropped weight or a mechanical device to set off an explosive charge in a mine or in oil-drilling; a child's homemade car; a human drifter; a playboy; a pressure brush used by oil riggers to clear pipes; and a hand-car on a railroad.

gold colic
Also **gold cholic.** Gold fever, the desire to find gold. (Weseen 1934; Ramon Adams 1944; Berrey and van den Bark 1942)

gold-hunter
See *prospector.*

goodnighting
The famous cattleman Charles Goodnight found that bulls on long, hot drives suffered chafing of the testicles, which could swell until the animal became sick and died. He learned to cut off the testicle bag, push the seeds into the body, and sew up the cut. The animals traveled well after this operation and their breeding capability was not impaired.

goose drownder
Also **fence lifter, gully washer.** A very heavy rain, a cloud-burst. (Weseen 1934; Berrey and van den Bark 1942; Ramon Adams 1944. Wentworth 1944 records the term in more easterly and southern states)

goose hair
A feather mattress or pillow. (Weseen 1934; Berrey and van den Bark 1942; Ramon Adams 1944, who confines the term to "pillow")

goosy
Also **goosey.** Nervous, irritable. A man jumpy under stimulus. Used as both

adjective and noun. (Weseen 1934; Allen 1933; Berrey and van den Bark 1942)

gophering
Digging, particularly with the exploratory digs a gold prospector made. Much the same as **coyoting** (see *coyote diggings*). (Ramon Adams 1944)

gotched ear
Also **gotch ear**. A cow's ear, the cartilage of which has been eaten away by ticks, causing the ear to droop. (Ramon Adams 1944). See also *mocho*.

gouge
(1) To cheat, to swindle. Weseen 1934 and Ramon Adams 1944 quote this as Western; Mathews 1951 records it in the East in 1845.
(2) In mining, the soft material along the wall of the vein. Mathews 1951 records the term in 1881.
(3) As a non-Western term it means, of course, to prise an opponent's eye from its socket in a fight.
(4) To spur a horse.

grab the apple
Also **grab the nubbin**. To hold the saddlehorn for greater security on a horse.

grace
One or two faintly blasphemous and humorous graces to be said before a meal in the West have come down to us; there are a number of versions:

> *Bless the meat an' damn the skin,*
> *Throw back your ears an' all pitch in.*

A variant on the same:

> *Eat the meat an' leave the skin,*
> *Turn up your plates an' let's begin.*

Another:

> *Yes, we'll come to table*
> *As long as we are able*
> *An' eat ever' God-damn thing*
> *That seems sorta stable.*

grade bull
A bull of a recognized breed, such as Durham or Hereford, used often to raise the standard of a low-grade or Longhorn herd while maintaining the hardiness of the range stock. (Osgood 1929)

grade horse

Usually a horse of mustang stock upgraded by crossing with quarter-horse stock, thus acquiring the ability to make quick starts necessary in a cow horse while retaining the stamina and hardiness of the mustang. (North 1942)

grade up

To upgrade or improve cattle by crossing with a superior breed. (Weseen 1934; Berrey and van den Bark 1942; Ramon Adams 1944)

blue grama

grama grass

(Sp). Also **gramma, gramma grass**. Webster's First New International Dictionary 1909 states that, in Spanish, *grama* is a certain species of grass: "The name of several kinds of pasture grasses found in the Western United States, esp. the *Bouteloua oligestachya.*" Farmer 1889 writes: "(Chondrosium). A Spanish name for a fine grass which, in Texas, grows to a height of two, and under very good conditions, of three feet." Dodge 1877 considers that the ***buffalo grass*** of the High Plains and grama grass, though entirely different in growth and appearance, are really identical: At Fort Dodge he had a small piece of ground covered with sods of buffalo grass taken from the high prairies. It was watered daily, and otherwise well cared for. To his great astonishment it appeared to change its whole nature, grew tall and rank, and in due time developed the seed heads of the true grama grass! Waters 1962 also equates the two. Ruxton 1849 writes: "The pasture, too, was good and abundant—being the rich grama or buffalo grass, which although rather dry at this time of the season, still retains its fattening qualities; and the animals soon began to improve wonderfully in condition and strength." See also ***gama grass***.

granger

A settler or farmer, as opposed to a cattleman. This name was the Northwestern equivalent to the Southwestern *nester*. All were referred to derogatively by cowmen as sodbusters, and there were other uncomplimentary terms. Granger was probably from *grange:* a farmers' union—which in turn took its name from *grange:* a barn. The word was in general use in the Eastern states and meant a rustic man, a hick. (Dykstra 1971)

granjeno

(Mex-Sp; SW). A thorned bush. A term that was used locally for a number of species (Dobie 1930), but more properly it referred to the edible berry-bearing hackberry (*Celtis pallida*). Mathews 1951 records the term in 1895.

grappling irons
Spurs. (Berrey and van den Bark 1942; Ramon Adams 1944; Gard 1954)

grass-bellied
Said of an animal whose belly was swollen from eating too much grass. Hence, pot-bellied. (Berrey and van den Bark 1942; Ramon Adams 1944)

grasses
These are, of course, an extensive study in themselves. Briefly, the distribution of grasses over the West was naturally dependent upon climate, altitude, rainfall, and general environment. The humid, low pasture of arable plains that stretched up through Texas and most of Kansas to the Canadian border was the home of the long, deep-rooted types such as the blue stem, needle, and wheat grasses. Farther west came the High Plains or dry prairie, supporting the short grasses: buffalo, mesquite, grama, and galleta. The galleta extended southwest of the grama area into parts of Utah, New Mexico, and Arizona. Grama and buffalo grass were seen in Wyoming, Nebraska, Colorado, west Kansas, parts of Oklahoma, and northwest Texas into New Mexico. Mesquite grass was found in Arizona, New Mexico, and west Texas. Most of these short grasses were sun-cured on the root and still nourished animals during the dry season. (Webb 1931)

grass freight
Goods shipped across the plains by ox-wagons (sometimes bull-wagons), the teams of which found *bait* on the grass by the way. This method of feeding made transportation cheap, though slow. But because they were slow, bulls and oxen were not such a temptation to Indians as were mules and horses: pursuit and recapture were easier. Majors 1893 writes: "Oxen proved the cheapest and most reliable teams for long trips, where they had to live upon the grass. . . . They did good daily work, gathered their own living, and properly driven would travel 2,000 miles in a season. . . . " (Berrey and van den Bark 1942; Ramon Adams 1944)

grass rope
Also **grass rope lazo, manila, ragline**. A rope originally made from *bear grass;* later manila hemp and sisal were employed. There are many pros and cons to its use and to that of the rawhide *reata;* in the old days fierce arguments were heard in favor of both kinds of rope. (Berrey and van den Bark 1942). See also *rope.*

grass-train
See *bull-train.*

graveyard shift
The trail-herd guard that circled the herd from midnight to two o'clock in the morning. This neat Westernism was obviously created by a man who had suffered such a fate. (Ramon Adams 1944)

greasebrush, greasebush, greasewood
Terms covering a number of resinous bushes in the more arid regions of the West. Prickly and usually growing in an alkaline soil, they burned with a bright flame when used as fuel. The **creosote** plant. (Mathews 1951)

greaser
A derogatory term for a Mexican. A return shot for **gringo,** as it were. Ruxton 1849 says in a footnote that the word *pelado,* which in Mexican-Spanish referred to a penniless and ill-bred person, was a "nickname for the idle fellows hanging about a Mexican town, translated into 'greaser' by the Americans." Greaser is indicative of the powerful racial feeling of the time, when Latins of all kinds were considered by the so-called Anglo-Saxons to be oily and greasy. However, there is a strong possibility that the term originated from the fact that Mexican freighters and even carriage-owners employed poor men to run beside their vehicles to grease the wooden axles. These men were called greasers and were regarded with some astonishment by the first Anglos who went into Mexican territory. Harby 1890 says: "A greaser, or the lower order of Mexican." (Weseen 1934; Ramon Adams 1944; Berrey and van den Bark 1942; Wentworth 1944)

greasy sack outfit
A poor cattle-outfit so needy that they were forced to carry their supplies in greasy sacks. Gard 1954: "In the earliest cattle drives from Texas, as in the cowhunts of that period, each of the few men involved carried his own food. He might take it in a saddlebag or in a sack tied behind the cantle of his saddle. . . . In the later years, one that persisted in this method was called a 'greasy sack' outfit." (Berrey and van den Bark 1942; Ramon Adams 1944)

Great American Desert
This title was given to the vast area which is now roughly the Midwest and which was then Indian country. Wagons headed for California and Oregon crossed it: men did not think to settle on the plains, for they were considered to be uncultivatable.

great seizer
A real treasure of a Westernism, meaning a sheriff. (Weseen 1934; Ramon Adams 1944)

greener
(1) Either an inexperienced cowboy or an Easterner strange to the West. Often the butt of earthy and sometimes rather cruel Western humor. Stan Hoig in his 1960 *The Humor of the American Cowboy,* a vastly entertaining book in which native Western humor is expressed at its best, writes: "The tenderfoot's gullibility was a red rag to the imaginative cowboy, and to him it was generally a matter of art to see how long he could 'string the greener.' " (Berrey and van den Bark 1942; Ramon Adams 1944). Also *greenhorn,* **pilgrim.**
(2) The generic term for a shot-gun, after the name of the maker of one of the finest shot-guns in the world, Greener, of Pall Mall, London, England, whose product was popular with lawmen and stage-guards.

greenhorn
Also **greener** (see *greener [1]*), **pilgrim.** A man inexperienced in the ways of the West or of cow-work. As Gard 1954 so neatly puts it: "a man who couldn't cut a lame steer from a tree."

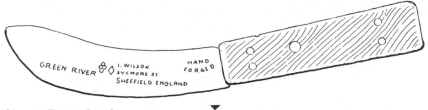

Green River knife
A heavy knife much favored by the early fur brigades and Mountain Men. The originals were probably in use by the Hudson's Bay Company and were marked GR for *Georgius Rex* (or so the tale would have it—believe as you will). One version relates that William Ashley's fur-hunters, going into the Green River beaver-country and finding the initials on the knife, named it for that area. While the bowie-knife-type weapon was not favored during the main Mountain-Man period, heavy knives were necessary tools for hunting, butchering, and fighting; and the Mountain Men made use of a number of models, among which was the Green River knife. For a fact, and in spite of the above, the knife was most certainly made in the Deerfield factory (established around 1832) of John Russell, near the Green River in Massachusetts. His knives were trade-marked GR. Competition caught on, and a number of makers, including at least one in Sheffield, England, produced knives bearing the words *Green River.* To **Green River a man** or to penetrate **up to the Green River** was to deliver a thrust so that the blade was buried up to the trade-mark. These phrases are vouched for by Ruxton 1849 and Barsotti 1956 but obviously did not apply to the later imitations, which had the words so near the point that the phrase lost its bite. The expressions were eventually extended to cover a job well done or, generally, the defeat of another. Carl Russell 1967 provides a detailed history of the knives. See also *skinner[1].*

green-up
Springtime on the range, when the grass turns green. (Berrey and van den Bark 1942; Ramon Adams 1944)

gringo
(from Sp *griego:* Greek, a term used for foreigners in past times). In the Southwest and Mexico, it was applied derogatively to Anglos, but one suspects it was employed at times to label any strangers other than Indians. Barrère and Leland 1897 state that it was applied to a newcomer, a johnny-come-lately. (Davis 1857; Weseen 1934)

grizzly bear
Before we even start on the nomenclature of this animal, I'll coyote out of the inevitable argument by quoting from Fitter and Leigh-Pemberton 1968: "Zoologists have wrangled over the naming of the grizzly bear more than over most animals. Most recent informed Old World opinion holds that it is really a subspecies of the widespread Palaearctic Brown Bear *Ursus arctus,* but many American zoologists like to think of it as an all-American bear, and call it *Ursus horribilis.*" Fighting words. However, the Westerner didn't have any doubts that a grizzly was a grizzly: an animal with many local races which ranged from Arctic Alaska and Canada down into Mexico, where the *Ursus arctus nelsoni* lived. Usually the giant grizzlies of the Northwest coastal areas were known as brown bears. The grizzly was so named simply because the texture of his coat was sometimes grizzled. There are many old-time tales of the animal attacking men, buffalo, and other large animals. In the case of wounded animals or old soreheads (bears with infected teeth), this may have been true, but generally the grizzly was a shy animal—although the female, in defending her young, could be ferocious. They were the targets of hunters of all varieties, as were the buffalo and pronghorn, and a number of local races are now extinct. The non-coastal grizzlies can weigh from as little as 350 pounds to 850 or 900 pounds, but the great coastal bear is much bigger and weighs up to 1,500 pounds or more. (The largest wild coastal grizzly actually tipped the scales at 1,656 pounds. Zoo specimens have weighed much more.) The grizzly was omnivorous—it would eat almost anything when in need. The Indians held the animal in great respect and gave it considerable religious significance. Occasionally, a cowboy would make chaps of a grizzly skin and leave the hair on: these were called **grizzlies.** They must have made

quite a show. Rossi 1975 reminds us that for Sunday sport the old California vaqueros roped the animals, took them back to the haciendas, and pitted them against bulls. He also notes that the bear usually won. It is on record that American cowboys of Colorado, Wyoming, and Montana also roped bears, and, though they did not match them with bulls, killed tlater.

ground cuckoo
See *road runner.*

ground-hitched
The partial immobilization of a horse achieved by dropping the loose end of a split rein to the ground while the other end was dallied (see *dally*) around the saddlehorn. If the animal tried to walk, it would eventually step on the line and stumble. Some learned to tread sideways and avoid it. Ramon Adams 1944 cites **grounding.**

grown stuff
Fully grown cattle. (Weseen 1934; Berrey and van den Bark 1942; Ramon Adams 1944)

grub
(1) Food; a meal, food-supplies. (Ramon Adams 1944)
(2) An *ear-mark* in which the entire ear was removed. (Ramon Adams 1944). In the 1870s, the famous Blocker outfit of Texas had for its ear-mark: grub, left ear; two under-bits (see *under-bit*), right ear.

grub-line rider.
See *chuck-line rider.*

grub pile
Cooked food; a meal. (Weseen 1934; Berrey and van den Bark 1942). Ramon Adams 1944 adds "often the call to meals."

grub slinger
The cook. (Weseen 1934)

grub spoiler
Possibly the most unkind reference to a cook yet recorded. (Ramon Adams 1944)

grubstake
To finance anyone, particularly a miner, for the purchase of supplies to enable him to start or continue with his activities. Hence, what was given or loaned was a grubstake. (Dobie 1930; Ramon Adams 1944)

grulla
(Sp). Crane bird. (Berrey and van den Bark 1942; Ramon Adams 1944)

grullo
(Sp: dark gray).
(1) A variant of *grulla.*
(2) One of the many Mexican words for a horse color which approximated the color of the grulla, or crane. There were a number of Anglo variants of this spelling: **gruya, gruyays, gruyo,** etc. Denhardt 1949 says: "The grullos are often mouse-colored, and could almost be called roans, as the hairs are often mixed, all the horse is a straight color to all appearances and is not spotted. The main part of the body is almost slate-colored, while the points [extremities, such as muzzle, tail, ears, and lower legs] are almost black. Zebra markings on the legs and the stripe down the back are the rule. Some vary from salt and pepper color to almost blue and mauve. They . . . have a reputation of being extremely tough and hardy." (Dobie 1952)

G.T.T.
In the Southeast, when a man wanted by the law could not be located, lawmen entered in their records "G.T.T."—Gone to Texas. Which was most likely correct, for Texas was a good place in which to make a new start with the slate wiped clean. The initials were also used by folks who upped stakes for a new start in the Lone Star State and left the information G.T.T. marked on their doors.

guajilla
(Mex-Sp *guaje* or *guage* from Nahuatl: a small kind of gourd; SW). Also **huajillo** (Mathews 1951), **huajilla** and **juajilla** (Dobie 1941), **juajillo** (Dobie 1964). A term loosely used for catclaw and a number of other plants such as acacia: *Acacia greggi,* etc.

guatamote
See *batamote.*

guayule
(Mex-Sp from Nahuatl; SW). *Parthenium argentatum.* A bush that yields a kind of rubber.

guia
(Mex-Sp *guía;* SW). A customs' pass or manifest; a safe-conduct. (Mathews 1951)

guide
See *scout.*

gulch
(origin uncertain). A deep-sided ravine, usually with a stream in the bot-

tom; a high-sided gully for a fast-flowing river. Often a place where gold was found, in which case the diggings and camps of the diggers would cover the sides, such as in the famous Alder Gulch. From the word were developed such terms as **gulch claim, gulch mining,** etc. To be **gulched** was to be caught up a gulch or in an impossible position by an enemy. Hence, possibly, to be **dry-gulched**: to be bushwhacked, caught by surprise in rough country, or jumped unexpectedly; a common expression. See also *dry-gulch.*

gully washer
Also **fence lifter, goose drownder.** A very heavy rain. (Dobie 1930; Ramon Adams 1944). Found in other parts of the United States besides the West.

gumbo grass
See *blue stem.*

gun
A word used in numerous combinations with other words, particularly in Western fiction. **Gun-fanner** (Ramon Adams 1944): a man who knocked back the hammer of his gun with his free hand while the trigger was depressed, so that a stream of bullets issued rapidly from the weapon— death for an enemy at close range, death for the fanner at a distance from a man who could shoot accurately in the conventional manner. Of late, Western fiction has developed a noted distinction between **gunman** and **gunfighter**—the first being a dirty word, the second a noble one—and "serious students of the West" have caught this habit. But fiction in the early twentieth century did not make this difference so obvious. **Gun-hand:** the hand that held the gun; also, a man who was hired for his expertise with a revolver and was not too particular whom he shot for his hire. To **gun down:** to shoot down. **Gun-hung:** to be armed with holstered gun or guns. **Gun-whip:** to hit and whip a man with the barrel of a revolver. To **go gunning for,** etc. The word *gun* more often than not referred to a revolver, but it could be used loosely to cover rifles.

gun-caps
Percussion caps used to ignite the powder charge of a cap-and-ball pistol or rifle. (Dunn 1886). See also *cap-and-ball gun.*

gunnysacker
During the wars between sheepmen and cattlemen, particularly in northern parts of the West, the cowmen on occasion attacked sheep-herds, wearing gunnysacks over their heads to hide their identity. Hence, the sheepman's name for them: **gunnysackers.** (Ramon Adams 1944)

gunslinger
A man who frequently resorted to the gun. Hence, the act of **gunslinging**. (Ramon Adams 1944)

gut-hooks
Spurs. (Berrey and van den Bark 1942; Ramon Adams 1944)

gyp
Short for gypsum. Used as an abbreviation of **gyp water**—water that was undrinkable from being heavy with alkali.

gypped
(1) Said of a man with a bellyache after drinking from one of the many rivers or water-holes contaminated with gypsum.
(2) In the common general slang of the period, the term meant "to be cheated."

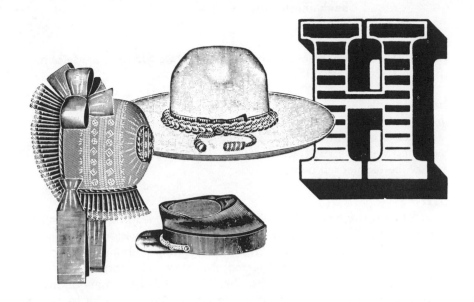

hacendado
(Sp; SW). The owner of a large estate or ranch.

hacienda
(Sp). The ranch or estate of a large landowner; the building thereon. (Ramon Adams 1944). Weseen 1934 defines it as "a cultivated farm, especially in the Southwest"—certainly domestic cultivation is implied in the term. The owner would be a stock-raiser, but he would also grow food for his family and hired hands. (Dobie 1950)

hackamer
A variant of *hackamore* (see **bridles [3]**), which was the Anglo corruption of the Spanish *jáquima.* (Ramon Adams 1944)

hackamore
See **bridles (3)**.

hackamore bit
A horse's bit, usually with a padded noseband, no part of which went into the horse's mouth. Used for a soft-mouthed horse, particularly in the training of young horses to bit and lines. (Mora 1950; Dobie 1952)

hackamore colt
A colt trained to the reins with the use of a hackamore and hackamore bit. (Mora 1950)

hackamore rope
A rope attached to a hackamore. Often a light-weight rope made of hair. (Branch 1926; Mora 1950)

hackmatack
(from the Algonkian). Referring particularly to the American larch, the tamarack, this term was also used to cover other coniferous trees such as the pine. (Mathews 1951, who records it as having been in use before the end of the eighteenth century)

hair
A scalp, as a war-trophy from the living or dead, taken by some Indian peoples, some Mexicans, and some U.S. citizens. At various periods, the authorities, both in Mexico and the United States, paid bounties for Indian scalps. One theory has it that taking scalps was not originated by the Indians but by the early English settlers, who placed a bounty on Indian scalps. There does not seem to me to be enough evidence for a firm opinion on the subject. The word *hair,* as used here, was originally Mountain-Man talk. (Ruxton 1849)

hair branding
Cold branding; the light branding of an animal (sometimes done through a wet blanket) in which only the hair was marked by the hot iron. Used for trail-branding or by cow-thieves. A not uncommon trick was to hair-brand a calf with the owner's brand, which meant that it escaped the proper branding; when this hair brand grew out, the animal would be rebranded by the thief. Hair branding was used quite considerably for legitimate trail-branding. (North 1942; Ramon Adams 1944)

hair lariat
Also **hair rope** (Ramon Adams 1944; Mora 1950), **hair reata**. A lasso made from hair usually taken from the tails of horses; hair ropes were on the whole too light for throwing.

hair pants
Chaps with the hair left on the hide. (Berrey and van den Bark 1942; Ramon Adams 1944)

halfbreed
A person of Indian and European descent, the male progenitor usually being white. In the early days, they were the go-betweens of the two races. The Indians usually accepted them as one of themselves, the whites usually regarded them as Indians. As civilization took over the West, so the status of the halfbreeds fell. It is worth noting that many families of high standing possess a mixed descent and are proud of it: distance in time, one might say, lends enchantment. A whole volume could and should be written on

halfbreeds and their part in the history of the West. The story of the French métis (see *mestee*) is of particular interest.

halfbreed bit
A corrugated bit that was hard on a horse's mouth. (Rollins 1922; Berrey and van den Bark 1942; Ramon Adams 1944)

halfbreed leggings
Leggins or gaiters that could be worn with shoes or moccasins and that were used by men afoot and by horsemen. Not liked much by cattlemen, but favored by later Mountain Men, freighters, scouts, et al. They were made of softened calf- or doeskin and were often highly decorated. Rossi and Hunt 1971 show a Charlie Russell painting depicting a freight-train boss wearing a pair in the saddle. (Mora 1950)

half-faced cabin
A temporary cabin with one side open to the elements.

half-faced camp
A tent-like construction with one side open to the elements.

hames
Two curved strips of wood or metal that formed part of either side of the collar of a draught horse or mule. The traces were attached to them. Not a Westernism.

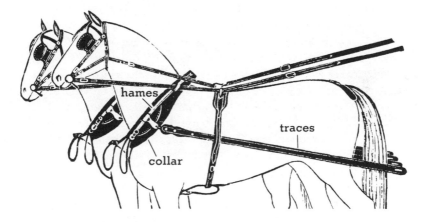

hand game
An Indian gambling game, much as played by children the world over, in which one player hides an object in the hand while the other player has to guess which hand is holding it.

handle
A man's name—whatever he chose to go by. It was not polite to ask for

a full name if it was not offered—or any other personal details, for that matter. You simply asked: "What's your handle?" Though this word is possibly not an original Westernism, it is very much associated with the West. (Rossi 1975)

happy hunting ground
A phrase used by the whites to describe what they thought was the Indians' version of heaven. Probably based on a term used by Indians. (Ramon Adams 1944)

hard-and-fast
See *roping.*

hardcase
Literally, a hard case: a hard and feelingless man, a criminal. Not necessarily a Westernism, but used frequently in Western fiction. (Weseen 1934)

hard money
(SW). Coin, as opposed to money notes (paper money). (Dobie 1930; Ramon Adams 1944)

hard tail
A mule. (Weseen 1934; Ramon Adams 1944)

hard twist
In the latter part of the period covered by this book, the rawhide *reata* was being replaced in many parts by the *grass rope,* either of hemp or maguey. Some of the hemp was manila; this was hard twist, which was a fair description of its nature. It was twisted, not braided like the reata, and it was hard. If I am not very careful, I shall get into the endless argument over rawhide versus hemp. And who made the best hemp that money could buy? Plymouth, Massachusetts, whence came the famous Plymouth hemp—not the supple tool that the reata was, nor as sensitive, but good-natured, hard-wearing, and easier to handle. (North 1942)

hardware
A belt-gun. (Weseen 1934; Berrey and van den Bark 1942; Ramon Adams 1944)

hasher
A cook. (Weseen 1934; Berrey and van den Bark 1942)

hatchet pipe
An Indian implement which was both tomahawk and smoking pipe. (Hodge 1907–10)

hatrack
A bony, tick-ridden calf or cow. (Berrey and van den Bark 1942; Hoig 1960)

hats

If any part of a cowboy's gear could be called a permanent fixture, it was his hat. He ate with it on and removed it only when hitting the sack (and maybe not even then). The only time he appears to have removed it voluntarily was for some purpose other than covering his head—such as fetching water in it, fanning a fire, or slapping a horse into action. To show how a cowhand felt about his hat, he'd spend up to 20 dollars or more on one—a good part of a month's wages. His models came in all shapes and sizes, but of course the John B. Stetson hat (which gave the cowland headpiece the generic term *Stetson*) reigned supreme from just before 1870 onwards. Many trail-drivers who first headed north out of Texas wore a hat modeled on the Mexican sombrero —wide-brimmed and with a sugar-loaf crown. Some probably also wore the low-crowned "planter's hat."

Any worthwhile hat had to protect the wearer against burning sun, rain, and hail and had to have enough brim for neck-shade and to wrap down around the ears with a scarf when the temperature dropped below zero. (Mora 1950; Foster-Harris 1955)

haul off
To depart. (Weseen 1934)

haw
The teamster's command when he wanted his ox-team to turn left. If he wanted them to turn right, he bawled "Gee." (Foster-Harris 1955)

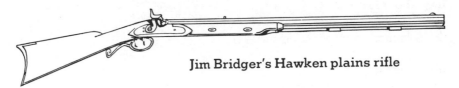

Jim Bridger's Hawken plains rifle

Hawken
No book on the West would be complete without a mention of this historic rifle. In brief: Jacob and Samuel Hawken made these guns in St. Louis from 1822 to 1849, when brother Jacob died. After that Samuel carried on alone till 1861, when he sold out to one of his men. The Hawken began life as a mountain rifle, especially made for the fur-trade; most of the American fur brigades were issued with them. Carl Russell 1967 writes of a Hawken percussion rifle of the later Mountain-Man period: "a heavy 34-inch octagonal barrel, about .53 caliber (½-ounce round ball, 214 grains), low sights, set trigger, percussion lock with a peculiar basket of steel (the 'snail') enclosing the nipple, half stock, ramrod carried under a

metal rib, sturdy butt stock, crescent-shaped butt plate, and the total weight of the piece 10½ to 12 pounds.'' By this time, it had developed into the *plains rifle,* no longer the mythical flint-lock that never failed a good man. It was the frontiersman's ideal weapon, uncomplicated and strong. The more powerful of the earlier models would stop a buffalo in its tracks. In the fastness of the Rockies, the trapper toted the best of the old Kentucky rifles, and some of them carried the same weapon for twenty years or more. The Hawken is legend and well it might be. There were other rifles of excellent quality made for the same trade, but none of them have survived with the glamour and romance that the Mountain Men gave to the Hawken. The collector who possesses one is a lucky man indeed. (Ruxton 1849; Barsotti 1956; Carl Russell 1967)

hay burner
(1) A stove that could be fueled by hay. In fact, a stove invaluable in treeless country; because it would burn almost anything available, including grass and weeds. Used particularly in Kansas. (Mathews 1951; Foster-Harris 1955)
(2) A horse. (Weseen 1934; Ramon Adams 1944)
(3) A smoking pipe—but this wasn't a Westernism.

hayseed
(1) A farmer.
(2) A rough, ignorant man.
(3) A green hand on a ranch. (Wentworth 1944)

hayseed country
Farming country. (Berrey and van den Bark 1942)

hay shoveler
(1) One who hay-fed cattle during winter.
(2) A farmer. (Ramon Adams 1944)

hay waddy
An extra hand on a ranch to cut hay for winter feed. (Weseen 1934). See also *waddy.*

haywire
Crazy, loco. (Berrey and van den Bark 1942; Ramon Adams 1944)

haywire outfit
An inefficient ranch or crew. (Berrey and van den Bark 1942; Ramon Adams 1944)

haze
To drive. The word implies driving slowly and gently. To **haze-in:** to

gather, to drive in. The cowboys would often use work-terms in their everyday speech: for example, a man would haze a pardner in the direction of a saloon. He could also haze the conversation in the direction he wanted. (Weseen 1934; Berrey and van den Bark 1942; Ramon Adams 1944)

hazer
A bronc buster's assistant. (Berrey and van den Bark 1942; Ramon Adams 1944). In later years, the term was applied to the rodeo rider who kept steers moving in a straight line for a steer-wrestler or bulldogger. (Rossi 1975)

head-and-tail string
A string of pack-mules that had been tailed up: that is, their lead-lines tied to the tail of the animal in front. (Ramon Adams 1944)

head-catch
The roping of an animal by the head or neck. (Ramon Adams 1944)

head-dress
See *war bonnet.*

headquarters
The ranch-house. (Ramon Adams 1944)

headstalls
See *bridles.*

headtaster
The ranch manager. (Weseen 1934; Berrey and van den Bark 1942; Ramon Adams 1944)

heap
Borrowed from the Indian's English, meaning "very much," "plenty," etc. (Ruxton 1849)

heap-walk-man
Also **heep-walk-man** (Weseen 1934), **walkaheap**. Allegedly the Indian name for an infantryman.

hediondilla
(Mex-Sp; SW). *Creosote* bush.

heel
To rope a cow by the hind feet. Rarely were horses heeled. (Weseen 1934; Ramon Adams 1944). Also found as **heeling.**

heeled

To be armed with a gun. A man's heels were said to be armed when they were spurred; this usage may have derived from the practice of arming the heels of fighting cocks with spurs. Francis 1887: "If I'd had any show, I'd've drawn on 'em right away—I wanted to ter'ble bad; but I hadn't got no Winchester along, and only two cartridges in my six-shooter, whilst they were well-heeled." Though widely used in detective thrillers, this term is thought to have originated in the West. (Ramon Adams 1944)

▶ **heeler**

A dog employed to catch and herd cattle, particularly in the early days of Texas. So called because the dog was trained to catch the heel of the cow in its jaws. (Dobie 1941). See also *dogs.*

heel-flies

Said to be the only living thing that could get the better of a wild Longhorn: when heel-flies attacked, they would run, usually to water, for protection. The fly attacked the back of the leg, just above the hoof, and laid its eggs there. (Ruede 1937; Dobie 1941; Ramon Adams 1944)

hemp fever

A lethally high temperature brought about by hanging with a rope around the neck—in short: a hanging. (Weseen 1934; Berrey and van den Bark 1942). Ramon Adams 1944 remarks pithily that the victim was "given a chance to look at the sky."

hen fruit

Eggs. (Weseen 1934; Berrey and van den Bark 1942)

Henry

Starting manufacture in 1860, this fine repeating rifle was the forerunner of the great Winchester, to which it gave way in 1866. It continued in use, however, conspicuous for being all metal from muzzle to stock. It had a tubular magazine under the barrel, holding 15 rimfire shells and loaded from the front. The lever-triggerguard ejected empty shells, inserted a fresh round into the breech, and cocked the trigger. (Bowman 1953; Peterson 1963)

hen-skin

(1) A sougan, a quilt, a bedcover stuffed with feathers. (Berrey and van den Bark 1942; Ramon Adams 1944)

(2) A poor saddle. (Berrey and van den Bark 1942)

herd
A considerable number of animals, usually gathered together: cows, horses, sheep—any animal that could be herded. However, a cattleman might refer to his stock as his herd even though the animals were scattered on the range. A smaller number of animals was a bunch. (Ramon Adams 1944; Mathews 1951)

herd-broke
Said of animals when they had become accustomed to being together in a herd, usually on a trail-drive. It could be applied to horses, referring to the stage before they became saddle-broke. (Ramon Adams 1944; Dobie 1952; Berrey and van den Bark 1942)

herder
(1) A tender of herds and flocks; a guardian and driver of cows, sheep, or any other beast that could be gathered and driven in herds.
(2) A foreman in charge of a gang of Chinese coolies working on railroad construction. (Barrère and Leland 1897)

Hereford
(1) One of the breeds of cattle (originating in this case in Herefordshire, England) which were brought into the West in the 1880s to replace the Durhams as breeding stock to upgrade the Longhorns. (Osgood 1929). The Wyoming Hereford Association was formed in 1883.
(2) Anything white: Hereford shirt, Hereford hat, even a Hereford man. (Bartlett 1877; Barrère and Leland 1897)

hern
An old form of the possessive *hers,* still to be found in British-English dialect. From *her one* or *her own.*

hickory
The word originally applied to a number of different trees of the genus *Carya;* and, this being a tough wood, the word was used in the same sense. Hence, a durable cotton cloth bore this name, and a cowboy would wear a **hickory shirt;** these were later displaced by flannel shirts, which were ideal for the range. (Mora 1950; Mathews 1951). Besides widely using hickory-nut oil, numerous Indian people found that for war bows the wood was as fine a material as ash or osage orange. In 1539–41 the Spaniards under de Soto discovered the lethal power of such bows in their fights with the Indians.

hidalgo
(Sp). A nobleman or proprietor of extensive land. Usually applied to a man of pure or near-pure Spanish descent.

hide and tallow factory
See *tallow factory.*

hide-hunter
A professional buffalo hunter in the 1870s and 1880s who shot the animals for their hides. The hunters often referred to themselves as buffalo runners, though they no longer hunted the buffalo by running them (see **run**); this label was a hangover, no doubt, from the days when the buffalo were so hunted. (Wellman 1939; Rossi 1975)

hide-thief
Also **hide rustler.** A man who killed another man's cows for the sake of their hides during the late 1860s and early 1870s, when cowhides were sometimes worth more than meat. One trick used by rustlers was to burn the grass, so that the cows starved to death. At one time, it was legitimate to skin a dead animal belonging to another man and take the hide.

hierba de vibora
(Mex-Sp *hierba de víbora;* SW). Also **snake-root** (Dobie 1965), **snake-weed** (Dobie 1941, 1965). Any number of weeds and roots which were said to combat the effects of snake-bite. (Dobie 1965)

highbinder
A vicious and unridable horse. Also applied to a man of vicious and mean nature. (Berrey and van den Bark 1942)

high-grading
The theft of ore from a mine—usually by those employed there. (Berrey and van den Bark 1942)

high lonesome
(1) A heavy drinker. (Berrey and van den Bark 1942; Ramon Adams 1944)
(2) A drunken spree. Wentworth 1944 records the term from 1891 in Nebraska. (Dobie 1930)

high lope
A swinging, fairly rapid horse gait. (Weseen 1934; Berrey and van den Bark 1942)

high poler
Also **high roller**. A horse that leapt high into the air when pitching. (Berrey and van den Bark 1942; Ramon Adams 1944)

high-tail
Surely one of the commonest yet most expressive of Westernisms. You can fairly see the lifting of the tail for yet another of the countless Western terms for departing in haste. It could also be applied to a bolting horse or a cow making a break for freedom. (Weseen 1934; Berrey and van den Bark 1942; Ramon Adams 1944; Wentworth 1944)

hill-nutty
A prospector of hill-country, a breed supposedly crazy from long months of solitude in the hills.

hinny
A mule, the offspring of a stallion and a she-ass; the usual mule had a reverse sire and dam. Not a Western word.

hisn
The old form of the possessive *his;* from his 'un: *his one, his own.*

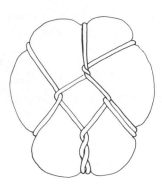

diamond-hitch

hitch
In the West, a knot was a hitch and nothing else. When you tied your horse to a post or rail, you hitched it to a hitching post or rail, or even to a hitching rack. When you tied a pack on a pack-saddle you used various hitches according to your taste. I do not profess to know the multitude of names applied to tying and knotting, but a few of them are: barrel-hitch, basco, basket-hitch, bed-hitch, double-diamond-hitch, half-hitch, Mexican-diamond-hitch, pack-hitch, prospector's hitch, squaw-hitch, and stirrup-hitch. When you fastened your team to a wagon, you **hitched up.**

hitching post
A post to which horses were tied—found sometimes in corrals, especially those used for the purpose of breaking horses or those in which horses were kept. This could also bear the name *snubbing post.* There might also be a hitching post outside a house for visitors' animals.

hitch pin
See *picket pin.*

hitch rail
Also **hitch rack, hitching rail, hitching rack.** A rail to which horses might be tied—found in front of houses, saloons, and places of business.

hit the breeze
Yet another phrase meaning to depart without loss of time. (Weseen 1934; Ramon Adams 1944)

hit the trail
To set out. (Weseen 1934; Ramon Adams 1944)

hobble
A shackle put on a horse's ankles so that he might move enough to graze but could not wander far. Hence, **to hobble:** to tie a horse's forelegs together while allowing it enough movement to rustle for graze. (Ramon Adams 1944). Allen 1933 distinguishes **hopple:** to tie both back legs.

hobble stirrups
Also **hobbled stirrups.** Stirrups that were tied under the horse's belly or fastened to the saddle girth, thus anchoring them. Such a dangerous practice that you may well ask why anybody should be crazy enough to do it. The rider was pretty well fixed in the saddle, but, if unhorsed, he would find it difficult to free his feet from the stirrup-irons. (Weseen 1934; Berrey and van den Bark 1942; Ramon Adams 1944)

hobble your lip
Hold your tongue, quit talking. (North 1942; Ramon Adams 1944)

hoe cake
Corn bread made of corn meal, salt, hot water, and bacon grease. The term probably came out of Texas, where it was the custom to bake bread on a hot hoe. (Rossi 1975)

hoe-dig
Also **hoe-down** (Weseen 1934; Berrey and van den Bark 1942). A dance, in the sense of folks gathering together for dancing. (Ramon Adams 1944)

hogan
A Navaho hut. Dunn 1886: "The dwellings of the Navahos, which they call hogans, are rude, conical huts of poles, covered with brush and grass, plastered with mud. They refuse to make any more substantial buildings on account of their nomadic habits and certain superstitions, which cause the destruction of their hogans at times."

hogbacked
Also **roachbacked.** Applied to a steep-backed horse; the opposite of sway-backed (Berrey and van den Bark 1942; Ramon Adams 1944). Also used to describe a ridge of land that was sharp or shaped like a hog's back. (Rossi 1975). See also *roachback.*

hog down
A variant of *hog-tie.* Fletcher 1968 writes: "The wildest we roped and hogged down by tying their feet together with small cords of rope until the herd could be brought to them."

hog down corn
To turn hogs loose to feed in unharvested corn. (Berrey and van den Bark 1942)

hogging string
Also **hoggin' string, hogging rope** (Berrey and van den Bark 1942; Ramon

Adams 1944), **hoggin' rope.** A short rope or cord for hog-tying animals, particularly a calf. (North 1942). See also *pigging string.*

hog-leg
A large, long-barreled revolver of the old type that was said to look like the leg of a hog. Ramon Adams 1944 states that it was originally a Bisley single-action Colt. (McCarthy 1936; Berrey and van den Bark 1942)

hog ranch
At the end of the 1870s, the Hayes administration banned the sale of liquor on military posts. Result: On the outskirts of military establishments in the West, so-called ranches for raising hogs appeared which were in fact drinking dens. They were a great nuisance to the military authorities, who, of course, had no power to stop their trade. (Foster-Harris 1955; Rossi 1975)

hogs
The flesh of the hog was repugnant to some Indian peoples, notably the Navaho. Hogs are usually avoided in Western fiction, and it is a general belief propagated by fiction writers that hogs and sheep were distasteful to all cattlemen. But trail-drives of large hog-herds are recorded, and it is interesting to note that most cattlemen in early Texas, for example, kept both hogs and sheep, which gave them a change of diet from beef. The sheep also supplied the wool from which their clothing and blankets were woven by the womenfolk. (Dobie 1929)

hogskin
An Eastern saddle, a postage-stamp-sized saddle. (Weseen 1934; Berrey and van den Bark 1942; Ramon Adams 1944)

hog-tie
Also *hog down.* The term is sometimes used loosely to signify the tying of anything so that no movement is possible, but it particularly meant the tying of an animal, especially a calf for branding or a troublesome cow. The two hind legs and one foreleg of the calf were tied together with a few half-hitches. A small noose was slipped over the foreleg and tightened; the loose end was put around the hind legs, and the knots were made; the hind legs were then pushed forward to be tied with the foreleg. (Weseen 1934; North 1942; Ramon Adams 1944; Mora 1950)

hog-wallow
A word about which there is some disagreement. What is certain is that it means a depression in the land and that in Texas there is a belief that these hollows were caused by the wallowing of hogs. Possibly the *razorbacks,* like the buffalo, wallowed in hollows that were already there and deepened them. (Dobie 1929)

hog wild
Excited, angry. (Weseen 1934)

hoja
(Sp: leaf; SW). A corn-shuck which was used as a cigarette paper.

hold down a claim
To occupy a claim, whether mineral or land, and establish legal ownership. (Berrey and van den Bark 1942)

hole up
(1) To take shelter in bad weather. *Line riders* holed up in their shacks in
winter. (Allen 1933; Weseen 1934; Ramon Adams 1944)
(2) To go into hiding when being pursued or hunted. It referred particularly to outlaws but could be used in reference to animals. (Ramon Adams
1944)

holler calf-rope
To acknowledge defeat, to throw in the towel. (Weseen 1934; Berrey and
van den Bark 1942; Ramon Adams 1944)

hollow horn
A belief that came to Texas from the Eastern states (where the term was
recorded early in the nineteenth century) that a poor condition in cattle
was due to the hollowness of their horns. The two common cures were to
bore a hole in each horn to "drain it off" or to saw the horn off. Dobie 1941
notes that, in fact, the pith in poorly nourished cattle does sometimes shrink
and that Texas cattle moving onto northern ranges increased their horn
growth. There is a nice saying about a dumb-head: "He ought to be bored
for the holler horn." (Dobie 1941, 1964; Mathews 1951)

holsters
See *scabbards.*

hombre
(Sp: man; SW and later in almost general use throughout the West—
Weseen 1934; Wentworth 1944). Ramon Adams 1944 adds: "Generally
applied by Americans to one of low character, or in conjunction with such
adjectives as *bad, tough,* etc." While I would not disagree with Mr.
Adams, who is an authority on Western words, I think his use of *hombre*
became more common in general American-English during the twentieth
century. I think it was used in the old Southwest as it is today in Spain and
Mexico—simply meaning "*man.*" (Dobie 1930)

hombre del campo
(Sp). Used not only in Mexico but in Texas and the Southwest, meaning

something more than a man of the wide-open spaces. Invariably a term of praise and respect, it referred to a man who was an expert in the life of the wilds, with a knowledge of animals (particularly those in the wild); a man who was adept at reading *sign,* at trailing, hunting, and trapping; or a man who possessed a great store of wild lore. A favorite term of J. Frank Dobie's.

home end
The end of the rope retained by the roper and dallied (see *dally*) around the saddlehorn. (Weseen 1934; Berrey and van den Bark 1942)

home range
The usual range for particular cattle. (Ramon Adams 1944)

homesteader
A farmer who took up land under the homesteading laws; but also a cowman's general term for a farmer.

honda
(Sp *hondón:* eyelet). A small loop or ring used as a slip-ring on a lasso. The honda of a *reata* was usually cleverly braided into the rope itself, while that of the *grass rope* was a securely tied slip-knot. (Wessen 1934 gives the masculine form **hondo;** Rollins 1922 gives both versions, as does Mora 1950, who adds **hondou** for good measure; Ramon Adams 1944 sticks to the above version)

hondo
(1) (SW). A deep arroyo—*hondo* is simply the Spanish word for *deep.* (2) See *honda.*

honey mesquite
See *algarroba.*

honkytonk
Also **honka tonk.** A rowdy, low place of amusement. Not strictly a Westernism, but a term found fairly frequently in Western literature.

hood
The driver of the *hoodlum* wagon on a trail-drive—usually the night-hawk (see *night-wrangler*). (Dobie 1941; Weseen 1934; Berrey and van den Bark 1942; Ramon Adams 1944)

hooden
Ramon Adams 1944 says it was a cabin where bachelor cowboys sometimes slept during bad weather; Weseen 1934 and Allen 1933 give the same definition. Berrey and van den Bark 1942 say: "line camp."

hoodlum
Also **hoodlum wagon.** The *bed-wagon* on a trail-drive, usually in addition
to the chuck wagon; not in use till the later days of the West. North 1942
writes: "With each outfit went its chuck-wagon, hoodlum or store-wagon,
and remuda of ponies." (Weseen 1934; Berrey and van den Bark 1942;
Ramon Adams 1944)

hooking cow
A cow-crittur with an inclination to hook innocent cowboys on its horns.
(Francis 1887)

hooks
(1) Spurs. (Berrey and van den Bark 1942; Ramon Adams 1944)
(2) The hip-bones of a thin cow. (Berrey and van den Bark 1942)

hookshop
A brothel. A piece of general American slang found in Western fiction.

hook up
To hitch a single animal or a team to a wagon. (Weseen 1934; Berrey and
van den Bark 1942; Ramon Adams 1944)

hooley-ann
(1) A corruption of *hoolihan(1)*. (Berrey and van den Bark 1942)
(2) A rope-throw made from afoot or from the back of a horse, composed
of movements that constituted a minimum of fuss and quietly necked a
horse without arousing others in the band. (Ramon Adams 1944). Authorities give various definitions of what actual motions were employed. Weseen 1934 gives the variant **hooligan** and says it was a rope-throw in which
the noose stood almost upright.

hooligan wagon
A wagon used on short drives to carry fuel and water when necessary.
(Ramon Adams 1944)

hoolihan
(1) The act of throwing a grown steer by hand, but without using the
twisting movement of *bulldogging.* Usually a rider would jump from the
back of a running horse across the back of a running cow, landing behind
its horns in such a way as to knock it down without using the usual wrestling
hold—a practice not regarded favorably and disallowed in most rodeos.
This term was sometimes mistakenly corrupted to hooley-ann. (Allen 1933;
Weseen 1934; Berrey and van den Bark 1942; Ramon Adams 1944)
(2) To behave roughly, to celebrate wildly in town. (Ramon Adams 1944)
(3) When a horse, in fighting its rider, somersaults. (Berrey and van den
Bark 1942)

hooraw

(1) To deride.

▶ (2) To ride through a town and raise hell. Maybe a window or two was shot in, the town marshal driven into a hole and told to pull it in after him, horses ridden on the sidewalk and even into the saloon, the town (probably in Kansas) generally terrified by the wild and woolly men from Texas. Very satisfying to the Texans after being defeated in the Civil War, but it happened more in fiction than in history.

hoosegow

(Sp *juzgado*; SW). Also **hoosgow**. Used in the West to mean jail, though the original Spanish meant "courthouse."

hooter

An owl. (Berrey and van den Bark 1942; Ramon Adams 1944)

hopper

A grasshopper. (Weseen 1934). Wentworth 1944 records **hoppergrass** as the term used in Texas.

hopperscare

Threat of a grasshopper plague. (Berrey and van den Bark 1942)

hopple

See *hobble*.

horn

The protuberance of the Western saddle, above the fork, on which a rope could be dallied (see *dally*) or tied. A development by the Mexicans and Californios which the Texans adopted and refashioned to their own taste. The horn used by the Anglos was smallish when compared with the broad horn of Chihuahua, which was common in east Mexico; but not all Mexican horns were broad, for in northwest Mexico the slim, very high horn is used to this day. See also *apple-horn*.

horn in

To push in, especially where you were not wanted. (Dobie 1930; Webb 1931; Ramon Adams 1944)

horning

(1) A gold-prospecting term meaning to assay pay dirt with a spoon. The term originated from the fact that the early spoons were made of horn; and

when metal spoons came into frontier use, the old term stuck. The phrase used was to **horn a prospect.**

(2) According to Weseen 1934, from to **horn a prospect** developed the meaning "to sell mine sites or stocks of questionable value."

horn-string

The thong at the side of the saddlehorn for securing a lariat. (Ramon Adams 1944)

hornswoggling

A classic Westernism: the movements of a cow by which it threw off or evaded a *catch rope;* the rope was said to be **hornswoggled.** (Weseen 1934; Ramon Adams 1944). It also meant hoaxing or swindling in general American usage.

horse pestler

See *wrangler.*

horse rustler

(1) In Texas, the horse-wrangler, the *remudero:* the man appointed to guard and control the horse-herd, or *remuda.* (Berrey and van den Bark 1942; Ramon Adams 1944; Dobie 1952)

(2) A horse-thief. This word *rustler,* both in fiction and factual writing, is sometimes seen as *russler.*

horse-thieves

Also **horse rustlers.** In the Old West the stealing of a horse was the most abominated of crimes, and a man caught at it or even suspected of it expected to be hanged. Called **horse-lifting** when referring to the Indian horse-raids, such stealing was a profitable if dangerous business. So great a public nuisance did white thieves become that in some areas vigilantes were formed to control them. To the cowman, or any other man who lived by his horse, to be deprived of it could mean in certain circumstances ruination or death. Even borrowing a horse from the string of another man in the same outfit was a breach of etiquette that could lead to fatal violence. A man might be tolerant of a little cattle-stealing, but horse-stealing— never. Even the Indians, some of whom prided themselves on their ability to lift the horses of other tribes, abhorred the man who would steal one from his fellow-tribesman: the very least the culprit could expect was banishment.

Dobie 1952 interestingly details the various techniques employed by Indians to steal animals belonging to other tribes and to the whites. One was to tie a dried cowhide full of stones to a horse's tail and run it into a herd, which then spooked and stampeded. John Woodhouse Audubon, son of the great ornithologist, gives an even more colorful account: "The scoundrels take a strong horse, cover him with the skin of an ox that has been newly killed, putting fleshside out, tie all the bells they have on the horse, fastening an enormous bunch of dry brush to his tail, set fire to it and start him off with yells and shouts through the camp to be stampeded. Horses and mules, keen of scent and hearing, receive warning through both faculties and are so frightened that they will break any ordinary fastening." (Audubon 1906)

horse-wrangler
See *wrangler.*

horsing
Also **horsin'**. Describes a mare when in breeding period. (Berrey and van den Bark 1942)

hostile
An Indian who did not agree to retire to a reservation at the invitation of the government and who fought if forced to do so. (Custer 1874)

hot-blood
A horse (and sometimes a cow) that had breeding, as opposed to a cold-blood, which would be hardy native stock, such as a mustang (or Long-horn). (Weseen 1934; Ramon Adams 1944). See also *cold-blooded stock.*

hot foot
(1) A particularly vicious trick practiced by some cow-thieves, in which a calf was burned between the toes so that it could not follow its mother. A similar ploy was to pare down a horse's hoofs so that it could not wander, a method depicted with vivid ghastliness in that fine Western movie *Tribute to a Bad Man* (1956), featuring James Cagney—one of the few movies to be adult about rustlers and to have the tang of the Old West. (Ramon Adams 1944)
(2) To depart in haste. (Weseen 1934)

hot iron
A branding iron heated in the fire at branding time. If the brander had an assistant and the iron became cold, his constant cry was "Hot iron." (Ramon Adams 1944)

hot rock
Biscuit. (Ramon Adams 1944)

hot roll
The bed-roll of a cowboy. A term found generally in the Southwest. (We-

seen 1934; Berrey and van den Bark 1942; Ramon Adams 1944; Rossi 1975)

howdy
A variant of **How do you do?** or **How d'ye do?** Also seen as **How d'e do?** Accepted by some now as a Westernism, but in fact a long-established rural Easternism. (Wentworth 1944)

huajilla
See *guajilla.*

huisache
(Mex-Sp; SW). *Acacia farnesiana.* Although now a Mexican word, it came originally from the old Nahuatl and has a number of variants. Dobie 1941 describes it with beauty: "In many places the huisache, golden and aromic-flowered in spring, its spined branches sweeping almost to the ground, has run out the mesquite. No vaunted 'dogwood trail,' however beautiful its turnings, ever led to a more gorgeous sight than huisaches in full bloom. If massed and arranged properly, a great highway-lining of them would at blooming time vie with the cherry-blossom drive of Washington."

hull
(1) Husk. Still to be found in East Anglia and North Essex, England.
(2) A saddle. (Berrey and van den Bark 1942; Ramon Adams 1944; Wentworth 1944)
(3) A cartridge case.

hump yourself
Also **hump your tail.** Hurry, get a move on, rustle. (Weseen 1934; Berrey and van den Bark 1942)

hundred and elevens
Spur marks on a horse's side. The cuts made by the rowels are, roughly: ||. (Berrey and van den Bark 1942; Ramon Adams 1944)

hundred and sixty
Also **quarter section.** A granger's legally registered land, so called because he was allowed 160 acres under the homesteading laws. (Ramon Adams 1944)

hung up
Describes a rider fallen from his saddle, with one foot caught in a stirrup-iron and in danger of being dragged.

hunker
To squat on one's heels or hams. **Hunkers:** the hams of the legs. Not a true Westernism.

hunt leather
To grab the saddle when in trouble on a horse. An act that did not exactly enhance your reputation as a rider. (Berrey and van den Bark 1942; Ramon Adams 1944)

hurricane deck
The back of a pitching horse. (Mora 1950)

Idaho brain storm
A dust twister, a **dancing devil**. (Weseen 1934; Berrey and van den Bark 1942; Ramon Adams 1944)

iguana
From this term for a type of lizard comes the mining term for an ore formation, the common factor being that they are both found in rocks.

Indian bread
(1) The term used by a number of writers to refer to certain fatty parts of the buffalo particularly favored by Indians and addicts of buffalo meat. Ramon Adams 1944 says: "This was the tasty strip of fatty matter starting from the shoulder blade and extending along the backbone of the buffalo. When scalded in hot grease to seal it, then smoked, it became a tit-bit the buffalo hunter used as bread. When eaten with lean or dried meat it made an excellent sandwich."
(2) Hodge 1907–10 says that the name also referred to the tuckahoe (*Scelerotium gigantum*), an edible root; but this was not a Westernism.

Indian broke
Said of a horse to be mounted from the right side, which was customarily used by Indians. Whites mounted from the left. (Ramon Adams 1944)

Indian lettuce
See *squaw cabbage.*

Indian liquor
See *Indian whiskey.*

Indian lover
A derogatory term applied to anybody who argued in favor of, supported, helped, or sympathized in any way with Indians.

Indian melon
The name given in Colorado to a species of *Echinocactus.* Only Hodge 1907–10 seems to mention this.

Indian pine
See *loblolly (2).*

Indian Police
Indians authorized by an Act of Congress on May 27, 1878, to preserve order on reservations, prevent traffic in liquor, and control distribution of rations. The pay was 10 to 15 dollars per month, and their loyalty, says Hodge 1907–10, was "well attested." They largely served among their own tribesfolk.

Indian pony
A small, hardy animal bred or caught in the feral state by Indians, of mustang stock and grass fed; particularly a paint-pony or pinto, which were favorites with the Indians.

Indian post office
One can do no better than quote Dobie 1956: "On a high point Gotch Ear stopped and pointed to what frontiersmen called an 'Indian post office' —a mound of rocks.

" 'These sticks and stones,' he said, 'meant three Apaches went by here two days back. They will return.' "

Indian potato
Bikukulla canadensis. Squirrel corn. As with **Indian melon,** only Hodge 1907–10 seems to note this. He also quotes Bergen as saying that it was a California name for *Brodiaea capitata* and reports that Barrett claimed the term was used indiscriminately for many species of bulbs and corns eaten by the Californian Indians. This last account sounds the most likely. (Mathews 1951)

Indian saddle
A form of saddle used by the Plains Indians which was a crude copy of the old Spanish saddle, often galling to a horse's back, as eye-witnesses have recorded. (Mathews 1951). Many early ones were merely pads filled with buffalo hair or grass, with a surcingle as a cinch. (Rossi 1975)

Indian scout
See *scout.*

Indian shod
A method of horse-shoeing employed at times by most Indian peoples. The usual procedure was to cover the whole foot with damp rawhide, which, when dried, fitted the foot snugly and became very hard. Most of the mustang stock of the Indians was hard-footed, but the best horse with unshod hoofs would suffer after working too long in rocky country. (Dobie 1952)

Indian side, Injun side
See *off-side.*

Indian sign
Tracks or traces of passage intentionally or unintentionally left by Indians. (Ramon Adams 1944; Mathews 1951)

Indian signboard
The shoulder-blade of a buffalo, on which Indians would leave *sign* messages. Mostly used on the Great Plains. (Ramon Adams 1944)

Indian trader
A whiteman who traded with Indians. (Mathews 1951)

Indian-up
To come close to someone without them being aware; to creep like an Indian. (Wentworth 1944 records its use in New Mexico, 1897)

Indian whiskey
Also **Indian liquor** (Hodge 1907–10). A cheap or adulterated whiskey

used by traders for sale to Indians. Teddy Blue, who claims it was invented by Missouri River traders in the early days, gives the following recipe for making it (quoted in Abbott and Smith 1939): "Take one barrel of Missouri River water and 2 galls. of alcohol. Then you add 2 ozs. of strychnine to make them crazy—because strychnine is the greatest stimulant in the world—and 2 plugs of tobacco to make them sick—because an Indian wouldn't figure it was whiskey unless it made him sick—5 bars of soap to give it a head, and ½ lb. of red pepper and then you put in some sagebrush and boil until brown. Strain this into a barrel and you've got your Indian whiskey."

iron
(1) A branding iron. (Weseen 1934)
(2) A gun, especially a revolver. (Ramon Adams 1944)
(3) A cowboy's knife, fork, and spoon; see **wreck tub.**

iron man
The man who heated the branding irons in the fire and produced one pronto at the cry of "Hot iron." (Weseen 1934; Ramon Adams 1944)

iron out
To ride the kinks out of a troublesome horse. (Berrey and van den Bark 1942; Ramon Adams 1944)

islands
See *motte.*

jacal
A primitive hut or shelter, particularly applied to those of the poor Mexicans or Apaches. Harby 1890 states how clean the Mexican women kept them in Texas: "indeed their cleanliness seems to show itself in this particular manner, for a broom is constantly in the hands of every Mexican woman." (Ramon Adams 1944). Dobie 1930 simply calls it a hut or cabin. See also *shack (3)*.

jackass mail
Also **jackass express**. A stagecoach pulled by mules; used, for example, on the El Paso–Yuma run established in the late 1850s because mules were more suited than horses to the hard desert trails. (Rossi and Hunt 1971)

jackeroo
See *buckaroo.*

jack-knife
The action of a wildly pitching horse in the middle of a jump, in which its back was bent while in the air and its forefeet put to its hindfeet. Also, of course, in general English, a knife with a blade that folds into the handle, from which action this term comes. (Berrey and van den Bark 1942; Ramon Adams 1944)

jack rabbit
Not a rabbit at all, of course, but a ubiquitous ◄ hare that came between many a traveler and hunger. This title could include the black-

tailed jack rabbit (*Lepus californicus*); the white-tailed jack rabbit (*Lepus townsendii*), which in the northern part of its territory assumed a white winter coat; and the rarer white-sided jack rabbit (*Lepus mexicanus*), which lived on the border and down into Mexican high country. The jack was a great survivor and developed a technique of opening up various kinds of cacti for water and nourishment during hard times in the desert. There was also an antelope jack rabbit (*Lepus alleni*), so called for its long legs and ability to execute very long jumps; its ears, a part of the animal's body-cooling system in hot weather, were extremely long, even for a hare. With his usual nonchalance over animal names, the Westerner also called the sage hare (*Lepus artemisia*) a jack rabbit. (Grzimek 1974)

jamboree
(origin unknown; the Shorter Oxford English Dictionary 1973 dates it in the United States at 1872). A wild celebration which certainly consisted of dancing and drinking—the fisticuffs and gunplay were optional. Not a Westernism. (Weseen 1934; Rollins 1922; Ramon Adams 1944)

jaquima
Also **jakoma** (Berrey and van den Bark 1942). (Mex-Sp *jáquima*). A headstall, a halter. Corrupted to **hackamore**. See also *bridles (3)*.

jarro
(Mex-Sp; SW). An earthen pot. (Dobie 1930)

java
Coffee. (Rossi 1975)

javalina
(Sp *jabalina*; Texas and SW). Also **javalino**. A musk hog, a peccary, native to the brush-country. Dobie 1950 writes: "Javalinas are easily domesticated but generally show emphatic hostility to any stranger."

jaw brand
A small brand on the jaw of an animal, usually a horse.

jayhawker
(1) As **Jawhawker**, a Kansas guerrilla fighter during the War Between the States.
(2) By extension, the lawless men who preyed on Texas cattlemen bringing the Longhorns north after the war.
(3) A tarantula. (Berrey and van den Bark 1942)
No doubt the reader will be aware that the term has other meanings, but

the three I have noted here are those employed in literature of the Old West.

jean
Twilled undressed cotton cloth. Hence **jeans,** garments made from that cloth. Not a Westernism.

jerked down
Said of a horse pulled down as its rider roped a steer. (Ramon Adams 1944)

jerk-line
A single line used to control a team of wagon horses or mules. The line went directly from the driver to the lead animal and was attached to the left side of its bit: one jerk turned it to the left, two to the right. A team of horses or mules so controlled was called a **jerk-line string** and could be hitched in spans or singly. The jerk-line driver (or **skinner**—Berrey and van den Bark 1942) might be mounted on a *wheeler* or on the wagon; in the latter case, he would hitch the line around the brake handle. The expression **to have a hold on the jerk-line** meant to be in command of a situation. (Weseen 1934; Berrey and van den Bark 1942; Ramon Adams 1944)

jerky
(Mex-Sp *charquí*). Jerked beef. Strips of beef, deer, or buffalo meat that were dried either in the sun or in the smoke of a fire. A staple article of diet among the Mexicans, the Comanches, and the Texan settlers. Among Mexicans of the Southwest it was known as **tasajo** or **tassajo** (Dobie 1952; Mathews 1951) and **carne asada.** (The Texans also salted or pickled beef, which was sometimes called *mess beef.*) The strips could be ground to powder, soaked, and mixed with berries, as by the Indians in making *pemmican,* and would keep indefinitely. (Dobie 1929; Berrey and van den Bark 1942; Ramon Adams 1944)

Jerusalem undertaker
A comb. Derivation unknown.

jewelry
Firearms, particularly a belt-gun. (Mathews 1951 quotes Robert M. Wright 1877)

jewelry chest
A storage box on the front of a chuck wagon. (Ramon Adams 1944; Jennings 1971)

jicara

(Mex-Sp *jícara* from Nahuatl; SW). It could refer to a vase or bowl, but also to very closely woven containers used by the Apache.

jigger

To over-run or over-heat a horse; a horse treated thus was **jiggered** or **bushed.** (Berrey and van den Bark 1942; Ramon Adams 1944)

jiggle

The normal pace of the cowpony. I have seen the gait described as being the same as the *fox-trot.* To me it conveys an easy waggling trot. A great word, rich in description; generally, *jiggle* means to jerk to and fro lightly, which definition helps a little with the Western word. (Weseen 1934; Berrey and van den Bark 1942; Ramon Adams 1944; Mora 1950)

jimpsecute

Barrère and Leland 1897 say: "In the Texas vernacular, this is the equivalent used, when a young man goes to pay his devoirs to a fair one, to signify the object of his attentions. She on the other hand calls her lover a 'juicy-spicey.' " All heady stuff. The authors follow this with a delightful quotation from *Overland Monthly:* "I knew a young man in Texas once who had no more sense than to have a *jimpsecute,* and this was all her name: Dionysia Boadicea Jeffalina Jacobina Christiana Buckiana Susannah Emily Wyatt Wilkinson Moore Wynne." Mathews 1951 also mentions the term and quotes authoritatively.

jinete

(Sp: horseman). Weseen 1934 explains the term as a bronco buster. Ramon Adams 1944 agrees and adds: an "excellent horseman." (Berrey and van den Bark 1942)

jingle bob

(1) The cattle *ear-mark* of John Chisum of Billy the Kid fame. It was a complete slitting of the ear from the tip to the base, giving the animal a

somewhat grotesque appearance, as if it had two ears on either side of its head, one standing up and the other drooping. Chisum cattle were so famous for this ear-mark that they were known as **jingle bobs** and the crew were known as the **jingle bob outfit.** (Wentworth 1944; Ramon Adams 1944). Weseen 1934 adds that the jingle bob could also be formed by the cutting of the dewlap.

(2) The jingles on a cowboy's spurs. (Branch 1926)

job
Also **jobbing** and **joshing** (Jennings 1971). To josh, to joke. The original meaning of the term was "to jab" or "poke," which seems to connect it to the act of goading, of poking fun. This makes a connection with the following entry.

jobbing
Roberts 1924: "I found this bull-punching a very wearisome and dangerous business. It is too frequently the custom of cattlemen to crowd the poor beasts, and put perhaps twenty-two where there is only comfortable room for eighteen or twenty. When a steer lies down, he often gets rolled over, and is stretched out flat without power to move, as the others stand upon him. It is the duty of the 'bull-puncher' to see that this does not occur, or to make him get up. For this purpose, he carries a pole, ten or twelve feet long, usually of hickory, and in the end of this a nail is driven, the head of which is filed off in order to get a sharp-point of half or three-quarters of an inch long which is used for 'jobbing' the unfortunate creature to rouse him to exert himself."

John B.
Any cowman's hat. After John B. Stetson, a maker of such hats. (Berrey and van den Bark 1942; Ramon Adams 1944)

John B. Stetson
A Stetson hat. (Berrey and van den Bark 1942)

John Chinaman
(1) A Chinese. Also **John.**
(2) Rice. (Berrey and van den Bark 1942; Ramon Adams 1944)

John Henry
A signature. (Weseen 1942; Ramon Adams 1944)

John Law
A law officer. (Ramon Adams 1944)

johnnycake
A flat corn cake baked either on a griddle or in any other way by the heat of a fire: for example, on a board before the fire or on hot stones. Corn bread. In use since the late eighteenth century. Of New England origin, it is not a Westernism, but is found often in Western literature. (Wentworth 1944)

johnny-come-lately
A newcomer to the country, a greenhorn, a pilgrim. (Berrey and van den Bark 1942; Ramon Adams 1944)

jonco
Also **junco thorn, junco.** *Koeberlinia spinosa.* The all-thorn. Dobie 1941: "Here and there like a pariah stands the 'accursed jonco', the leafless all-thorn, which the Mexicans say furnished Christ's crown and on which, they claim, only the butcher-bird will to this day alight. However, I have seen mocking bird nests in jonco bushes."

jornada
(Sp). A long, waterless drive with cattle or wagons. (Stewart 1964)

Joshua tree
(SW). The yucca palm (*Yucca brevifolia*), growing in desert regions only. (Mathews 1951)

juajilla, juajillo
See *guajilla.*

Judas steer
A steer trained to lead others to the slaughter-house. (Weseen 1934; Dobie 1941; Ramon Adams 1944)

jug-handled dewlap
Also **jug-handle.** An identifying cut made in the loose flesh of a cow's throat (probably in place of an *ear-mark,* but not necessarily so). Often cut to hang like a pendulum, the dewlap could also be merely slashed to form a jug-handle; the brisket could be cut similarly. (Wellman 1939; Ramon Adams 1944)

jug-head
(1) A horse without horse-sense, one that did not understand what was wanted of it. The term could also be applied to a man. (Weseen 1934; Berrey and van den Bark 1942; Ramon Adams 1944)
(2) A mule. (Berrey and van den Bark 1942)

jump
To attack unawares; to take by force or by intimidation. The word gives a sense of suddenness or surprise: a man could jump another's mining claim or he could jump another man by getting the drop on him on the street; a wagon-train could be jumped by Indians—that is, attacked from ambush, or simply attacked. (Barrère and Leland 1897; Ramon Adams 1944)

jumping cholla
See *cholla.*

jump up a lot of dust
To raise the dust, to get going or depart in a hurry.

juniper
A pilgrim, a greenhorn. (Berrey and van den Bark 1942)

Justins
Also **Justin's.** Cow-country boots. Named for a superlative maker of boots, Joseph Justin, who began business in Old Spanish Fort, Texas, in 1879. The firm exists to this day in Fort Worth, Texas. (Ramon Adams 1944; Mencken 1948)

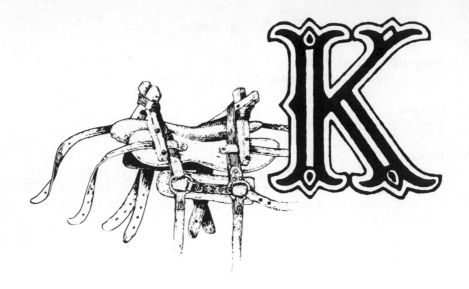

kak
Also **kack** (McCarthy 1936; Berrey and van den Bark 1942; Ramon Adams 1944; Mencken 1948). A saddle. Found in Western popular fiction. There are suggestions in some mentions that the term refers to a pack-saddle, possibly due to its similarity to *kyack.* (Allen 1933)

kamas root
Bartlett 1877: "(*Camassia esculenta*). Breadroot. The *Pommes des Prairies* or *Pomme Blanche* of the Canadians, and the Prairie Turnip of the hunters and trappers of the West. It is very extensively used by the Digger Indians." (Mathews 1951). See also *camas (1).*

kamus
See *camas (1); kamas root.*

Kansas brick
See *Nebraska brick.*

Kansas neck blister
A bowie knife. (Weseen 1934; Berrey and van den Bark 1942; Ramon Adams 1944). See also *Bowie knife.*

karimption
Also **rimption.** Bartlett 1877: "A squad. Western." A bunch, a small crowd. (Wentworth 1944; Mathews 1951)

kayack
See *kyack.*

keep that dry
Keep it secret. (Barrère and Leland 1897)

keep your eyes skinned
Be wary, keep a sharp lookout. A phrase that has now entered into the general language of English-speaking peoples. But, according to the dictionaries of the last century, it was Western slang.

Kellys
Bits and spurs hand-made by P. M. Kelly and Sons, El Paso, Texas. (Ramon Adams 1944)

keno ◄
(1) A gambling game similar to bingo and housey-housey. The cry of a winner was "Keno"; hence:
(2) All right, okay. (Ramon Adams 1944)

kershaw
Farmer 1889 gives: "a pumpkinlike fruit." Cashaw, which is the Algonkian name for pumpkin, was corrupted in the West to kershaw. Dobie 1941 writes: "To begin with, a man by the name of Kerr had a little ranch on Esperanza Creek in Frio Country, in the mesquite lands south of San Antonio. . . .Grew corn, water melons and 'kershaws'—except when the season was droughty."

ketch dogs
See *dogs*.

ketch hand
Catch hand. A man who had the duty of roping calves for the brander.

ketch rope
See *catch rope*.

kettle
To pitch, to buck. (Weseen 1934; Berrey and van den Bark 1942; Ramon Adams 1944)

kettle-bellied
Pot-bellied, having a distended belly. (Ramon Adams 1944)

kick like a bay steer
The Texas version of "to kick like a mule." (Weseen 1934; Berrey and van den Bark 1942; Ramon Adams 1944)

kick the frost out
To get the kinks out; to unlimber a horse. (Berrey and van den Bark 1942; Ramon Adams 1944)

kick the lid off
To break into violent action. Said of a horse that started pitching or bucking. (Ramon Adams 1944)

kid
This implies a boy or a young man and was a fairly common nickname in the Old West: the Oklahoma Kid, the Apache Kid, Billy the Kid. The name might be stuck on a boy and stay with him into manhood. But I am not satisfied that it originated solely from the meaning of youth: there might also be a suggestion of the bearer being a dude, a sharp dresser. (Barrère and Leland 1897). Londoners used the word in the American sense at the same period and possibly even earlier, both with reference to childhood and with the meaning of deceiving or joshing.

killpecker guard
The guard on a cow-herd from sundown to 8:00 a.m. (Berrey and van den Bark 1942; Ramon Adams 1944)

kinks
That which was found in the backbone of a cowpony when first saddled and mounted. The animal was said to pitch and generally act up to get these out of his back. Found frequently in Western fiction.

kinnik-kinnik
A substance added by Mountain Men to tobacco for pipe-smoking. Probably a habit learned from the Indians. (Ruxton 1849). According to Hodge 1907–10, the Indians used a smoking mixture by this name that was made up of tobacco, dried sumac leaves, and the inner bark of a species of dogwood. The original Chippewa word indicates a mixture, and there were a great many varieties of such. One involved the use of red osier and bearberry.

kip pile
Buffalo hides—one of the three assortments of buffalo hides made by the hunters, the other two being those derived from bulls and calves. (Ramon Adams 1944)

kite
To depart hurriedly; literally, to fly. (Hoig 1960)

kiuse
A variant of *cayuse.* Bartlett 1877:

In the States of the Far West and on the plains, a native pony.
"As if some devilish infection invaded the atmosphere, one of our horses, a kiuse, took a fit of 'bucking' soon after we left, and was particular to select the most dangerous portion of the road for the display of his skill in that line." McClure, *Rocky Mountains.*

kiva
Pueblo Indians' ceremonial chamber. (Simmons 1942; Waters 1950)

klooch
Also **klootch.** (Chinook; NW). An Indian woman. Hence, **kloochman,** a *squaw man.* (Wentworth 1944; Mathews 1951, who dates it back to at least 1860)

kneeing
An operation in which a tendon was cut between the ankle and the knee of a cow's foreleg to prevent it from running. This unpleasant operation was also carried out by mustangers on mares, so that the mares, though they could no longer run, could be driven slowly and bear foals. (Berrey and van den Bark 1942; Ramon Adams 1944; Dobie 1952)

knob
The chap guard on the shank of a spur. (Mora 1950)

knobhead
A mule. (Weseen 1934; Berrey and van den Bark 1942; Ramon Adams 1944)

knothead
A brainless creature; an unskilled cowboy; an untaught or unteachable horse. (Weseen 1934; Berrey and van den Bark 1942; Ramon Adams 1944)

kyack
Also **kayack.** A pack-saddle. Often the panniers on either side of the pack-saddle were so called. (Berrey and van den Bark 1942; Ramon Adams 1944; Wentworth 1944; Mathews 1951)

ladino
(Mex-Sp: learned—knowing Latin, cunning). Originally, a wild Longhorn, usually one in the *brasada.* The word came to mean a cow-critter of dangerous nature and was sometimes used in reference to animals other than cattle. (Berrey and van den Bark 1942; Ramon Adams 1944; Dobie 1941)

ladron
(Sp *ladrón;* SW). A thief, a robber. (Dobie 1930)

ladies of the line
See *girls of the line.*

lamp
To **blow out a man's lamp** was to kill him. (Ramon Adams 1944)

land shark
A land speculator, one who seized public land for commercial purposes. Not a true Westernism. (Mathews 1951)

laneing
Also **laning.** This took place when one rider, coming to help another who was trying to turn a cow, approached the animal not on the same side but on the opposite side, forming a lane down which the animal could escape and thus preventing it from being turned. (Ramon Adams 1944; Mora 1950)

lariat
A throwing rope with a running noose used for catching or throwing animals. Anglo variant of the Mexican-Spanish *la reata;* there were many

other variants and forms. (Weseen 1934; Berrey and van den Bark 1942; Ramon Adams 1944). See also *lasso; reata.*

lariat pin
See *picket pin.*

larigo
See *latigo.*

larrup
(1) To flog or beat.
(2) Molasses. (Ramon Adams 1944; Mathews 1951)

larruping
Great, wonderful. (Rossi 1975)

lasher
An assistant to the driver of a *jerk-line* team. He applied the whip and operated the brake. (Berrey and van den Bark 1942; Ramon Adams 1944)

lash rope
Rope used to tie packs on animals. (Ramon Adams 1944; Mathews 1951, who quotes it from the early nineteenth century)

lasso
Also **lassoo, lazo.** (Sp *lazo*). A rope (Weseen 1934; Berrey and van den Bark 1942; Ramon Adams 1944). In the early days, usually of rawhide made from the skin of a buffalo or cow. It had a running noose and was used for a multitude of purposes, usually to catch and bring down cattle or simply to catch horses. Normally 40 to 50 feet in length, it was sometimes as much as 70 feet, depending on the country: in the deep *brasada* it would be much shorter than one used on the open plains. It is not known how or when various Indian-peoples came to use rope for catching

horses, but Lewis and Clark found the Shoshone expert at it, and certainly the Nez Percé were using a noose before then. Dobie 1952 says that in their art the Sioux, after 1812, show the lasso as a symbol for wild horses. In the very early period it is known that the Indians sometimes used a noose at the end of a long stick. (Mora 1950; Bartlett 1877). See also *reata; rope.*

lass rope
A rope, a lariat. (Ramon Adams 1944)

last round-up
Death. (Berrey and van den Bark 1942; Ramon Adams 1944)

latigo
(Sp *látigo*). Also **larigo, latigo strap.** A strap that attaches the rigging of the saddle to the cinch. (Ramon Adams 1944; Mora 1950)

lay
(1) A ranch, a spread.
(2) A cowhand's bed.
(3) An opportunity to make a throw with a rope. (Ramon Adams 1944)

lays 'em down
Dies. (Allen 1933)

lead ox
A good lead ox might be used for two purposes, particularly in the brush-country of southwest Texas. First, he might be used again and again to lead trail-herds north to Kansas. Second, he might be used for *necking,* which meant that an intractable Longhorn from the thickets, refusing to be driven to the main gather, could be tied neck-to-neck to a powerful trained ox which would bring him home or die in the attempt. J. Frank Dobie, in *The Longhorns* (1941), that classic of the brush-country, tells some delightful stories of lead oxen and necking.

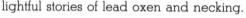

leather
(1) A saddle. (Berrey and van den Bark 1942)
▸ (2) A revolver holster in the expression **to slap leather;** that is, to draw the gun from the holster.

leaving Cheyenne
Going away. From the cowboy's song "Goodbye, Old Paint, I'm leavin' Cheyenne." (Ramon Adams 1944)

legaderos
Farmer 1889: "A Spanish term for stirrup-straps." One cannot help suspecting that this term is based on the Anglo *leg,* with *rosaderos* in mind. I suspect, too, that the word was used also for a leg guard.

leggin
To **give a leggin** was to take a cowboy who merited punishment, bend him over a wagon-tongue, and beat him with a pair of leggins or chaps. His was a **leggins case.** (Allen 1933; Berrey and van den Bark 1942; Weseen 1934; Ramon Adams 1944)

legging
Separating sheep of different brands. (Berrey and van den Bark 1942)

leggins
What the remainder of the West referred to as *chaps* were also called leggins by south Texans. The word was used more rarely in southwest Texas. Fiction writers, and they may well be right, use the term to cover *shotgun chaps* rather than *bat wing chaps.* They were fairly tight-fitting over-trousers used particularly in brush-country when working cattle in the chaparral and mesquite. They came in several styles and went through evolutionary changes. (Dobie 1929)

Le Mat
A strange and formidable belt-gun that found its way into the Old West after its popularity during the Civil War. It could be said that, if you bought a Le Mat, you had two guns for the price of one, for this nine-chamber, single-action, cap-and-ball revolver (see *cap-and-ball gun*) delivered its conventional shots through the rifled .40-caliber upper barrel and a load of buckshot through its smoothbore .66-caliber lower barrel. I have heard it said that all a lawman with mob trouble had to do was to share the buckshot out among them with the lower barrel and pick off the survivors with the upper. Originally manufactured in France, this weapon was copied by a number of makers in the Confederacy. (Bowman 1953)

lent
An inexperienced cowhand. (Weseen 1934; Berrey and van den Bark 1942; Ramon Adams 1944)

lenty
Green. Applied to an inexperienced man. (Weseen 1934; Allen 1933; Berrey and van den Bark 1942)

lepero
(Sp *lépero;* SW). A low and dishonest type of Mexican. (Ruxton 1847)

leppy
A motherless calf. (Berrey and van den Bark 1942; Ramon Adams 1944)

let out
When a horse lets out, he kicks. (Weseen 1934; Ramon Adams 1944)

Levi's
Also **Levi Strausses, Strausses.** The term usually referred to pants or trousers—a bibless overall, in fact—but originally it described the jacket also. Named for Levi Strauss, a tailor who made pants and coats strong enough to withstand the hard wear they were subjected to by a cowhand. The

pockets and joints were riveted with metal. Strauss sailed from the East around the Horn to California in 1849 with supplies of cloth. He sold his stock on arrival in California, except for some bales of canvas which he had intended to sell to miners for tenting. Apparently clothes were needed more than tents. However, there is another story which says that Strauss took on a bet that he could make clothes strong enough to stand up to a cowboy's wear and thus produced Levi's. (Ramon Adams 1944; Mora 1950; Mathews 1951)

Lewis grass
See *mesquite grass.*

lick
(1) Used by a cowboy when he could get it as a substitute for butter on flapjacks and biscuits—in short, molasses. (Weseen 1934; Ramon Adams 1944; Wentworth 1944; Emrich 1951)
(2) A salt lick, a place where cattle went to lick salt. Many would walk incredibly long distances to find the salt they lacked in their diet. (Dobie 1941)

life preserver
(1) A revolver. (Hoig 1960)
(2) A small club, a *billy.*

light out
To leave, often in a hurry: "There were men in town looking for him, so he saddled up and lit out." Connected with the expression to **light a shuck:** to depart. Not to be confused with **'light,** which was the imperative of *alight:* **'light and set,** meaning "dismount and sit." (Ramon Adams 1944)

Lincoln shingles
The army word for hard-bread. "Thereupon the Indians were all taken to the cookhouse, where everything had been kept in readiness, and they were given all they could eat, which was an enormous amount. The boiled beef and coffee and *hard-bread* (which the boys called 'Lincoln shingles') were spread out with panfuls of molasses, and things went along all right." (Captain Eugene F. Ware, *The Indian War of 1874,* quoted in Rifkin 1967). Rossi 1975 writes that they were also called **Lincoln pies, McClellan pies, teeth-dullers,** and **sheet-iron crackers.** Erudition indeed! He adds they were roughly 3⅛″ × 2⅞″ × ½″ in size. Common ration for frontier troops during the period of the Indian wars.

line
(1) The boundary, fenced or not, of a range or ranch.
(2) Prostitutes' line of cabins or tents in a town. (Emrich 1951). See also *girls of the line.*

(3) A horse's rein. (Ramon Adams 1944)

line-back
A horse with a dorsal stripe, such as found on dun horses. (Dobie 1952). The term was also applied to cattle. (Dobie 1941)

line boss
A man in charge of a detachment of cowboys. (Weseen 1934; Berrey and van den Bark 1942)

line camp
A boundary camp of a ranch. In the early days, line camps housed riders who turned away neighbors' cattle and contained those of their own outfit and who tended and doctored herds remote from headquarters. Later, the camps became quarters for the men who not only tended herd but tended fences—which sometimes needed as much watching as the cattle. Such camps, of course, were necessary only on large ranges, on which boundaries were a long ride from the main house. See also *line riders; line shack.* (Weseen 1934; North 1942; Rossi 1975)

line house
The cabin of a *line camp.* (Mathews 1951)

line riders
First called **outriders,** these were cowboys who rode the boundaries of a ranch to make certain that cattle of their own brand did not stray and that cattle from other ranges did not wander to eat the grass of the riders' range. They roped cattle from bogs, watched out for cow-thieves and sickness among stock, and warded off wolves. They lived in a *line camp.* Later, after fences were introduced, they were also called **fence riders** and would inspect and make repairs on damaged fences. If cattle had drifted through a break they would gather them, if possible, and drive them back

to their home range. (Allen 1933; Berrey and van den Bark 1942; Ramon Adams 1944; Mathews 1951; Rossi 1975)

line shack
A building constituting a *line camp;* a *line house.*

line-up
The time of the round-up on a range. (North 1942)

lining his flue
Feeding—refers to a man eating. (Berrey and van den Bark 1942; Ramon Adams 1944)

linsey woolsey
A cloth made from a combination of linen and wool. (Mora 1950; Mathews 1951)

lizard
A sled used for short hauls in place of a wheeled vehicle. (Dobie 1941)

lizard bird
See *road runner.*

llano
(Sp; SW). A plain; sometimes a prairie. (Dobie 1930)

loading corrals
Pens in which cattle were held prior to being loaded into railroad cars.

loafer wolf
Timber or gray wolf; lobo wolf. (Rossi 1975)

loblolly
(1) A muddy puddle. Andy Adams 1909: "The preceding outfit, so he reported, had dug a shallow well in the bed of the creek, from which he had filled his kegs, but the stock water was mere loblolly." Not a true Westernism.
(2) The name of a variety of pine tree, *Pinus taeda.* Also **Indian pine.**

lobo
(Sp; SW). A wolf. Sometimes **lobo wolf,** to indicate a gray or timber wolf. (Dobie 1930)

lobo stripe
(Texas). The dark stripe down the spine of some Texas and Mexican Longhorns. (Dobie 1941)

locate
To settle cattle on a new range. (Weseen 1934; Ramon Adams 1944)

locked spurs
Spurs, the rowels of which were tied so that they could not move. A cowboy might lock these into a cinch on a bronc so that it was difficult for him to be thrown. (Rossi 1975)

loco weed
Astragalus. A plant with purple or white flowers, poisonous to cattle and said to drive them crazy. (North 1942)

lodge
An Indian habitation. A word used loosely by writers, but usually meaning the buffalo-skin tent of the Indians. In reality, the term was often applied to the stoutly built houses of the Indians of the near West, such as the Osage and Kansas, who resorted to the buffalo-skin teepee only when on the hunt. Many other tribes, before they were reduced by the whites, built substantial houses: for example, the Mandans, the Sacs and Fox, the early Sioux, etc.

logging
(1) The tethering of a horse to a log light enough to be moved (so that the animal could graze) but heavy enough to stop it from going too far. Used in lieu of a hobble. (Ramon Adams 1944)
(2) The cutting of timber, the felling of trees, the making of logs. Not a Westernism.

loggy
Also **logy** (Andy Adams 1909). Said of an animal that had become heavy through drinking too much water. Horses do not have the same sense as mules, who seldom if ever drink themselves into this condition. (Dobie 1952)

loma
(Sp; SW). A small hill or rise in the land. (Dobie 1930)

lonesome
A drink on one's own. (Berrey and van den Bark 1942)

long
A long-aged *yearling,* as opposed to a short-aged yearling. (Berrey and van den Bark 1942)

long-ear
(1) A method of amplifying sound employed by plainsmen. Instead of

placing an ear to the ground to hear the distant sound of hoofs, they would first put a silk handkerchief against the ground and listen through it. I like the idea of a plainsman carrying a silk handkerchief. (Ramon Adams 1944) (2) A cow-crittur lacking an *ear-mark* or brand. (Dobie 1941; Berrey and van den Bark 1942). Wentworth 1944 applies the term to unbranded cattle. See also *orejanos.*

Longhorn

▶ (1) The Longhorn cattle—which originated in Texas so far as the Western trail-herds were concerned, though their origin was Spanish through Mexico. A book could be written about them and indeed has been—J. Frank Dobie's *The Longhorns* (1941), which I can do no better than recommend. It should be remembered, however, that all long-horned cattle in the United States (including Texas) are not solely descended from this old Spanish breed, for long-horned cattle were brought in from England and elsewhere by settlers on the Eastern Seaboard; there is no question that some of their blood ran in the veins of the famous Texas Longhorns. When the southern cattle met the cattle of the immigrants in such territories as Montana and crossed, it was often the crossing of two long-horned types. Also **Texas Longhorn.**
(2) An old-timer. (Berrey and van den Bark 1942; Wentworth 1944)
(3) A Texan. This term was applied on the northern ranges to the Texans who came up the trail. (Weseen 1934; Ramon Adams 1944)

long-horned
Experienced. The opposite of a greener. Applied to an old cowhand, in fact. (Berrey and van den Bark 1942)

long horse
A horse possessing endurance, one that could run a long distance. (Berrey and van den Bark 1942; Ramon Adams 1944)

long-line skinner
The driver of a long *jerk-line* team or more than one team—as when teams are doubled on a hard haul. (Berrey and van den Bark 1942)

longrider
An outlaw. (Ramon Adams 1944)

long tom
(1) A long-barreled, large-caliber rifle sometimes used in buffalo hunting. (Mathews 1951)
(2) A long, inclining trough down which water would run to wash gold from dirt or gravel. (Weseen 1934)

loose herd
To loose herd was to allow a herd of animals to spread out but not to scatter at will, usually so that the animals might graze. Hence, one could have a loose herd. (Dobie 1930; Weseen 1934; Berrey and van den Bark 1942; Ramon Adams 1944)

love apples
Canned tomatoes. (Rossi 1975)

lucifer
A strike-on-anything match introduced in the first half of the nineteenth century. (Foster-Harris 1955)

lump oil
Coal oil, kerosene. (Berrey and van den Bark 1942; Ramon Adams 1944)

lye
A soap substitute. Sometimes called **lye-soap**. Usually alkaline salt and water mixed with wood ash. Not a Westernism.

lynching
Illegal hanging, usually by a mob, a vigilance committee, or by a rancher taking the law into his own hands. Sometimes preceded by the semblance of a trial. From Charles Lynch (1737–96), a Virginian farmer who summarily executed lawless people by hanging during the American War of Independence against Britain. Not a Westernism.

lynch law
Summary punishment of lawless or suspected men by hanging, carried out by unauthorized persons. These might be vigilantes dissatisfied with a corrupt lawman, a mob finding a scapegoat, or ranchers cleaning out cow-thieves.

macheer
See *mochila*.

machero
(Sp *mechero;* SW). A fire-making implement carried on the person. Not used generally for lighting fires, but for cigars and cigarettes. The Spanish word was altered to sound like the Anglo *match*. (Mathews 1951)

machete
(Sp; SW). A heavy chopping knife, described by Dobie 1930 as a cutlass. Mention is made of this word from the 1830s onward. Not a Westernism.

machilla
See *mochila*.

macho
(Mex-Sp; SW). A mule. (Dobie 1930)

Mackinaw
(1) A flat-bottomed boat. Tilden 1964: "It was the first of the Missouri River boats that required sawn boards. . . . The mackinaw, with a flat bottom, a pointed bow and a rudder, was a one-way boat; it would carry cargoes only down stream, and indeed continued to do so even after the steamboats arrived. It could be built to any size desired, from a small boat to a craft fifty feet long, for four rowers and a rudderman, able to transport fifteen tons. These boats were cheaply made and broken up or sold, just as were the flatboats of the Kaintuck boatmen who went down the Ohio and the Mississippi to New Orleans." Lavender 1969 calls it a barge.
(2) A *Mackinaw blanket* or *Mackinaw coat.*

Mackinaw blanket
A term found throughout the early West, certainly from the 1830s onward. Farmer 1889: "A superior kind of blanket which derived its distinctive name from the island of Mackinaw, formerly one of the chief posts at which Indian tribes received their grants from the Government. A provision of one of the Indian treaties was that part of the payment made to the redskins should be in these superior blankets, and from that fact the name *Mackinaw Blankets* or *Mackinaws* simply was derived."

Mackinaw coat
A coat made from a Mackinaw blanket. Sometimes simply called a Mackinaw. It later came to mean any blanket-coat.

maguey
(1) The century plant, from which rope and ◀ liquor (see *mezcal*) were made. Farmer 1889: "(*Agave Americana*)—a species of aloe, and otherwise called Century Plant. These abound in the south-western states, and, according to species, furnish sisal, hemp, bagging, and in one or two cases an intoxicating drink called pulque. . . ."
(2) A cowboy's rope made from maguey fiber. (Weseen 1934; Ramon Adams 1944; Mora 1950)

mahala
Farmer 1889: "A term used in California for an Indian squaw, and thought to be a corruption of the Spanish muger (pronounced mu-her), a woman." Mathews 1951 points out that the origin was the Yakuts word *muk'ela* (a woman).

major domo
(1) A ranch foreman. (Weseen 1934). Also **mayor domo**.
(2) The Mexican butler or head-servant in a household.

make meat
Farmer 1889: "a term by which the frontiersman denotes the process of drying thin slices of animal flesh for future use." It sounds to me identical to *jerky.* Wentworth 1944 says: "To cure meat."

make sleepers
To steal calves by ear-marking them only (see *ear-mark*), then branding them falsely at a later date. There were other methods of **sleepering** (see *sleeper [1]*). (Weseen 1934)

make smoke
To shoot with a gun.

makings
Also **makins**. Material for cigarette-building. Not a Westernism. (Berrey and van den Bark 1942; Ramon Adams 1944)

maleta
(Sp; SW). A bag, often of rawhide and used on the saddle. In later years, the term was often applied to a satchel improvised from a sack. (Weseen 1934; Dobie 1930)

mal pais
(Sp *mal:* bad, *país:* country). Also **malpais**. Volcanic rock; bad country. (Ramon Adams 1944)

manada
(Sp). A band of mares as kept in the old Spanish-American style, in which a lead stallion and colts also ranged. Farmer 1889: "This term, which, in California is especially applied to breeding mares, is elsewhere more generally used of a herd of cattle or drove of horses. It comes from the Spanish." Dobie 1930 describes the term as a "bunch of mares with stallion."

mañana
(Sp; SW). Tomorrow; any time in the future. An indication of action being put off in what was considered by the Anglos to be a typically Mexican manner.

manga
(Sp; SW). A poncho, a cloak, a cloth covering the shoulders and upper part of the body as a protection against rain and cold. (Mathews 1951)

mangana
(Sp: lasso; SW). Forefooting: the roping of a horse by the front feet or legs. (Weseen 1934; Ramon Adams 1944). Mora 1950 states: "An overhand flip, the loop opening in front for the forefeet to step into."

manila
See *grass rope.*

mankiller
A horse with lethal tendencies. (Weseen 1934; Ramon Adams 1944)

mano
(Sp: SW).
(1) Hand. Hence:
(2) A stone held in the hand to grind corn on a *metate.* (Dobie 1930)

mantilla
(Sp; SW). A head-shawl worn by women. (Dobie 1930)

manzana
(Sp: apple; SW). The horn of a saddle. (Mora 1950)

marker
(1) A branded cow. (Weseen 1934)
(2) A cow with easily distinguishable natural markings. (Ramon Adams 1944)
(3) See *butcher.*

marrons
Also **maroons**. Dobie 1952: "About 1840, a traveler in the Osage country found frontiersmen calling the wild horses **marrons** or **maroons** manifestly from *cimarrones,* but this Americanism made no headway against the mustangs."

martingale
From British-English, a breast-collar or strap used with a saddle, with attachments running to the cinch between the horse's forelegs and one running to the noseband on the bridle. It checks a horse from throwing its head up and rearing. Not a Westernism. (Ramon Adams 1944; Rossi 1975)

marvick
Weseen 1934 gives this as the most frequently used version of *maverick* heard on the range.

mas alla
(Sp *más allá;* SW). Further on. (Dobie 1930)

mascal
See *mescal.*

mash
(Texas). To press down on something; hence, to press with a smoothing iron, to iron clothes. (Wentworth 1944, who records the word from the end of the nineteenth century)

massena partridge
A name covering several varieties of quail in the Southwest.

matalija
(Mex-Sp; SW and California). Also **matiliga**. *Romneya coulteri.* A beautiful variety of giant white shrub poppy.

matanza
(Mex-Sp; SW and California). The slaughtering of cattle or the place where cattle were killed. (Mathews 1951; Stewart White 1933)

mauvric
A variant of **maverick**. McCoy 1874: "Unbranded animals over a year old are, in ranchman's parlance, called 'mauvrics.' Which name they got from a certain old Frenchman who began stock raising with very few head and in a very brief space of time had a remarkably large herd of cattle. It was found that he had actually branded fifty annually for each cow he owned. Of course he captured unbranded yearlings." There are several other versions of the origin of the word *maverick*.

maverick
Unbranded stock. Seen spelled in a number of ways, including **mavoric** and **mavorick**. The word *maverick* is the least understood and most corrupted of Western words that have survived to late-twentieth-century general English speech. The most acceptable version of the origin of the word is that it derives from the name of a Texas lawyer, one Samuel A. Maverick, who collected a herd of Longhorns on Matagorda Island in lieu of payment of a debt in 1845. Not being a cattleman, he took little interest in them and they multiplied. In 1853, he had the herd brought to the mainland and found to all appearances that the stock was not increasing: as unbranded cattle were ready for anybody's rope, many had fallen on Maverick's stock. The cattle were mavericks—not stolen, mind you. And the men who took them were **maverickers**. A new word had enriched the Anglo-American language. If you don't believe me, see J. Frank Dobie, *The Longhorns* (1941). If Dobie didn't know the true story, nobody did. (McCarthy 1936). See also *mauvric.*

maverick brand
An unrecorded brand. (Ramon Adams 1944)

mavericking
To take possession of unbranded cattle. In the early days, a perfectly legal activity, and many a big cowman started his herd this way. When later the laws regarding unbranded cattle were tightened, the maverickers continued to maverick—this made them cow-thieves. Hence mavericking came to mean stealing cows.

mayor domo
See *major domo (1).*

McClellan pies
See *Lincoln shingles.*

meat biscuit
(1) Bartlett 1877: "The concentrated juice of beef, mixed with flour and baked. It is chiefly used to make soup for travelers and soldiers etc." I have not seen this definition elsewhere, but have found the word defined as a kind of biscuit in its finished form. Bartlett's explanation sounds reasonable. Not a Westernism.
(2) Canned beef, first produced (so it is said) in Texas in the early 1850s by Gail Borden, who later made a fortune canning condensed milk. (Wellman 1939). See also *airtights.*

meat in the pot
A rifle—the weapon with which the hunter shot for the pot (Ramon Adams 1944)—or a revolver (Mathews 1951).

mecapal
A basket used by miners for carrying ore from a shaft. It could be carried on the back and the weight taken by a band around the forehead. (Dobie 1930)

mecate
A hair rope. Varied by Anglos to **McCarty**—as nice a Westernism as ever I saw. Mora 1950 says that such ropes were made from horse-mane or -tail (the former being the softer and better), mohair (very silky), or cow-tail (stiff and prickly). (Ramon Adams 1944; Berrey and van den Bark 1942, who spell it **mecarte**)

medicine
Bartlett 1877: "This word is used in translating certain terms in the language of the American aborigines which denote not only 'medicine' proper, but any thing the operation of which they do not comprehend, that is, any thing mysterious, supernatural, sacred. . . . " This shows some real understanding on the part of the writer, which seems commendable for a man of that period. Medicine in this sense is said in some ways to be the equivalent of the Maori *mana,* itself a word much misunderstood. However, now that esoteric religions and philosophies are being more understood by the Western world, or at least read about more widely, something of the meaning of these words may be conveyed to the reader. They are rather more than aura or reputation, yet their meaning contains both. They cover the whole spiritual strength and courage of the man in question, his contact with the spirits, his inner and outer vision, his influence and his standing with his fellow men, his luck, his ability to survive in dangerous situations, and more. From *medicine* we have **medicine man** to cover anything from a holy man to a magician; **medicine bag,** a bag containing

holy relics or venerated objects considered to have spiritual influence; **medicine feast,** a religious festival; **medicine lodge** or **hut, medicine pipe,** etc. The whites adopted some of these terms and some survived well into the present century. In white use, ***bad medicine*** indicated a bad or dangerous man. Weseen 1934 translated the word simply as "information."

medicine tongue
A deluge of talk from a man—or woman. (Weseen 1934; Berry and van den Bark 1942; Ramon Adams 1944)

mequit grass
See *mesquite grass.*

mesa
(Sp; SW). Roughly the equivalent of the plateau of the Northwest. A table; hence, a flat-topped eminence of land. (Dobie 1930; Dunn 1886)

mesa oak
Oak trees growing in mesa country, usually of a stunted nature.

mescal
(Mex-Sp from Nahuatl). The agave or century plant. A term also used loosely to cover the ***peyote*** plant and also the liquor obtained from the agave (see ***mezcal***). From it was obtained a vegetable for eating and the vision-making drug in the form of a peyote button. (There is a tradition of socially controlled drug-taking among certain Indians of the Southwest.) The word *mescal* is found in literature with a multitude of spellings, such as **mezcal, mascal,** etc. The Mescaleros (Spanish: the mescal people) were so named for their eating of mescal. (Hodge 1907–10; Safford 1916)

mescal bean
The bean of the *Sophora secundiflora,* an evergreen bush with violet flowers. Safford 1916 writes: "The plant, usually avoided by animals, is eaten by deer and goats, and the hard glossy beans, when swallowed whole, are apparently harmless. In the early days they were used by certain tribes of Indians for making a narcotic decoction, and when ground to powder and put in mescal, or Agave brandy, to make it more intoxicating; hence the name 'mescal bean,' which was formerly applied to them."

mesquital
(Mex-Sp; SW). The final *-al* of this word makes it collective: a thicket of mesquite. Dobie 1952 writes: "I take the saddle off her and hide it in the mesquital." (Mora 1950)

mesquite
(Mex-Sp from Nahuatl). *Prosopis juliflora,* or other related species. This tree has been likened to the peach, though, when old, it can look like an ancient apple tree. It generally does not grow tall and has a very short trunk with deep-V  forks and branches that come low to the ground. Its thorns sit upon "black and warty bases," and its leaves are a blessing in the desert, where there are so few. The twigs, closely knit, become knotty and weighty; green in the spring, they are edible by cattle. Flowers appear a little later, in April, after the winter rains. The tree flowers again in June and July and off and on into the fall. In western Texas, where bees were raised, the insects fed upon the catkin-like flowers. Indians used the bean-pods as food and also to make a mildly alcoholic drink. The beans were also beneficial to horses as *bait.* Webster's First New International Dictionary 1909 says *mesquite* covered two kinds of trees in the Southwest: the honey-mesquite and the screw-pod mesquite. Bartlett 1877 gives two spellings, **mesquit** and **muskeet,** and provides the Latin name *Algarobia glandulosa,* stating that it belonged to the locust family. The gum was used as an adhesive by the Indians.

mesquite grass
Webster's First New International Dictionary 1909: "a rich native grass in Western Texas (*Bouteloua oligostachya* and other species); so called from growing in company with the mesquite tree;—called also **muskit grass, gramma grass**" (see *grama grass*). Bartlett 1877 says: "MEQUIT GRASS (*Stipa spata.* Algonkin, *maskeht, maskit,* grass). A fine short grass, called also **Lewis Grass,** which grows with great vigor and beauty on the western prairies. It is usually found in very thick tufts and patches, interspersed with other grasses. It is very nutritious and palatable to cattle, horses and sheep; it has the great advantage of preserving its sweetness, to a certain degree, through the winter. Sometimes called **muskeet** and **muskete.**"

mesquite prairie
A prairie of *mesquite grass.*

mess
A meal.

mess beef
The salted or pickled beef of the early Texans. Dobie 1929: "The pickled

beef was sometimes called 'mess beef,' and as early as 1844 'mess beef' was quoted on the Galveston market at $10 for a barrel of 200 pounds. At the same time dried beef was offered by Galveston stores at ten cents a pound."

mess room
The cowboys' dining-room on a ranch, where the cook ruled supreme. (National Livestock Historical Association 1904)

mess wagon
The chuck wagon: the term preferred by Charles Goodnight. (Berrey and van den Bark 1942; Ramon Adams 1944; Newton and Gambrell 1949)

mestang
An early variant of *mustang.*

mestang court
A kangaroo court, such as one that might be set up in the absence of official law in early Texas or in the mining districts of the Rockies. (Mathews 1951)

mestee
The parallels and variants in English, French, and Spanish appear as **métis, metif, mustee, mestizo,** etc.—some of which show the Old Westerner as carefree in his speech as in his hearing. In different parts the words had slightly different meanings and had connections with varied origins, but in whatever place or form, it meant a person of mixed descent. The famous métis of Canada were of mixed French and Indian descent. The mestizos of Mexico were of Spanish-Indian descent. (Dobie 1930). The mustees or mestees of the United States were of Anglo-Indian descent generally, though most European groups at one time or another cross-bred with Indians. Dunn 1886 uses the form mustee, which Farmer 1889 places in the West Indies. The French form métis was known in what is now Wyoming/Montana in the early days and probably down the Missouri, but was not generally used in the Southwest. Stegner 1963 writes: "Like the Plains Indian culture, the *métis* were a white creation; ethnically and culturally they were the product of the white and the Indian. . . . And like the Plains culture, they were obliterated eventually by what made them."

metate
A hollowed stone in which nuts, corn, and wheat were ground, used by Indians and Mexicans in the Southwest. The word is derived from the Nahuatl *metatl,* and in Harby 1890 the word is spelled **metal.** (Dobie 1930)

mex
A common abbreviation of *Mexican,* used by Anglos as noun and adjective.

Mexican
A Mexican dollar; a **'dobe dollar** (see *adobe [2]*).

Mexican badger
See *badger.*

Mexican bean
The frijol or **Mexican black bean.**

Mexican bit
A horse's bit which used a curb-ring in place of the Anglo curb-chain and *curb-strap.*

Mexican iron
See *rawhide (1).*

Mexicano
A Mexican—a general term on the ranges. (Weseen 1934; Berrey and van den Bark 1942)

Mexican pack-saddle
See *aparejo.*

Mexican saddle
Generally, a heavy saddle with a high cantle and bow and a flat, wide-based saddlehorn which was adopted by the Texans in the early days. While this was the prototype of the Western saddle, there were many other varieties.

Mexican spur
A spur of a type with a large rowel, favored by Mexicans. There were some who claimed this spur to be cruel; indeed, it could be if it were used cruelly—but no more so than a simple barbed spur used cruelly. See also *spurs.*

Mexican strawberries
Beans. (Berrey and van den Bark 1942; Ramon Adams 1944). See also *Arizona strawberries.*

mezcal
(Mex-Sp; SW). An intoxicating liquor. The *aguamiel* of the **maguey** or

century plant when fermented became pulque, which, in turn, when distilled, became mezcal.

mill
The formation of a herd in the act of *milling.* (Mora 1950)

milling
The action which brought about a situation called a mill, in which cattle circled tightly. This was sometimes done intentionally by drovers to stop the movement of stampeding cattle. The leaders were turned and the animals driven in an ever-tightening circle. The mill had to be halted at the right time or the animals could injure each other. Some experienced trail-bosses were against the practice and believed in allowing stampeding cattle to run till spent, concentrating on holding them together. (Harger 1892; Weseen 1934)

milpa
(Mex-Sp from Nahuatl: cornfield; SW). A small patch of cultivated ground. (Mathews 1951)

miner's
Silicosis, the dreaded lung disease of the miner—known as **the miner's.** (Emrich 1951)

miners' lettuce
See *squaw cabbage.*

missed hole
Also **sleeper.** A hole drilled for and packed with explosives which failed to go off. (Emrich 1951)

mission Indian
An Indian converted to Christianity (sometimes only nominally) and attached to an established religious mission. Under the Spaniards in California and New Mexico they were detribalized people who were often used as serfs. However, these were not the only Indians to have their cultures eroded by an alien religion. Among the Navahos (who were not mission Indians) there were tragic cases in which Indians were taken East for schooling only to be returned to their reservations not quite as white people, but certainly no longer Indians. Sometimes they were children taken against their parents' wishes. There is a considerable literature on the subject. Some of the writings of the missionaries themselves, without their being aware of it, make appalling reading. Two of the works which most movingly describe these distressingly misguided efforts are *Sun Chief,* edited by Leo Simmons (1942), and D'Arcy McNickle's *The Indian Tribes of the United States* (1962).

Missouri mule
The animal famed for its endurance and hauling power. Originally bred in the Southwest in the old Mexican possessions. (Gregg 1844)

mite
A little. Some fiction writers mistakenly spell this word **might**. Used as follows: "I'm a mite mad at you," meaning "I'm a little angry with you." Not confined to the West, but used generally in U.S. dialect. (Wentworth 1944)

moccasin
Also **mocassin, mocasin, moccason**. An Indian shoe that came in a variety of designs, often skillfully made and beautifully decorated by women. They were preferred by many white hunters and trappers, who claimed that in winter wearing them made frost-bite less likely. (Farmer 1889). Invariably, the sole was soft and pliable. On hard journeys, the wearers would carry material for keeping the footgear in repair; such repairs might have to be made each day in rocky country. Doddridge 1912 gives the following description of one version of the moccasin: "made of dressed deer skin. . . . mostly made of a single piece with a gathering seam along the top of the foot, and another from the bottom of the heel, without gathers, as high as the ankle joint or a little higher. Flaps were left on either side to reach some distance up the legs. These were nicely adapted to the ankles and lower part of the leg by thongs of deer skin, so that no dust, gravel or snow could get within the moccasin. . . . In cold weather the moccasins were well stuffed with deer's hair, or dry leaves, so as to keep the feet comfortably warm."

mochila
(Sp). Also correctly **machilla**. A loose skin or cloth cover for a saddle. Common in the early days when various parts of the saddle, particularly the wooden tree, were covered only with rawhide. Corrupted in many forms, such as **mochiler** or **mochile**. In the case of the Pony Express riders, it could contain pockets, or **cantinas**. As **macheer**, it was mentioned in Western literature from the 1840s onward. (Berrey and van den Bark 1942; Ramon Adams 1944). See also *saddles.*

mocho
(Sp: cropped, shorn). Referred to a cow with a gotched ear, a drooping horn, or a damaged tail. (Dobie 1930; Ramon Adams 1944)

mockey
(1) A wild mare. (Ramon Adams 1944)
(2) A young mare was a **mocky**. (Wentworth 1944)
I think that the first meaning was the one prevalent in the second half of the nineteenth century.

mogote
(Mex-Sp; SW). A thicket. (Dobie 1930)

Montana rig
A three-quarter single saddle-rig with the cinch just forward of the center-fire position (see *center-fire rig*). (Foster-Harris 1955)

monte
(Mex-Sp).
(1) Country heavily thicketed, usually with chaparral, but sometimes with mesquite, particularly applied to the foothills of California. (Dobie 1941)
(2) A card game played with 45 cards, introduced from Spain and Mexico, in which bets were made on a bottom and top layout of two cards to each player. Three-card monte, thought to be of purely Mexican origin, was played with three cards only.

mooley cow
See *muley (1)*.

moonshine
(1) Dobie 1941: " 'I was working for the Quien Sabe outfit on the Pecos,' Horace Wilson used to relate, 'while Barnes Tillus was boss. One night we made what we called a "moonshine"—that is a night ride and a dry camp —with the intention of starting at daybreak on a fifteen-or twenty-mile drive back to the roundup ground.' " (Berrey and van den Bark 1942; Ramon Adams 1944)
(2) Rice. (Weseen 1934; Berrey and van den Bark 1942)

moose
Alces alces shirasi. In nineteenth-century literature there must have been as many moose stories as grizzly bear stories and most of them just about  as true. The moose may be a homely hombre, but anybody who has seen one will admit he's pretty impressive—occasionally with a six-foot spread of massive palmed antlers, always with heavy shoulders and a pendulous upper lip. A shy creature, he's a tree-browser and loves to live near water, in which he is an incredible swimmer. He likes to eat water plants and in winter rustles a living on tree bark—maybe he passed on that tip to the mustangs. Dark brown in color, they were once plentiful in the northern Rockies and still exist in fair numbers. Though shy, they will turn savage if cornered or worried at the wrong time of year. A man who had a lip like that of a moose was either said to look like one or was given the name of Moose. The name was also sometimes laid on a man of large stature.

Morgan
An Eastern breed of horse descended from a stallion belonging to Justin Morgan of Massachusetts (1747–98). A strong, lively breed, which crossed well with the mustang and the Spanish horse of the West.

Mormon brake
A log attached to a wagon as an extra brake when going down a steep slope; used by the Mormons on their westward travels. (Foster-Harris 1955; Mathews 1951)

Mormon wagon
Also **mover's wagon** (Mathews 1951; Rossi and Hunt 1971). A strong wagon, lighter than a Conestoga, used by settlers in crossing the Plains. So called through its use by the Mormons. See also *wagons.*

moro
(Mex-Sp). A horse of bluish hue. (Ramon Adams 1944; Mora 1950)

morral
(Mex-Sp; SW and Texas). A fiber bag usually carried hanging from the saddlehorn. Also a feed- or nose-bag. (Dobie 1930; Weseen 1934; Berrey and van den Bark 1942; Ramon Adams 1944)

mosey
Farmer 1889: "To depart suddenly and involuntarily; to sneak away. This, with some degree of plausibility, is said to be a corruption of the Spanish VAMOSE . . . often used in the primary and simple sense of to go, and *to mosey along* with anyone is employed idiomatically in the sense of to agree with." Bartlett 1877: "To be off; to leave; to sneak away." Which makes one think that Farmer had been reading Bartlett. In Western literature the term is generally used in the sense of "to go easily," "to drift." Originally from the Appalachians. (Wentworth 1944)

moss back
An old Longhorn, usually knowing and skilled in taking refuge from the questing rope. The name implies that the animal is so old that moss grows on its back. Hence, the term could be applied to a man. Similarly, one finds **moss head** (Weseen 1934; Berrey and van den Bark 1942), **moss horn** (Weseen 1934; McCarthy 1936; Mencken 1948), and **mossy horn** (Berrey and van den Bark 1942; Ramon Adams 1944). (Berrey and van den Bark 1942)

mota
(Sp; SW). A clump or *motte* of trees. (Dobie 1930)

Mother Hubbard
Old-style saddle with a removable cloth cover. The cloth had slits through

which the horn and cantle appeared. So named because of its long skirting by the cowboys of Texas, where it originated probably in the late 1860s or early 1870s. (Ramon Adams 1944; Mora 1950; Rossi 1975)

Mother Hubbard loop
A very large loop of a lasso. (Berrey and van den Bark 1942; Ramon Adams 1944)

mother lode
In mining, the main part of a vein of ore. (Willison 1952)

motte
Also **mota, mott.** A clump of trees, usually on a plain or prairie land. Farmer 1889 gives both motte and **mot**—"A Texas term for a clump of trees on a prairie. These oases are also called **islands.**" Farmer followed in the footsteps of Bartlett 1877, apparently. (Wentworth 1944; Ramon Adams 1944; Dobie 1930)

mought
Might. (Bartlett 1877; Farmer 1889)

mount
A cowhand or cattle-drover's string of saddle-horses. In popular fiction, a single horse is often referred to as a mount. (Weseen 1934; Berrey and van den Bark 1942; Ramon Adams 1944)

mountain beaver
See *boomer (2).*

mountain boomer
(1) A cow-crittur of the hill country. (Ramon Adams 1944)
(2) A mountain lizard. (Ramon Adams 1944)
(3) A mountain beaver. Also called simply *boomer.* (Wentworth 1944)

mountain buffalo
See *buffalo.*

mountain canary
A burro, a donkey. (Wentworth and Flexner 1960; Weseen 1934; Berrey and van den Bark 1942)

mountain goat
Oreamnos americanus. The **Rocky Mountain goat,** sometimes called the **goat antelope** or **antelope goat.** Not a true goat, but a relative of the chamois. An awkward-looking animal, it is four feet high at

the shoulder and noticeably shorter at the rump, weighing up to 300 pounds. Male and female have small, upright, backward-curving horns and long shaggy white coats all the year around. They inhabit the high remote crags above the tree-line.

mountain lion
See *cougar.*

Mountain Men
Although, strictly speaking, the term applies to men who ranged the West before the period covered by this book, no work on this subject would be complete without mention of them. Broadly, the name covers the men who invaded the Rocky Mountains, either as free hunters or trappers or as employees of the fur companies, approximately in the period 1820–40. The breed first comes to our notice with the Lewis and Clark expedition of 1804–06, which employed men already experienced in the wilderness of the Old Northwest (northwest of the country settled at that period)—men from the Kentucky mountains and New Englanders who had retained their taste for the free life and skills of forest and hills. The expertise of these men in trapping and shooting, their general hardiness, and their ability to survive in an often hostile environment was tempered in the Rockies where the true Mountain Men were forged.

Various writers may have led us to believe that these men were uncontrollable, wild, murderous illiterates who lived from one drunken debauch at annual rendezvous to the next, but the facts do not bear this out. Like most groups of men, this one comprised all kinds, and U.S. history rightly regards many of them with pride. The list of Mountain Men whose names, without any degree of exaggeration, may be listed in the heroes' honor roll is long, but as examples one can cite Jim Bridger, Tom Fitzpatrick, Joe Walker, Kit Carson, Josiah Gregg, Jim Beckwourth, Jed Smith, Dan Potts, the brothers Sublette, the brothers Chouteau, and Joe Meek—as good a racial mixture as ever you could find.

All breeds of men give rise to new ones. The Mountain Men begat the best of the frontier scouts and guides of the era that followed, many of them serving honorably with exploration and surveying parties, wagon-trains, and the army. Whether the term should be written *Mountain Men* or *mountain men* is argued by the purists; the capital letters appear mostly in twentieth-century literature—but I do not think it matters much.

mountain rifle
See *plains rifle.*

mountain sheep
See *big horn.*

mountain wagon

A light, durable wagon of various designs, suitable for use on mountain runs. It possessed, and needed, a very powerful brake. (Mathews 1951)

mouth

The end of the gold miner's *rocker,* to which a sieve was attached. (Buffum 1850)

mover

This was one of the many words in the West that altered its meaning according to time and place. Originally it was used as an exact equivalent of *emigrant.* Later, it sometimes gathered to it a derogatory air and was used in reference to failures, people who were incapable of settling and making good their land. I suppose that, as land became more settled, movers coming in from outside were considered with suspicion, much the same as gypsies would be. (Mathews 1951)

mover's wagon

See *Mormon wagon.*

mozo

(Mex-Sp: a youth). Used in Spain for a waiter, in the West its meaning varied a little according to time and place. It might refer to a domestic servant, a clerk, or an assistant of any kind. Sometimes *muchacho* was used in much the same sense. (Ramon Adams 1944; Mathews 1951)

muchacho

(Sp; SW). Literally, a boy. A term of familiarity that might be applied to a servant. (Mathews 1951)

muckamuck

(NW). Chinook jargon for food. (Ramon Adams 1944; Mathews 1951)

mud

To chink or fill gaps between logs of a cabin with mud.

mud wagon

Also **mud coach, celerity wagon.** This has been described as the poor man's *Concord.* An open-sided stagecoach in which, presumably, the unfortunate passengers were plastered with mud. The vehicles were usually light and drawn by two or four horses or mules. The term appears as early as 1835 (according to Mathews 1951) and was used during the California–Nevada runs in 1896. (Foster-Harris 1955; Rossi and Hunt 1971)

mujer

(Sp; SW). Woman, wife. (Dobie 1930)

mulada
(Sp). A drove of mules. (Dobie 1952; Ramon Adams 1944; Berrey and van den Bark 1942)

mule
Western fiction of the twentieth century has a curiously superior air when writing of the mule, and it is rare to find a hero mounted on one. This may be because the Anglo-Saxon American mostly employed the animal for draft purposes. The Spaniards took another attitude and valued a good saddle-mule: while the trot of a mule is not usually a thing of delight when you're on its back, there were certainly excellent saddlers among them. Mules often ran with mustangs on the plains; indeed, Dobie 1952 remarks that in some manadas the chief sentinel was a mare or mule. The mule, in fact, was the great unsung hero of the West. The offspring of a jackass and a mare, it was often preferred to a horse for its hardiness, particularly in hot climates that could be trying to horses. A mule could survive on rougher fare than a horse—but not as rough as some writers of Western fiction would have us believe. (The toughness of the mule is graphically illustrated in William Manly's 1927 *Death Valley in '49*.) Oxen were possibly preferable for the long prairie hauls, on which the mules required grain that had to be carried, but mules were considerably faster. Good muleteams fetched amazingly high prices during the commercial use of the Santa Fe Trail, and freighters chose individual animals carefully for their position in the team. The strongest pair was chosen as wheelers, the span hitched directly to the wagon. Smaller and smarter animals were chosen as leaders. The nigh- (left-hand) leader was the smartest of all. Being faster than oxen, mules could be driven off with horses by raiding Indians, who not only valued mules as saddle-animals and pack-animals, but possessed palates which were not too delicate to appreciate mule steaks. Lewis and Clark found that both the Flatheads and Nez Percé possessed large and fine mules. (Rossi and Hunt 1971)

mule deer
Odocoileus hemionus. The black-tailed deer that ranged from Canada to Mexico in large numbers, hunted by Indians and whites alike, and so called because it had long ears like those of a mule. There are a number of subspecies, among which are the Rocky Mountain mule deer (*O. hemionus hemionus*) and the **blacktail deer** (*O. hemionus columbianus*). The main difference is that the former has a white tail with a black tip and the latter a wholly black tail.

mule-ears
(1) The pull-on straps of a pair of boots, often worn outside the boots.

(2) Boots that possessed mule-ears that flapped as the wearer walked. (Berrey and van den Bark 1942)

(3) *Tapaderos*, because of their shape. (Ramon Adams 1944)

mulero
(Sp; SW).

(1) A muleteer, a man attending a mule-train of pack-animals. (Dobie 1930)

(2) A driver of a mule-team, a muleskinner. (Berrey and van den Bark 1942; Ramon Adams 1944)

muleskinner
Also **skinner**. The driver of a wagon pulled by a mule-team. Such men rode on the wagon, whereas bullwhackers usually walked. (Weseen 1934; Berrey and van den Bark 1942; Ramon Adams 1944)

muley
(1) A hornless or one-horned cow-crittur. The word appears to be a variation of the Scottish and Anglo-Irish *moiley*, which comes from *moil, moll* (bald). On a trail-drive, muleys were inclined to congregate when it came to bedding down and usually isolated themselves from horned cattle. A lone muley, hesitating on the fringe of the herd, could unsettle the remainder of the animals. Andy Adams 1909 writes: "I remember there were a number of muleys among the cattle, and these would not venture into the compact herd until the others had lain down. Being hornless, instinct taught them to be on the defensive, and it was noticeable that they were the first to rise in the morning, in advance of their horned kin." (Wentworth

muley (3)

1944; Ramon Adams 1944; Berrey and van den Bark 1942). Also **mooley cow, muley cow, mulley.**

(2) A *mule deer*.

(3) A hat with a small brim; the hat of a dude or city man. (Rossi 1975)

mule-yeared rabbit
Also **mule-eared rabbit**. When a man didn't know nothin' more than a mule-yeared rabbit, he was pretty damned . ignorant.

muley saddle
From *muley (1)*, a hornless saddle. Westernisms have their own sweet logic. (Ramon Adams 1944)

muskeet
See *mesquite; mesquite grass.*

muskete
See *mesquite grass.*

muskit grass
See *mesquite grass.*

mustang
(Sp *mesteño, mestengo,* from *mesta,* an association of graziers in Old Spain). A stranger, a wild one. Dobie 1952 says: "It is the English corruption of *mesteño* or *mesteña* (feminine), a word already legalized in Spain when Copernicus asserted diurnal rotation of the earth. In 1273 the Spanish government authorized the *mesta* as an organization of sheep owners. On the long 'walks' between winter and summer ranges, many sheep were lost. They were called *mesteños* (belonging to the *mesta*). They were also called *mostrencos* (from *mostrar,* to show, to exhibit). The estrayed animal had to be *mostrado* (shown) in public to give the owner a chance to claim it. *Bienes mostrencos* were, in legal terminology, goods lacking a known owner. . . . *Mestengo,* a later form of *mostrenco,* is a word nearer to mustang than *mesteño,* and some etymologists have regarded it as the origin." Certainly the word was in use at an early date in Anglo-Saxon North America—I think as early as the beginning of the nineteenth century. These animals were descended from the original Spanish stock in Mexico, either escapees or animals stolen by Indians—but not to be confused with the **Spanish horse,** which breed was kept up to standard. The

mustang often degenerated through inbreeding of poor characteristics; however, there were no doubt some fine animals among them. In the wild they ran as bands of mares (usually small in number) with a lead mare and a stallion which allowed estrayed geldings and mules to join without objection. By the time the whiteman moved into the West in force, the mustang population, including that of Texas, must have been immense. They were mainly of small build and, though descended from the solid-color Spanish horses, were (through inbreeding) often multi-colored. They kept to established ranges, were hardy and durable, able to rustle for food in bad winters, and ideal mounts for Indians and cowboys. Crossed with such Eastern stock as the quarter horses, they made perfect cutting horses. (Dobie 1952)

mustang cattle
Generally in Texas, these were untouched, black wild ones, as opposed to branded stock. See also *black cattle.*

mustanger
Also **mustang hunter.** A man who, for sport or trade, hunted and caught mustangs. It could be a disappointing trade, since the animals were often hard to catch and, when caught, might kill themselves or prove indifferent beasts in the captive state: too often the heart went out of them. Those captured were often small and runty, for the big and fast ones were the most likely to escape. However, the trade could earn a man a fair living, for the little animals were in great demand during the first part of the period covered here, both as saddlers and light draft horses. There were various ways of catching them, for which see *mustanging.* Mathews 1951 records the word in 1849.

mustang grape
A small red grape of Texas. (Mathews 1951)

mustanging
There were probably as many methods employed in catching mustangs as there were mustangers. Some believed in running them down: one suspects that, in many cases, the poorer animals were thus caught, which only proved that a good horse without a rider could out-run a good horse bearing one. Some believed in patiently walking the mustangs down on foot, day in and day out, never letting them rest or drink; this must have been trying for the mustang and hell for the man on foot. Others walked them down with buggies (see *walk-down*), most from the backs of horses —which made good sense. Many men laid traps at water-holes visited regularly by the feral animals. Another trick was to play upon their curiosity, for horses are the most curious of animals—the theory being that while their attention was held you dropped a noose over them. There was

also a trick of stampeding them into a pen down an ever-narrowing lane of stakes, brush, or men. (A usually lethal method was *creasing[1]*). Mustangs kept to an established range and left only when it became untenable —a fact that made the hunter's difficult task a little easier. Movies, TV, and fictional stories usually draw an inaccurate picture of the size of the wild bands such men hunted. They were bossed by a stallion, led by a wise old mare, and were made up of mares, young geldings, and mules that had escaped from domesticity. The mares might number from a half-dozen to possibly twenty.

mustangler
A herder of mustangs. The words *mustang* and *wrangler* and their connection with horses were irresistible to the cowboy. He had to unite them, and how right he was: the result is a beauty. (Weseen 1934; Berrey and van den Bark 1942; Ramon Adams 1944)

mustard
To unsettle cattle, to disturb and excite them. (Ramon Adams 1944)

mustee
See *mestee.*

mutton-puncher
A sheepherder, in the eyes of a cowboy. (Berrey and van den Bark 1942; Ramon Adams 1944)

naja

(Mex-Sp; SW). A small decoration hanging from the headband of a bridle onto the horse's face, rather like an inverted horse-shoe or crescent moon, reminding one of a similar decoration worn by the Moors. (Foster-Harris 1955)

naked possessor

In Texas, a person who, though without title, undisputedly occupied land for a long period. (Bartlett 1877)

nankeen

A cloth (originally brought from Nanking, China) made from cotton, usually of a pale-yellow or fawn color. A word to be found in Western fiction which may puzzle a modern reader. (Bartlett 1877)

navy model

This term, applied to a revolver by such makers as Colt and Remington, simply meant that the weapon was supplied to the navy specification. Compared to the *army model* of a specified type, this usually meant a slightly shorter barrel and smaller caliber: for example, the Remington New Army Model revolver (single-action) 1861, made from 1863 to 1875, had an 8-inch barrel and was a .44 caliber, while the New Navy Model revolver (single-action), patented 1858 and manufactured in the years 1863–88, had a 7⅜-inch barrel and was a .36 caliber. Similarly, Colt and Starr had varied barrel and caliber measurements. The navy models were popular with civilians for their comparative lightness and slightly smaller size. (Karr and Karr 1960; Bowman 1953)

near-horse
Also **nigh-horse**. The left-hand horse in a pair on a wagon team. In a four-
or six-horse team, you had the **near-wheeler** and the **near-leader,** the latter
the smartest member of a *jerk-line* team. (Rossi and Hunt 1971). See also
off-horse; wheeler.

near-side
See *off-side.*

neat cattle
Bovine cattle.

Nebraska brick
Also **Kansas brick.** Squares of prairie turf that were used in the building
of a *soddy (1).* (*Harper's Monthly Magazine* 1888)

necking
Said when the neck of a difficult animal was tied to that of one better
behaved. In the brush-country of Texas, for example, intractable Longhorns were necked to tame steers. Wild mus-
tangs were sometimes necked to another horse
or to a burro. The word was recorded in use in
the 1850s. (Dobie 1941; Weseen 1934; Gard
1954; Ramon Adams 1944; Berrey and van
den Bark 1942)

neck-reiner
A horse trained to neck-reining—in which a
saddle-horse was turned not by a rein-pull on
the bit, but by slight rein-pressure on the neck.
If pressure was applied to the left side of the
neck, the horse turned right. (Berrey and van
den Bark 1942; Ramon Adams 1944)

neck-roped
Roped by the neck. At round-up and branding
time, if a calf was neck-roped it would then be
thrown by hand for the actual branding. (North
1942)

neck-tie party
A hanging. (Weseen 1934, who, with Mathews 1951, provides **neck-tie
sociable**)

green
needle grass

needle grass

The common name given to about 30 species of the genus *Stipa,* a grass favored in the Western ranges because of its abundance, long growing period, and capacity to cure well when cut for hay. Each spikelet ends in a sharp, feathery bristle (awn), which in some species can be injurious to grazing cattle. Needle-and-thread grass (*Stipa comata*) gives the appearance of a threaded sewing needle because of the sharp-pointed seed and the long, twisted, threadlike awn.

Green needle grass (*Stipa viridula*), sometimes known as feather bunchgrass, also has conspicuous awns, approximately an inch long, but they are not as bothersome to livestock as those of other species. (United States Department of Agriculture 1948)

nester

Really a squatter, one who settled on land without permission; but a term also used by cowmen in the Southwest when referring to farmers. (Weseen 1934; Mencken 1948)

nigger brand

A saddle-sore on a horse's back. (Berrey and van den Bark 1942; Ramon Adams 1944)

nigger catcher

A leather tab on a saddle, with a slit in which the free end of the *latigo* strap is retained. (Berrey and van den Bark 1942; Ramon Adams 1944; Rossi 1975)

nigh-horse

See *near-horse.*

night-guard

Men assigned to watch a trail-herd at night. Andy Adams 1909 writes: "The guards ride in a circle about four rods outside the sleeping cattle, and by riding in opposite directions, make it impossible for any animal to make its escape without being noticed by the riders. The guards usually sing or whistle continuously, so that the sleeping herd may know that a friend and not an enemy is keeping vigil over their dreams. A sleeping herd of cattle make a pretty picture on a clear moonlight night, chewing their cuds and grunting and blowing over contented stomachs. The night horses soon learn their duty, and a rider may fall asleep or doze along in the saddle, but the horses will maintain their distance in their leisurely sentinel rounds."

night horse
At night a trail-driver needed the quietest and most reliable member of his string or mount, a horse that would not disturb sleeping cows, would not spook in a stampede, and would follow surely after running cows even in the pitch-dark. (Berrey and van den Bark 1942; Ramon Adams 1944; Mora 1950)

night wrangler
Also **night-hawk** (Allen 1933; Mora 1950). The night-guard for the horses of a trail-crew. (Weseen 1934; Berrey and van den Bark 1942; Ramon Adams 1944)

nogal
(Sp: walnut tree; Texas and SW). A walnut tree; a pecan tree; the hickory. (Mathews 1951)

No Man's Land
(1) Farmer 1889: ''the strip lying between Colorado and Kansas on the North, and Texas on the South. It was ceded by Texas to the United States, and has been classed geographically with Indian Territory for convenience. It extends from the 100th to the 103rd meridian, and is about seventy-five miles in width.'' This was not the only piece of country to bear the title in the United States.
As **no man's land**:
(2) Land claimed by nobody, or where no man dared go.
(3) Soil washed from one farm to another. (Weseen 1934; Berrey and van den Bark 1942)

no medicine
Lack of information. (Weseen 1934; Ramon Adams 1944)

nopal
(Mex-Sp from Nahuatl). A cactus (genus *Napolea*). Tuna cactus, Indian fig. Used as a hedging plant, also to purify water for drinking; sometimes referred to as a prickly pear. (Mathews 1951). Dobie 1941 agrees that it bears prickly-pear fruit and says that it is also called the **Devil's Head.**

norther
A cold wind blowing from the north over Texas and the Southwest. This could be a cold, wet wind before which cattle would drift for many miles. A bad one was a **blue norther.** (Ramon Adams 1944; Mathews 1951)

Northwester
Besides meaning a man from the Northwest territories, this was also the kind of story such a man would tell—a very tall story indeed. First cousin, in fact, to the straight-faced lies told to any gullible listener by the Texas cattlemen.

nose paint
Whiskey. (Ramon Adams 1944; Rossi 1975)

nubbing
Also **nubbin'**. The saddlehorn. (Berrey and van den Bark 1942; Ramon Adams 1944)

nueces
(Mex-Sp; SW). Pecan, nut. (Dobie 1930)

nut pine
Any one of a number of pine trees bearing nuts, such as *Pinus monophylla*. (Mathews 1951)

ocotillo
(Mex-Sp from Nahuatl *acote;* SW). *Fouquieria splendens.* A variety of cactus that looks rather like a collection of dry sticks, until rain brings out its green leaves. In late March, a red tassel of flowers appears on the tips. Seen also as **ocotilla.**

off herd
Resting from herd-duty while on a trail-drive. (Berrey and van den Bark 1942; Ramon Adams 1944)

off-horse
The horse on the right side of a pair in a wagon team. In the same way, an off-mule, off-ox. See also *near-horse; wheeler.*

off-side
Also **Injun side** (Berrey and van den Bark 1942), **squaw side** (Mencken 1948), **Indian side.** The right side of a horse, the side on which an Indian mounted. Other riders mounted on the left, or the **near-side.** (Ramon Adams 1944; Mora 1950)

oiler
A Mexican. (Weseen 1934)

ojala!
(Mex-Sp *ojalá;* SW). A cry of surprise, pleasure, or encouragement. (Dobie 1930)

ojo
(Sp: eye). Used by the Mexicans and Anglos in the Southwest for a spring

of water instead of the Spanish *fuente* or *manantial.* (Dunn 1886; Ball 1970)

Oklahoma rain
A dust or sand storm. (Weseen 1934)

Old Reliable
So did the cattlemen rightly name the *Sharps* rifle. (Ramon Adams 1944)

▶ **olla**
(Sp; SW). A pot, a jar. (Dobie 1930)

open range
Range which, legally, had no restrictions or controls put upon it; range for common use—an ideal that was too great a temptation for range-hungry men. The reality was that the large cattle outfits often laid claim to it and held it by simple possession. (Mathews 1951)

opera
A horse-breaking surveyed by the fence-sitters. (Weseen 1934)

Oregon
One finds this word added to *horse* and *cattle.* After the settlement of the Oregon country, a form of native cattle developed from the domestic stock brought to the Northwest by the Oregon Trailers. The **Oregon Horse** was used and ridden in the Northwest outside the Oregon area, particularly where it was recorded in the 1880s (as noted by Mathews 1951). The word *Oregon* was used in conjunction with other words, such as *Trail*, the famous trail that led to the Oregon country.

orejanos
The old Tejano word for the *mustang cattle,* meaning "the eared ones": those that had not been marked or cut on the ears. They were also called *black cattle, cimarrones,* mesteñas (mustangs), mustang cattle, *Spanish cattle,* wild cattle. See also *long-ear(2); mustang.* In later years, orejanos became the Southwestern equivalent of the Northwestern *slick-ear,* meaning an unbranded and un-ear-marked cow-crittur. (Dobie 1941; North 1942). Weseen 1934 gives the form **orejana.**

Osage orange
Maclura pomifera. A tree or bush used widely by the Osage and Kansa Indians, particularly in the manufacture of bows. Used by white farmers as a durable hedge. (Mathews 1951). See also *bois d'arc.*

Osage orange hedge

An agricultural field hedge of *Osage orange* bushes. Discussed in Osgood 1929. In most areas its place was largely taken by barbed wire.

osoberry

Osmaronia cerasiformis. A white-flowered shrub found in California and Oregon, or its blue-black fruit. Sometimes seen as **oso berry,** for it is composed of the Anglo word *berry* tacked onto the Spanish *oso* (a bear).

ourn

The old form of the possessive *our,* which still survives in American- and British-English dialects. Really *our one* or *our own.*

outfit

(1) Almost any organized group of cowmen. The whole organization of a ranch could be called an outfit, or the term could apply to the men only. On a large ranch, where hands were divided into parties for better working, each might be termed an outfit. Hence, any organization outside the cattle-trade came to be called an outfit. (Ramon Adams 1944; Berrey and van den Bark 1942)
(2) A cowboy's personal gear.
(3) Weseen 1934 says: "A group of cowboys and their equipment."

outlaw

(1) A man wanted by and outside the protection of the law.
(2) An unmanageable horse. (Weseen 1934; Ramon Adams 1944)
(3) A Longhorn that managed to evade capture and was dangerous to man. The word is possibly suggested by the Mexican *ladino.*

outriders ◀

Cowboys who rode a general circuit of inspection around a range. The term was mostly replaced by *line riders,* **fence riders.** (Rossi 1975)

over-and-under

A small, twin-barreled pocket pistol of the derringer type, with one barrel above the other. (Bowman 1953)

over-bit

A cattle *ear-mark* made by cutting a small piece from the upper part of the ear. (Ramon Adams 1944; Mathews 1951)

over-hack
A cattle *ear-mark* made by a clear cut downward on the upper part of the ear. (Ramon Adams 1944)

over-halfcrop
A cattle *ear-mark* made by cutting halfway down the ear from the tip and then cutting away the top quarter of the ear. (Ramon Adams 1944)

overland coach
Also **overland stage.** A stagecoach system operating from what was then the United States across the Great Plains and the mountains to the Far West and California. The word *overland* was taken up by a company operating a stage-line, but the term was used generally to cover any such service. *Overland* was also used, in the 1830s, to describe the traders on the Santa Fe Trail: they were called **overland traders.**

overland trout
Bacon. Wentworth 1944 notes this in Arthur County, western Nebraska, in 1940. I have no firm evidence that the expression existed in the nineteenth century, but it is such a fine Westernism that I can only hope it did.

over-round
A cattle *ear-mark* made by cutting away a part of the upper ear with a curving cut. (Ramon Adams 1944)

over-sharp
A cattle *ear-mark* made by a large curving cut that took away a substantial part of the upper ear.

over-slope
A cattle *ear-mark* made by making two cuts, one down from the tip and the other in from the upper edge to meet it, thus removing the upper corner of the ear. (Mathews 1951)

over-split
A cattle *ear-mark* made by cutting a simple or splitting cut in the upper part of the ear. (Ramon Adams 1944)

over-stocked
A range was so called when there were more cattle than there was grass to feed them. Such range was also termed **over-grazed.** It may be imagined that when a range was over-stocked, big cattlemen did not welcome the cattle of smaller or shirt-tail outfits.

over the jump
A range term for "killed," "dead." (Rossi 1975)

owl hoot
(1) To **hear the owl hoot** is described by Dobie 1930 with a pawky "To have many and varied experiences." Ramon Adams 1944 says exactly the same, but adds a little spice with "to get drunk."
(2) The **owl-hoot trail**—indicating some night-riding on the wrong side of the law. (Ramon Adams 1944). Hence, outlaws were sometimes known as **owl-hoots** and said to be **on the owl-hoot.**

ox-bow
(1) The part of an ox-yoke that went around the neck of the animal. This shape gave rise to:
(2) The bend of a river making that shape and, consequently, the land contained within it.
(3) The fastener that connected the stirrup-iron to the stirrup-leather.
(4) The old-time wooden stirrup.

ox-bow stirrup
A wooden stirrup in the shape of an ox-bow.

pack
For historical reasons, nothing in the West was carried—it was packed. The simple explanation is that in the early days of the frontier, goods *were* packed over rough country, on the backs of either humans or beasts. So, in the West, supplies were not carried over the hills, they were packed. A man didn't wear a gun, he packed it. (Ramon Adams 1944; Berrey and van den Bark 1942). Mathews 1951 records this use of the word at the start of the nineteenth century.

pack-burro
A donkey that carried goods or supplies.

packer
A man in charge of pack-horses. His duty would be to load and unload the animals—as all those who have undertaken this task will know, it takes skill to balance a pack and secure it. He would also care for the horses. His employer might be a surveyor, a freighter, a wealthy traveler, or even the army. His beasts of burden might equally be mules or burros.

pack-horse
A horse employed in carrying loads.

pack iron
To carry a revolver.

pack-mule
A mule employed in carrying loads. In a train, the animal would be in the charge of a muleteer or mulero.

pack rat
(1) Numerous species of *Neotoma.* A common Western rodent also called
trade rat, because it is said to always leave something behind when it
steals. It will pack the most unexpected articles off to its hole, and was an
even greater nuisance to campers than the camp robber, the jay.
(2) As an extension of the above: a petty thief.
(3) As a play on the word *pack* in this term: a packer.

pack-train
A number of animals—usually horses, mules or burros, but sometimes
oxen—used to carry supplies or equipment over terrain too rough for
wheeled vehicles.

padre
(Sp: father; SW). A priest or monk of the Roman Catholic faith. (Dobie
1930)

paho
(Hopi). Also **baho, bahoo.** A prayer stick.

pail
Wentworth 1944 has two interesting notes on the term **pailing the cow,**
(milking it): the indications are that the term existed from Texas to Montana
and Wyoming at the end of the nineteenth century; and he notes that in
Wyoming the phrase covered watering a cow from a pail. (Weseen 1934)

pail feeds
Hand-reared calves; those fed on skim-milk, often by farmers sold or given
calves by the trail-drivers from Texas, who frequently discarded calves that
could not keep up. (Weseen 1934)

painter
See *cougar.*

paint-horse
These days there are strong opinions about the difference between a paint-horse and a *pinto;* but the old-timers didn't distinguish the two. The name may well have come from the Spanish *pinto* (from *pintar:* to paint). A horse of more than one color, with the colors usually in generously sized patches, it could be brown and white, black and white, or even brown, black, and white. Of no particular breed, they were common among the inbreeding mustangs and greatly favored by the Indians (especially if studs). But they were often despised by white horsemen, who suspected that the colors denoted weakness—a dislike probably coupled with the Old Westerner's suspicion of any horse too fancy-looking; or perhaps this was the heritage of the Spaniards, who liked solid bays and sorrels and blacks. North 1942 says that cowboys avoided choosing paint-horses for their *string,* believing that they lacked stamina because of inbreeding. Also called **paint, paint-pony** (which Weseen 1934 refers to as "a piebald Indian pony").

paint the tiger
Much the same as "paint the town red." Possibly connected with the tiger painted on the front of the faro box in gambling dens.

paisano
(Sp; SW).
(1) A peasant (Weseen 1934); a compatriot. In general use among Mexicans and Anglos, but usually with rather different meanings: the Anglos used it with some contempt in referring to a Mexican as a peasant, but also in the sense of "fellow-countryman," as used by the Mexicans.
(2) A name for the *road runner.* (Dobie 1930)

palaver
Talk, discussion.

pale-face
Extremely popular in dime novels in the second half of the nineteenth century. All whitemen were pale-faces to the Indians. The Old West buff winces a little when he reads it.

Palo Alto hat
A wide-brimmed "slouch" hat, this was the forerunner of the famous Stetson. (*Harper's Monthly Magazine* 1856)

palo amarillo
(Sp; SW). A term used loosely to describe a number of shrubs having a leaf similar to a holly. A mahonia, also called chamiso. (Dayton 1931)

palo blanco
(Sp; SW). *Celtis reticulata.* The white bark hackberry. Bears a bright flower and a bean which the Indians used as a food.

palodura
(Sp: hard stick; SW). *Sapindus saponaria.* A shrub, the soap-berry, the wood of which is hard and durable.

palo hierro
(Sp; SW). Also **palo fierro.** *Olneya tesota.* A desert tree of hard wood. Also known as ironwood. (Dayton 1931)

palomilla
(Sp; SW). A white or cream horse with a white mane and tail. (Ramon Adams 1944). Contemporary descriptions in the nineteenth century show some confusion with the *palomino* and with the *paint-horse.*

palomino
(Sp: dove). Also **California sorrel.** A horse of a particular golden color, originally thought to have been the grayish-golden shade of the dove. Known in Old Spain as *Isabellas,* after the queen.

Palouse
See *Appaloosa.*

palo verde
(Sp: green stick; SW). *Cercidium microphyllus.* When this plant blooms in April and early May, it attracts insects to its nectar and bees to its bright yellow flowers. While consuming moisture for the rest of the year, it is more or less leafless. In Arizona, it is found in washes and arroyos, and in places throughout the desert country in spring flood areas, from sea level to 3,500 feet. When it blooms, the entire area is covered with yellow. (Rossi 1975)

panhandle
A narrow extension of a state or territory sticking out from that area as a handle sticks out from a pan. For example, the Texas panhandle. Not necessarily a Westernism.

panning
The act of washing soil or sand in a water-filled pan (see *batea*) so that the unwanted dirt was washed away, leaving the desired gold behind. Usually applied to gold, but could also apply to the panning of silver and other metals. (Winslow 1952)

panocha
(Mex-Sp; SW). Also **panoche**. Unrefined sugar. It was also used as a term for sweetmeats or candy. (Mathews 1951)

pansaje
(Mex-Sp; SW). A social meal taken in the open air. Not quite a picnic, more a barbecue including groaning tables and animals roasted whole. (Mathews 1951)

panther
See *cougar.*

▶ **papoose**
Originally an Algonkian word, but used generally by Westerners to refer to an Indian child. (Mathews 1951)

parada
(Mex-Sp). A main herd of cattle. Probably the basis of the Anglo *parade.* (Weseen 1934; Ramon Adams 1944)

parade
A main herd of cattle on a drive or gather. (Andy Adams 1909). Probably connected with the Mexican term *parada.*

parara
An old variant of *prairie.*

pard
A very common abbreviation for *pardner,* a term in itself in common use, especially among cow-crews. A direct equivalent of the more modern *buddy.* (Wentworth 1944)

pardner
Comrade, friend, side-kick. Not truly a Westernism, but as commonly used as its abbreviation *pard*—in the earlier days, probably more so. See also *partner* (*2*). (Wentworth 1944)

parfleche
A word that came into the West from Canada. Mathews 1951 says authoritatively that it is made up of *parer* (to parry) and *flèche* (arrow), because it could be applied to a shield which was made of hide. The term was used widely to refer to a hide, usually one of buffalo, which had been cleaned, dehaired, and dried. By extension, it referred to an article made of that hide, such as a container or a plain hide saddle. Spelling it **parflesh** (a nice and pointed transition brought about by misunderstanding), Rux-

ton 1849 used it to mean the soles of footwear made of buffalo hide. Seen as **parflesh** and **porflesh,** it is used by Berrey and van den Bark 1942 to cover a cowboy's tucker-bag or *warbag.* Today it is generally accepted as a term once used by *voyageurs* and Mountain Men for an Indian packing-case or portmanteau. Rarely used in the Southwest. (Schultz 1935; Ramon Adams 1944)

parihuela
(Mex-Sp; SW). A hod for carrying ore.

park
A term most used in the Rocky Mountain regions, particularly Colorado, referring to meadow land in the midst of timber.

parker
A cowboy's heavy bed-quilt. Probably from *parka,* the hooded garment of the Canadian Northwest and Alaska. (Weseen 1934; Wentworth 1944 records the term in camp use in the Texas panhandle in 1933)

partida
(Mex-Sp). A band, a small bunch. Could be applied to men or cattle.

partner
(1) In a land largely lacking women, partnership could take on a deep significance and often bring to life spiritual and moral values in men who would have laughed if such things had been mentioned to them. A partner was a man to be trusted, who sided with you against the rest of the world; hence, if treachery showed itself in the relationship, the bitterness that resulted was great. Some of the major quarrels in the West were between men who had been partners.
(2) A term used in addressing another in familiarity and friendship, but not necessarily to one's partner. Also **pard, pardner.**

pasear
To walk. Although pure Spanish, it was handled nonchalantly and commonly both as a noun and a verb: "He took a pasear down the street" or even: "He paseared around town." It could also be used generally as a noun, to cover a trip. (Weseen 1934; Ramon Adams 1944; Berrey and van den Bark 1942)

paseo
(Sp: a walk or ride). To walk or ride for pleasure. (Mathews 1951)

paso
(Sp; SW). Dobie 1930 describes it as:
(1) A pass, a ford.
(2) A double-step, six feet.

pastor
(Sp). A sheepherder of Mexico or New Mexico, usually an Indian or a Mexican, though some were Basques. In use in the 1840s to the present time. (Dobie 1930)

patch
Also **patching.** The greased or waxed piece of cloth used to seat a ball for firing a muzzle-loader. Not a Westernism.

patron
(Sp *patrón;* SW).
(1) The owner of a large estate or ranch would be so addressed by his Mexican hands and servants.
(2) A patron saint. (Dobie 1930)

paulin
See *tarp.*

pay dirt
Earth or the bed of a river with gold or silver in it; also the gold or silver itself. To **hit pay dirt** was also used to describe the act of anybody suddenly coming into possession of a large sum of money. The word *pay* was used in conjunction with a number of other terms in the same sense, such as **claim, gravel,** and **ledge.**

payote
See *peyote.*

peace dance
A dance performed in various forms by most Indian tribes to celebrate and give thanks after war for a state of peace.

Peacemaker
The Colt Revolver Model 1873. The innovation that helped make this the finest and most famous weapon of its kind was that its .44 ammunition fitted the Winchester repeating carbine made in the same year. (Bowman 1953)

peace pipe
Also **pipe of peace.** A pipe smoked by Indians ceremonially to seal a peace in a sacred manner between warring people.

peace talk
Negotiations between warring Indian peoples or between Indians and whitemen, or even between whitemen themselves, to decide if a state of peace was possible between the opponents.

peacherino
Something excellent—a good horse, a pretty girl. (Wentworth 1944)

peal
See *pial.*

pear
See *prickly pear.*

peck
On the peck: on the prod, aggressive, looking for trouble. (Weseen 1934)

pecos
(SW). To kill by drowning; literally, to throw into the Pecos River. (Dobie 1930)

pedregal
(Sp: stony place). Throughout the West the Anglos gave the same meaning as the Mexicans to this word. Dunn 1886: "It is what is known in scientific parlance, as also locally in the West, as a pedregal (pay-dray-gahl), a name adopted from the Spanish, meaning a stony place."

peel
To peel a horse was to break him. (Weseen 1934). Hence, **peeler:** a horse-breaker; **peeling:** to ride or stay on a bucking horse. (Mora 1950)

peeps
Chicks. (Weseen 1934)

pegger
A *cutting horse* trained and skilled in the art of turning sharply. (Berrey and van den Bark 1942)

pelado
A term of contempt for the lower order of Mexican; a shiftless man of doubtful honesty and no visible means of support. (*Harper's Monthly Magazine* 1875; Dobie 1930)

pellote
See *peyote.*

peltry
Also **pelt**. The skin and fur of an animal (such as fox, beaver, etc.) which was sold by trappers for profit. (Farmer 1889; Carl Russell 1967)

pemmican
Farmer 1889 says that the name "consists of the two Konestino words *pemis,* which means fat, and *egan,* the general substantive inflection, so that the whole implies 'fat-substance.' It consists mainly of buffalo meat— though other meat is sometimes used in the same manner—dried in flakes and then pounded between two stones." The powder was put into skin bags and fat poured in. Sometimes berries or cherries were included in the mixture. It constituted the staple winter diet of many Indian tribes. (Schultz 1935)

pen
A corral; an enclosure in which to hold cattle, sheep, horses, or hogs. The term implies a somewhat limited size.

peon
(Sp). In the original sense, a man who was one grade above a slave among the Mexicans, held by debt in the employ of a landowner. The word is roughly the equivalent of *peasant,* but unlike peasants in most countries, a peon did not possess land. Later, the name was used to cover any lowly Mexican laborer. (Dobie 1930)

pepperbox
Also **coffee mill**. An early development of the revolving pistol, in which the cylinder consisted of a number of barrels consolidated into one moving part. This gave it the appearance of a pepperbox, hence the name. They were cap-and-ball (see ***cap-and-ball gun***). (Bowman 1953)

peraira, perara
See *prairie.*

persuader
(1) A bull whip. (Willison 1952)
(2) A six-gun. (Ramon Adams 1944)
(3) A spur. (Ramon Adams 1944)

peyote
Lophophora williamsii. A variety of spineless cactus from which a hallucinatory drug sometimes referred to as ***mescal*** can be made. The drug is used by devotees of various Indian religions under socially controlled conditions to attain spiritual experience and vision and can be taken as a drink or in the form of a button. Peyote is a corruption of the Aztec word *peyotl* and is seen in such various written forms as **payote, pellote,** etc.

Dobie 1930 says it is the *raíz diabólica* of the Southwest. (Waters 1950; Safford 1916)

pial
(1) Also **peal, piale** (Weseen 1934). A classic rope-throw, made usually from the back of a running horse. Who better to describe it than Jo Mora 1950? "The 'piale' was a throw tossed underhand right back of the front legs under the belly of the running quarry, the loop opening up so that the hind legs stepped into it."
(2) A rope.

picked brand
A cow-thief's trick, in which the owner's brand mark was removed by picking out the hairs, leaving a bare spot which later would grow over. (Berrey and van den Bark 1942; North 1942; Ramon Adams 1944). See also *sleeper (1)*.

picket pin
Also **lariat pin** (Mathews 1951), **stake pin** (Dobie 1930), **hitch pin**. A pin or stake, usually of metal but sometimes of wood, carried by horsemen on the plains, where there was no other means of tying a horse. This pin could be driven deeply into the ground, leaving a few inches above the surface, probably with a ring on it to which the horse's line could be fastened. Hence, **to picket:** to tether a horse by such a stake. The pin would seem secure enough to hold any animal, but horse-stealing Indians had methods of so alarming mules and horses that they would pull their pins and stampede ahead of the raiders. Longer pins could be placed at some distance from each other and be connected by a **picket line,** to which a number of horses could be tied. Such a line was also called a **picket rope** (Vestal 1939) or **stake rope,** and was best made of hemp or such, because wolves and coyotes like to gnaw through rawhide. To **cut your picket pin** was a phrase expressing the act of departing. (Ramon Adams 1944; Berrey and van den Bark 1942)

Picket Wire
The Purgatoire River, which flowed through what was once northeast New Mexico and is now Colorado; it joined the Arkansas River near Bent's Fort.

piebald
A horse with patches of white and black coloring.

pigging string
Also **piggin' string**. A short length of string, usually of rawhide, used to tie three legs of an animal together to assist in immobilizing it while being branded. When this was done, the animal was said to be hog-tied. A cowman would invariably carry a number of such strings in his pockets. (Wentworth 1944)

piket
The polecat (see *polecat [1]*). (Weseen 1934)

pile the rope into
To rope an animal. (Weseen 1934)

pilgrims
(1) Cows of Eastern stock. Also **barnyard stock, States cattle.**
(2) Men inexperienced in the ways of the West. Greenhorns. (Ramon Adams 1944; Weseen 1934)

pimple
The cowboy's name for the postage stamp the Easterners called a saddle. (Weseen 1934; Berrey and van den Bark 1942; Ramon Adams 1944)

pine-straw
Dead pine needles. (Weseen 1934)

pin grass
See *alfilaria.*

pinnacle
(Texas). A hill of any kind, large or small. (Andy Adams 1909; Allen 1933; Weseen 1934)

pinole
(Mex-Sp from Nahuatl *pinnoli*). Parched corn flour mixed with flour from the mesquite bean (sweetened) or with sugar and spice. Seen also as **pinol, pinola.** Pinole was also made from the flour of any edible bean, and from pinole frijoles were made. (Gregg 1844)

piñon
(Sp: pine nut). Also **pinion, pinyon.** Any of a number of dwarf pines (including *Pinus edulis, Pinus monophylla,* and *Pinus parryana*) which bore edible nuts that were part of the Indian diet. The nuts were sometimes referred to as **piñones.** (Dobie 1930)

pinto
(1) A horse colored brown and white, black and white, or white with brown and black. See *paint-horse* for the long argument about the differences between that and pinto. Richard Glyn's *The World's Finest Horses and Ponies* (1971) lumps paint, pinto, and calico together, quite rightly in my opinion. This authority, it should be noted, contradicts my entry under

paint-horse and says that this horse was greatly favored by cattlemen in the West. (Weseen 1934; North 1942; Wentworth 1944)
(2) A spotted bean. (Dobie 1930)
(3) A kidney bean. (Mathews 1951)

pipe of peace
See *peace pipe.*

pirooting
(SW). Fooling around. One of my favorite Western words. Dobie 1930 thinks that it is probably from *pirouetting.*

pita
(Mex-Sp; SW). Fiber obtained from a number of different plants, but usually the agave, to make hemp, nets, bags, ropes, etc. (Gregg 1844)

pitahaya
(Mex-Sp; California and SW). A term used freely by the Mexicans and Californios for a number of organ-pipe cacti, but more properly applicable to *Lemaireocereus thurberi* (called by the Mexicans also *Pitihaya dulce*) and *Carnegiea gigantea,* also correctly called the **sagarro, saguaro, suhuaro,** etc.

pitcher
A horse given to bucking. (Rollins 1922)

pitted
Said of cattle that were caught in deep holes from which they could not escape without aid. They were usually roped out. (Berrey and van den Bark 1942). Ramon Adams 1944 says: "When cattle are caught in a corner or a draw during a snowstorm."

P.K.
Polecat (see *polecat [1]*). (Weseen 1934)

placer mining
The mining of gold-bearing gravel or sand. A **placer** was a location of sand or gravel in which gold was found. (Willison 1952)

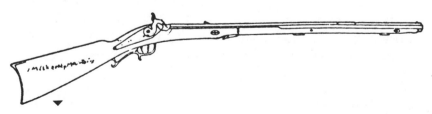

plains rifle
There are two explanations of this term, and I have little doubt they

are both correct. The original requirement was for a "plain rifle," a utilitarian weapon for use on the plains and for trade with the Indians by the companies crossing the plains. This did indeed develop into the "plains rifle," a name which took the place of the "mountain rifle." The latter was long-stocked and long-barreled, the former short-stocked and short-barreled. Shortening of the barrel probably took place because steel was scarce on the plains and, when the muzzle was damaged, it was simply sawn off. The plains rifle was not confined to any geographic locality, in spite of its name: many manufacturers made many types of rifles under this category, all of which (notably the *Hawken*) are listed and described in remarkable detail by Carl Russell 1967. (Sawyer 1920; Barsotti 1956)

plateau
Dunn 1886: "A divide or watershed is called a coteau; table-land or mesa is always a plateau; a hill is a butte; a gulch, ravine or arroyo is a coulie." He was writing of the Northwest country; the equivalents were all of French origin.

platform spring wagon
See *spring wagon.*

play a lone hand
To act alone on one or every occasion. (Weseen 1934)

played out
To be spent, finished. A gold vein could **play out,** become worthless.

plew
(1) Mountain-Man term for the whole skin of a beaver. (Ruxton 1849)
(2) Pipe plug tobacco. (Rossi 1975)

plow chaser
A farmer, from a cowboy's viewpoint. (North 1942)

plug
A broken-down horse. (Dobie 1930)

plumb
Complete, full, very, absolutely: "He hit the target plumb center." The language of the Westerner at its simplest and best. (Ruxton 1849; Rossi 1975)

poco pronto
(Mex-Sp). A little more than pronto—in fact, immediately. (Weseen 1934)

point
To **ride point** was to lead the trail-herd and keep it directed. The two point-riders (see *pointers*) were the most trusted of the trail-crew.

pointers
Also **point-riders** (Ramon Adams 1944), **point men.** Trail-drivers riding *point.* Whereas other men might change their positions during the drive, usually the pointers did not. (Mathews 1951)

poke
A small sack; a small leather, rawhide, or skin container such as that used to hold gold dust. This word has altered somewhat in its general use in U.S. dialects and local language to mean a paper sack, etc., but in the West of 1850–1900 it had the first meaning. An old word from British-English dialect. (Moor 1823; Wentworth 1944)

polecat
(1) A loosely used term for skunk creatures of genus *Mephitis.* Mostly called skunk in the Southwest; also, rather neatly, **wood-pussy** (Weseen 1934; Berrey and van den Bark 1942; Ramon Adams 1944), also **essence pedlar, piket, P.K.** This smart animal amused early travelers with his handstands, but they were not amused when, on feeling threatened, it secreted a nauseous liquid. (Mathews 1951). Not a polecat in the European sense.
(2) The line-back cattle of Texas. (Dobie 1941)
(3) Polecat flowers, the wild lantana. (Dobie 1965)
(4) A low-life, no-good hombre.

pole fence
Much the same as *snake-fence.* A fence constructed without uprights. The horizontal poles rested upon each other almost end on end and, to maintain support, were set at a slight angle to each other, forming a zigzag. (Mathews 1951)

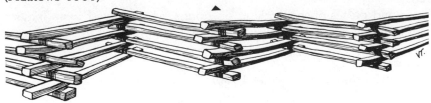

policeman
See *town marshal.*

polled
Hornless; referring to hornless cattle, **muleys** (see *muley [1]*). Not a Westernism; still used in British-English. (Rossi 1975)

pommel
Front portion of a saddle (the fork), attached to the side-bars. Andy Adams 1909 seems to extend the meaning to include the horn when he writes: "and within the hour, brush began to arrive, dragged from the pommels of saddles, and was piled in the stream." Not a Westernism.

pommel bags
Saddlebags up front of a saddle. Sometimes **cantinas** (see *cantina [3]*). (Rossi 1975)

pomo
(Mex-Sp: apple). The pommel of a Mexican saddle. The Mexicans also called it *manzana* (apple), a term which included the horn. **Apple** was also used by Anglos to refer to the horn.

poncho
(Mex-Sp). Also **ponchar**. Usually a blanket with a hole in it, through which a man put his head and neck so that it served as a cloak. Some, such as those used by the U.S. army, were made of oiled cloth. (Ramon Adams 1944; Mathews 1951)

pony
As in *cowpony*. Rather rare among Old Westerners.

Pony Express
An express mail service that created records in carrying light-weight mail and papers across the continent during the years 1860–62 from St. Joseph, Missouri, to Sacramento, California. The riders were mostly young boys, who experienced great dangers. The service proved uneconomical and could not compete with the telegraph. The exciting story of the Pony Express is told by Robert West Howard in *Hoofbeats of Destiny* (1960).

pook
Shells and pieces of shells, slung on strings, which served some Indian peoples, such as the Mohawks, as money. (Whipple 1855)

poor doe
Any inferior deer meat. (Dobie 1930)

poppers
In the early days, cattlemen were to be found driving cattle with whips having a popper—a separate strip of buckskin—attached at the end of the lash to add a louder note to the cracking of the whip. For this same reason, it was not uncommon through all the trail-driving years to find drovers with buckskin poppers at the ends of their ropes. It is interesting to note here the difference in the driving and catching techniques

of the American cowboy and the Australian stockman: the latter retained the whip as the main tool of his trade. The popper, however, was most commonly seen on the tips of whips in the hands of muleskinners and ox-team drivers.

porflesh
See *parfleche.*

porcion
(Sp *porción*). An allotment or portion of land. (Dobie 1930)

possible sack
Also **possible bag.** Originally indicating an Indian form of saddlebag, this term was not a Westernism but one used by the Mountain Men when referring to a sack in which they carried their personal effects. The term was retained by the cattlemen. (Rossi 1975; Ruxton 1849)

'possum belly
(Texas). Also **bitch, caboose, cooney, cradle.** A cowhide slung under a chuck wagon for carrying fuel—wood, buffalo chips, or cowchips. (Dobie 1941)

potrero
(Mex-Sp; SW).
(1) Pasture land, sometimes fenced and sometimes not. Jo Mora 1950: "We were first going to hunt in the Forest Reserve and had emerged from the woods into a fine potrero that stretched before us like a great bowl in the mountains." (Dobie 1929)
(2) A herder of young horses, based on the word *potro* (colt). (Mathews 1951)
(3) A narrow ridge between canyons. (Mathews 1951)

potro
One sees various interpretations of this word. The Spanish meaning is a colt, and this was its general meaning in the West. Anglos in the Southwest also used it sometimes to mean an unbroken young stallion and, by extension, wild horses in general. (Berrey and van den Bark 1942; Ramon Adams 1944)

pot rustler
See *rustler (4).*

powders
Orders from the boss. (Weseen 1934)

prairie
(Fr: meadow). Generally, open land—either rolling or flat—covered with wild grass. Variously interpreted. A word that became established when the French occupied parts of North America from Canada to the Caribbean. Seen also as **peraira** (Ruxton 1849; Mathews 1951), **parara, perara, prer-ie, priory,** etc. It took on the meaning of the country in which it was used: for example, a plainsman would mean a vast expanse of grassland; a brasada Texan might mean a large opening or glade in the brush-country. (Wentworth 1944)

prairie butter
The fat and juices left after cooking meat. Prairie farmers would spread this on bread—when they had bread. (Shepherd 1884)

prairie chicken
A term covering several species of grouse that inhabited the prairie country:
(1) The **sage grouse** (*Centrocercus urophasianus*), a fairly large bird and almost wholly dependent on the fruit, leaves, and twigs of the sage (*Artemisia tridentata*).
(2) The **greater prairie chicken** (*Tympanuchus cupido*), a blackish-brown bird with a light tawny color above, white with barring underneath, and an erect feather "ear" on each side of its neck.
(3) The **lesser prairie chicken** (*Tympanuchus pallidicinctus*), which inhabited semi-desert country and was smaller and paler than the greater prairie chicken.
(4) The **sharp-tailed grouse** (*Pedioecetes phasianellus*), possessing a higher-pitched voice than the ordinary prairie chicken. (Mathews 1951; Grzimek 1974)

prairie chips
Buffalo chips (and possibly later, cowchips), used for fuel in the treeless prairie country of the Great Plains. (Hough 1897)

prairie clipper
A large wagon used in the trade with New Mexico. Obviously some connection with the idea of the clipper ship and the term *Prairie Schooner* for a plains wagon. (Vestal 1939)

prairie coal
Buffalo chips and, by extension, cowchips, used as fuel. (Dobie 1941; Ramon Adams 1944)

prairie dog
The ground squirrel of the prairie. There are
several species, but the main one is *Cynomys ludovicianus.* Burrowing animals, they live in settlements called **prairie dog towns,** which at one time extended for a number of miles and covered vast areas. The holes were a menace to horsemen: many a horse broke a leg or fell as a result of stepping into a hole belonging to these little animals. Sandoz 1958 uses the verb **to prairie dog.** (Mathews 1951; Dobie 1965; Grzimek 1974)

prairie feathers
Prairie grass used as bed-tick stuffing. (Rossi 1975)

prairie grass
The several varieties of grass found originally on the Great Plains.

prairie oysters
Bulls' testicles—a delicious fry. (Jennings 1971)

prairie schooner
A boat-shaped wagon in which it is popularly,
but wrongly, supposed all westward migration took place. Drawn commonly by oxen, but also by horses and mules.

prairie strawberries
Beans. Fletcher 1968: "We bought a supply of provisions in Dodge City, including a keg of pickles. During the entire trip we had tasted no vegetables other than beans or 'prairie strawberries' as some called them." (Ramon Adams 1944)

prairie turnip
See *camas (1).*

prairie wolf
See *coyote.*

prairie wool
Grass. (Weseen 1934; Ramon Adams 1944)

praties
Potatoes. (Weseen 1934). Originally found in Anglo-Irish.

prayer book
A packet of cigarette papers.

prer-ie
See *prairie.*

presidente
(Sp). The owner of a ranch. (Weseen 1934)

presidio
(Sp). A fort. (Dobie 1930)

▶ **prickly pear**
The fruit and cactus of the genus *Opuntia.* Dobie 1941: "The prickly pear leaves, on which
the Longhorns could go indefinitely without
drinking water, analyze up to eighty per cent
fluid, though in droughts the percentage shrinks to a much lower figure."
The author informs us that a poultice may be made from it against its own
and other cactus thorns. Burned, to remove the thorns, it could be fed to
Longhorns; Mathews 1951 states that the cattle could eat prickly pears
with the thorns *on.*

priory
See *prairie.*

prod
Anyone or anything—whiteman, Indian, or cattle—wanting to do battle
was **on the prod.** This phrase was certainly in use during the 1870s and
probably a good deal earlier. It must have originated with the Texas cattle,
which showed a tendency to go on the prod after they had been roped
out of the brush or thrown; that's why cowboys wore spurs or carried quirts
around their wrists: they were the cowman's only means of sudden acceleration out of trouble. One of the best and most descriptive of Western
expressions. Man or beast in a prodding mood was said to be **proddy.** A
man could also be said to be **on the peck.** (Wentworth 1944)

prod pole
A long-hafted pole for prodding cattle, usually with a headless nail on the
tip as a goad. Employed by cow- or bull-punchers on cattle-trains to keep
cows on their feet during the long journeys on the railroad. (Ramon Adams
1944)

pronghorn
Antilocapra americana. Male: **prongbuck.** Although called an antelope,
it is not one, but a unique survivor from the past. Notable for its great

speed, it is too fast for greyhounds, wolves, and coyotes, and its agility is illustrated by the fact that it can leap over or through barbed-wire fences. Although their herds were of enormous numbers, they never over-grazed a range and, feed-for-animal, were economically produced meat, far more so than cattle. You could say that their curiosity killed them. They even followed wagon trains, offering themselves as targets. Not surprisingly, they were reduced from approximately 40 million to about 19,000 but have now risen to about 400,000. Their slaughter must have equaled

that of the buffalo, though writers have dealt slightly with the subject. Grzimek 1974 writes: "Along the line from Denver to Cheyenne in the winter of 1868/9, daily wagon-loads of dead pronghorns were brought to town. Along the rail line lived three to four million head. Three to four of the animals were sold for 25 cents. . . . When the p[ronghorn] perceives a wolf, or coyote or something unusual in his environment, he spreads the long stiff white hairs on the rear flatly apart so that they flash . . . actually reflect the light. Other pronghorns can see this signal over a distance of several kilometres." Added to this signal is a gland secretion which can be smelled even by humans over 100 meters. (McHugh 1972)

pronto
(Sp). Quickly. In the sense: "Do it now." Common among Anglos. A man might say: "Vamoose, pronto." (Dobie 1930)

prospect
The place where a search for minerals occurred; also, the actual searching for the minerals—also seen as **prospecting** (Buffum 1850). (Mathews 1951)

prospector
One who searched after minerals—and, in the West, this usually meant gold or silver, and more likely gold at that. What kind of a man a prospector was depended much on the time and place. In the goldrushes, many of them were ordinary Easterners of all walks of life, trying to get rich quickly; most of them knew little about the finding of gold and went where the rush went. Rather than prospectors, they were **gold-hunters**. A prospector often worked alone or with one or two partners. In dangerous country, he might search the hills in carefully selected company for mutual protection against Indians. Prospectors usually employed burros as their beasts of burden, and most of them preferred to travel afoot. (Buffum 1850)

prove
(1) To sample a vein of ore while mining in order to find its worth.
(2) To **prove up** on a land claim: to carry out the conditions of the home-steading laws and other land laws, by improvement of the land and by a recognized period of residence, so that legal claim could be made.

prowl
To hunt cattle. (Weseen 1934; Ramon Adams 1944)

public land
Also **public domain**. Land which was considered to belong to a territorial, state, or federal government. Some of the local troubles in the West were caused by cattle barons holding such land against all comers: settlers naturally considered that they had the right to settle it. Trouble also could be caused by the fencing in of such land without any legal claim. In literature, the term is closely connected to that of **free range** (see *free grass*), range upon which anybody could throw his cattle or sheep.

puddle-jumper
See *rattler (2)*.

pueblo
(Mex-Sp; SW and W). A Mexican village or town. It was also employed by the Spaniards in reference to Indian villages in which the buildings were of adobe or brick or stone. The Spaniards extended the word to cover those Indians who lived in such villages—Pueblos, Puebleños. (Cooke 1878)

pull leather
To hold on to the saddle while riding a pitching horse. (Weseen 1934; Ramon Adams 1944; Wentworth 1944; McCarthy 1936). Weseen adds: "To feel insecure in any matter."

pulperia
(Mex-Sp *pulpería*). In the old sense of this word, a store in which liquor was not only sold but drunk. It was anglicized without the accent on the penultimate syllable and applied more to a Mexican establishment than to an Anglo one. Certainly in use during the first part of the nineteenth century in the Southwest. (Mathews 1951)

pulque
(Mex-Sp from Nahuatl; SW). An alcoholic liquor fermented from the agave. (Ball 1970)

pulqueria
(Mex-Sp *pulquería*, from Nahuatl; SW). A store selling *pulque*. (Ruxton 1847)

puma
See *cougar.*

punch
There is much controversy over the origin of this word and its true original meaning. One theory is that it began with the punching or prodding of cattle with long poles on the railroad cars to keep them on their feet. However, as early as 1870, the word was recorded in Virginia as referring to driving loose cattle with sticks. Hence, we have the words **cow-puncher** or **puncher** from some source unknown, which came to mean a cowhand. (Weseen 1934; Wentworth 1944; Ramon Adams 1944)

punk
(1) Described variously in old dictionaries as touchwood or wood made rotten by the growth of fungus: in short—tinder. The word is said to be of Indian origin, and Mathews 1951 points out that the Delaware word *punk* means "ashes." (The word has also been related to *spunk*.) In the days before lucifers and self-igniting matches, every man carried steel, flint, and punk for making fire. The word was used by the early-seventeenth-century settlers on the Eastern Seaboard. Speaking of the Mountain Men, Ruxton 1849 explains: "Their bullet-pouches always contain a flint and steel, and sundry pieces of punk," which the author describes as a "pithy substance found in dead pine-trees." Though matches were in fairly wide use in the 1840s, men in far places who had to rely on their own resources still used flint, steel, and punk for their fire through the 1860s and probably into the following decade as well. Dried buffalo dung, powdered with the fingers, also served as punk.
(2) The word was also used generally in the United States to refer to a blow with the fist or something second-rate and rotten: a low person, a petty thief. (Captain Eugene F. Ware, *The Indian War of 1874,* quoted in Rifkin 1967; Dobie 1941; Bartlett 1877)

pup
(1) A small side-branch of a main gulch or stream.
(2) A single-shot percussion pistol. A Mountain-Man term. (Barsotti 1956)

pure quill Indian
A pure Indian; a wild Indian, one independent of the whiteman. Of the former sense, Dobie 1956 writes: "Among the Indians . . . was a young Mexican man. Unconsciously, he soon turned all interest upon himself. Both in dress and feature, he looked a 'pure quill' Indian." Dobie 1930 also gives **quill:** a pure-blood Indian, adding "of Mexico."

put on tallow
In reference to cattle, to put on fat. The word *tallow* was used no doubt because in Texas, before a good market was found for live cattle, men who owned Longhorns had to find other ways of turning cows into cash, and one of them was to send them to the tallow factories. Many a Texas candle burned on the tallow of cattle. (Weseen 1934)

put on the morral
To eat. To **put on the nose-bag** or **feed-bag.** (Weseen 1934). See also *morral.*

put the string on
Also **put the loop on.** To rope. (Weseen 1934; Ramon Adams 1944)

put up
To **put up a herd** was to gather a herd of cows for the trail. While this term could be used to cover the activity of gathering the cattle of *one* outfit, it could also imply the gathering of several. Osgood 1929: "About all we know is that by the summer of 1866, herds of considerable size were crossing the Red, in some cases in charge of the owners, in others, in the hands of drovers, who 'put up' a herd, taking the cattle on credit and giving a list of brands and amounts due to the owners."

quail

The quail appears fairly frequently in the literature of the Old West and came in a number of varieties. In the more arid areas of Texas, Kansas, Colorado, and central Mexico was the scaled quail (*Cellipepla squamata*). In the dry areas of Mexico and the Southwest was the crested quail, the best-known species of which were the California quail (*Lophortyx californica*) and Gambel's quail (*Lophortyx gambelii*). These were common in the chaparral of oak and hardwood on the slopes and in the valleys of the Pacific coast. In New Mexico could be found the small harlequin or Montezuma quail (*Cyrtonyx montezumac*).

quamash

See *camas (1)*.

quarantine line

One of a number of lines drawn north to south in Kansas during the 1860s and 1870s, east of which Texas cattle were forbidden for fear of **Texas fever.** The most detailed account of these lines I know appears in Robert Dykstra's detailed 1971 study *The Cattle Towns*. (Sandoz 1958)

quarter section

See *hundred and sixty*.

quartillo

(Sp *cuartillo*). Also **quartilla**. A quarter of a *real,* a Mexican coin; said to be worth three cents. (Beadle 1878)

querencia

(Sp *querer:* to love). Used by Dobie 1941, meaning the place where one was born. The author referred to a cow that returned persistently to such a spot and says that the vaqueros used the word in Texas specifically for a Longhorn's birthplace.

querida
(Sp; SW). Dear, darling, sweetheart.

quick-draw artist
A man adept at producing his six-shooter quickly from leather. (Ramon Adams 1944)

quick on the trigger
Hasty, a human at half-cock. (Weseen 1934)

quien sabe?
(Sp *¿quién sabe?*).
(1) Who knows? (Dobie 1930)
(2) The Texan's term for a Mexican cattle-brand which was so complicated that at the sight of it a man would scratch his head and say: "Who knows?"
(3) Weseen 1934 gives: "A secret brand used on mavericks," meaning, possibly, an unknown brand used by cow-thieves.

quill
See *pure quill Indian.*

quirly
Originally a cigarette made with a corn-shuck for paper. Thus, something that has been twirled. Ramon Adams 1944 says it is merely a cowboy's term for a cigarette.

▶ **quirt**
(Sp *cuerda:* cord; Mex-Sp *cuarta:* horsewhip). Also **cuerta**. A short-handled riding whip with the butt often loaded; essentially a horseman's tool. Andy Adams 1909: "If a rider carried a quirt, he usually dispensed with spurs. . . ." Like whittling, the plaiting of quirts was a great spare-time occupation of the more skilled of the working cow-hands, and some produced beautiful work. Most Plains Indians (possibly because they were bootless and did not wear spurs) also used the quirt. Like their saddles, these were of a rather cruder pattern than those of the whiteman, usually composed of a simple wooden handle, from one end of which hung several rawhide lashes, each about one foot long. Both whiteman and Indian employed a wrist-loop at the butt so that the quirt could be carried while the whip-hand was otherwise employed. In his painting *Salute to the Fur Trade* (for which see Rossi and Hunt 1971), Charlie Russell (1864–1926) shows a Blackfoot carrying a quirt made from an elk-antler, as was common among Indians of the northern plains.

ragline
See *grass rope.*

raiz diabolica
(Mex-Sp *raíz diabólica:* devil root; SW). The drug **peyote,** or **mescal**
buttons. (Dobie 1930)

ramada
(Sp; SW). A shelter of brush or some similar material; an arbor. (Dobie
1941). Hence, **ramaderos:** thickets. Dobie 1941 writes: "They acquired
about ten thousand acres of land. There were prairies on them then,
though *ramaderos* of dense brush and montes of chaparral [see **monte**
(1)] bordered and cut into the openings."

ranahan
The Northwest equivalent for the Southwest's *top-hand* on a cow-spread.
Shortened to **ranny.** (Weseen 1934; Berrey and van den Bark 1942;
Ramon Adams 1944)

ranch
(Sp *rancho*). At first, this word referred to the land on which stock was
raised in the West and the buildings on that land, but it came to be applied
to any building or establishment on the trail. Often a trading post, stage
station, or even an eating place or whore-house would bear the name.
Finerty 1961: "Some ranches appeared at intervals . . . bearing the legend 'saloon' on their dingy fronts. As a rule it would be better for a traveler
to have some Indian lead in his carcase than a glass of ranch rot-gut in his
stomach." (Ramon Adams 1944; Weseen 1934; Berrey and van den Bark
1942)

rancheria
(Mex-Sp *ranchería:* settlement, camp; SW). An Apache encampment. In California, the word applied to any Indian camp. (Buffum 1850). Occasionally the term referred to the headquarters of a ranch. (Weseen 1934)

ranchero
(Sp). Rancher—particularly in the Southwest and California. (Dobie 1930; Hawgood 1967)

rancho
(Sp; SW). A ranch. The land or building thereon, where cattle and horses (and sometimes other animals) were raised. (Weseen 1934)

range
Generally employed in reference to a tract of land supporting cattle or sheep. In fact, land was not range till it was in general use for free-moving cattle, whether wild or not. A cattleman would refer to his range—meaning his spread, the land over which his cows grazed—although he might not have legal title to it. This would be free range (see *free grass*) and, in fact, anybody would have the right to graze his cattle on it. The word appeared in conjunction with other words which were self-explanatory: **cattle-range, sheep-range,** etc. One thing range could not be was cultivated; it was a place over which animals could wander in search of graze. (Osgood 1929)

range boss
The manager of a ranch who bossed the outfit so far as range work was concerned. (Ramon Adams 1944; Berrey and van den Bark 1942)

range bum
A man riding from ranch to ranch for free meals; a *chuck-line rider.* An out-of-work cowhand. Depressions hit the cattle-trade as they did any other in the last quarter of the nineteenth century. (Ramon Adams 1944)

range delivery
If a man bought cattle range delivery, he bought cattle on a range, accepting the estimate of the seller. This was a gamble taken fairly frequently, and sometimes great profit was made—as much as a 1,000 head over the estimate. The term is indicative of the times—the word of a man of good reputation was trusted. (Dobie 1941; Aldridge 1884)

range horse
As opposed to a wild horse or *mustang,* a broken, half-broken, or completely unbroken but branded horse allowed to roam the range until he was needed and caught up. Such a horse might have the attributes of survival belonging to the mustang and few of the disciplined characteris-

tics of the civilized horse. Both range horses and mustangs were great homers and would rather circle on the range they occupied than wander off it, unless, of course, times were bad and they pushed into strange country in search of food and water. Both kinds of animals were capable of surviving a bad winter by pawing through the snow to grass and eating the bark of trees. Some writers, not incorrectly, use the term to denote a horse trained to range work. (North 1942; Ramon Adams 1944)

range rights
One of those terms that varied with time and place. In early post–Civil War days, it could mean the rights a man demanded to public range (see *public land*), possibly based on a single land-claim or a checker-boarding of the range with claims, with as many as possible taking in water rights. (Osgood 1929; Webb 1931)

ranny
See *ranahan.*

ransation
I have found this word recorded only by Wentworth 1944, who dates it 1896 in north Texas: "Spiritual excitement at a revival."

rassel
Wrestle. For steer rasslin', man-fighting, etc. (Weseen 1934)

rastra
See *arrastra.*

ratonera
(Sp: mousetrap; SW). A snake's den. (Dobie 1965)

rattler
(1) A rattlesnake.
(2) Rossi 1975 adds: "A railroad train. Still used in western Nebraska in 1950s and probably elsewhere. Also called a **puddle-jumper.** A short-run train."

rattlesnake
A viper including numerous species of the genera *Sistrurus* and *Crotalus,* varying in size from the very small to the big diamond-back, which may be well over six feet long. Through the years, sightings of giant rattlers equal the  catching of giant fish, tempting one to ask the traveler in snake-country: "Seen any rattlers, you liar?" Whatever the old-timers may tell you, the age of a rattler cannot be told from its rattles, because the creature sheds them.

Rattlesnakes were one of the most generally hated and feared creatures of the West: the men of the Old West habitually killed them from a sense of duty. The rattlesnake's bite can be lethal, and the folk-medicine of Texans, Indians, and Mexicans is full of sure-fire antidotes. The most entertaining book on these snakes I know of is J. Frank Dobie's *Rattlesnakes* (1965). One of the rattler's pseudonyms is the **sidewinder,** which the wit of the Westerner applied also to a man of treacherous character.

rattlesnake milkweed

(SW). Also **Texas milkweed.** *Asclepias texana.* A weed which, when mashed, may be applied to a snake-bite or taken internally to combat the effects of a rattlesnake bite. (Dobie 1965)

rattlesnake root

A term used to cover any number of roots used locally as antidotes to the bite of a rattlesnake.

rattlesnake weed

Any number of wild plants which were used in the West and throughout the rural United States for the cure of rattlesnake bite. (Mathews 1951)

rattle your hocks

Get a move on, rustle. (North 1942)

raw bronc

An inexperienced or unbroken horse. (Weseen 1934)

rawhide

(1) This was just what it said it was—raw hide. It is difficult to imagine how the frontiersman would have managed without it. To answer the question: "What was it used for?" calls for the answer: "Everything." Which is not far short of the truth. It was the skin of, usually, a cow-crittur, dried in the sun. It could be used for ropes, whips, chaps, or anything else you fancied. It expanded when damp and contracted when dried. So you could mend a broken wheel with it; use it as joining material in the construction of a corral; make it into hinges for a door or a gate; sole your boots with it; even torture an enemy with it. Indians in the Southwest used playing cards made of it. Once hardened it was almost as tough as iron—hence the name **Mexican iron** (Berrey and van den Bark 1942; Ramon Adams 1944). The nearer you got to Mexico, the more rawhide you saw. Punishment in a trail-camp could be inflicted by beating a man with a rawhide; thus the expression **rawhiding.** The word *rawhide* could be combined with a number of other words to indicate anything in its raw and unprepared state: **rawhide lumber,** for example, was wood still green when used for carpentering.

(2) In the Northwest the word denoted a man up the trail from Texas. In

short, the Northwesterners not only noted that Texas men widely employed the material, they found the Texans as tough as rawhide. Also **rawhider**.
(3) By extension of *rawhiding*, above, came the meaning "to tease," "to annoy"; for a boss to drive a man hard.
(4) To catch up cattle on one's own.
(5) An old-timer.
(Dobie 1941; McCarthy 1936; Weseen 1934; Mora 1950)

rawhider
(1) A general term in the West, particularly in Texas and the Southwest, in application to movers (see ***mover***), who were often penniless and suspect. They used rawhide for every possible purpose, and their wagons seemed to be held together with the stuff.
(2) The owner of a shirt-tail cow-outfit (see ***shirt-tail outfit***).
(3) See ***rawhide (2)***.

raw one
A green, untrained saddle-horse. (Ramon Adams 1944)

razorbacks
Wild or near-wild hogs, the boars of which, when cornered, could be as dangerous as Longhorns. They were not native to America and are said to be descended from the animals, including 13 sows, brought in by the Spaniard de Soto—although most were but recently descended from domestic swine gone wild. In Texas they were rounded up each year and roped, cut, and marked like cattle. Like cattle, they also constituted an essential part of Texas economy: when the salting industry grew up in south Texas, along with the skinning trade (hide and tallow), the razorbacks throve and multiplied greatly. They were useful stock—the boars were long-tusked and could defend themselves against natural enemies; Indians and thieves found them almost impossible to run off. They usually fattened in the woods on mast in the fall; during the hot, lean months, they rooted enough to survive. They were speedy, slender-bodied, ridgebacked, and long-legged. When fat, they were immune to snake-bite. The only thing they had in common with the domestic pig was that their meat tasted something like pork. An unglamorous, unsung essential character of the Old West.

reach
The first hand-action in drawing a revolver. (Ramon Adams 1944; Dobie 1930)

reach for the sky
Put your hands up. (Weseen 1934)

ready-mades
See *tailor-mades*.

rear jockey
Sometimes called **back jockey** (Ramon Adams 1944; Rossi 1975). The top skirt of a saddle under the cantle.

reata
(Sp *reatar:* to tie again, to bring together). Also **riata** (Wentworth 1944). Like the ***grass rope,*** this was variously called and miscalled **lariat** (a variant of *la reata*), ***lasso,*** **lass rope, lazo, string,** etc. The reata, however, could only properly be made of rawhide, although the grass rope was sometimes given the term. It was braided, usually in four, six, or eight strands; the common rope for everyday heavy use was usually of four strands. This, if cared for, would last far longer than a grass rope, though rawhide could not take the great strain that a grass rope in good condition could. The making of good reatas was, and still is, a craft of the highest order and a reata-man would choose an evenly braided one of good young heifer skin for flexibility and to avoid the curse of the roper: kinks in the string. (Dobie 1930; Mora 1950). See also *rope; skin-string.*

reatero
(Mex-Sp; SW). A maker of reatas.

rebozo
(Mex-Sp; SW, west Texas, and California). A head and shoulder shawl worn by Mexican and some Indian women. (Ober 1885)

red eye
One of the many terms for whiskey. (Rossi 1975)

redman
Also **red man**. An Indian. (Ellis 1882)

regulators
Loosely speaking, another name for men who organized themselves in committees of vigilance when regular law had broken down. Such committees were always somewhat suspect and could often be the means by which old scores were paid off, but they filled a need. Not a Westernism.

reloading outfit
A cowboy term for fork, spoon, knife, cup, and plate. Another delightful Western term which I would have missed without the watchful eye of Paul Rossi 1975.

Remington
Although the name of this designer and manufacturer of fine guns never became a part of the popular imagination and language as did that of

Colt, his guns had their devotees among men who knew good weapons. Eliphalet Remington of Ilion, New York, made his first flint-lock muzzle-loader in 1816; by 1828, he had a thriving business. In 1845 his works produced his first standard arms in large batches for the armed forces, and at about this time his three sons joined him. The Civil War saw both sides using weapons of his pattern, but he manufactured exclusively for the North. After the war, more veterans purchased their Remingtons to take into civilian life than did the users of Colts (see also *colt [2]*).

Early war models, built to the Beal's patent, were massive but beautiful in design and good in balance, easily recognizable by the slope from the trigger to the tip of the lever-hammer. They weighed 2 pounds 14 ounces and were cap-and-ball (see *cap-and-ball gun*), single-action. A sample description of Beal's Army Model revolver: .44 caliber; eight-inch octagonal barrel; six shots, five-groove rifling; brass oval trigger-guard; walnut grips; blue finish. An estimated 3,000 were made between 1860 and 1862. This gun and those that followed were extremely popular in the West. It is interesting that the New Army and Navy models, patented in 1858 (see *army model; navy model*), were in manufacture till 1888 and 1875 respectively, showing the continued demand for cap-and-ball revolvers. Often, however, this type was converted for metal cartridge use. The firm produced a conversion system so that the gun-owner could exchange chambers and use the weapon for either loading. Remington also produced "derringers" (see *derringer*), pocket-revolvers, shot-guns, rifles, and carbines—all to be found all over the Old West. (Karr and Karr 1960; Bowman 1953)

Remington's old slide-action, Model 14

The story of the Remington rifle is as important to the West as it is to all lovers of good rifles. The firm took an important step in the evolution of the rifle with the introduction of the rolling-block breech, which not only greatly increased loading speed, but which, through the nature of its construction, became stronger at the moment of ignition. (See also *Springfield*.) The greater the recoil, in fact, the more tightly the parts of the breech were interlocked. Remington made variations on this basic design from 1867 to 1890. The early model met immediate popularity in the West. Nelson Story (a trail-driver) and his crew proved its capability when they fought off a large body of Sioux under Crazy Horse. The rifle became an international success, and you might say that Remington has never looked back. Today, it is difficult to find a peer of the Remington bolt-action rifle. (Peterson 1963)

remuda
(Mex-Sp). The saddle-horses of a ranch or a trail-outfit. Such horses were said to be **in remuda**. Occasionally, since about 1900, the term has been used in a slightly different sense to refer to a man's own string or mount. The remuda was in the charge of the wrangler (horse-wrangler, horse rustler, remudero), usually a less experienced and younger hand. (Dobie 1930; Weseen 1934; McCarthy 1936)

remudadero
(Mex-Sp; SW). The corral or pen in which a remuda was kept. Somewhat rare. (Mathews 1951)

remudera
(Mex-Sp; SW). A *bell-mare.* (Berrey and van den Bark 1942; Ramon Adams 1944)

remudero
(Mex-Sp; SW, Texas, and California). A *wrangler,* the man or boy who cared for the remuda, or horse-herd, of a ranch or cattle-drive. Dobie 1964: "I turned back towards our cattle, telling the cook to follow, which he did at a gallop. Then I halted the wagon, and had the remudero bring up the horses." (Mora 1950)

renig
To back out of an agreement, to welch. (Weseen 1934)

rep
(1) A cowhand who represented his outfit at a round-up or other ranches. Also used as a verb: "I **rep for** Charlie Goodnight." (Dobie 1930; Mora 1950)
(2) Reputation.

repeater
Sometimes, in the early days, used in reference to a revolver, but usually to a rifle capable of firing a number of shots without reloading.

resaca
(Mex-Sp; SW). A marsh. (Dobie 1930)

revolver
One cannot help wondering if the Old West as we know it would have existed without the revolver. Certainly the defeat of the Indians would have been delayed. And just as certainly fewer men would have accidentally shot themselves and innocent bystanders. Flint-lock revolvers were in limited use both in the United States and Europe at the beginning of the

nineteenth century, but they made no great impression on gun-handlers till Sam Colt came along with his adaptation of the cap-lock to the principle of the revolver. In 1835, at the age of 21, Colt patented it in England and the following year in the United States. His Paterson Colt was first used by the Texas Rangers in action against some astonished and, shortly after, mostly dead Comanches in 1844. (See *colt (2)* for the rest of the story.) These early guns were cap-and-ball (see *cap-and-ball gun*), and such weapons were used right into the 1870s. For a number of reasons, some gun-toters were reluctant to change to the new-fangled metallic cartridges which came into use in the late 1850s: they knew the old guns well; cap-and-ball, because it limited their shots, made them careful; the loading of the old guns was more economic; and cartridges were not always easily obtainable. There were a number of pretty good guns beside Colts, guns that seldom seem to get a mention outside specialist books—Remington, Starr, Smith and Wesson, Le Mat, Irving, Trantor, Adams, and a good many others. Some of these ancient hog-legs were like young cannon and often weighed two to three pounds. It is said that the guns of 1850–70 could not be fired very accurately, but tests have shown that in good hands they compare quite favorably with modern weapons. However, their size prevented them from being drawn with the speed of modern guns. Most men, even at quite a late period, wore their weapons pretty high on the hip; most carried one gun on the right side for the orthodox draw. Incidentally, a much-favored position for a mounted man's gun was high on the left with the butt forward.

riata
See *reata.*

rib up
To persuade. (Dobie 1930)

rico
(Sp; SW). A rich man. (Dobie 1930)

ride herd
To herd cattle. Hence, to ride herd on anything was to guard it, to manage it. (Weseen 1934; Ramon Adams 1944; Wentworth 1944)

rider
(1) Although applied generally to a horseman, it was used in many instances for cowboy, cowhand.
(2) See *stake and rider.*

ride the fence
Also **riding fence.** To fence-ride on a cattle-ranch to check and repair the fence. (Weseen 1934). See also *line riders.*

ride the river with
A man to ride the river with was a man worth having along, one who would not fail you.

ridge runner
An inhabitant of high country. The term originally referred to cattle or horses but was later extended to men. An animal that stayed in high country to watch for danger. Thus, an outlaw on the run. (Ramon Adams 1944; Wentworth 1944)

riding line
Also **ride the line** (Weseen 1934; Ramon Adams 1944). Riding along the boundaries of a brand's range to see, from their *sign,* if cattle had strayed beyond the line or to catch animals in the act of straying and to turn them back onto their home range. In the later days, with the arrival of fences, the act became fence-riding or riding fence, but the old phrase stayed in use. See also *line riders; riding sign.*

riding sign
Riding the cattle-range in search of tracks and *sign* which would indicate that animals had strayed from their home range. It might also be applied to the act of following sign to come up with estrayed or stolen cattle. (Ramon Adams 1944). See also *riding line.*

riding slick
Riding a bucking horse without benefit of *bucking roll,* locked spurs, or other cheaters. (Rossi 1975)

riffle
A bar at the bottom of a *sluice-box;* so called because it caused riffles or ripples in the water. There might be a number of these bars in a box, and they were used by miners to catch the particles of gold and prevent them from being washed away. Such a sluice-box was called a **riffle-box** (Mathews 1951) or **ripple-box.** Certainly in use in the mid-nineteenth century. In general American-English, a *whiffle* referred to a similar obstacle (such as a small sand bar) in a waterway. (Buffum 1850)

rig
A saddle. Variously as *center-fire rig,* **Texas rig,** etc. (Ramon Adams 1944)

right-hand man
Strawboss, or second-in-command to a foreman. (Weseen 1934). Berrey and van den Bark 1942 and Ramon Adams 1944 disagree with Weseen and say "foreman."

rildy
A quilt. (Weseen 1934; Ramon Adams 1944; Wentworth 1944)

rimfire saddle
Also **rimmy**. A saddle with a forward-placed cinch. A *Spanish rig.* The rear of the saddle was inclined to rise when a rope-*dally* was made on the horn and there was a lot of steer on the other end of the rope. (Ramon Adams 1944; Foster-Harris 1955)

rimption
See *karimption.*

rincon
(Sp *rincón:* corner; SW). A sheltered nook—say in a canyon or a place protected by the spur of a hill.

ring bit
Also **chileno** in California and the Southwest. A metal ring used in place of a *curb-strap* around the lower jaw of a horse. Perfectly acceptable in the hand of a skillful horseman, torture for the horse with a rider who "rode the reins." (Mora 1950)

ring herd
To herd cows (usually troublesome ones) by keeping them moving in a circle to prevent their scattering. (Dobie 1941)

ringy
Also **ringey**. Riled up, mad, angry. (Rossi 1975)

rio
(Sp; SW). River.

ripple-box
See *riffle.*

roachback
A grizzly bear (Wentworth 1944)—a roach being a mass or line of hair that stands on end. The term **roachbacked** was applied to any animal whose hair stood out or was humped over its shoulders. Roosevelt 1964 used the term to cover any bear with long hair on its back and shoulders. (Mathews 1951). See also *hogbacked.*

road agent
A highway robber, a thief who generally at gun-point stopped stage-coaches to rob passengers of their possessions; or, if the vehicle carried

mail or bullion, that. Taking mail, of course, was a federal offense. There were few successful operators on a large scale. (Wentworth 1944)

road agent's spin
Also **Curly Bill spin** (Ramon Adams 1944). This move with a gun was said to have originated with "Curly Bill" Brocius (or Graham), who, when pretending to hand his gun to a lawman, reversed the weapon into his own hand by keeping his forefinger in the trigger-guard and shot the unfortunate lawman. (Cunningham 1934)

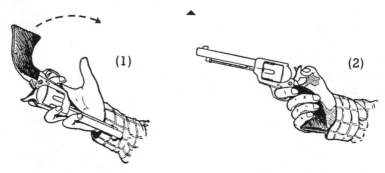

road branding
See *branding.*

road-broke
Also **trail-broke.** Cattle that were used to being herded and drifted slowly along in a drive. (Gard 1954)

road runner
Also **runner, runner bird.** *Geococcyx californianus.* The **chaparral cock.** Also **chaparral bird.** One much mentioned in Texas tales. Mexicans called it the *paisano* and *faisano,* also *corre camino, churrea,* and *churella.* Never did a small bird collect so many names. To remind us how like the cuckoo it was, it was also called the **ground cuckoo;** also **cock of the desert; lizard bird** (it ate lizards and other small creatures), **snake-killer** (Dobie 1929; Berrey and van den Bark 1942) and **snake-eater** (appropriate, as it was known to take on and kill rattlers). Best known for its habit of running through the chaparral ahead of horsemen and wagons on trails, hence its most popular name. However, it was not confined to the bush and was found in large numbers on the plains. There is a saying: "As crazy as a paisano." Dobie 1958 states that in Chihuahua, Mexicans used to capture the birds young and train them to catch rats and mice. The New Mexico state bird.

robes
Indian robes were either blankets (in the later years) or made from the whole hide of any large animal, made soft and pliable by much dressing.

Buffalo cow was the most common, but pelts from foxes, wolves, martens, and other animals were used. Among certain tribes, rabbit skins and the more delicate skins of birds were cut into ribbons and woven or twisted into material. Skin robes were much used by whites both in the East and West, as bed-covers, etc. (Hodge 1907–10)

rocker
A primitive instrument used in sorting gold from dirt, employed by small-scale miners. There were two methods—*panning* and rocking, both known to man for many hundreds of years. Winslow 1952: "A rocker, a Chinese invention, was a box worked like a cradle. The top of it was a hopper made with a perforated sheet-iron bottom. Two shovelfuls of dirt were thrown in, several dippers of water were poured on and the rocker moved back and forth until all the mud slid through onto an apron made of a double thickness of blankets. The holes in the hopper were a quarter of an inch in diameter, so that any nuggets in the dirt remained behind to be gathered up. Any grains which escaped the blanket fell upon a plate containing quicksilver, which retrieved the last trace of color before the water ran off. The water was caught and used over and over again. From time to time the mud was scraped from the blanket and washed in the pan. The blanket was rinsed eventually in water containing quicksilver. The gold and quicksilver formed an amalgam which was heated to reclaim the gold." Now, that's a pretty thorough description of the whole process, but I don't suppose that the average Easterner who took part in the early goldrushes was familiar with the whole process. Probably, lacking the quicksilver, the prospector failed to retain the finest dust. Buffum 1850 says that the rocker was a wooden box or cradle made from a hollowed log. The sieve end was called the mouth, the other end where the dirt was washed out was the tail.

rock hopper
A parallel to the Texas *brush-popper,* applied to the cowboys of Arizona who went after the wild cattle in rocky country. (Rossi 1975)

Rocky Mountain canary
A burro. (Ramon Adams 1944)

Rocky Mountain goat
See *mountain goat.*

Rocky Mountain sheep
See *big horn.*

rodeo
(Mex-Sp). The original Spanish meant "to encircle," "to round," or "to round up," and the word was used during the first and major part of the

period covered by this volume to mean a rounding-up of cattle. But as contests of riding, roping, and cow-throwing were established toward the end of the century as sources of local entertainment, the word was extended to cover these contests. Quite rapidly, of course, they became public entertainments and later big business. Now the second meaning has overtaken the first in the English-speaking world. (Ramon Adams 1944; McCarthy 1936)

roll his tail
(1) A cow that intends to run will hump up its tail at the body end, a telltale sign. Berrey and van den Bark 1942 cite **rolling their tails** to describe stampeding cattle. Hence:
(2) The act of a man departing on the run. (Rossi 1975)

roll up
Said of a horse rolling on its back when unsaddled. (Rossi 1975)

romal
(Mex-Sp *ramal:* rope strand, halter, also a railroad branch-line; take your pick to find the connection with the Anglo form). Used in the Old West in reference to an extension of a pair of saddle-horse reins at the place where they were joined. This did away with the convenient split rein, but it provided the rider with a quirt. Quite a popular addition among the Californios. Often very finely worked. (Ramon Adams 1944; Mora 1950)

rookus juice
One of the many nicknames for the lethal whiskey of the frontier.

rooter
A hog. (Ramon Adams 1944)

rootin' tootin' (or shootin') son-of-a-gun
A heller, a gunslinger. (Berrey and van den Bark 1942)

rope
Broadly speaking, there were two kinds of rope used by cattlemen: the *reata,* a rope of braided rawhide, which was the original of the braided rope developed by the Mexican vaqueros; and the **grass rope,** which was twisted instead of braided, made in the early days of manila hemp and maguey, but later of sisal and even cotton. (There was also, of course, the **hair lariat.**) The grass rope was stronger and cheaper than the reata, but scorned by reata men—which didn't mean that grass-rope men didn't have a powerful argument in favor of their own rope. Though the weaker of the two, the reata, with due care and use, could outlast a grass rope. Reatas were braided with a varying number of strands, usually four, six, or eight. The common number was four for a working reata, while

six- and eight-strand ropes were reserved for light roping and were often the finest examples of the reatero's art. The diameter of the reata varied, but the most common in use this century has been the ⅜-inch. Ropes, whether grass or reata, had to be cared for in much the same spirit as an archer cared for his bowstring.

One of the great truisms of the Old West is that whatever article of clothing or tool of his trade the cowman possessed, he had more than one use for it, probably a hundred. You can't carry much on a horse, and everything had to serve more than one purpose. A rope was no exception. Primarily a tool for catching up horses, busting down cows, and roping calves, it was also used as a whip for driving cattle, to construct a temporary corral, drag bogged cows to safety, haul firewood, add extra pulling power to a wagon team, rescue drovers from drowning at river-crossings, kill snakes, fashion a hackamore, and even, when it seemed like a good idea, to bring justice (or injustice) to a supposed horse- or cow-thief.

roping

There were two fundamental roping systems: the "hard-and-fast" method, in which a short rope was used with one end secured to the saddlehorn before the throw took place; and the **dally** method, in which a longer rope was used, free in the roper's hands until he was sure that the noose had reached its target. Then the dally was made as the roper took several turns around the saddlehorn with the free end of the rope. It was said you could tell a dally man for sure if he had a thumb missing. When a cow horse drove its feet into the dirt and a fast-moving Longhorn hit the end of the rope, there was enough pressure from the rope on the saddlehorn to remove more than a thumb. Men using the "hard-and-fast" method commonly used **grass rope,** while the dally men used both the grass rope and **reata.** Many old-timers sometimes favored a rope of more than 60 feet, occasionally as long as 100 feet, and a big loop besides. They could find their marks at 50 feet and more. However, length of rope was mostly dictated by the kind of country being worked: a long rope would not have been much use in parts of the brasada. One of the tricks of the dally man was to leave enough of the rope so that the loose end could be tucked under his right leg after the dally had been made.

The words *roper* and *roping* were certainly in use in the United States at the beginning of the nineteenth century, and a good roper was a man on the top rung of his professional ladder. The acts of skill carried out by such men in the ordinary course of their work are incredible to laymen. To contemplate such performances standing on your two feet is difficult enough—from the back of a running horse in difficult country, almost impossible. The accent today, with the help of the various communications media, is on the Westerner's skill with guns. This skill was a nice thing to have, but the emphasis should be on roping, for in that art lay the cowman's pride. In the successful throwing of a rope lay the multiple co-ordination of a man with his faculties of eye and hand and also with the horse under him. There were a good many recognized and named rope-throws, all used with varying-sized loops, according to the technique of the roper. A good man could decide the fate of a cow based on the need of the moment—he could catch it and hold it, throw it with comparative lightness, bust it hard, or, if he wanted meat without a shot being fired, kill it by bringing it down in a particular manner. The roping of a calf would generally be accomplished by one competent man. A feisty steer was another matter. This fellow might call for a rope around his horns and a second roper making a heel-catch. That brought the fightin'est Longhorn down with a bump. But don't get the wrong idea about cowhands dumping cows in the dust too violently just for the hell of it: cows were worth money and the over-enthusiastic roper who damaged the investment didn't last too long.

rosaderos
(Mex-Sp, in the same sense as [1]).
► (1) The fenders of a saddle, under and to the rear of the *stirrup-leathers.* These were made of leather and were almost the length of the stirrup-leathers, of which, on occasion, the rosaderos were a part. (Ramon Adams 1944; Mora 1950). Also *sudaderos.*
(2) Bed-rolls. (Weseen 1934; Berrey and van den Bark 1942)

roughing out
The first riding of a bronc. (Rossi 1975)

rough neck
Any employee of a dude ranch, with the exception of the owner. Known also now as a **dude wrangler** (a nice one), also a **savage**. This term may have come into being right at the end of the period covered by this volume, possibly in this century. (Rossi 1975)

rough string
Since a string or mount referred to the horses allotted to a hand for normal ranch work, on round-up, or on a trail-drive, the rough string was the left-overs, the horses nobody else wanted—all of them no more than half-broken. Tradition has it that most outfits had one such string, and God help the man who drew it by lot or was given it—nobody else would. The **rough-string rider** must have been the most miserable man in creation as he crawled from his hard bed on the trail in the cold, small hours to saddle and get the kinks out of his first horse of the day. Even at this distance in time, my heart bleeds for him. (Weseen 1934; Ramon Adams 1944)

round-up

(1) It is not possible to give a general description of a round-up that would apply to all ranges in all historical periods, but the general meaning is "the gathering of animals by men," often several together, usually a goodly number. The round-up of cattle was generally well organized, keeping strictly to the quickly developed custom of a given locality. The original round-ups (if they can be called such) in east Texas were known as *cow-hunts,* and took place at a time when most men who ran cattle also farmed and raised cotton. Several, with their families, would combine to gather cattle that had run wild and multiplied in the brush: it really was a hunt.

After the Civil War, when Texas men started to suspect that they could obtain a price for their cows, the bigger ranchers got together in associations and made rules. There was a recognized round-up boss, whose word was law while the round-up lasted, and agreement on the branding of mavericks. Later, when the cattle industry developed colonies in Wyoming and Montana, the associations organized round-ups. This followed a season or so of organized gathers, during which cattle might be rounded up as many as half-a-dozen times by various cattlemen searching for their stock on the open range. Since the animals were worn down by this, the need for range discipline increased. Nobody writes more authoritatively about this than E. S. Osgood in his classic *The Day of the Cattleman* (1929).

In the early 1880s, in Wyoming, the associations organized district round-ups, with territorial laws demanding that mavericks be sold by auction every ten days during the round-up and branded with the association and buyer's brands. Calf-branding was one of the factors that forced organization, for the most desirable end-product of the round-up was the calf-crop. Previously, the man who got out first on the gather got the most calves; once the brand was on the calf it made for bad feelings and legal difficulties when it followed a cow with another brand.

As said already, it is difficult to lay down hard and fast rules for the conduct and timing of round-ups over the wide period covered here, but it is safe to say that when the cattle industry settled down on the open range that ran from Mexico up into Canada, there were generally two round-ups a year—the spring calf round-up and the beef gather around the middle of the year. Each outfit involved sent its representatives (reps) who reported at an agreed spot to the man chosen to be the round-up boss. He might be one of the ranchers concerned or a foreman who attracted local trust and respect. There were rules of etiquette which were closely observed. One remark that has always amused me is that to ride a stallion to a round-up was like wearing brown boots with tie-and-tails. The purpose of the beef round-up was, of course, to send beef to market—which was what the cattle industry was all about. If somebody else's beef got among yours, you might sell it along with your own and later hand the money gained to the owner—which is a nice indication of the values of that time and place.

Round-up was a period of exhausting and intense labor, particularly the calf gather, when there was branding to be done. Complete co-operation was needed from all who took part. If it was hard on the men, it was harder on the horses, and the cutting horses were changed frequently. The horses employed during the early part of our period had not been bred-up by heavier Eastern stock and were often small and only grass-fed. Some of them were carrying a lot of man and saddle, and a few turns at holding a reluctant cow at the end of a rope could take the stuffing out of the most willing horse. Added to which, the animal was called upon to make endless sudden stops and starts so violent that stamina was sapped fast. The word *rodeo,* originally used solely to refer to the annual round-up of cattle, burrowed directly into American-English from the Mexicans and Californios in the first half of the nineteenth century. Only toward the end of the century did it take on its present meaning. (Weseen 1934; Berrey and van den Bark 1942; Ramon Adams 1944)

(2) A social gathering. (Weseen 1934)

rowel
A rotating disc with sharp points at the end of a spur—used for goading a horse.

rouser
Anything employed to keep a weary cowhand awake in the saddle when riding herd at night, particularly on trail-drives. It usually took the form

of tobacco juice rubbed in his eyes. This was said to make the eyes smart so much that sleep was impossible. (Andy Adams 1909; Dobie 1941)

rubbed out
Killed. **To rub out:** to kill. A phrase taken directly from Indian languages by the Mountain Men. The phrase survived among cattlemen and lived on to become a part of the language of city hoodlums in the twentieth century. (Ruxton 1849)

run
A common word in the West and one used in a number of senses, though the context seldom left doubt of the sense intended. As a noun, it stood for a stampede of cattle or horses and also a stampede of people in a landrush—for example, the Oklahoma Run of 1889. To *run meat* or to **run buffalo** was to shoot them at a gallop from the back of a horse, Indian-fashion, as opposed to establishing a *stand* and killing them on foot. Catlin 1851 cites this sense of the word in use as early as the 1830s. You could also *run mustang*— that is, run them down and rope them. The word was also used in the general American sense of "operating": a man was said to be **running a ranch, running horses** or **cattle,** meaning that he operated an outfit for the raising of stock. (Hawgood 1967)

run meat
To shoot down buffalo in a chase on horseback in the old way, when men shot for meat or plain sport and before the killing of buffalo became an industry. (Vestal 1939). See also *run.*

run mustang
To hunt wild horses from the saddle. (Weseen 1934). See also *run.*

runner, runner bird
See *road runner.*

running-iron
A plain iron, the tool of the illicit *brand artist.* In the early days many a cowman wrote his brand free-hand on the hide of his own (and possibly other men's) cows, but in the 1870s and 1880s, varying according to locality, anyone caught with a running-iron was dealt with as a cow-thief. The usual dodge was for a running-iron artist to carry a very short iron in a boot-top. A running-iron was also used legally during round-up to brand a calf that belonged to an outfit without a rep when there was no iron available bearing the outfit's brand. (North 1942; Ramon Adams 1944). See also *brands; stamp iron.*

rustle
Sometimes spelled **russle**.
(1) To get busy.
(2) To provide for oneself.
(3) To steal cows. The third meaning derived from the other two, for a cow-thief was certainly a man who provided for himself. All three meanings survived alongside each other on the range.

rustler
(1) A cow-thief. (Ramon Adams 1944; Mathews 1951)
In Texas, the word *rustler* was not in general use to denote a thief, and the horse-wrangler was referred to there as a **rustler** (Ramon Adams 1944) or **horse rustler**. So we find the following meanings for the word:
(2) A mover, a busy man, a hustler (Ramon Adams 1944). This relates to the idea of a cow-thief who moved cattle along sharply to put distance between himself and the irate owner.
(3) A cow or horse turned out and capable of looking after itself in the way of feed; one that in freezing weather could find feed by pawing through the snow to grass or gnawing the bark of trees.
(4) A ranch cook. Berrey and van den Bark 1942 give **pot rustler**.

rustler's brand
An expression common in the 1880s when, for example, the Cattlemen's Association of Wyoming made determined moves against range thieves and anybody but themselves who lived by cattle: a brand that was not officially recognized by the association. Probably it sometimes referred to the brand of a regular but small cattleman. (Osgood 1929)

sabina, sabino
See *savino.*

sacaguista
Also **sacuista.** (Mex-Sp from Nahuatl; SW). A variety of coarse *salt grass.*
Also correctly **sacahuista.** (Dobie 1930; Dayton 1931 says it is also called
bear grass).

sachel
Also **satchel.** A *wallet* often used by horse-riders to carry food-supplies.
It came in different forms—as a *parfleche,* a hide bag, or hessian bag. The
last was commonly carried in early Texas days tied behind the saddle. The
open end was sewn or tied closed and the sack slit in the middle for access.

saddlebag house
See *Texas house.*

saddle-blanket
Although in the West of the twentieth century many forms of saddle-
blanket were developed, in the Old West the average cowman used an
ordinary blanket, folded according to taste to protect the horse's back
against the chafing of the saddle. It was preferably made of wool, but if
made of cotton it was larger and folded more to produce the necessary
thickness. The finest saddle-blanket (or ordinary blanket, for that matter)
ever produced was the Navaho article. A saddle-blanket had to be of the
right quality, and the Navaho had it—less inclined to crinkle than a common wool blanket and yet possessing pliancy. Riders who used the *double
rig* or *Texas rig* generally covered a larger area of the horse with their
blankets than those favoring a single-cinch rig.

saddle-bow
The arched forepart of a saddle-tree. (Mora 1950)

saddle-broke
Said of a horse that was sufficiently broken to suffer a saddle on its back.

saddle-bum
An out-of-work cowboy riding from ranch to ranch for free grub. (Berrey and van den Bark 1942)

saddle-gun
A rifle or carbine, one that was attached to and carried on the saddle either by a sling over the horn, in or out of a scabbard, or booted under the leg

of a rider (the latter was unsatisfactory for long trips, as it chafed the horse). Earlier the term covered horse-pistols. (Ramon Adams 1944)

saddle-pocket dogies
(Texas). Runty cattle.

▶ **saddle pockets**
Saddlebags, cantle bags, cantinas (see *cantina [3]*). On the front of the saddle they were called **pommel bags**. (Rossi 1975)

saddles
A full account of the evolution and details of the Western saddle would require a great number of pages. Briefly, it was a development of the *Mexican saddle*, itself an adaptation of the Spanish war-saddle. The Spaniards probably got this general-European pattern of saddle from the Moors of Spain, who no doubt developed their own design from that of the Arabs. A number of different rigs were used in the West, and to a great extent, in the early days, a man's rig could indicate whence he came. For example, a *Texas rig* had two cinches; the *center-fire rig* belonged fundamentally to California, while the El Paso–Albuquerque was a *three-quarter rig*, a style that belonged also to the Northwest (for example the *Montana rig*). In the later days a man could more easily use the rig of his fancy. Every part of the saddle had its identifying name, most of which may be found in this book.

The very early saddles of the Mexicans in Texas had a broad-based *horn* that instantly identified it: the *apple* was flat-topped. The early Anglo saddles constituted the bare minimum to separate a man's butt from his saddle-blanket. The *saddle-tree* was covered with rawhide only and the over-all housing was a loose detachable cover, known as *mochila*, with a slit at each end for the horn and *cantle*. The Mexican models were adopted by the Mountain Men and frontiersmen, modified further by the

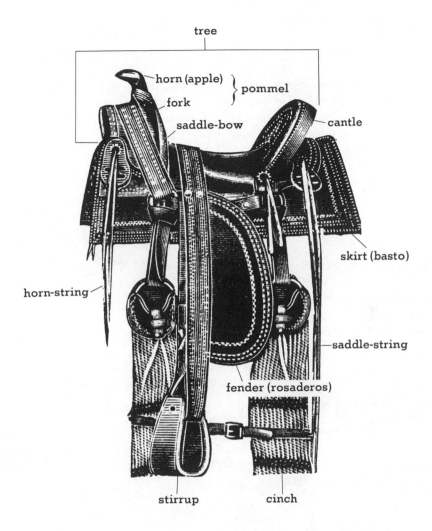

tree

horn (apple)
fork
saddle-bow
pommel
cantle
skirt (basto)
horn-string
saddle-string
fender (rosaderos)
stirrup
cinch

Texans and others to their own needs. The saddle-types of the Mountain Men were used by the early cattlemen in the north (about whom there is not enough written), whose first herds were not Longhorns but the cattle traded by travelers on the Oregon Trail and California Trail back in the 1840s and 1850s. One early type of saddle with the loose cover was the **Mother Hubbard**—named for obvious reasons; under this, most of the rigging disappeared from view. Toward the end of the century, once again most of the rigging was revealed, though the style did not revert entirely to the earlier model that had only an upper skirt and no **fenders.** The new style retained the deep fender that had been used with the mochila and had a full squared skirt under the tree. Swelled forks (see **swell-fork**) came in at the end of the century and some riders had adopted the roll cantle by this time. It is scarcely necessary to say that the old-timers were disapproving, and many stayed with the old *slick-fork.* With the high cantle and swelled fork, they didn't know how a self-respecting bronc could throw a rider.

The saddle was the cowboy's most valuable possession monetarily and was often worth more than his horse. A common sight, as they said, to see a "fifty-dollar saddle on a ten-dollar horse." In the process of going broke, the last possession a man parted with was his saddle—understandable in a land of horsemen. The expression "he sold his saddle" told the world that a man had reached rock-bottom. On a working cow-pony, a saddle was a man's workshop, and on it he hung the tools of his trade: his lariat, tie-rope, sachel or saddlebags, slicker, bed-roll, maybe a rifle, and, under some circumstances, a canteen of water or a water-skin.

saddle stock
Horses broken for riding; the remuda.

saddle-string
The string on either side of the saddle, on the rear skirts, for fastening bed-rolls, etc. (Mora 1950)

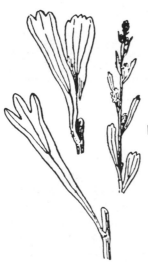

saddle tramp
A *saddle-bum,* a *chuck-line rider.*

saddle-tree
 Also **tree** (Rossi 1975). The frame and foundation of the saddle, usually wood covered with rawhide. It was measured from the top center of the cantle to the rear of the horn. (Mora 1950)

sagarro
See *saguaro.*

sage
The open range, sage country. (Weseen 1934)

 sagebrush
Any brush of the many varieties of *Artemisia,* found over vast expanses of country in the Southwest and up through Nevada to Nebraska. In New Mexico and Arizona large cattle-outfits ran stock in sagebrush country. The term was used with other words to extend their meaning: **sagebrush country, sagebrush range,** etc.

sagebrusher
A man living remotely, 'way out in the sagebrush. Weseen 1934 and Ramon Adams 1944 further define the term to mean a tourist—a meaning which I think developed in the twentieth century.

sagebrush men
Cowboys of Colorado, Wyoming, and Montana; men from the sage country. (Rossi 1975)

sagebrush philosopher
A talkative, phonily wise man; a crackerbarrel philosopher.

sagebrush whiskey
A lethal alcoholic drink allegedly distilled from sagebrush. The mind boggles at the thought.

sage cock
Also **sage grouse, cock of the plains.** *Centrocercus urophasianus.* A grouse of the sagebrush country. See also *prairie chicken (1).*

saged
Said of stock made crazy by the eating of sagebrush. (Weseen 1934; Berrey and van den Bark 1942)

sage hare
Also **sage rabbit.** *Lepus artemisia.* A pale-gray hare that blended well with the sagebrush; one of the several hares referred to as a *jack rabbit.*

sage hen
(1) The female of the *sage cock.* Also **sage chicken, sage fowl.**
(2) A woman. (Weseen 1934; Ramon Adams 1944)

sage rat
Something like a *hill-nutty,* a loner in sage country or desert, a prospector. (Weseen 1934)

saguaro
(Mex-Sp). Also **sagarro, suaro, suhuaro, suwarro.** A giant cactus of the genus *Carnegiea.* Its fruits were eaten by Indians and it also provided a consumable syrup. Also correctly **sahuaro.**

sail away
To depart in a hurry. (Weseen 1934)

sala
(Sp; SW). A salon, a spacious room or hall.

salado
Also **salowed** (Ramon Adams 1944), **sallowed**. A wind-broken horse.
(Berrey and van den Bark 1942; Ramon Adams 1944)

salea
(Mex-Sp; SW). A softened sheepskin placed between a saddle-horse's
back and the saddle-blanket. Ramon Adams 1944 also places it between
a pack and the back of a pack-animal.

salina
(Sp; SW). A salt-lick for cattle; a salt-bed. (Mathews 1951)

salinera
(Mex-Sp; SW). A salt-bed or salt-pit. (Mathews 1951)

saloon
Not a Westernism, of course, but a word which demands a few lines, for
the picture of the Western saloon in the mind of the modern reader is often
incorrect. It's true that the nature of these places varied greatly and they
did at times attain heights of opulence, but they were too often the reverse.
Liquor was sold in all of them, but they ranged from the plank across two
barrels, to the *shebang* of green lumber with sawdust on the floor and no
chairs and tables, to the comparative luxury of the Alamo in Abilene and
the well-set-up Long Branch in Dodge City. In the trail-towns, at the height
of the shipping season, they were open day and night. A good many of
them were used as gambling dens, dance halls, and whore-houses. No
respectable woman would have been seen dead in one. Trail-towns often
had local laws demanding that drovers hang their guns up in the saloon.
Many a rear wall behind the bar was festooned with hog-legs (see *hog-
leg*). While such surrenders might ruin a fictional story-line, they saved the
lives of many a town marshal and serious drinker. No denying that some
pretty wild scenes have been recorded, some of them even true. When
a cow-crew hit town after several months on the trail, often on bad food
and little sleep, they needed to let some of the tension out. There wasn't
much to do in a cow-town except to buy some new duds, eat a decent
meal, have one of the scarce women, and get drunk. You could also
gamble all your wages. This many a man did and returned home to Texas
dead-broke. Believe it or not, the now traditional face-to-face meeting of
gunmen in saloons was extremely rare.

salowed
See *salado*.

salt
(1) A word often used as a substitute for *alkali*. Salty and alkaline country
was known, say, as **salt flat, salt plain,** or **salt prairie. Salt sage** was a

greasewood found growing in such country (see **greasebrush, grease-wood**).

(2) To **salt a mine** was to scatter mineral dust or ore in a worthless mine in order to fool some poor sucker into believing it valuable and buying it. A number of normally smart businessmen were caught in this way. A quick chance of something-for-nothing blinded men then as now.

(3) The West also used the word *salt* as a verb in the same sense as the rest of the world; that is, to preserve food by salting. Salt pork was part of the staple diet of the Texans, even though we have been led to believe they lived on straight beef to a man.

salt grass
Sedgy grass growing on salt land. See also *salt (1)*.

salt horse
Corned beef. (Rossi 1975)

Saltillo blanket
A blanket of a type originally made in Saltillo, Coahuila, Mexico, which was commonly used in Texas as a poncho before the introduction of the slicker or *fish*.

salty dog
(1) A tough man.
(2) Salty ham, bacon. (Rossi 1975)

sand
Sand is grit and *grit* is another word for guts or courage. If a man had **sand in his craw,** he had what it took.

sand cherry
Prunus besseyi. A cherry of the West.

sand creek
A dry creek or a creek which had sand bars in its bed, causing the water-flow to be impeded. (Mathews 1951)

sandia
(Sp *sandía;* SW). A watermelon. (Mathews 1951)

sand painting
An artistic religious ritual adopted by the Navahos from the Pueblo Indians, using colored pigments and sands to create "healing-harmony" patterns of great beauty and with esoteric meaning. The Navahos show a remarkable manual and artistic discipline, which, to some extent, is exhibited in their blanket-weaving, an art also learned from the Pueblos. Some

California tribes also practiced a crude form of sand painting. (Underhill 1956; La Farge 1956)

santo
(Sp). A sacred image, the statuette of a saint. (Fergusson 1940)

sarape
A band of wool or silk, possibly a foot wide, that went several times around the waist and was sometimes fringed at the ends. (Rossi 1975). See also *serape.*

sash
Fashions come and go in fictional depictions of the West. I remember in Western movies of the 1920s cowboys wore leather cuffs all studded and decorated, angora chaps, and high-pointed hats. They wore their hair short in the 1920s style, so one could settle in a split second whether a person was a boy or girl. In the late 1960s and 1970s heroes (when the plot had one) wore long hair, never wore leather cuffs, and went in for pants (skin-tight) tucked in boots. The sash never had much vogue except in the Old West itself, where it enjoyed a fair popularity. They might seem to have been borrowed from the Mexicans, but soldiers in both North and South during the war used sashes, which had long been established as an article of clothing in Europe. You may be sure that when an early range-rider wore a sash, he made a dozen uses of it. It held guns and knives, it could bind injured limbs and tie up an enemy. It could also add a touch of color to the dress of the range dandy.

sashay
(Fr *chassé*). To travel, to go; to walk mincingly; to bow to a partner in a square dance. Weseen 1934 says "to walk, especially with a gliding step." (Wentworth 1944)

satchel
See *sachel.*

savage
See *rough neck.*

savanero
(Mex-Sp). A herder of animals, a man in charge of animals, and also one such as a packer or muleteer. The term was used loosely in the early part of our period and seemed to indicate a *plainsman,* for *sabana* is a treeless plain, such as the Anglicized *savanna.* (Gregg 1844)

savers
Stout leggings (see *leggins*) which were secured above the knees.

savino

Also **sabina** (Ramon Adams 1944), **sabino**. A Texas Longhorn sprockled white and red. (Mora 1950)

savvy

Anglo variant of the Spanish *sabe*. To know, to understand. Very common in the Old West, both in the Anglo and Mexican form. (Weseen 1934)

sawbuck saddle

A pack-saddle, the cross-piece front and back of which suggested a sawbuck or stand for supporting wood while it was being sawn. A simple and easily extemporized pattern for packing; very useful for quick loading and also for hanging small afterthoughts on when the packing was complete.

sawdust crew

The saw-mill crew in a lumber camp. (Weseen 1934)

scabbards

The word *scabbard* was used more commonly in its general sense than it is today, covering gun holsters, rifle boots, and sword- and knife-sheaths. So all sheaths and holsters are placed under this head.

Gun Holsters. Holsters after the Civil War had flaps to retain the gun and to keep out dust, but in the decade after the war, flaps were mostly discarded as encumbrances. Till the mid-1870s holsters were plain and not cut away for quick-draws. Roughly, they came in two styles: those with loops holding the holster to the skirt (the flat leather between the holster and the wearer's leg) and those which were stitched to the skirt. The cutaway for the trigger-finger was not so vital to the user of a single-action gun, for whom the thumb-cock was the first move, so cutaways became necessary only when double-action guns came into use. For the cross-draw, the scabbard was worn high with the gun close to the body; for the side-draw, the holster was slung at a slight angle to the body, leaving the butt clear. In the 1880s and 1890s, 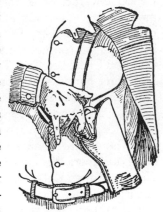 holsters were often artistically tooled, and, by then, hideaways were in being and were usually worn under the left armpit suspended in a shoulder harness. The design of the gun dictated the holster shape. It was not until the Colt Peacemaker, with its compact shape, that a holster could be made for the classic quick-draw. Gun-handlers had holsters trimmed and fashioned to their own tastes: one had his hip pockets lined with leather to hold his guns. Holsters were constructed with open fronts, necessitating a clip to retain the gun. One type was pivoted so that the gun could be elevated to be fired while still in the holster. But the average cowman kept his gun in a deep, safe scabbard so that whatever might happen to him his gun would still be there when his gun-hand went looking for it.

Rifle Scabbards. Dust was the great enemy of every Westerner who cared for his weapons, and when a saddle-gun was taken on a trip, it had to be protected as much as possible. Much favored in the 1850s was the decorated doeskin Indian scabbard, used by Indians and whites alike. Most models covered the whole barrel and stock of the rifle, leaving all or part of the butt exposed. During the Civil War, the cavalry did not employ a scabbard, but a **spider**—a small socket affair attached to the *off-side* cinch- (safe) ring and encircled by a strap. The barrel of the carbine went through this and was attached by a ring and swivel to the trooper's shoulder-strap. (Rossi 1975). Solid-leather scabbards were official issue in 1885 and were probably in use by civilians in the West before that. There were many and varied ways of carrying a scabbard on a saddle, including hanging it from the horn loose and hanging it from the horn with the barrel secured by a latch under the rider's leg. A few riders foolishly cinched their carbines under their legs, which was uncomfortable for the rider and galling for the horse.

Fast-draw Holsters. We cannot leave scabbards without a word about the fast-draw, if for no other reason than that's what a reader will be looking for. Some of the old-timers may have pulled iron from leather a sight faster than some of the opposition, but, with the scabbards in use during the period covered here, they could never compare with the quick-hand merchants of the twentieth century. Possibly because Tio Sam Myres, master saddlemaker of El Paso, did not match his unequaled skill with leather to the requirements of master gun-handler and lawman and full-blooded Cherokee Tom Threepersons until the twentieth century. Under Tio Sam's hands a holster was produced of thick, hard leather that left hammer, trigger, and butt clear of that leather. The scabbard tilted slightly forward, and it never lost shape once it was molded wet to the gun it was made for. Simple enough ingredients, but they made a near-perfect holster. There have been a number of fine craftsmen and gun-fighters who have designed and made good holsters since, but Tio Sam was the first. Then and then only was a good man with a gun able to do (on rare occasions) what had been no more than a wild dream for the old-timers —to draw and fire faster than a man holding a gun on him could react and squeeze the trigger. (Askins 1956)

scab-herder

(1) A sheepherder. (Ramon Adams 1944). Wellman 1939 writes: "Many a humble Mexican, Basque or American sheepherder paid with his life for trying to protect his flock—but it should not be thought that the shooting was by all means on one side. A good many cowboys, too, have been knocked off their horses from a distance by 'scab-herders' proficient with

Winchesters, and left to the coyotes under the wild Western skies."
(2) Later this term was applied to anti-strike guards in lumber camps.
(Weseen 1934)

scaffold
To lay out your dead, Indian-fashion, on a scaffold of poles.

scalawag
(1) A horse of no use for cow-work because of its wildness or age. The term could also be applied to humans sometimes because of their bronco attitude. (Weseen 1934)
(2) In the defeated South after the Civil War, a collaborator with the North.

scalp
There are two main schools of opinion on the origin of scalping: one, that the collecting of scalps as war trophies started with the Indians; the second, that they adopted the practice from the Europeans. When the two races met on the Eastern Seaboard, both societies lived by the dual code that demanded a man be nice to the members of his own group and nasty to those outside it. They both recognized that it was permissible to be cruel to the enemy. Early white settlers offered bounties on Indian scalps, Woodland tribes took scalps as trophies. In Europe during the same period the Albanians were taking heads for the same reason—which puts such atrocities in the right perspective. As the whiteman progressed across America, he found the scalping custom among almost all the tribes he contacted. Those whitemen who lived among the Indians also often took scalps, and this included Mountain Men. Mexican authorities put bounties on Apache scalps. Indians scalped extensively among themselves—lodges, belts, and horses were decorated with the scalps of enemies. U.S. soldiers, on more than one occasion, took Indian scalps after battle, and both sides were prone to taking scalps of the enemy's women. In the Southwest, Indians generally regarded scalps with abhorrence, even though they took them, and the act called for a ceremony of purification. Whites claimed the Apaches scalped, the Apaches themselves denied it. Most Plains Indians glorified in the act; they stretched, dried, and decorated scalps to be handed down to posterity. The habit might well be a substitute for the taking of heads, but some of the Eastern tribes took heads as well. Among the Yumas of the Southwest, a lock of hair was taken in place of a scalp. So important was the taking of scalps among the Indians that there were a number of words used in conjunction with the word *scalp*: *scalp dance,* scalp hunter, *scalping knife,* etc. (MacLeod 1928; Hoig 1960; La Farge 1956; Wellman 1956)

scalp dance
Among Indian tribes this is usually taken to mean a dance of victory after battle. Certainly warriors danced after returning home from a fight; scalps

were exhibited and their taking described in song. But there were also scalp dances held at regular intervals, particularly among the tribes of the Southwest. These were of deeply religious significance, for the accumulated tribal store of scalps represented the dead.

"scalping" knife

Any knife used for taking scalps. We are told that it was generally curved, mostly used by the Plains and Woodland Indians, and was occas-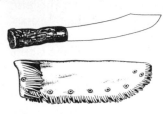ionally carried by the white frontiersman. But it is highly improbable that more than a very few men of either race reserved a knife exclusively for scalping. As Carl Russell 1967 writes in reference to Indians: "When there was an occasion to take scalps, the same knife which pared tasty morsels from hump ribs at meal time loosened the scalp of the victim destined to provide the trophy."

scaly

Rough, unpleasant, difficult. Andy Adams 1909: " 'While I know every foot of the trail through here,' said the foreman, 'there's several things that look scaly.' "

scattergun

A shot-gun. Not a Westernism. (Wentworth 1944; Ramon Adams 1944; Rossi and Hunt 1971)

scorcher

A branding iron. A word used only in the later part of our period. (Berrey and van den Bark 1942)

scout

Also **Indian scout** (Mathews 1951). A white civilian or an Indian with knowledge of the country campaigned in, employed by the army usually in action against what were termed "hostiles"—Indians who fought for their territory against invading whites or whites who had already occupied their country. They were also called **guides**. Often the white scouts were of doubtful value: for fair pay and keep, a man who had lived for some years on the frontier could pass himself off as possessing local knowledge. Some, however, such as Jim Bridger and the unfortunate Tom Horn (see *badman*), Major North, Bill Williams, and Al Sieber (master of Apache scouts), were highly skilled and greatly respected men; and there were many more who received little publicity. Bridger and Williams were veteran Mountain Men, and scouting against Indians was merely an extension of their long-used survival tactics in Indian country. Indian scouts were sometimes wrongly named, for, in certain campaigns, particularly those launched against various Apache bands, they were used as guerrilla troops. On some occasions the Apache government scouts outnumbered the Apache hostiles. Some tribes were regarded as particularly recruitable as army aides because they were hereditary enemies of the hostiles. The Arikara and Crows were employed around the time of the last Custer fight against the Sioux, Cheyenne, and Arapaho. A company of Pawnees served under Major North against the Sioux. The Christian Delawares, although Eastern Indians, served all over the West as loyal lone scouts. It has always seemed curious and tragic to me, and a subject calling for further study, that such race-conscious people as the Sioux and Cheyenne, once the tribal circle had been broken by the whiteman, acted willingly as scouts against their own people.

scratch
To spur a horse. Ramon Adams 1944 takes the explanation further with "to spur a horse backward and forward while riding."

screw
A cowhand. (Weseen 1934)

scrub
An animal of such poor quality that one would not wish to breed from it. The term was applied to both horses and cattle.

sea-lions
See *coasters.*

section
Six hundred and forty acres or a square mile. A ranch was and still is often measured thus—so many sections rather than so many acres. Not a Westernism. (Mathews 1951; Rossi 1975)

seegar
Cigar. Not a Westernism, but seen frequently ◀ in Western literature and used in the East by Mark Twain and others. (Wentworth 1944)

see the elephant
See *elephant.*

segundo
(Mex-Sp). A *strawboss;* an assistant trail-boss. Often used for the second-in-command in any situation. (Weseen 1934; Ramon Adams 1944)

sell your saddle
So broke you had to sell your saddle—always the last thing a man parted with; the all-time low. (Weseen 1934)

señor
(Sp; SW). Sir, mister. (Dobie 1930)

serape
Also **sarape** (Weseen 1934). A blanket used by Mexicans as a cloak, often worn folded narrowly and neatly on one shoulder as an adornment. (Buffum 1850; Dobie 1930)

service berry
Amelanchier alnifolia. June-berry. A North American shrub bearing a fruit rather like a huckleberry.

set back
To pull back. (Dobie 1930)

set brand
A branding iron with a head in the shape of some brand—as opposed to a *running-iron.* (North 1942)

set down
To be fired from a job on a ranch and have to hitch a ride to town; to be told to get off the place on foot. Rossi 1975 adds wryly: "Not a good way to go."

set fast
A sore on a horse's back. (Weseen 1934)

sewellel
See *boomer (2).*

shack
(1) A bunk-house. (Ramon Adams 1944)
(2) A ranch headquarters, the main ranch-house. (Rossi 1975)
(3) A poor house or hut. (Mathews 1951). Mathews adds an interesting note on the origin of the word as the Spanish-American **jacal** (pronounced *shacal*), earlier written *xacal,* from the Aztec *xacalli:* a wooden hut.

shadow rider
I cannot date this term confidently, but it is too good to miss—which I would have done if it had not been brought to my attention by Paul Rossi 1975. He describes the term as applying to a vain cowboy who admires

his reflection in store windows, one who even finds his own shadow fetching.

shank of the afternoon
Late afternoon. (Dobie 1930)

sharpen his hoe
Another way of cleaning a man's plow (see *clean his plow*)—to beat him, to thrash him. As nice a Westernism as ever was. (Weseen 1934)

Sharps
One of the greatest rifle-makers in the world, who marketed almost forty different models between the 1840s and 1881. Usually associated with the *Big Fifty* of the last days of the buffalo slaughter, Sharps made many other guns that were used in war and buffalo hunting before that model appeared—notably the Sharps-Borschardt .45, which could take a heavy load and could penetrate the thick hide of the buffalo in a way such repeaters as the Henry and Spencer could not. The Big Fifty was *said* to be capable of hitting a target at five miles, but this takes a large pinch of salt in the swallowing. It could be fired today, men remarked, and would kill tomorrow. The hunters allegedly called it "Old Poison Slinger." With the production in 1875 of his .50–90 (.50 caliber, 90 powder weight), Sharps responded to the demands by hunters for a gun that could carry powerful charges. This charge could vary to 100 and 110 according to personal taste. This was the charge the old-timers were talking about when they spoke of the Big Fifty. No thanks to Sharps that the buffalo survived at all. (Bowman 1953; McHugh 1972)

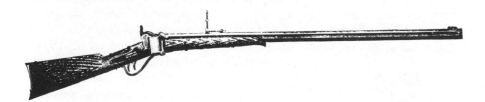

Bowman 1953 describes the Sharps of 1848 as one of the outstanding firearms of the mid-nineteenth century. The action of the rifle calls for a description. I quote from Bowman: "The Sharps' action consisted of throwing forward the trigger guard, which dropped a sliding block at the rear of the barrel and uncovered the breech for loading. Paper and later Sharps' linen cartridges . . . were then inserted and after the trigger guard was drawn back, the rising block sheared off the rear end of the cartridge, exposing the powder charge. When the trigger guard was fully returned to position, the sliding block effectively covered the breech." This was the pre-metallic cartridge Sharps. The Buffalo Sharps were chambered for various metallic cartridges, .44, .45 (the 2 $^1/_{10}$ Sharps is the same as the .45–70 U.S.), and finally in several .50-caliber loads.

shave-tail

(1) A horse with its tail plucked. Cowmen did not like full tails and plucked hairs from those of their mounts. This made them the opposite of broomtails (see *broomie*). Shave-tails were easily distinguishable from broomtails when running free on the range.

(2) Later, in lumberjack's parlance, this term was applied to a mule. (Weseen 1934). Rossi 1975 tells us that this was also an army mule with its tail shaved short and square. Later applied to second-lieutenants in World War II.

shebang

Usually a poor shelter or hut, but used later to apply to a shack. Became part of the phrase **the whole shebang,** meaning "the complete works," "the whole kit and caboodle."

sheep

Without sheep, fiction writers would have been hard put to find plots. A substantial part of pulp-Westerns rests upon the hatred of the cattlemen for sheepmen, a hatred said to have been based on the fundamental difference between their modes of life and the belief that sheep killed the land for cattle: sheep ate the grass to its roots, and their small hoofs killed off what was left. Undeniably, there were sheep and cattle wars—but this is not the whole picture. The two interests did resort to violence when range was contested, as in the Pleasant Valley War, Arizona, in the late 1880s; but in many situations, sheep were as necessary to a local economy as any other animal. Most Texas frontier settlements possessed sheep, and most womenfolk wove homespun cloth for the family's clothes. Often sheep and cattle occupied adjacent ranges without too much friction. In 1870,

Colorado Territory had something like one million cattle and two million sheep. The Colorado cattlemen of that period seemed more hostile to Texas Longhorns than to the woollies. Sheep from California, Utah, and Oregon were reaching northern ranges by the early 1870s. The last sheep war was fought in the Ten Sleep Country of Wyoming as late as 1905–09. Sheepherders were Mexicans, Indians, Basques, and occasionally Anglos. They were not as meek as fiction would have us believe and were often the aggressors.

sheeped-off

A country was said to be sheeped-off when its grass had been nibbled down to the roots by sheep, thus making it useless for cattle. It was not really sheep themselves that were the trouble, but sheepmen sometimes misused the land by over-grazing. (Dobie 1941)

sheep-puncher
A sheepherder. A later development from the already established word **cow-puncher**. (Wentworth 1944)

sheepskin
In spite of fiction writers who claim that the cowman decried everything appertaining to sheep, the latter-day cattlemen of the nineteenth century did not scorn to wear sheepskin coats nor, for that matter, sheepskin chaps, particularly in the intense cold of the Northwest. Sheepskin gloves—that was another matter; the usual wear of the cattleman was the finest doeskin.

sheep-wrangler
A sheepherder. (Wentworth 1944)

sheet-iron crackers
See *Lincoln shingles.*

she-stuff
As the word *cow* referred to all cattle in the West, irrespective of sex, this word had to come into use to cover the females of the species. (Weseen 1934; Ramon Adams 1944; Wentworth 1944)

shindig
A barn dance, a ranch dance, usually with ladies present and hard liquor not overlooked. One didn't happen every day, so the most was made of it and it could last all night. When all's said and done, there's no sense in going home in the dark! (Weseen 1934; Ramon Adams 1944)

shinnery
An expanse or deep thicket of scrub oak. Mathews 1951 mentions it. Dobie 1929 writes: "One of the range sayings was: 'If you want beef to kill, go to the shinnery.' "

shirt-tail outfit
A small cattle-ranch, implying that it was so diminutive that it could be placed on the tail of a shirt.

shooting fixings
Guns and ammunition. (Weseen 1934)

shooting iron
A pistol, a revolver. (Farmer 1889; Farmer and Henley 1890-1904; Ramon Adams 1944)

shoot square

To be straight-dealing, aboveboard, honest, and forthright. An honest man was also referred to as a **straight shooter**. The implication was a man who was not devious but who went straight to the mark. Left-overs from the Mountain-Men days.

short

A short-aged *yearling,* as opposed to a long-aged yearling: a calf short of its first birthday. (Berrey and van den Bark 1942)

short bit

See *bit house.*

shorthorn

(1) An Eastern cow with short horns. (Ramon Adams 1944). Hence:
(2) A cattleman who was unused to Longhorns and worked shorthorns. And:
(3) A pilgrim, a shorthorn, a greenhorn.
(4) Something inferior, second-rate. (Weseen 1934)

short horse

The American quarter horse, so called for its ability to sprint short distances. A quick starter, hence the usefulness of its blood when crossed with a mustang to produce cowponies.

shot-gun

(1) Known as a **scattergun** or **greener**—the latter from Greener, the maker of superlative weapons in London, England. The greener may have impressed its name on the West and put an extra word in its vocabulary, but there were other excellent shot-guns in use, muzzle- and breech-loader, single- and double-barreled, with full barrel and sawed-off barrel. Whitney produced a good cheap single-barrel, breech-loader; Remington, good as ever, marketed muzzle- and breech-loaders accessible to every pocket;

 Winchester was naturally in the market—though I blush to say that some were English imports with the firm's mark on them. But, by the 1880s, this famous firm was making its own repeating shot-guns.

No reader of Western literature has to be told that, at fairly close quarters, the shotgun is a devastating weapon. When sawed-off it must have quelled many a crowd convinced that the man holding the gun would use it.

Usually 12-gauge, the shot-gun, historically, was a development of the old fowling piece. It was always a smooth-bore and fired a load of small shot. The gauge was arrived at by taking a ball that would exactly fit the

barrel: the number of such balls to the pound gave the gauge. Twelve balls to the pound gave you 12-gauge or 12-bore, the diameter of which was 0.729 inches. The usefulness of the shot-gun was that, within reason, you could load it with anything you fancied or had handy. Nails with a good charge of black powder behind them could be formidable. The weapons were the favorites of stage-guards and some lawmen.
(2) A *shotgun messenger.*

shotgun chaps
Closed chaps or leggings that encased the whole leg. They were in use from the 1870s to the 1890s. Also called the **Texas leg.** See also *leggins.*

shotgun house
A house built with all the rooms in a row, without a *dog trot* between them. (Rossi 1975)

shotgun messenger
Also **shotgun guard.** Stagecoach guard, so called because he was often armed with a shot-gun. Often simply referred to as the **shotgun.** (Horan and Sann 1954)

shotgun wagon
The wagon of a few ranchers sent out as a round-up wagon independently of the main round-up. (Ramon Adams 1944)

showt'l
See *boomer (2).*

shuck
(1) A cigarette with a corn-shuck wrapping. (Dobie 1930)
(2) A Mexican. (Dobie 1930)
(3) See *blue backs.*

side-kick
A man's partner. The allusion is to a member of a team-span of a wagon.

sidekicker
A step or platform in front of a house from which a horse could be mounted.

side-line
The hobbling of a horse or mule by fastening fore- and hindfeet together, as opposed to the more usual hobble which fastened forefeet together and hindfeet together. (Weseen 1934; Ramon Adams 1944)

sidewinder
See *rattlesnake.*

sierra
(Sp). A large range of hills or mountains. Found in titles of Western mountain ranges, as in **Sierra Madre, Sierra Nevada,** etc. Also seen in conjunction with other words: **sierra juniper, sierra pines,** etc.

siesta
(Sp; SW). The noon forty-winks. (Dobie 1930)

sign
A word used on the frontier certainly since the seventeenth century to
denote the evidence of the passage of a man or beast. This could be in
the form of crushed grass, snapped twigs, hoof- or foot-prints, lines scoured
in the dirt by travois ends, the droppings of animals, etc. Some writers have
differentiated between tracks and sign, using sign as a term for droppings
and man-made marks. Dobie 1930 designates the two signs as tracks and
droppings. In spite of the claims of fiction, not all Indians were expert
readers of sign, though many possessed amazing skill, as did a number
of whitemen. From the cowman's point of view, sign was mostly the tracks
of cattle and those of predators (man and beast) that preyed on cattle. The
lives of Mountain Men often depended on their ability to read sign and
to tell to a matter of hours—or smokes (see *smoke [1]*)—how old it was.
It was said of a good Apache tracker that he could follow sign over bare
rock, and certainly the iron shoes of a whiteman's horse could leave marks
even on the *mal pais.* Rock and water were the two media which a man
used to lose his sign when he had no wish to be followed. There were a
number of words connected to *sign,* such as **cutting for sign** (cutting across
the suspected line of the quarry's travel in the hope of finding trace of its
passage), **bear sign** (which also meant "doughnuts"), **buffalo sign, cow
sign, Indian sign,** etc.

sign language
This subject, of course, needs a volume to do it justice. Basically, it was a
method of communication employed by the Indians in which speech was
not needed. There were three methods: One aided communicators close
to each other and employed only the hands. This enabled fairly detailed
exchanges involving basic facts to be made—but not, let it be noted,
nearly so detailed as fiction writers would have us believe—between people who did not share the same language. The second method was used
by communicators who were, one might say, at middle distance from each
other and employed wide gestures of a general nature. The third was a
method used to communicate at great distances. This could involve ma-
neuvering a horse or using smoke. The great Francis Parkman in *The
Oregon Trail* (1872) writes: "Not long after, a black speck became visible

on the prairie, full two miles off. It grew larger and larger; it assumed the form of a man and horse; and soon we could discern a naked Indian, careering at full gallop towards us. When within a furlong he wheeled his horse in a wide circle, and made him describe various mystic figures upon the prairie; Henry immediately compelled 'Five Hundred Dollars' to execute similar evolutions. 'It *is* Old Smoke's village,' said he interpreting these signals, 'didn't I say so?' '' Trail-driving outfits, unable to converse by voice because of the distances, had their orders signaled by the boss in a series of arm and hand signs which amounted to a sign language.

sign riders
Much the same as *line riders.* Cowhands who rode the range boundaries in search of the *sign* of straying cattle.

silk
(1) Barbed wire. (Weseen 1934)
(2) The lash of a whip.

silk grass
See *bear grass.*

silk-popper
A stagecoach driver, so called because he popped a silk (the lash of a whip). See also *poppers.*

silla
(Sp). A chair or seat; hence, a saddle. (Allen 1933; Weseen 1934)

silver tip
A grizzly bear with silver-tipped fur.

sin-buster
A preacher. (Berrey and van den Bark 1942; Ramon Adams 1944)

sinch
A variant of *cinch.*

single-barreled, single-rigged
See *center-fire rig.*

single-fire rig, single-fire saddle
See *center-fire rig.*

single-foot
A horse pace halfway between a trot and a canter. Mathews 1951 gives several quotes from the nineteenth century. Webster's American Dictionary of the English Language 1864: "between a pace and a trot."

single-tree
Truly a single tree: the cross-bar to which the traces of a horse- or mule-team were attached for drawing a wheeled vehicle. A corruption of **swingle-tree,** no doubt because of its association with *double-tree.* Not a Westernism.

sinkers
Biscuits. (Berrey and van den Bark 1942; Ramon Adams 1944)

sit her
To stay in the saddle on a wild one. (Weseen 1934). A cowboy habit to use *her* for *it.*

sitio
(Mex-Sp; SW). A substantial titled piece of land; a land grant. (Dobie 1930)

siwash
To sleep unsheltered in the open, supposedly like an Indian. Probably from the Siwash Indians. (Wentworth 1944; Mathews 1951)

Siwash coat
(NW). A long, loose dress, rather like a Mother Hubbard, as worn by the women of the Siwash Indians.

siwash onion
An edible root of the Northwest.

six-shooter
Also **six-gun** (Ramon Adams 1944; Weseen 1934). A revolver with six chambers. (Weseen 1934; Wentworth 1944)

skeebald.
Also **stew-ball** (Berrey and van den Bark 1942; Ramon Adams 1944). Piebald (Weseen 1934). Though, in general English, *skeebald* and *piebald* have different meanings, Weseen, in this case, means of white and other colors in fairly substantial patches. Thus, a **skew ball**: a horse of such coloring.

skeer
Scare.

skim diggings
Shallow diggings for gold.

skimmies
Calves raised on skim milk. (Weseen 1934)

skinned
To keep a sharp lookout, to **keep one's ears skinned.** (Farmer 1889)

skinner
(1) A buffalo skinner. When buffalo hunting became a highly organized industry, the hunters, the men who actually shot the animals, became the aristocrats of the trade. Lower down the scale were the skinners, men able to skin buffalo at an incredible speed, using a very sharp knife. Some, but not the best, made their first cuts with the knife, then finished the job by pulling the hide from the corpse with mules or horses. Not a good practice, for it could tear the hide. For an excellent description see Mari Sandoz's *The Buffalo Hunters* (1954). The famous tool and weapon of the skinner was the knife of the Mountain Men, the ***Green River knife,*** or skinner. (Rossi 1975)
(2) Cow skinner. Sometimes a *hide-thief.*
(3) A *muleskinner.* (Wentworth 1944)

skinning season
If a man could not find a market for his cattle, he could at least have a skinning season and earn cash from the sale of their hides. A *die-up (1)* could be followed by a skinning season.

skin-string
Since all ropes could be referred to as strings, the word skin was added to specify a *reata* or rawhide rope. (Ramon Adams 1944; Mora 1950)

skookum
(from Chinook jargon; NW).
(1) A devil, an evil spirit; sickness (which might be regarded as the same thing). (Mathews 1951)
(2) Bread, food. (Mathews 1951)
(3) Strong, well. (Weseen 1934)
(4) **skookum-house**: jail-house. (Weseen 1934; Ramon Adams 1944; Mathews 1951)

sleep
A measurement of time after the Indian manner, indicative of a 24-hour period. (Gregg 1844)

sleeper
(1) A calf marked by a thief in such a way that it could be overlooked by its owner, who would fail to brand it. There were various methods. One was to *ear-mark* the animal with the owner's mark, which at a glance would cause him to think the animal had been branded, since, normally, animals were not ear-marked without also being branded. The following year, if the trick had not been discovered, the thief would put his own

brand on the animal. The ear-mark was the sleeper mark. A second method was to brand the animal lightly with the owner's mark so the mark would grow out. Another was to pick out a brand mark by plucking the hairs; the spot would later grow over and the thief could slap on his own brand. (Wellman 1939; Weseen 1934; Mora 1950). Thus, **sleepering:** the act of making a sleeper of an animal. (North 1942)

(2) A bet in a game of faro. (Mathews 1951)

(3) An explosive charge that failed to go off in a mine; a missed hole. (Emrich 1951)

sleeper brands
Brands that were unrecorded and therefore largely unrecognized. Sleeper branding could also refer to the fadeable brands that were employed by thieves **sleepering** cattle (see *sleeper [1]*). (Ramon Adams 1944; Mathews 1951)

sleeper mark
Any mark put on an animal that made it a sleeper (see *sleeper [1]*). (Ramon Adams 1944; Mathews 1951)

slick
(1) Smooth, tidy. "Old St. Vrain went out of Santa Fe with a company of Mountain Men and the way they made 'em sing out was 'slick as shooting.'" (Ruxton 1849)

(2) A horse or cow that was unmarked or unbranded. So far as cows were concerned, it meant a *slick-ear,* one that had not been ear-marked (see *ear-mark*). (Weseen 1934; Ramon Adams 1944)

slick-ear
(1) A cow that had not been ear-marked (see *ear-mark*). Also **full-ear** (Ramon Adams 1944). In later years, in Texas and the Southwest, "eared" cattle were called *orejanos.* (North 1942)

(2) Used on the northern ranges to denote an unbranded calf. (Weseen 1934; McCarthy 1936; Mora 1950)

slickens
The useless residue or washings from hydraulic mining; fine powdered washings. Late nineteenth century. (Mathews 1951)

slicker
See *fish.*

slicker-roll
See *fish.*

slick-fork
The fork of a saddle that curved down smoothly, as opposed to a *swell-fork*. (Berrey and van den Bark 1942; Ramon Adams 1944; Mora 1950)

slick-heeled
Said of a man not wearing spurs. (Berrey and van den Bark 1942; Ramon Adams 1944)

slipper
A smooth horse-shoe, one lacking calks. (Ramon Adams 1944)

slow brand
An unrecorded brand, a cow-thief's brand. (Dobie 1929; Ramon Adams 1944)

slow elk
Meat from another man's cow. Surely Western speech at its most pithy.

sluice-box
Also **sluice**. In gold-mining, a flume or **riffle-box** (or line of such boxes) used in washing gold. Also: **to sluice**. (Mathews 1951)

Smith and Wesson
Horace Smith and Daniel B. Wesson were two great names among U.S. gunsmiths. Although a number of famous gun-toters packed Smith and Wessons at one time or another, these guns never found the market they deserved among Westerners. However, Wells Fargo supplied their guards with weapons of this make, and Wild Bill Hickok made them his

final choice after years of using Navy Colts and was carrying one when Jack McCall shot him from behind in 1876.

As early as 1857 (when Colt's patent on the revolving cylinder ran out), Smith and Wesson at their Springfield, Massachusetts, factory made a revolver that fired a metallic cartridge—they were the first in their field to do so. This was done on a patent licensed to them by the inventor Rollin White. Their early models did well, but they were complicated and frail and failed to rouse the interest of the army, where the best market lay. The firm held the monopoly on the metallic-cartridge gun market until 1869, when White's patent expired. However, it must have been hard to find a better gun than the Model 1869, with which Smith and Wesson abandoned their sheathed trigger for the conventional trigger-guard and exposed trigger. The firm then went in for the large caliber of .44. The gun held six shots and was single-action. An innovation was that, when the gun was "broken" for reloading, the C. A. King shell-extractor came into action automatically and in one movement emptied the chambers of their expended loads. When army officer George Wheeler Schofield came along, the Schofield–Smith and Wesson was developed: a heavier, simpler, and altogether stronger weapon. The army bought some, but not in sufficient numbers to prevent the firm from turning its attention to foreign trade. The weapons did well in Russia, Turkey, and Mexico. The Smith and Wessons did indeed have a more European look about them, and I suspect that Westerners were conditioned to the shape and feel of the Colts and Remingtons. The Schofield–Smith and Wesson model 1875 was single-action in the larger and then more popular caliber of .45. (Bowman 1953; Peterson 1963)

smoke
(1) A cigarette. Rolled by hand and of various components. Time was often measured by the duration of a smoked cigarette.
(2) Among Indians, to hold talks under peaceful conditions.
(3) To dry meat or to harden something in smoke.
(4) To **read smoke**: to understand the smoke signals of Indians.
(5) To **smoke up**: to shoot at something or somebody. (Ramon Adams 1944; Hoig 1960)
(6) To **smoke out**: to drive an enemy or quarry from cover with smoke.
(7) To **make smoke** or to **come out smoking**: to shoot, to break out of somewhere with guns in action.

smoothbore
Usually a shot-gun, but could apply to any gun whose barrel is not rifled. Not a Westernism.

snake
To drag an object—say a log of wood—along the ground by means of a rope, which would usually be fastened to the horn of a saddle.

snake-eater
See *road runner.*

snake-fence
Also **Virginia Fence, worm-fence.** A zigzag rail fence that could be largely constructed without upright posts. (Mathews 1951). See also *pole fence.*

snake-headed
Mean, ornery, unpleasant—applied to a man.

snake-head whiskey
A crude form of whiskey such as might be sold to Indians. So called because, as the story has it, one of the original makers nailed snake-heads inside the barrels to give it flavor. (Ramon Adams 1944)

snake-killer
See *road runner.*

snake-root, snake-weed
See *hierba de vibora.*

snakes
Cunning Longhorns that evaded capture and were left behind in the thickets and gullies after the gather was complete. (Dobie 1941)

snare
See *trap (1).*

snaring
(Texas). The unexpected catching of cattle in wild country. (Dobie 1941). Or, simply, to catch with a rope.

snow-birds
Men who enlisted in the army for food and shelter during the winter months and deserted in the spring. (Vestal 1939). Rossi 1975 says this term is now used in the Southwest for northerners who come south for the winter months.

snow-shoe rabbit
Also **snow-shoe.** *Lepus americanus.* A common hare of the northern regions that moults to white fur in winter. (Mathews 1951)

snub
Also **snub up.** To tie to a post or other object. Farmer 1889: "to tie up, to secure." Bartlett 1877: "SNUB UP: An expression used by canal-boatmen,

meaning to 'tie up their boats.' " North 1942: "Down at the corral two of the boys are engaged in blindfolding the animal's eyes and they have not found it necessary to throw him for he already has a hackamore on his head and they have snubbed this sternly close to the horn of a saddle on the back of a staid old cowhorse of powerful build."

snubbed
Dehorned. (Ramon Adams 1944)

snubbing post
A post to which a horse might be tied. Farmer 1889 does not note it as a Westernism, but says: "A post to which horses and cattle are tied." (Weseen 1934; North 1942; Ramon Adams 1944)

snuff
Not **up to snuff.** Not competent, not up to scratch. Andy Adams 1909: " 'I was selling a thousand beef steers one time to some Yankee army contractors,' Pierce was narrating to a circle of listeners, 'and I got the idea that they were not up to snuff in receiving cattle out of the Prairie.' "

snuffy
Jumpy, sniffy, suspicious. Dobie 1941 says: "The steer was alone. He approached very, very slowly, often stopping to look behind him and to all sides—listening, alert in the nostrils. He was 'snuffy' at his own shadow." (Berrey and van den Bark 1942; Ramon Adams 1944)

soda-butte
(NW). A butte of alkaline composition. (Mathews 1951)

soda-prairie
Prairie land covered by soda. (Mathews 1951)

soda-sinkers
Doughnuts in which soda was an ingredient.

soda-spring
A spring giving off soda-impregnated water. (Stewart 1964)

sodbuster
A cattleman's name for a farmer. Though commonly used in fiction of the twentieth century, it was not found widely in contemporary literature, but was in use colloquially. (Havighurst 1957; Ramon Adams 1944)

soddy
Also **soddie.**
(1) Often the house of the early *sodbuster,* made from pieces

of turf, cut and usually piled one upon the other in the manner of bricks. If a hill or a ridge was available, it would probably be built in the form of a *dug-out (1)*. The roof in all likelihood would also be of sods. This made a cool house in summer and probably a warm one in winter, but in rainy weather it must have been hell to live in: soddies leaked like sieves. Houses were made this way, of course, because of the absence of wood on the plains. (Berrey and van den Bark 1942; Ramon Adams 1944; Wentworth 1944; Hawgood 1967)

(2) Short for *sodbuster.* (Ramon Adams 1944)

sod-fence
A retaining wall of a field made up (in the absence of wood for normal fencing) of sods cut from the prairies. (Osgood 1929)

soft-horn
A tenderfoot. (Berrey and van den Bark 1942)

soft-mouthed
Also **sweet-mouthed**. Said of a horse sensitive to the bit.

soiled dove
A prostitute. A Victorianism beloved of newspapermen and contemporary literature. Not truly a Westernism, but found fairly frequently in Western writings.

soldier
Among some Indian tribes, such as the Cheyenne, there were warrior societies, the members of which were known to the whites as soldiers. They

were used by the tribes in the manner of police—though that term simplifies their role greatly. They restrained the impetuous young men on the buffalo hunt and in war. Among the Cheyenne, there were several such societies—the *dog soldiers,* the kit foxes, etc. These societies extended beyond the tribal boundaries, and a Cheyenne might find himself a fellow society member with Sioux, Arapaho, and Mandans. (MacLeod 1937–38; Catlin 1851; Utley 1963)

sombrero
(Sp; SW). A broad-brimmed Mexican hat. Sometimes used in reference to any wide-brimmed male headgear. (Weseen 1934)

some
A little; but also in a sense, a large quantity. The meaning depended on the context: A man, when asked if he could rope, might reply with modest understatement, "Some." On the other hand, to lay emphasis on a statement one could tack on "and then some": "We covered a hundred miles an' then some." A small word, hard to define. (Mathews 1951 confirms both meanings historically.)

son-of-a-bitch stew
Also abbreviated to simply **son-of-a bitch.** The only true name that this fine veal dish could answer to, though it was known in polite society as **son-of-a-gun stew.** Rightly the most renowned of Western dishes, there were as many variations as there were cooks—as it should be. (I now paraphrase unashamedly part of Ramon Adams's charming "Cookie" [1957].) All versions included sweetbreads, marrow gut, and kidneys added to the best meat of the calf—calf meat possibly because, on trail-drives, calves were expendable. The best of the species was made of the meat of un-weaned calves; in these animals the marrow gut between the two stomachs is tender and flavored the dish well. Some cooks added onions or chilis or both. The recognized thickening was made of brains and flour. Also, in the later days, known among cattlemen as **district attorney** (Ramon Adams 1944; Foster-Harris 1955) and **county attorney.** The implication is obvious. (Wentworth 1944; Weseen politely refers only to **son-of-a-gun stew,** but that was in 1934)

sooner
This word could be applied to any man who "jumped the gun" by moving into territory or a situation before the allotted time: for example, those men who went ahead of the starting time during the land-run on the Cherokee Strip in 1889. (Berrey and van den Bark 1942)

soopollalie
(from Chinook *olallie;* NW). *Shepherdia.* The buffalo berry. (Mathews 1951)

sop
Gravy. (Weseen 1934)

sopapilla
Biscuit fried in fat. Called **buñuelo** in New Mexico.

sorrel
A reddish horse color, which some writers describe as having a slightly golden tinge. Not to be confused with *bay (1):* the mane and tail of such a horse are never dark as with a bay.

sotol
(Mex-Sp from Nahuatl; Texas and SW). One of the several *Dasylirion.* A member of the yucca family with long stiff leaves, which Dobie 1955 says were used as flares or torches.

sougan
Also **sugan** (Berrey and van den Bark 1942), **suggan** (Ramon Adams 1944; Wentworth 1944), **sugin** (Weseen 1934), **soogan, suggans.** A closely woven blanket or quilt, used particularly by cattlemen. (Emrich 1951)

sourdough
(1) The dough from which the cow-crew cook made bread and flapjacks, particularly on the trail. How he managed to make bread under cattle-trail conditions, I shall never know. However, a batter was mixed of flour and water with a pinch of salt. Potatoes or cornmeal were sometimes added to increase fermentation and often molasses and sugar were also. The container was then covered and stored in a warm place, for it was essential to maintain the correct temperature or fermentation would cease. When baking time came, this starter  was added to flour with a little more salt, some soda, and warm water. Lard or bacon grease was thrown in as fat. If you favored a brown crust you could put in some sugar at this stage. You then mixed thoroughly; this process may have given rise to: "We got fresh bread, men—cusie [see *cocinero*] has clean hands." When the mixing was completed, the dough was laid on the work table at the rear of the mess wagon and rolled and kneaded to a fine consistency. Next, the mixture was placed in a well greased Dutch oven with hot coals above and below it. (The secret was to keep the oven well greased to prevent sticking.) The last vital step was to place the starter in a safe place so that you had the right ingredient for your next baking.
(2) A biscuit.
(3) A cook. (Ramon Adams 1944)

(4) A bachelor. (Ramon Adams 1944)

(5) A prospector, rather indicating that he was a tough old-timer who used sourdough for his baking. (Mathews 1951)

sowbelly
Salt pork; fat pork from the belly of a pig. (Mathews 1951)

sowbosom
Salt pork, *sowbelly.* One of a number of Western euphemisms to be used in the presence of ladies. (Ramon Adams 1944; Wentworth 1944; Dobie 1930)

spade bit
See *Spanish bit.*

span
A pair of draft animals hitched side by side in the traces of a wagon or plow. Not a Westernism.

Spanish bayonet
See *datil.*

Spanish bit
More properly perhaps **Spanish spade bit**. A bit with a large port, which, if wrongly used, could agonize a horse's mouth. Often there would be a roller or cricket on the port, which the horse could play with its tongue. In California horses were broken with a hackamore and so were soft-mouthed for a gently used spade bit. (Mora 1950)

Spanish cattle
A term loosely used by some writers to refer to cattle of Mexican origin, but applied by the purists to the wild *black cattle* of Old Texas. (Dobie 1941)

Spanish dagger
Several varieties of cactus, but especially *Yucca gloriosa.* Dobie 1929: "The hardy Spanish dagger will not retreat one inch for animal or plant, but sends its flower-stalk like a flag to victory overtopping the plain of thorn and leaf." The author also informs us that if the poison from this cactus is inserted into the flesh above a snake-bite, the snake venom is counteracted. (Mathews 1951)

Spanish fever
See *Texas fever.*

Spanish horse
The number of references found concerning this term lead only to confusion, but there's no doubt that the Old Westerner knew what he meant when he used it. As indicated by its name, the animal was a descendant of the horses brought over by the Conquistadores—which could mean a horse that came of a long line that led back to Old Spain; it could also mean an animal of mustang lineage. However, it was used mostly to denote a horse of Mexican or Californian origin, of light conformation and generally a solid *bay (1)* or *sorrel.*

Spanish needle grass
Also **Spanish needles**. *Stipa spartia.* Prairie porcupine grass, extremely painful to the mouth of cattle. (Mathews 1951)

Spanish rig
A saddle with one cinch directly beneath the saddlehorn.

Spanish supper
The tightening of the belt over an empty belly. (Ramon Adams 1944)

Spanish trot
A horse's gait: an easy swinging trot. (Weseen 1934; Berrey and van den Bark 1942)

Spencer
Manufactured by Christopher Spencer's Spencer Repeating Rifle Co., this was one of the handiest little repeating carbines to come out of the Civil War into the West. It gave the Union forces great superiority of firepower, and the Confederates said wryly that you could "load it on Sunday and shoot all week." Its lever action was easy to handle, and the weapon itself was ideal for the mounted man. The early models were loaded with individual shells through the butt-plate, but the later ones were loaded with a tube packed with seven rounds. It came in various calibers, from the early .52 to the later .56. (Peterson 1963; Bowman 1953)

spider
See *scabbards: Rifle Scabbards.*

spike team
A three-horse team used to pull the prairie schooners on the westering migrant trails. (Rossi and Hunt 1971)

spilled
Thrown from a horse. (Weseen 1934; Ramon Adams 1944)

spilling stock
Allowing stock to scatter while driving them. (Rossi 1975)

spinner
A horse given to bucking in tight circles. A term developed in the later
bronc-riding competition days. (Ramon Adams 1944; Clinton 1967)

split-ear bridle
See *bridles (1)*.

spondulix
(origin unknown—to me, at any rate). Money. Spelled variously **spon-
dulicks, spondulics, sponduliks,** etc. Not a Westernism, but it became a
part of the Western vocabulary toward the end of our period.

spook
To frighten or be frightened—particularly horses and cattle, but the word
could be applied to humans also. (Ramon Adams 1944; Mathews 1951)

spooky
Liable to be easily scared. Said of cattle likely to be stampeded, or of a
nervous horse. (Branch 1926; Wentworth 1944; Ramon Adams 1944)

spot cord
As the soft *hair lariat* was to the rawhide *reata,* so was the spot cord to
the *hard twist* manila rope. A light rope of twisted cotton, which was
introduced latterly with *grass rope* in cow-country. (North 1942)

spotted horse
A variety of this animal was known in Europe in prehistoric times. In the
Western states of the United States, it was represented by the *Appaloosa*
and the **Colorado Ranger** (a later development).

spread
An established range, the land of a cattle- or sheep-outfit and the buildings
thereon. Hence, a **cattle-spread, sheep-spread,** and the names of outfits
which might include the owner's name, the brand, or the *ear-mark:*
Chisum Spread, Jingle Bob Spread, Rocking Chair Spread.

Springfield
The Springfield rifle was very much a part of the Old West, if for no other
reason than that it was the weapon of the army in its fights with Plains
Indians for many years. Its official life was long, for it was used during the
Spanish-American War and was even carried by some state troops at the
start of World War I. Springfield really came into its own in 1866, when
the army in the West was demanding a faster-loading rifle with more

fire-power. Such a weapon was created by converting muzzle-loaders to hinged breech loading, an operation designed and carried out by Erskine H. Allin, the firm's master-armorer, and developed into the renowned Springfield .45–70 side-hammer of 1873 (the Trap Door or Trap Door Model), which made single-loading a quick and comparatively easy process. The weapon stayed sturdy and serviceable. The movable breechblock (including a firing pin) was hinged at the front so that it could easily be raised to expose the chamber and eject a spent cartridge. It was then a simple matter to reload, close the block, and cock the side-hammer. (Peterson 1963; Rossi 1975)

spring round-up
The calf round-up in the spring. (North 1942; Ramon Adams 1944)

spring wagon
A light wagon, sometimes called a **platform spring wagon,** which was something of a luxury in a land of rough trails and rutted roads. The wagon-bed was shallow and the driving seat high above the sides. Each wheel was

sprung individually on steel springs; the front wheels were smaller than those at the rear. See also *wagons.*

spur leathers
Also **spur straps.** Straps which went over the instep of the boot and held the spur in position, sometimes beautifully tooled with intricate designs. (Ramon Adams 1944; Mora 1950)

spurs
The spur is composed of a heel-band, a shank, and, commonly, a rowel. Roughly speaking, the fashion in spurs showed some difference east and west of the Rockies, as in so many other things concerning horses and horsemen. The California spur, true to the Spanish-Mexican influence, tended to be more highly decorated and larger. Shanks could be straight or curved, the curves described according to their depth: one-third, a quarter, half, or full curve. The Old Californios favored so great a curve that the spur had to be removed on dismounting if the owner wished to

walk. The Mexican style fitted to the boot-heel, the Anglo to the foot-heel. The Californians wore their spurs loose with a chain under the instep of the foot, while most Anglos wore a tight strap (see *spur leather*). Rowels were of various design but usually took the shape of wheels and stars.

Most spurs look much alike to the uninitiated, but to the horseman there is a great difference between them. In fact, bring two Western horsemen together and raise the subject and you'll get as good an argument as you would if you started comparing the dally system of *roping* with the hard-and-fast style. To the modern city man, the spur seems a cruel and barbarous piece of equipment, but, as with a bit, a spur is as cruel as the man using it. A large, savage-looking Mexican spur used to be no more painful to a horse than a small one; indeed, the small spur with a single spike is more likely to be cruel. The horseman of the Old West, particularly the Californian, used the spur for guidance and as an emergency starter.

 In fact, the judicious use of his armed heels saved many a vaquero from coming off worst in a disagreement with a *ladino* on the prod. (Mora 1950; Foster-Harris 1955)

squad
A small bunch of cattle. Andy Adams 1909: "Strayhorn explained to us that the cattle had struck some recent fencing on their course, and after following down the fence for several miles, had encountered an offset, and the angle had held the squad until The Rebel and Blades overtook them."

squat
(1) To occupy land without legal claim. The meaning was extended at times to include the occupation of land, whether claimed or unclaimed. (Mathews 1951)
(2) A piece of land, a land-claim. (Dobie 1930)

squatter
(1) A man, settled without legal claim on land either legally claimed by another man or simply occupied by him.
(2) A term applied in the brush-country of Texas to a Longhorn that sat tight in the deep thickets when a *cowhunt* was mounted. (Dobie 1941)

squaw
An Indian woman, rather implying that she was either married or living with a man. (Schultz 1935; Berrey and van den Bark 1942). As distasteful a term as buck for a man. See also *buck (1)*.

squaw cabbage
Also **Indian lettuce, miners' lettuce.** *Montia perfoliata.* Greens; a succulent herb. (Mathews 1951)

squaw dance
Among Indians, a dance in which the women were by tradition free to choose their partners from among the men. (Mathews 1951)

squawman
A whiteman either married to or cohabiting with an Indian woman, a practice frowned upon when white women became more common in the Old West. In the early days, squawmen, like halfbreeds, were an invaluable medium of liaison between the two races. (Ramon Adams 1944)

squaw saddle
A horse saddle such as that used by squaws; a padded blanket or quilt after the fashion of the old *aparejo.*

squaw side
See *off-side.*

squaw talk
Inconsequential women's talk.

squaw wood
(1) Dried cowchips or buffalo chips used as fuel. (Ramon Adams 1944)
(2) Wood that was easily gathered without chopping. (Mathews 1951)

squeezer
A small pen or corral in which cattle could be close-herded for a short period—for example, to be branded. Also applied to the branding chute itself (see *branding*). (Ramon Adams 1944)

squeeze them down
Newton and Gambrell 1949 quote Charles Goodnight: "Under normal conditions, the herd was fifty to sixty feet across, the thickness being governed by the distance we had to go before resting. When the signal was given to start the herd, the foreman would tell the men what width to make the herd. Therefore, the order might be ten or twenty feet. Narrowing the string was called 'squeezing them down.' Ten feet was the longest limit, for when the line was this width, gaps came and cattle began trotting to fill the spaces. Then the pointers would check them in front. The fastest steppers would naturally go up a little; but they were never allowed to trot. After a herd was handled a month or two they became gentler and it was necessary to ride a little closer to obtain the same results." (Ramon Adams 1944; Berrey and van den Bark 1942)

squinch owl
See *burrowing owl.*

squirrel can
Weseen 1934 states this is a general cooking utensil, but Ramon Adams 1944 claims it as a receptacle carried on a chuck wagon for throwing odds and ends into. The term itself suggests that, in its general use, Adams must be right.

stags
(Texas). Male cow-brutes castrated late in life. Their horns could be pretty long, but were seldom as long as those of steers that had lost their bull-hood early in life and seemed to make up for their loss by growth of horn. The Mexicans believed that an animal should not be castrated until it had reached or passed maturity. (Dobie 1941; Ramon Adams 1944)

stake
(1) As a verb it referred to financing somebody in an enterprise. **To grubstake**: to supply the food or wherewithal for a venture such as a gold-hunt. To **make a stake** meant to make enough money to give oneself a start in life or in a certain enterprise.
(2) To **pull** or **pull up stakes**: to depart; to pull up one's hitch pins (see *picket pin*) or claim-stake. (Dobie 1930; Mathews 1951)

stake and rider
Bartlett 1877: "A species of fence higher and stronger than a 'worm fence.'" Farmer 1889: "A kind of high fence." It zigzagged, with the intersecting horizontals resting on each other at the ends. At these intersections were two high stakes that crossed above the horizontals; where they crossed, top horizontals rested, greatly heightening the fence. The additional top rail was called the **rider**. Not a Westernism. (Mathews 1951)

stake pin
See *picket pin*.

staked plain
A wide plain so devoid of landmarks that it was necessary to mark a trail with stakes to avoid being lost. The term implies an extensive barren treeless plain. Hence, the famous Staked Plain, Llano Estacado, once a great grazing ground of the buffalo (till 1879) and the refuge of the Comanches, stretching between the Pecos and Canadian rivers across the Texas–New Mexico line. Here the great cattlemen, such as Goodnight and Slaughter, drove in their Longhorns and claimed their empires on grassland of some 40,000 square miles.

stake rope
See *picket pin*.

stallions

Most fighting Indians preferred stallions as war-horses and claimed they had more staying power and fighting spirit than any other. Whitemen mostly preferred geldings, as stallions could cause damage to geldings and were a nuisance to mares.

stampede

(Sp *estampida*). Also *stompede.* The mass bolting of cattle when alarmed. Although Longhorns, once running, would often stampede at the slightest unusual sound, sight, or smell, it was generally considered that they held together and did not scatter singly as did more domesticated cattle such as Durhams and Herefords. Longhorns were known to take to their heels at the snapping of a twig, the approach or arrival of a storm, or the sudden movement of a rabbit. Some herds stampeded a dozen times on the trail from Texas to the railhead in Kansas, with the unfortunate trail-boss losing animals each time he rounded them up. There were various opinions on what should be done by riders in a stampede, opinions that may be divided roughly into the majority who thought a *mill* was the answer and the minority who believed that if you let cattle run and stuck with them, fewer would be injured and lost by the time they had run themselves out.

J. Frank Dobie, that marvelous man so rich in Western lore, suggests in *The Longhorns* (1941) that the man who really knew cattle would, at the outset of the stampede, leave all his men in camp except one besides himself and act on the assumption that Longhorns would stay together if left alone. The trick was to ride in front of them, singing to them and making himself their leader. In this way he could gradually slow them by reducing his own pace, riding zigzag to control the direction of the herd. Speaking for myself, I can think of more enjoyable occupations on a dark and stormy night. Dobie adds that some cowmen liked to have a few calves on a drive: in the event of a stampede, if a cow became separated from her calf, the she-crittur would bawl for her young and the sound would steady the other animals. However, he points out, a herd composed of animals of uneven ages was often disjointed because of the different traveling speeds of the animals. Added to this, in a stampede, very young stock could be injured or killed.

Charles Goodnight, as might be expected, had something interesting to say on stampedes: "When cattle are first started, the risk of stampedes is great. They are nervous and easily frightened, the slightest noise may startle them into running. Some cattle are stampeders by nature. The greatest losses occurred in the night when all was utter confusion. A herd was more likely to run on a dark night than on a moonlight night. The remarkable thing about it was that the whole herd started instantly, jarring the earth like an earthquake. We could not divine the course they were taking until they had gone far enough for the sound to guide us—unless they were coming toward us. In that case, I led the herd, holding them back as much as possible. As soon as the herd was strung out, we would turn the leaders back. They would circle and go into what was called a 'mill,' invariably moving to the right (if any old trailman ever heard of a herd moving to the left, I would like to hear from him). The cattle would run until they were tired and we gradually spread them and they would settle down. We never took the cattle back to the same bed ground for we knew they would run again. We also tried to find the highest ground. Once they settled they would generally be quiet. As a rule it took several days to rid the cattle of the effect of a stampede. The most successful way I found was to drive them all night. This way had them under control with the men all around them. I placed two of my most skillful men behind at what we called the corners and four more in front. If it was dark and the cattle had been badly stampeded they would not go far until they began to run again; not all of them would be running, however. Strange to say, there would be about one-third the herd that were marching along as though nothing had happened, while the rest of the herd would be going at a mad rate. The stampeders would come up one side at full speed, but when they reached the front the men in the lead would catch them and turn them back on the other side; then the men on the corners would drive them back again. These cattle would run until they were in great distress; we followed this method again the next night and the cattle were cured. They never stampeded again." (Quoted in Newton and Gambrell 1949)

Writers of fact and fiction have occupied themselves mostly with the stampede of Longhorns, which, heaven knows, was formidable enough, but hardly to be compared with that of the buffalo. Cow-panic among 500 or 1,000 head of half-wild cattle was sufficiently bad, but when 5,000 to 10,000 buffalo took off, it must have been as if the surface of the earth itself reared up and charged insanely at everything in its path. Buffalo ran blind. When the railroad first pushed its way across the plains of Kansas, the engineers thought their iron-horses a match for any hump-backed ruminant, but they soon learned better. Stampeding buffalo neither avoided nor stopped for anything. Maybe many buffalo were killed in the process, but the railroadmen soon learned to give the Lord of the Plains best and stopped to let his hordes pass. The Indians knew well that, once spooked, the buffalo would stop for nothing; and before the Indians learned the excitement of running the great animals down and killing them from horseback, they would stampede them over cliffs and into blind canyons to kill them more easily.

The verb **to stampede** meant to cause a stampede and to take part in one. By extension, of course, the word could be employed to describe the actions of humans; thus we have **land stampede** and **gold stampede**. Causing a stampede was one of the techniques employed by both Indians and whites to lift the stock of other men.

stamping ground
Bartlett 1877 says: "S. and W. The scene of one's exploits, or favorite place of resort." Dobie 1930: "Home range."

stamp iron
Also **stamping iron**. A branding iron with the brand formed at one end of the tool. So called to differentiate it from a *running-iron*. (Ramon Adams 1944)

stand
Stand of buffalo or **buffalo stand**. What a buffalo hunter prayed for. It was not long after the whiteman abandoned the old Indian custom of running buffalo, dropping them from the saddle, that white hunters discovered that the buffalo herd, given the right wind, could not smell the blood of a slaughtered fellow nor the hunter and would not stampede. Which meant that the hunter could keep right on shooting, knocking over animal after animal without the rest taking flight. Phenomenal kills were made in this way, often twenty to thirty animals being shot without alarming the others. Far bigger stands are recorded, some of which run into hundreds. With this technique, Joe McCombs is said to have killed over 4,000 animals in one season in 1878. (Ramon Adams 1944; Sandoz 1954; McHugh 1972)

stand up
To hold up, to stop a stagecoach and rob it. Wellman 1939: "Curly Bill Brocius stepped into the leadership of the rustlers after Old Man Clanton's death. One of the collateral activities of the gang was 'standing up' the stages which often carried gold from Tombstone and Bisbee."

Starr
Eben T. Starr (of the Starr Arms Company of New York) was a maker of revolvers that were eclipsed only by those of Colt and Remington. Supplies of the .44-caliber, six-shot gun to the Union Army reached nearly 40,000. And it is usually a good measure that if a gun was popular with the army, it later became pretty common in the West. While it was not so handsome as the Colt or Remington, it was a highly efficient pistol, capable of being employed as a double-action gun by the use of one trigger and as a single-action weapon by the use of another. It possessed a top-breaking action and weighed about three pounds. The company also produced a six-shot, single-action .36 gun. The butt-base was of the narrow type not generally favored by Colt and Remington, but found in the Smith and Wessons and English guns. (Bowman 1953)

starve-out
A corral or pen for horses, lacking natural water and grass, into which

horses were thrown for easy catching. (Allen 1933; Weseen 1934; Ramon Adams 1944)

States blood
Eastern blood introduced into the mustang strain. (North 1942)

States cattle
Also **pilgrims, barnyard stock.** Eastern cattle, meaning cattle from the United States, which to the Westerner of the territories was the proper name for the Eastern states. (Osgood 1929)

States fruit
Also *States eggs* (Ramon Adams 1944). Simply hen's eggs, rare on the cattle-range. One of the few commodities for which the cowman envied the Easterner. The hen's egg was not considered a product of the Western territories, but of the United States proper. Hoig 1960: "Many a café 'biscuit shooter' [see *biscuit-shooter (1)*], upon seeing a cowboy crew hit town, would dig out all his 'States fruit' even before he heard the inevitable 'Keep mine bright-eyed' or 'I'll have 'em dirty on both sides.' "

stay
There were a number of admonitions to a man to stay on a pitching bronc: "Stay on your ellum fork," "Stay in your pine," "Stay with 'er," "Stay in your tree." (Weseen 1934; Ramon Adams 1944)

steeple fork
A cattle *ear-mark.* A cut into the under-curve of the ear below the tip. (Ramon Adams 1944)

steer
Generally, in the West, an ox or bullock, a grown castrated male cow-critter. Among the Longhorns, they grew longer horns than the bulls or cows. In the West, of course, they were also known simply as cows, for to impart masculinity to anything in the presence of ladies was considered disgusting. Most cattle sold to the markets, were beeves, steers raised for that purpose.

steer rassling
Throwing a steer by hand; it later became an established rodeo term. (Weseen 1934)

St. Elmo's fire
Also **fox-fire** (Berrey and van den Bark 1942; Ramon Adams 1944). The phosphorescent light seen on the horn-tips of cattle and ears of horses during stormy weather, described by many chroniclers of the trail-drivers.

(Some Mexican vaqueros wore a ball of beeswax on the crown of their hats as a protection against lightning.) (Dobie 1941)

Stetson

A wide-brimmed, high-crowned Western hat. John Batterson Stetson (1830–1906) founded his famous firm in 1865 in Philadelphia. The name became synonymous for a cow-country hat, as did the name Colt for a belt-gun. Crown and brim could be molded by hand and the elements shaped to the owner's fancy. The hats were often referred to as JBs, after the maker's initials, and came in a variety of dimensions, some wider in brim and higher in crown than  others. The first model was called the Boss (see *boss [3]*), followed by the Carlsbad (the most popular line). If a man wanted something higher, wider, and handsomer, there was always the Buckeye. The Stetson virtues were durability and adaptability: you could dance on it, water-soak it, and even shoot a hole in it and it would still reflect the character and taste of the wearer—a battered crown with a corrugated brim, round-crowned, part-crowned, four-finger-pinch-crowned in the Montana peak (the favorite early shape), curly-brimmed, or straight-brimmed; it did as you wished. (Mora 1950; Ramon Adams 1944; Foster-Harris 1955)

stew-ball

See *skeebald.*

stick-and-mud chimney

A chimney of adobe and sticks. (Dobie 1930; Foster-Harris 1955)

stick-poker

An Indian guessing game played with sticks. Among adults, high stakes were played for. (Mathews 1951)

stirrup-iron

Sometimes referred to as simply **stirrup,** which correctly is the *stirrup-leather* plus the stirrup-iron. To make matters more confusing, in the early days this support for the horseman's foot was not made of iron at all, but was carved  from a single piece of wood. Later the wood was bound with rawhide or wrapped with metal; eventually the support was made from iron. Compared with the Eastern or European stirrup-iron, those of the West were heavy and utilitarian. They were an essential part of the working equipment of the cattleman, and great strain could be put on the leather and iron during the working of cattle. See also *tapaderos.*

stirrup-leather
The broad strap hanging on each side of the saddle which supported the *stirrup-iron*.

stock association
Cattle became worth stealing when they became worth selling, so, when Texans discovered that it was profitable to drive their cattle to the Kansas markets and to the northern ranges, they found it necessary to form associations for the mutual protection of their stock. The first were formed after the initial post-war drives in 1868. In the early 1870s strong stock growers' associations sprang up in Wyoming. (Osgood 1929)

stock detectives
Men hired by cattlemen's associations (see *stock association*) to hunt down cow-thieves. They were particularly active in Montana and Wyoming in the second half of the 1870s and through the 1880s.

stock horse
A brood mare. (Weseen 1934)

stock inspectors
Men hired by cattlemen's associations (see *stock association*) to inspect ranges, stock, and brands as a protection against theft. The term might also be applied to those men who were employed by large ranchers and associations to cut trail-herds for local brands. At times the dividing line between an inspector and detective was slight. (Osgood 1929)

stock saddle
A saddle especially made for the working of cattle, strong enough in the horn and tree to withstand the enormous stress and strain laid on it by roping animals. A term certainly in use by 1880.

stogie
A particularly foul black cigar which was carried by traders on Conestoga wagons, of which the term is a shortened form. (Wentworth 1944)

stomp
To stamp. (Dobie 1930)

stompede
A variant of stampede. Among other writers, J. Frank Dobie uses this form, notably in *The Longhorns* (1941). This recalls the version of *stomp* for *stamp*.

store-boughten, store-broughten
See *boughten*.

stove up
Also **stove in**. Ruined, worn out. Particularly applied to the bronc buster who has topped off one too many broncs, rather like a boxer who has taken one too many punches.

straddle bug
A land- or mine-claim marker made up of three boards standing upright in a triangular form. A term that probably existed at the end of the nineteenth century and certainly at the start of the twentieth. (Mathews 1951)

straight iron
A *running-iron* with which a brand was drawn free-hand (rather than stamped) on the hide of a cow. (North 1942)

straight shooter
See *shoot square.*

stranger
The West retained the ancient habit of calling a stranger a stranger to his face and thought to give no offense in so doing.

Stranglers
The Stranglers was a name given to a group of powerful Montana cattlemen who in 1884 organized themselves as vigilantes in order, it is said, to clear the country of small-fry opposition, sheepmen, small ranchers, and horse- and cow-thieves. Possibly a good many honest men died of an overtight necktie. Some of the atrocities laid at their door make ghastly reading. The leader of the Stranglers in Montana was Granville Stuart, a cattleman of power and good reputation. There are strong arguments both in his favor and against him. Strangler was also a general term for vigilantes given by those who disapproved of them. (Sandoz 1958; Richard Brown 1969)

strawberries
Beans. So called by lumberjacks. (Weseen 1934). Noted by Berrey and van den Bark 1942 as a term used by lodgers. Also seen as *Arizona strawberries,* Arkansas strawberries, Mexican strawberries, prairie strawberries.

strawberry roan
A horse with a coat of a distinctly red color.

strawboss
Also **straw**. The foreman of a ranch; an assistant foreman. (Weseen 1934; Ramon Adams 1944)

stray
Also *estray.* An animal that had wandered from its herd or customary range. (Osgood 1929; Ramon Adams 1944)

stray man
(1) A cowhand searching for stray cattle beyond the boundaries of his range. (Weseen 1934)
(2) A hand representing his brand at a round-up outside his own area looking for strays bearing his outfit's brand. (North 1942; Ramon Adams 1944; Mora 1950)

stretch hemp
To be hanged by the neck. (Weseen 1934)

string
(1) The team of saddle-horses allotted to one cowboy either on a ranch or a trail-drive. (Weseen 1934; Ramon Adams 1944). Also **mount**.
(2) A rope, a lasso; applied to both reatas and grass ropes. You could distinguish it as a *reata* by calling it a **skin-string**. (Mora 1950)
(3) Saddle-string on the flank skirt of a saddle for fastening bed-rolls and other equipment to the saddle. (Mora 1950)
(4) A line of pack-animals, either tied together or loose.

string up
To hang by the neck. A punishment that could be awarded summarily by an isolated and irate cattleman to cow- or horse-thieves, or legally by official upholders of the law. (Dobie 1930)

strip
A narrow length of country. Also found in such names as the **Cherokee Strip**.

strong talk
Andy Adams 1909 writes: "Finally Robert, seeing that I was overanxious to go, came to me and said: 'I've been thinking that if I recommended you to Jim Flood, my old foreman, he might take you with him next year. He is to have a herd that will take five months from start to delivery, and it will be the chance of your life. I'll see him next week and make a strong talk for you.' "

stud
A stud-horse, a stallion.

study
To consider, to think about. (Wentworth 1944)

stuff
(1) (SW). Buried treasure. (Dobie 1930)
(2) Cattle. (Weseen 1934; Ramon Adams 1944)

suaro
See *saguaro.*

sudaderos
(Mex-Sp). Often used for *rosaderos.* More properly, the lining of a saddle-skirt. (Ramon Adams 1944; Mora 1950)

sugan, suggan, suggans, sugin
See *sougan.*

sugar-eater
A pampered horse. (Weseen 1934)

suhuaro
See *saguaro.*

suicide gun
A gun that lacked the power to stop a man dead, notably the Colt .32. (Willison 1952)

sull
Farmer 1889 says: "(Texan)—to have the sulks. An obvious corruption." Dobie 1941: " 'I rode that steer myself,' Rhodes inscribed on the flyleaf of a copy of the story that he gave away—'a brindle steer with big horns. Seven miles I made him go before he sulled on me. I wasn't particular where he went, you see, or he might have sulled sooner. Where I wanted to go was away.' " (Wentworth 1944)

sumach
Also **sumac.** A bush of the genus *Rhus.* Andy Adams 1909: "We had every horse under hand before the sun peeped over the eastern horizon, and when returning to camp with the *remuda,* as I rode through a bunch of sumach bush, I found a wild turkey's nest with sixteen eggs in it."

Sunday horse
A cowhand's horse chosen for "occasions" because of its good appearance and behavior, possibly a single-footer (see *single-foot*) and usually a horse with a handsome gait. (Weseen 1934; Ramon Adams 1944)

sunfish
A dangerous jumping twist sometimes made by a bronc in the process of being broken by a rider. During the movement, the animal has first one side toward the ground and then the other. Such a horse was said to be **sunning his belly** or **sunning his sides.** (Weseen 1934). Ramon Adams 1944 uses the term **sunfisher** for a horse that sunfishes.

surcingle
A strap or girth, with or without saddle, that goes around a horse's barrel. Rossi 1975 reminds me that it often went around and over the old McClellan army saddle and side-saddles as an extra precaution. A surcingle could also be used by a rider who wished to use stirrups without a saddle. Not a Westernism and still common in general English.

surface coal
(west Texas). Cow-dung fuel. (Wentworth 1944)

surrey
A light, two-seated, four-wheel, horse-drawn vehicle based on a design imported from England in the early 1870s. The sides were open; the roof was soft, rectangular, and had a fringed frieze around its edges.

surround
A method of hunting wild animals in which they were completely encircled, then either killed as they broke for freedom or driven over a cliff or into a trap-pen. The method was employed by Indians and occasionally by whites. (Catlin 1851)

suwarro
See *saguaro.*

swag
(1) A quantity, a load.
(2) A low place, a coulee. (Ramon Adams 1944; Dobie 1930)

swallow fork
(1) A certain *ear-mark* of cattle in which the shape of a swallow's tail was cut out of the ear. (Wentworth 1944; Ramon Adams 1944)
(2) To wander, to travel without purpose or care. (Dobie 1930)

swallow his head
This expression described the action of a horse when it pitched or bucked by putting its head between its forelegs and bending its back. (Ramon Adams 1944)

swamp angels
(Texas). Runty cattle. Dobie 1964: "Shanghai brought the boy to Texas where he could hear runty cattle called 'swamp angels' or 'saddle-pocket dogies.' "

swamper
A cook's aide; a handyman; a cleaner in a saloon. Not a Westernism.

swear paper
An affidavit sworn before a justice of the peace. (Sandoz 1958)

sweater
A man, not a member of the outfit, who hung around sweating on a free meal. (Weseen 1934; Berrey and van den Bark 1942)

sweat house
An Indian form of sauna bath, the steam being created by dampening heated stones.

sweet-mouthed
See soft-mouthed

swell-fork
The fork of a saddle which swelled out on either side below the horn. The opposite of a *slick-fork.*

swing a wide loop
(1) To be so free with your rope that it sometimes fell on other men's cows. (Mora 1950)
(2) To live freely; high, wide, and handsome. (Dobie 1930)

swingle-tree
See *single-tree.*

swing riders
Members of a trail-crew who rode behind the point (see *pointers*) and in front of the *flank riders.* (Mora 1950). See also *trail-drives.*

swing team
Any one of the spans of animals between the wheelers and leaders in a *jerk-line* team. (Ramon Adams 1944)

switches
Thorny thickets in which cattle could hide and from which they would have to be winkled in the brush-country. Dobie 1941: "True to promise, the prairie hand had his chance, but though he was minus some of his clothes and a great deal of skin when he came back out of 'the switches,' the tie rope was still on his saddle."

switch grass
Panicum virgalum. A wiry grass of the Great Plains. Havighurst 1957:

"Matt tilted the plow and bit in. With a tearing sound the first furrow curled over. In the hollows where the wiry switch grass tangled with rank bluestem it would take three teams to open the stubborn sod."

Sydney Birds
Australians who found their way into the Californian goldfields after the discovery of gold in 1849. They supposedly contained a large criminal element and were of evil reputation. Also known as **Sydney Ducks** and **Clipped Ears** (based on the punishment of clipping criminals' ears).

tabasco
(SW). A strong liquor which took its name from the state in southeast Mexico. (Mathews 1951)

tablas del fuste
(Mex-Sp; SW). Saddle-tree bars or slats.

tackaberry buckle
Also **tackberry buckle**. A cinch-buckle that took two wraps of the *latigo* and hooked into the cinch-ring. (Ramon Adams 1944; Mora 1950)

tail
(1) To tail a cow (see *tailing*).
(2) To **roll one's tail**: to leave in a hurry. (Rossi 1975)
(3) The end of a gold miner's rocker or cradle, out of which the dirt was washed. (Buffum 1850)

tail crop
The shortening of a cow's tail by cropping, sometimes used as an additional mark of ownership beyond the brand and *ear-mark*. Fletcher 1968: "After we had branded the imprisoned cattle through the fence of the chute, we cropped their tails as an additional mark to indicate they were trail cattle."

tail down
To bring a cow down by the tail. (Berrey and van den Bark 1942). See also *tailing*.

tailers
Men riding at the *drag* of a trail-herd. (Ramon Adams 1944)

tail flume
Also **tail sluice**. A mining term meaning a flume that carried away waste material.

tailing
Obviously at different times and in different places, man had various ways in which this activity was carried out; but always the main implement was the tail of the unfortunate cow. Allen 1933: "To seize a calf by the tail after the other fellow ropes it and when it makes a jump to give a quick jerk throwing it on its side." This plainly indicates it to be a part of the branding process. Dobie 1941 augments this statement when he describes maverickers using this method to save roping a cow when they wanted to brand it. The animal was busted hard on the ground when it was tailed down and was presumably branded before it recovered. Dobie adds that a well-trained horse was required, which shows that this was done from the saddle after the Mexican fashion, which was not a game for boys. It took nerve and skill. A rider, coming up behind a cow on the animal's left, leaned from the saddle, grasped the tail in his right hand, released his right foot from the stirrup-iron, and threw his leg over the tail. Men were said to do it actually for sport at times. The horse was turned abruptly to the left and the tail released. This action busted the cow pretty thoroughly; it sometimes busted the rider pretty well too. Gard 1954 says the rider gave the cow's tail a twist around the saddlehorn—which would replace the leg-move above. He would then spur his horse and jerk the cow from the ground. Usually he could tie the cow before it recovered. Note that he says *usually*. (Mora 1950; Foster-Harris 1955)

tailings
A trail-drive's cow-stragglers. (Ramon Adams 1944)

tailing up
(1) The fastening of the lead-line of one pack-animal to the tail of the animal ahead of it on the string.
(2) The twisting of a recumbent cow's tail until the pain forced it to its feet in a cattle-car on the railroad. (Roberts 1924). Ramon Adams 1944 says that it was used mainly to get cattle from bog holes.

tailor-mades
Also **ready-mades**. Commercially made cigarettes. This term probably got in at the end of the nineteenth century. (Rossi 1975)

tail out
To depart, to leave hurriedly. (Weseen 1934; Ramon Adams 1944; Berrey and van den Bark 1942)

tail rider
A drag rider on a trail-drive; one at the rear of a driven herd of cattle. (Ramon Adams 1944; Mora 1950)

tail-wagon
See *caboose (2)*.

take it on the run
To 'light out fast, to break down timber (see *timber [1]*) out of a situation.

talache
(Mex-Sp; SW). A hand hoe. (Dobie 1930)

talking iron
A pistol or revolver. (Farmer and Henley 1890–1904; Weseen 1934; Berrey and van den Bark 1942; Ramon Adams 1944)

tall-grass country
The prairie country, as opposed to the short-grass, high-plains, and sagebrush country. (Webb 1931; Weseen 1934)

tallow
(1) The weight and fat put on a cow on good ◀ feed. (Weseen 1934)
(2) The fat boiled down from cattle for candle-making, etc. That and the hides were often the sole means of income for many Texas cowmen before the great cattle-drives of the 1860s. (Dobie 1941; Gard 1954)

tallow factory
Small factories for the production of tallow appeared in Texas well before the Civil War as some sort of outlet for the over-abundance of cattle in the state. The tallow went for candles, the hoofs for glue, the hides for leather. In the early days, the meat was mostly left to rot, but some of the establishments salted the beef down for export to Mexico and the Southern states. These places were also known as **hide and tallow factories**. (Wellman 1939)

tally
A count of stock; a record of such a count. A cattle count usually performed by two men, perhaps representing seller and buyer, on either side of a checking gate. After the count, they would check their arithmetic. The notched stick may well have been one method, but stockmen used various mnemonic systems—a handful of stones, each stone representing ten or a hundred animals; a knotted string; matches; marks on paper. In the ordinary way, when a cattleman checked his herd, the result was noted in

a **tally book.** Andy Adams 1909 gives a good description of such a count in *The Log of a Cowboy,* in which an American uses a string with ten knots and a Mexican uses ten pebbles. (North 1942)

tally branding
Counting your cattle. (Ramon Adams 1944; Berrey and van den Bark 1942). See also *tally.*

tallyman
Also **tally hand** (Ramon Adams 1944). A member of a cow-crew detailed to make a count of cows, to make the *tally.* (North 1942)

tamale
(Mex-Sp from Nahuatl; SW). A Mexican dish which consists of minced meat rolled in corn-husks and baked. Often highly seasoned with red peppers. (Mathews 1951)

tame Indian
A peaceful Indian, one who did not oppose the whiteman with force: a term that put Indians on an animal level. To continue the animal analogy, the other kind were known as **wild Indians.** Did they call their opponents "wild whitemen," I wonder?

tangle-leg
The lethal rough whiskey of the Old West. Also **Taos lightning** (Mathews 1951), **forty rod** (see *forty rod lightning*), **tarantula juice,** and so forth. (Emrich 1951; de Quille 1876; Dobie 1930).

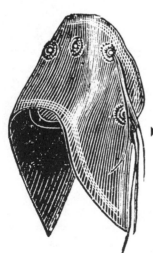

tank
A pond or reservoir for the storage of water; usually a dug-out catch basin. It could, however, refer also to a natural formation or to a metal tank, usually raised on four legs, (Wentworth 1944)

▶ **tapaderos**
(Sp). Also **taps** (Mora 1950), **tapaderas.** A covering on the forepart of the stirrup to protect the foot from brush and other obstacles. A very necessary piece of equipment in brush-country. In Spanish, literally, a "thing that covers," which is precisely what it was—a cover for the foot. But it was also more than that, for it prevented the foot from being put fully through the stirrup-iron. Should that happen, and a man fell from his horse, he could be dragged. In what might be called pre-gringo days, the Mexi-

cans and Californios, putting only their toes in their stirrup-irons, used a shallow tap, which lay flat against the broad stirrup-iron. (Mora 1950; Ramon Adams 1944; Berrey and van den Bark 1942)

tapajos
(Sp *tapar:* to cover, *ojos:* eyes; SW). Also correctly **tapa ojos.** A blind for horses and mules. Used on both saddle- and pack-animals. Pack-animals, particularly mules, wore them high on the forehead, ready to be pulled down over the eyes so that they could not see while being loaded or unloaded. Tapajos were also used in horse-breaking to blind a difficult animal while being mounted. (Ruxton 1847; Ramon Adams 1944 and Mora 1950 spell it **tapaojos**)

tapalo
(Mex-Sp *tápalo;* SW). The shawl of the Mexican women. (Harby 1890)

tar bucket
An essential part of a freight or emigrant's wagon: the container that hung from the rear axle and held axle lubricant—tar, or resin mixed with tallow. If this supply was exhausted, which it invariably was, it was replaced by animal fat or mineral oil available along the way. (Stewart 1964)

tarp
An early abbreviation for *tarpaulin.* The later abbreviation was **paulin.** Used as a windbreak or shelter on the back of the chuck wagon by the trail and round-up cook. Sixteen to eighteen feet of the material was used by the latter-day cowboy to contain his bedding in a bed-roll and as an under-and-over for his bed. (Ramon Adams 1944)

tarpoleon
A variant of *tarpaulin,* which I find wholly delightful. (Berrey and van den Bark 1942). See also *tarp.*

tasajero
(Mex-Sp from *tasajo:* jerked beef; SW). A building in which beef was smoked and dried. (Mathews 1951)

tasajillo
(Mex-Sp; SW). Also **tassajillo.** A variety of cactus of the genus *Opuntia.* (Mathews 1951)

tasajo, tassajo
See *jerky.*

tata
(Mex-Sp; SW). A title of respect applied by Indians to certain whitemen,

such as missionaries or Indian agents. It was possibly applied also to Indians, but I have not found it used thus. (Mathews 1951)

taxel
See *badger.*

techy
A variant of touchy; sensitive, prickly. It could be applied to man or beast.

tecolote
(Mex-Sp from Nahuatl; SW). *Speotyto cuniculania hypogaea.* The small ground or *burrowing owl.*

teepee
The older accepted spelling of **tepee, tipi, tipee,** etc. The early fiction and travel writer's word for the Indian hide lodge. From the Siouan language.

teeth-dullers
See *Lincoln shingles.*

tejano
(Mex-Sp). A Texan. Although writers in the second half of the twentieth century seem to use this term for a Texan of Mexican descent, in the second half of the nineteenth century it seems to have been applied generally to Texans of Anglo-Saxon descent. The others were simply Mexicans. (Owen White 1945)

temescal
(Mex-Sp from Nahuatl; SW). A *sweat house* or sweat bath, built usually of adobe. (Mathews 1951)

tenderfoot
A newcomer from the East; a greenhorn, a pilgrim. Originally, the term probably applied only to Eastern cattle, the feet of which were tender, unaccustomed to walk long distances to water as were the Longhorns. The word was stretched to cover male newcomers of the human species. Farmer and Henley 1890–1904 give some delightful quotes from nineteenth-century literature. (Wentworth 1944)

ten-gallon hat
(Sp *galón:* braid). Also **ten-gallon.** A Western hat, high-crowned and wide-brimmed, typically a *Stetson;* named not so much for its capacity but from its braid decoration. (Wentworth 1944)

tepary
Also **tepary bean.** A bean that was cultivated in arid country.

tequila
(Mex-Sp; SW). An alcoholic drink produced from the *maguey*. (Dobie 1930)

teshuino
See *tiswin*.

teton
A hill. Dunn 1886, referring to the vocabulary of the Northwest as compared to that of the Southwest: "a hill is a butte . . . The name Teton (a breast) is also sometimes given to hills, and the probability is that the Teton tribes had their name from the French fur-traders."

Texan
(1) An inhabitant of the state of Texas. Also **Texas** man, **Texian**, **Texican**.
(2) Longhorn cattle, cattle of Texas origin.

Texas butter
A kind of gravy made from flour, water, and melted animal fat. (Berrey and van den Bark 1942; Ramon Adams 1944)

Texas fever
Also **Spanish fever** (Gard 1954), **Texas fever tick, Texas tick.**
(1) Splenic fever in cattle. Popular literature tells us that in the 1860s, after the Civil War, when the farmers of Kansas (besides the vagabonds, who were generally known as Jayhawkers) first stopped Texas cattle crossing the state line from Indian territory, they gave as their reason the fear of the Texas Longhorns spreading Texas fever or Texas tick among the northern domesticated cattle. On the farmers' part it was a genuine grievance, but on the Jayhawkers' part it was an excuse: often Jayhawkers stole the cattle they accused of being a menace. The origin of this fever was then unknown; later it was discovered that the ticks the Texas animals bore (*Margoropus annulatus*) were responsible. They were blood-sucking and created havoc among the cattle of the Civilized Tribes and Kansas, while the Longhorns remained more or less immune to them. In fact, the Missourians were complaining of the ravages caused among their own cattle by Texas fever as early as 1859, and 1866 saw the state pass laws to control the passage of cattle. As early as 1855 Kansas had formed bands of armed men to stop the cattle and, since the Texans were armed, matters looked ugly. In 1866 quarantine statutes were brought in forbidding the importation of Texas cattle into eastern Kansas (see *quarantine line*). For the next few years there were powerful factions for and against the laws. For an excellent account, see Robert Dykstra's *The Cattle Towns* (1971). The various and mobile quarantine lines affected the routes taken by the northing herds, pushing them ever westward. (Dobie 1941)
(2) A powerful desire to go to Texas. (Lord 1961)

Texas gate
A gate introduced after the appearance of barbed wire in the West. There were no horizontal wooden spars, but usually three strands of wire wound around widely spaced perpendicular stakes which were clear of the ground. The stake at the opening was wired to and detachable from an upright stake driven into the ground. (Ramon Adams 1944; Foster-Harris 1955)

Texas house
Also **double cabin** (National Livestock Historical Association 1904), **saddlebag house**. Wherever Texas men went in the Old West, so, it seemed, went the Texas house. A typical frontier construction, which was a natural progression: a man built a one-room cabin; when he wanted more accommodation, he built another cabin; he joined the two together with the roof, creating a *dog trot*—and he had a Texas house. Often the back of the dog trot was filled in to make an open-fronted room in which tackle could be kept.

Texas leg
Shotgun chaps—those that went all around the leg. (Foster-Harris 1955)

Texas Longhorn
See *Longhorn (1)*.

Texas milkweed
See *rattlesnake milkweed.*

Texas Rangers
If any man fails to be stirred by the legend of the West generally, he cannot fail to be moved by the never-dying story of the Texas Rangers. Even in their own day, this body of men aroused the deepest respect and admiration. They were, when they needed to be, a rough and tough crew, and they rank in history with any small troop of men who dedicated themselves to impossible tasks, bore hardship, faced overwhelming odds, and received as a reward the gratitude of the folk they protected. First formed as a loosely organized semi-military police force in 1823, while Texas was still a part of Mexico, they provided settlers a minimal protection against Indians. With regard to their Indian-fighting, modern writers have sometimes condemned them for ruthlessness, and I for one have no doubt that at times they showed it; but one should remember that these men had witnessed atrocities of an appalling nature against settlers (whatever the right and wrong of the situation) and were behaving in a manner fully understood by their adversaries. Let it be said that the Rangers were invariably outnumbered—which is not something one can say often for white forces against Indians. Sam Houston re-organized them in 1844 to the strength of over 1,500. Every man provided his

own mount, did not wear a uniform of any kind, and did not participate in formal drill. Nor were the Rangers subject to formal police discipline—which does not mean that they behaved in an undisciplined manner, for their dedication to duty was high: they were picked men, and it was considered an honor to serve in their ranks. Ranger Captain John C. Hays in 1844 astonished a large party of Comanches when he and his small outfit produced the first Paterson Colts to see action in battle. On through the 1870s, the Rangers brought what law they could to a lawless frontier and numbered many great Westerners among their ranks: Captain L. H. McNelly, who went south of the border after Mexican cow-thieves; Charles Goodnight of the Goodnight–Loving Trail fame; and many others who patrolled the vast Texas frontier from the Colorado line down through the Staked Plain and west Texas, through the brush-country and along the Mexican border against raiders of all races and colors. Later, of course, they were formed into military units and served as a part of the national army of the United States.. (Webb 1935)

Texas rig
Also *double rig,* **Texas saddle.** Basically, this was the double-rigged saddle favored by Texans—that is, a saddle with two cinches. A *stock saddle,* always with a high cantle and horn. (Mora 1950)

Texas skirt
A square saddle-skirt such as that found on a *Texas rig.* (Ramon Adams 1944). Popular east of the Rocky Mountains from Texas to Canada, including part of western Canada, while the Spanish style of rounded skirt prevailed in the coastal states. Around 1900, the two styles were combined, generally speaking, by the Miles City, Montana, saddlemakers; from that time on, the styles were mostly mixed throughout the West. (Rossi 1975)

Texas tick
See *Texas fever.*

Texas tie
The fastening of a rope to the saddlehorn as employed by the hard-and-fast ropers (see *roping*), so many of whom were Texans. (Ramon Adams 1944). The alternative was to use the loose rope and to employ the *dally.*

Texas tree
A *saddle-tree* of a kind used on a *Texas rig.*

Texas wing chaps
See *winged chaps.*

Texas yell
Much the same as the **Comanche yell** and the **Rebel yell.** A high-pitched, blood-chilling yell which some say may have been taken by the Texans from the Comanches. It was used in moments of combat—a blood-rouser for the yellers—and must have struck terror into the enemy. It had about it a note of defiance and ferocity and could also express triumph. Writers have tried to represent it on paper with such inanities as "Yaaaaheeeo" and "Yah-hoo." None of them gets anywhere near the Texas yell. Rossi 1975 agrees and adds his belief that it came from the Creek Indians and loosely combined the turkey gobbler's cry with a series of yelps. The only man he knows who gives the original is Chief "Dode" McIntosh, former principal chief of the Creeks, in his eighties and living in Tulsa. "Dode" agrees that the South's Rebel yell used in the Civil War had been picked up from the Creeks and the Texans adopted theirs from that, both undergoing changes along the way.

Texian, Texican
See *Texan.*

that
At that. Added to a sentence to create emphasis: "An' he's plumb loco at that." Both Bartlett 1877 and Farmer and Henley 1890–1904 agree that this was a Westernism.

theodore
See *fiador.*

thirty and found
The going rate of pay for the old-timey cowboy—30 dollars a month plus board.

three-quarter rig
A saddle with its cinch just forward of the center-fire position (see *center-fire rig*); the *Montana Rig;* also found in the El Paso–Albuquerque rig.

three saddles
The professional bronco buster was required to ride a horse three times before it was considered broken; thus, he saddled it three times. This was the case in the last quarter of the nineteenth century. Ramon Adams in his unique *Western Words* (1944), which is essential reading for all students of the West, is the only man, to my knowledge, who recorded this neat term.

three ways from Sunday
To analyze this phrase is beyond me, but it does not leave its meaning in doubt. Gordon Shirreffs, in *Now He Is Legend* (1965), writes: " 'Little ol' lizard,' said Ross as he mounted, 'you got us humans beat three ways from Sunday.' "

throw a buffalo in his tracks
Vestal 1939: "to 'throw a buffalo in his tracks,' which is the phrase for making a clean shot, he must be struck a few inches above the brisket. . . . " (Ruxton 1849). The heart shot described by Ruxton will sometimes drop an animal in its tracks, but the only shots that can be depended on to do this are the brain shot or a hit in the neck vertebra or spine. Hide hunters usually used a high lung shot.

throw a hitch
To make a hitch on a pack-saddle. (North 1942)

throw back
(1) To drive stray cows back onto their home graze from one's own range.
(2) The act of a horse throwing itself backward to crush its rider.
(3) To revert to ancestral type. (Ramon Adams 1944)

throw down on
To draw a gun and aim at a man; to throw down on a man. (Ramon Adams 1944)

throw off
To drive off, to move livestock. Andy Adams 1909: "The next morning by daybreak the cattle were thrown off the bed ground and started grazing before the sun could dry out what little moisture the grass had absorbed during the night."

throw out
(1) To move a herd off the trail.
(2) To cut out unwanted stock from a herd. (Ramon Adams 1944)

tie-hacks
Also **tie-whackers.** Lumberjacks, tree-fellers—because they hacked out the ties for the railroads. (Weseen 1934)

tie-man
A roper who kept his rope attached to his saddlehorn, as opposed to a *dally man,* who, after making a throw, took a turn with the *home end* of the rope around the saddlehorn. (Ramon Adams 1944)

tienda
(Sp; SW). A shop or store. (Harte 1884)

tie-strings
Also **tie-straps**. The thongs or straps on the upper flank saddle-skirts by which bed-rolls and other equipment were fastened behind the cantle. (Foster-Harris 1955)

tiger
The gambling game of *faro,* so called from the tiger painted on the faro box. Hence, the expression to **buck the tiger,** to **fight the tiger.** Not a Westernism.

tight
A tight or difficult situation; to be **in a tight**: to be forced into a corner. Not a Westernism.

tilma
(Mex-Sp from Nahuatl; SW). A loose, unshaped garment, cheaply woven and worn by the poor. (Mathews 1951). Wentworth 1944 quotes **tilpah,** a varicolored blanket or rug, and I think it is possibly the same word.

timber
(1) to **break down timber**: to get out of anywhere fast, implying panic or at least a powerful inclination to put distance between oneself and a source of danger. A phrase that I love and that is, I think, the Anglo West expressing itself at its best. (Emrich 1951). Also **bust down timber.** (Cunningham 1934)
(2) To **take to tall timber**: to run for cover. (Dobie 1930)

timberline
The line in mountainous country above which trees would not grow.

timothy
Also **timothy grass, timothy hay.** *Phleum pratense*. A fine grass that provided good hay, named for Timothy Hanson, who grew it, though he was probably not the first to do so. Not a Westernism. (Mathews 1951; Foster-Harris 1955)

tinaja
(Mex-Sp, in the same sense as [1]; SW).

(1) A large earthen water-urn. (Mathews 1951)
(2) Both a man-dug water-hole and a natural tank of water in arid country. Dobie 1930 says: "A rock water hole."

tinhorn
Any man who was cheap and flashy; a fake; a dude. A common phrase: "a **tinhorn gambler**." (Wentworth and Flexner 1960; Ramon Adams 1944)

tipee, tipi
See *teepee.*

tipsinah
The prairie turnip, part of the diet of the Northwestern Indians; also known as the Dakota turnip. (Bartlett 1877; Hodge 1907–10). See also *camas.*

tire
To frighten. (Roberts 1924)

tiswin
Also **teshuino.** A mildly intoxicating liquor of the Apache people, the brewing of which had certain ritualistic or religious significance. Safford 1916 says it was made from "sprouting maize and other grains, and also mesquite pods or cactus fruits. . . . " The same scientist makes the point that the Spaniards recorded "disgusting drunken debauchery" among the Indians long before the whiteman appeared on the scene.

to
In place of *at:* "Is the boss to home?" Strange to some modern ears; not necessarily a Westernism.

tobosa
(Mex-Sp; SW). *Hilaria matica.* A coarse grass. (Dobie 1930)

tomahawk
This Algonkian word for a hatchet spread ◀ throughout the West in the English language. It could also be used as a verb—for example, **to tomahawk** someone: to axe him. (Dobie 1930)

tongue oil
(1) Whiskey, strong drink. (North 1942)
(2) The ability to talk easily. (Ramon Adams 1944)

tongue-slitting
Also **tongue-splitting**. A cow-thief's trick; or, more properly, a trick of maverickers (see *mavericking*), who would slit a calf's tongue so that it could not suck. It would not follow its mother and thus would not be gathered at round-up by its mother's brand.

tongue-splitter
The cow-thief who practiced tongue-splitting or *tongue-slitting.* (Ramon Adams 1944)

toothpick
A knife. Used alone and in conjunction with other words, as in the term *Arkansas toothpick.*

top-hand
A full-skilled cowhand. Also, later, **top-waddies, top-waddy**. (Berrey and van den Bark 1942). Ramon Adams 1944 points out that the cowboy adds the word *top* to a number of others to denote superiority.

top-horse
The best horse in a cowboy's string or mount; the best horse in a remuda. (Berrey and van den Bark 1942)

top-screw
A strawboss, a foreman. A later development. (Ramon Adams 1944; Berrey and van den Bark 1942)

top-waddie
Also **top-waddy**. A *top-hand;* or, as Wentworth 1944 notes it, a ranch-foreman.

tornillo
(Mex-Sp; SW). *Prosopis pubescens.* The screw-pod mesquite; and, by extension, the bean of this, which was good *bait* for horses and cattle. (Gregg 1844)

toro
(Sp). A word from the Southwest which became used for a bull on the range, though not too frequently. (Ramon Adams 1944)

tortilla
(Sp). Bread made of ground corn in the shape of a flat, thin disc which could be rolled to contain any food you wished—chilied beans or meat, for example. A Mexican staple, but many Anglos in the Southwest were addicted to the diet.

tote
To carry. Probably one of the earliest Americanisms recorded, certainly in use in the seventeenth century. Most likely an African word originally, brought to America by slaves. Eventually, its meaning was extended slightly—to **tote a gun:** to wear a gun in a holster. Hence, a **gun-toter,** etc. (Mathews 1951; Rossi 1975)

town marshal
Either a lone police officer employed by the town authorities or the chief of police, with anything from one to a half-dozen deputies; his authority did not go beyond the boundaries of a town. At times called a **policeman** or **town constable.** From this official, fiction has created an archetype which is often a long way from the truth. However, though there were a number of venal marshals, some little more than bullying gun-toters, among their ranks were brave and honorable men, many of whose names are lost to us. Towns that hired their marshals for their ability with firearms and their willingness to use them, frequently found them a little more than they had bargained for. Some, such as Wild Bill Hickok, were greatly feared, and rightly so. Others, like Ed Masterson (brother to Bat), who was shot down point-blank on a Dodge City street, were far from being promiscuous gunmen. Many rose to fame in the struggle to control the Kansas cow-towns when they were shipping points for Texas cattle. One of the pleasures of the incoming Texans was to hooraw a marshal (see *hooraw [2]*), but one should not exaggerate the frequency of this pastime. (Dykstra 1971; Frantz 1969; O'Connor 1957)

trace
(1) A trail. A track beaten out by the feet of men and beasts. So we find such terms as **buffalo trace** and **wagon trace.** As the frontier moved farther West, this term became less used.
(2) One of two harness straps or leather-covered chains that attached a horse to a wagon or other vehicle.

tracks
To **make tracks:** to leave, to travel. (Dobie 1930)

trader
Usually the term was synonymous with **Indian trader.** With the missionary, he was usually in a country ahead of the soldiers. Either as whites or halfbreeds, they were often the medium of communication between the authorities and the Indians, though there was seldom much sympathy between them and the authorities. Though they were diverse kinds of men, and it is impossible to give a comprehensive account of them in a small space, many were dishonest in the extreme and worked in cahoots with venal Indian agents, playing on Indian ignorance of white values, charg-

ing extortionate amounts for trade goods, and paying low prices for Indian pelts. Some traders caused great havoc among the tribes by selling them bad strong liquor and using the stuff as a lever to facilitate trade. However, it must be said that there were traders who had a hard-headed but very real understanding of the Indians. Two such were the brothers Bent, who were men of standing and power in Anglo, Mexican, and Indian worlds.

trade rat
See *pack rat.*

trading post
The establishment of a white trader, one usually in commerce with Indians. Some of the traders engaged in this business were the best authorities on the customs and habits of the tribes concerned. In the West, from Canada to the Mexican border, these posts were, in the early days, veritable forts set up for defense; but in the Southwest they developed into open establishments which were in some sense the center of exchange and intercourse of the area. Some bore the title of fort—such as the famous Fort Laramie and Bent's Fort—and they were indeed fortified places in every sense of the word.

trail-boss
The man given charge of a trail-herd. (Gard 1954; Ramon Adams 1944)

trail-broke
Also **road-broke**. Cattle were trail-broke when they became accustomed to being driven on the trail. (Ramon Adams 1944)

trail count
The counting of cattle while they were being driven on the trail. (Ramon Adams 1944)

trail cutter
When a trail-herd was being driven through the range of other outfits, the local cattlemen might send a rep to inspect the herd for local cattle which might have been drawn into the massed strangers—which often happened. If you had to eat your own beef on a drive, that was your bad luck, or bad judgment. (Ramon Adams 1944; Berrey and van den Bark 1942)

trail-drives
Also **cattle-drives**. Although herds of cattle could be driven from any one location to another, the classic route for trail-driving was north from Texas. Before the Civil War, there had been a few drives over considerable distances, such as from southwest Texas to Shreveport, Louisiana, and into Mississippi; and also as far north as Sedalia, Missouri, and Quincy, Illinois. Possibly the first recorded long-trailing was done by Edward Piper, from

Texas to Ohio, in 1846. But the main Texas trail-driving period was after the war, from 1866 to about 1885. This took cattle to various trail-towns on the railroad that bisected Kansas, on which cows were shipped to the Eastern states. The trail-driving was pushed west, eventually to California, by a quarantine against the Texas cattle (see *quarantine line; Texas fever*) and the westward expansion of the railroad. The trails became famous: the Shawnee Trail, the Chisholm Trail, the Western Cattle Trail. Herds were taken as far north as Nebraska, Wyoming, and Montana and were pushed along the lethal stretches of the Southern Trail and up the Goodnight–Loving Trail into Colorado.

The start of such drives was usually made in the spring, so that cattle could feed on the fresh grass as they slowly went north. If the drive was to the northern country, the cattle had to meet the new grazing grounds before the hard winters set in. Spring was also early enough to avoid rivers in flood: at that time most of them were shallow and fordable; a late-started drive could encounter serious trouble at river-crossings.

In the very early days, as was to be expected, the techniques of driving vast herds of wild Longhorns were crude and sometimes wasteful. Men had to learn the hard way, by doing. Specialists continued to argue about the best way to do the thing, right up to the time when long-distance drives came to a halt. It was never agreed, for example, how best a trail-boss should handle a *stampede.* The trouble was that every trail-drive faced different difficulties provided by crews, cattle, and the elements. Some herds got through with scarcely a loss; others suffered stampedes almost every other day and also lost cattle, men, and horses to an alarming extent due to robbery.

One school of thought maintained that a herd of like cattle was the easiest to drive. A herd of steers, without cows or calves along, could maintain a rate of about 15 miles a day, which was the drover's favorite speed: though the driving could be hard at the start, and covered about 20 to 25 miles per day so that the herd could be trail-broke, when it settled down there would be no hurrying, because the cows had to be well-fleshed when they reached their destination. The cattle would be strung out in a long fore-and-aft line and could be drifted along rather than driven. The cook and his wagon would go ahead to look for a spot for noon dinner. The trail-boss would find a good bedding ground for the night. Dinner was around 11:00 in the morning so the cattle could graze through noon. Ideally, a herd was well-fed and -watered before they were settled down for the night.

A herd of 3,000 would need something like 10 to 15 drovers, one of whom would be the foreman, or trail-boss, who was appointed by the owner or owners and was usually, at least in later years, an experienced professional who had made several such drives. How he gathered his herd depended upon time and place. During the early days in Texas he or his employer would gather all the cattle on a range and road-brand them (see *branding*), taking careful note of all the brands gathered so that the owners could be reimbursed when the entire herd had been sold in Kansas. (See also *drive*.)

The cook was one of the most important men on the drive: he had to be good or the crew would be bad. The men were hired in pairs so that two-man watches could be made up. A hand's status could be seen from his position on the drive. First came the pointers at the head of the herd, then the swing, followed by the flankers. In the rear was the drag. Among some trail-crews, some men might change positions, but usually the pointers kept their posts for the entire drive. The pay of all hands was generally somewhat better than that of a cowboy on the range, and the cook received a higher wage than the ordinary drover.

In the best outfits, each hand would have a string or mount of eight to ten horses (the boss, who rode farther and harder than any other member of the crew, would have a few more). He would need every one of them and had to know each of them well. With a number of rivers to cross, each man preferred to have at least one good swimming horse and one to use for a hard run. He also had what he called his "night horse," one that was sure-footed and confident in the dark. The choosing of these horses was an important occasion: probably lots would be drawn for the first choice; after that the men could choose freely. And God help the man who helped himself to another man's horse. The horse-herd was in the charge of the wrangler or remudero (known in Texas also as the horse rustler), usually a young and comparatively inexperienced hand. He had to know every horse in his band and to which hand it belonged, and was expected to be able to rope whichever one was called for at any time of the day or night. When he slept is a matter for puzzlement.

To give some idea of the number of cattle that went up the trail into Kansas from Texas, in 1866, the first year of the big drives, something like 260,000 head went north. The total fluctuated from year to year, but in 1871, the all-time high of about 600,000 was reached. As late as 1885, 350,000 went north.

Texas abounded not only in cattle but in horses and burros. Large herds of both are well recorded. Texas cowponies were in great demand in Wyoming and Montana, and it was said that in 1884 some 100,000 were exported from Texas; throughout the range period a total of one million went to supply the needs of the cattle industry. Burros were driven in vast herds to the mines of Colorado. This note could not end without mentioning that both turkeys and **razorbacks** found themselves driven in herds over the long trails by intrepid Texans. (Gard 1954; Dobie 1929, 1941, 1952; Osgood 1929; Newton and Gambrell 1949; Andy Adams 1909). See also *drive; trail-town.*

trail-town

Equally well-named as **cattle-town** and *cow-town.* All three terms denoted a town concerned with the cattle industry. The terms cow-town and cattle-town had much the same value, although the former was rather indicative of a sleepy market town in the heart of cattle-country. Such a term became derogatory in the mouths of Easterners, suggesting that the town was a one-horse affair inhabited by unsophisticated hicks. But a cattle-town could equally be a trail-town and I shall treat it here as such. It was usually a town to which cattle were trailed and then shipped on the hoof to market— though, on occasion, the term could refer to a town on the main cattle trail which profited from trade with the transient drovers. The most famous of the early railroad trail-towns were, of course, in Kansas. They blossomed briefly like the prairie flowers they were—though maybe they didn't smell so sweet. Typical of such towns was Abilene, at the head of the Abilene Trail, an extension of the famous Chisholm Trail. It shipped cattle on the Kansas Pacific Railroad, flourishing with ups and downs but in fairly rude health from 1860 to 1872. Then there was Ellsworth, at the top end of the Ellsworth Trail, a cut-off from the same Chisholm Trail starting at Pond Creek on the Cherokee Strip. This town fattened on the cattle-trade from 1871 to 1875. Vying with these towns was Wichita, standing at the head of the Chisholm Trail proper and at the commencement of the Abilene Trail; its inhabitants filled their pockets with cow-money from 1872 to about 1877. Dodge City, probably the most famous of its kind, was already established as a buffalo town before the Longhorn stream turned in its direction to escape the quarantine of the rest of Kansas (see *quarantine line, Texas fever*). Until 1875, it was reached up the Chisholm Trail, which turned off through the Cherokee Strip, where it became the Eastern Trail; after that date, it could be reached up the Western Trail, which cut across the extreme western part of the Strip. Other towns also claimed the honor of being the queen of cattle-trade, such as Caldwell, Baxter Springs, Newton, Hays City.

The northern ranges also had their great shipping centers, which are just as much a part of the trail-driving legend. To name only two that have the true ring of the period about them: Ogallala, Nebraska, was on the map when the Texas herds first reached it in 1867; it shipped vast numbers of cattle east right into the 1890s. Nor should we forget Cheyenne, Wyoming, which was in the cattle-trade as early as 1867. (Dykstra 1971; Osgood 1929). See also *trail-drives.*

trampoose
To walk, to wander. Possibly a mixture of *tramp* and *vamoose.* Farmer and Henley 1890–1904: **trampoos, trampous.** One wonders if Trampas, the famous character in Owen Wister's 1902 *The Virginian,* was named after this word.

Trantor
A British revolver—percussion, double-action, .43-caliber, five-shot—popular in the 1860s and 1870s. One of the first guns to be supplied to the Pinkerton Detective Agency. An efficient gun, narrow-butted and without the graceful lines of the Colts and Remingtons of the same period.

trap
(1) Any contrivance other than a **snare** (a loop of hide, string, or wire in which an animal's neck or foot was caught) in or by which animals could be captured. In the West, traps ranged from simple deadfalls and pits to sophisticated mechanical devices of iron and steel. In their quest for furs and skins, the Indians employed simple but ingenious methods—the common deadfall worked when the animal stepped on a tread-bar; the rarer spear deadfall caused the animal to be stabbed to death. For beaver, Indians sometimes employed a funnel trap in which a funnel of poles, narrow at one end and broad at the other, was positioned in a break in the beaver dam. Upon investigating it, the beaver would swim to the narrow end, thrust its head through the opening that, being made of pliant poles, would close on its neck and prevent the animal from withdrawing, thus drowning it.

The steel trap with sprung jaws was probably brought to North America in the seventeenth century by English settlers. Almost all such traps consisted of jaws activated by a spring released when the animal stepped on a metal plate. In various sizes, they were used throughout the West to catch and hold a variety of animals, with the purpose either of wiping them out as vermin (for example, wolves in cattle country) or of obtaining their pelts.

The decline of the beaver and the passing of the Mountain Men did not see the total finish of fur-trapping in the West, for there was still some demand for such furs as marten and fox. See also *beaver (1).*

(2) In the later part of our period, the term was used for a small pasture for saddle-horses. (Webb 1931)

traps
Personal gear, personal effects. (Duffield 1924)

trash a trail
To lose your own trail or *sign* by taking to water or rock—or in any other way, such as by wiping it out. To mislead your pursuers by your sign. (Bartlett 1877)

travail
Probably the original of *travois* but now fallen out of use in literature.

travois
Also **travee.** Both were variants of **travail,** which form became rare and gave way primarily to its variant **travois.** A wheel-less Indian draft vehicle of the simplest form, consisting of two poles criss-crossed over the withers of a draft animal, mule or horse, making a V-shape going away and widening from the hind legs of the animal. Across this V were supporting strips of hide or a full *'possum-belly,* on which were laid the folded tents or whatever else needed to be carried. The women's saddles had a small fork under the horn to which the crossed poles were tied. (Rossi 1975). Before the coming of the horse, dogs were employed for this service, which restricted the amount of camp goods that could be moved and, in fact, kept the sizes of the tents small. With the advent of the horse, teepees increased in size and children could even ride on the travois. In time of war, the travois could also be used for the transportation of wounded.

treaty
This term was used to cover not only an agreement made between Indian tribes and the government but also the actual council at which the terms of agreement were made.

Treaty Indian
An Indian whose people had made a treaty with the government and were therefore considered "tame." It should be added that some of the so-called Treaty Indians carried out the same kind of depredations as the non-Treaty Indians. This may often have been because individuals did not feel themselves bound by the words of their chiefs. Indian tribes had powerful emotional and spiritual bonds, but a man was a man for all that and could

go his own way. For example, battle discipline was not imposed to stop men from running away—which they were perfectly free to do if their *medicine* was bad—but to prevent the bold ones from charging too soon.

tree
(1) **To tree** or **to be treed:** to force or be forced into an inescapable position, analogous to an animal climbing up a tree from a hunter or a man so fleeing from an animal.
(2) See *saddle-tree.*

trick
Also **tricks.** Belongings, baggage; traps. (Farmer and Henley 1890–1904)

trigueño
(Mex-Sp: brunet, swarthy, brown; SW). Applied to a brown horse. (Dobie 1930)

trim
A similar meaning to *cut (2).* Dobie 1941: "After we had been cutting and classifying steers nearly all day, we still had forty or fifty head to trim."

trinchera
(Mex-Sp; SW). A fortified or entrenched position. (Mathews 1951)

trompillo
(Mex-Sp). *Solunum eleaginfolium.* A common deadly nightshade of west Texas. (Mathews 1951)

Tucson bed
Towne 1957: "lying on your stomach and covering that with your back." (Ramon Adams 1944; Berrey and van den Bark 1942)

tulare
(Mex-Sp from Nahuatl). A place where *tule* or bulrushes grow. (Mathews 1951)

tule
(Mex-Sp from Nahuatl; SW and California). Bulrushes. Used for the thatching of Mexican jacals (see *jacal*). To **pull freight for the tules** was an expression that referred to running for cover from the law. (Buffum 1850; Dobie 1930; Ramon Adams 1944)

tumbleweed
(1) Any of a number of varieties of bush which, when dry, break off from their roots late in the year and roll before the wind.

(2) A fiddle-footed man. (Mathews 1951; Ramon Adams 1944)

turnip grass
Panicum bulbosum. Panic grass, found across the Southwest. Turnip because of its bulbous base. (Mathews 1951)

tumbleweed (1)

twine
(1) A rope. (Ramon Adams 1944; Berrey and van den Bark 1942)
(2) To rope. Dobie 1941: "He had to cross some open ground, and here two punchers 'twined' him about the same time."

twister
(1) A rather cruel implement used on an unmanageable horse. A cord encompassed the animal's lower lip and a stick was thrust through the loop for twisting, after the manner of a tourniquet. (Ramon Adams 1944; Berrey and van den Bark 1942). Also **twitch.**
(2) A horse-breaker. (Berrey and van den Bark 1942; Ramon Adams 1944; Mora 1950)
(3) A cyclone or dust-twister. (Ramon Adams 1944)
(4) A doughnut.
(5) A liar. (Weseen 1934)
(6) The tack or nail at the end of a bull-puncher's pole. Roberts 1924: "These are small tacks driven into the pole and round the end, not on the flat top, where the sharp point is. By means of these small tacks the pole catches in the hair of the steer's tail, and it can be twisted to any desired extent. This method is effectual but very cruel, for I have seen the tail twisted until it was broken and limp; but, as a general rule, as soon as the twisting begins, the steer gives a bellow and makes a gigantic effort to rise. . . . " The author was describing his work as a bull-puncher on the railroad.

twisthorn
A Texas range name for a Longhorn, given because the animal's horns took many curious shapes—ox-bow, corkscrew, etc. Often two horns on the same animal could be quite different in shape. (Dobie 1941)

twisting down
In the act of bulldogging, to force a steer down onto its side by twisting its neck. (Ramon Adams 1944)

two-gun man
A man foolish enough to wear two guns. (Ramon Adams 1944)

two whoops and a holler
Not far, short distance, within spitting range. (Weseen 1934; Ramon Adams 1944)

under-bit
A cattle *ear-mark* made by cutting a small piece from the lower part of the ear. (Ramon Adams 1944)

underbrush
(Texas). Undergrowth, brush. (Wentworth 1944)

under-hack
A cattle *ear-mark* made by a plain cut upward from the bottom of the ear. (Ramon Adams 1944)

under-halfcrop
A cattle *ear-mark*. If you wanted to make this cut, you started to crop the ear and stopped when you had cut away the under-quarter of the ear. (Ramon Adams 1944)

underhand pitch
A throw that could be made to *heel* cows from saddle or afoot. The loop was whirled mildly so that the animals in the bunch were not disturbed. When thrown, the loop stood vertically under the animal's belly so that its hind feet stepped into it. The noose was tightened and the slack taken up immediately. Such throws, not considered difficult by the experienced cowhand, showed his understanding of the animal's natural movements. These rope-throws to me are one of those things that sound improbable in print. (Ramon Adams 1944)

under-round
A cattle *ear-mark* made by a half-circle cut from the under part of the ear. (Ramon Adams 1944)

under-sharp
A cattle *ear-mark;* the shallow cutting off of the under-curve of the ear.

under-slope
A cattle *ear-mark* in which the tip under-quarter was trimmed away with a cut sloping across from the top. (Ramon Adams 1944)

under-split
A cattle *ear-mark* made by cutting the ear open with a split at right angles to the under-edge of the ear. (Ramon Adams 1944)

uneducated
Said of an unschooled horse. (Weseen 1934)

unexception
A cowboy of a particularly remarkable skill. (Weseen 1934)

unhook
To unhitch a wagon team. (Ramon Adams 1944)

us uns
See *we uns.*

vaca
(Sp; SW). A cow. (Dobie 1930; Ramon Adams 1944)

vacada
(Sp; SW). A band of cows. (Ramon Adams 1944)

vaciero
(Mex-Sp; SW). A man who had charge of a number of sheepherders in a large sheep-outfit. As the *pastores* (see **pastor**) could not leave their sheep, he brought supplies to them. (Dobie 1955)

vamose
(Mex-Sp *vamos:* let's go). Also **vamos** and **bamoose** (Weseen 1934), **vamoos, vamoose, vampoose**. To go, to clear out. A word that reached the Eastern states, where it became common slang. (Farmer and Henley 1890–1904; Mathews 1951)

vaquero
(Sp). Also **baquero, vacquero**. A Mexican or Californio cowboy. When used by Anglos, the term would in a certain sense refer to a man of Mexican origin; but to this day in some areas of southern California, south Texas, and southern Arizona, all cowboys, including Anglos, are called vaqueros. (Remington in Harby 1890; Dobie 1930; Weseen 1934; Rossi 1975)

vara
(Sp; SW). A linear measurement that varied, but usually just under three feet. Often used by Anglos as well as Mexicans.

vayeta
See *bayeta.*

vega
(Sp; SW). A large plain or valley, a stretch of open grassland. Conrad Richter in *Sea of Grass* (1937) writes: "Most of the way across the vegas I could have reached out my hand and touched the fragrant rows of bee balm starting to bloom on either side of the trail." Dobie 1930 describes it as: "A meadow, a stretch of low, flat country."

velduque, verduque
See *belduque.*

vent
(Sp *venta:* sale). To **vent a brand** was to cancel it out and apply another brand to the hide of the animal, as when cattle were road-branded for a drive (see *branding*). So we have a verb, **to vent;** and the nouns **vent** and **vent-brand.** Certainly in use in the early nineteenth century. (Ramon Adams 1944; Mora 1950). See also *counter-brand; cross-brand.*

vereda
(Mex-Sp; SW). A trail. (Dobie 1930)

vigilance committees
Known also as **vigilantes, committees of vigilance,** or **regulators,** they were composed of citizens who organized, without the official recognition of law, to eliminate elements they considered to be a danger to life and property in the absence of peace officers or effective law-enforcement. Such committees were already a native institution in the United States before the need for them arose in the West. They had been set up in the East in defense of the country against external danger and for the internal protection of society against horse-thieves and counterfeiters. In the West, they were set up against the activities of horse- and cow-thieves and killers. As the name *regulator* implies, they attempted (and often succeeded) in regulating society when it was necessary. Sometimes the ideal went sour and the organizations became the implements of power and privilege. Their characteristics were a short individual existence; usually some semblance of legality, such as a trial of sorts; and a few violent deaths—after which the badmen against whom they were aimed lit out for parts distant and unknown.

Though they came into being when bad elements made it impossible for ordinary folk to carry on a normal way of life, vigilantes sometimes acted from sheer impatience with law. Their activities then became what one could call "regulated lynchings." It is interesting to note that their leaders were, in such places as Bannock and Virginia City, Montana, the most responsible and respected members of the community. They cleared out the ruthless Sheriff Henry Plummer and his network of cut-throats after a few brisk hangings. Illegal, maybe, but it is doubtful if lawmen attempting the job according to the book could have cleaned society so thoroughly or rapidly. But there were times when vigilantism became a dirty word: The San Franciscan movement of 1856 smacked of anti-Catholicism. The Montana organization of 1884 did a goodly number of stock-thieves to death, but there were also tragic losses among possibly innocent settlers and sheepmen. (See also *Stranglers.*) Almost every Western area knew vigilantes at one time or another, post-war Texas spawning the most. Butler County, Kansas, operated a short-lived but massive movement when men became impatient with open ruffianism, and Dodge City organized in 1875. (Granville Stuart 1925; Dimsdale 1953; Gard 1949; Frantz 1969; Richard Brown 1969)

village
A colony of prairie dogs, an area pitted by their burrows—a menace to horses and cattle. (Mathews 1951)

Virginia fence
Also **snake-fence, worm-fence.** A fence built in a zigzag form to provide support for itself without upright posts. Not a Westernism. (Farmer and Henley 1890–1904). See also *pole fence.*

viznaga
(Mex-Sp; SW). A kind of cactus. (Dobie 1930)

volante
(Mex-Sp; SW). A light two-wheeled, horse- or mule-drawn passenger vehicle. (Mathews 1951)

voucher
(SW). An Indian scalp (removed from its owner, of course). The term implies a scalp taken for a bounty payment. (Dobie 1930; Ramon Adams 1944)

vug
(1) A room-like pocket of gold ore in a mine. (Emrich 1951)
(2) A small cavity in a rock. (Weseen 1934)

wabash
(1) To talk freely, maybe even to suffer from verbal diarrhea. (Farmer and Henley 1890–1904)
(2) To defeat, to cheat. (Bartlett 1877)

waddy
Also **cow-waddy** (Wentworth 1944), **waddie.** Originally thought to be a temporary hand taken on at round-up, to **wad out** the normal outfit. Several authorities state that the term was originally applied to a cow-thief, but later was used to cover all cowhands. It has been suggested that it originated from chewing a wad of tobacco; generally, however, it is accepted as being of unknown origin. (McCarthy 1936; Berrey and van den Bark 1942; Ramon Adams 1944)

wagh
Indian and Mountain Man expression of emphasis, anger, or surprise. (Ruxton 1849)

wagon
The **mess wagon** (as Charles Goodnight preferred to call it) or *chuck wagon.* (Ramon Adams 1944)

wagon-boss
(1) The man who managed a cattle round-up, usually delegated by a number of outfits taking part in the round-up. He was not necessarily one of the owners, but any man who was respected for his skill with cattle, his knowledge of local feelings, and his understanding of men. (Weseen 1934; Ramon Adams 1944; Mora 1950)
(2) The captain of a wagon-train. (Mathews 1951)

wagons

Conestoga is the name that conjures up a picture of the lines of wagons moving westward across the prairie. Early movie-makers and fiction writers made it the vehicle of the Western migration: it was not, but the legend stays with us. It was used in a somewhat modified form for the New Mexico trade down the old Santa Fe Trail during the 1830s and 1840s. Drawn by oxen and capable of carrying immense loads, it was ideal for this long and arduous trip. The Pittsburgh wagon, a similar mammoth, was also in use. Both stood high off the ground for rough-country travel, with water-tight wagon-boxes for river-crossings and tires about five inches wide to prevent bogging and sinking. As the trade expanded, the vehicles grew larger and the teams increased upward from four span of mules or oxen (eight animals). These wagons could be large because, for one thing, the traders could afford them and needed to carry heavy loads; for another, the traders had a fairly large force of disciplined men to handle them. But in the second half of the century, the commercial wagon changed. The freighters found smaller, tough wagons and used two to three of them in tandem and a team of, say, 10 to 12 yoke of oxen (20 to 40 animals). These were Murphies, Studebakers, etc. They weighed about a ton, were high-sided, and about 14 feet long and 4 feet wide. They did not have the aesthetic beauty of the Conestogas, but they were right for the job.

The westering folk had to use a smaller team and a smaller wagon for good reasons: a long team could not pull effectively on rapidly varying gradients nor maneuver on a twisting trail. If an emigrant could afford it and wanted to carry more, he was better off with two wagons. There were roughly two types in use—the medium-size wagon (the ***prairie schooner***), which was more or less a smaller version of the Conestoga, and the light wagon, which was commonly used. Both, however, were referred to as "light wagons." About ¾ ton was the recommended load. The wagon-box was about nine to ten feet long, about four feet wide, and with sides about two feet high. Sometimes there was a false floor under which supplies were stored. The canvas top, supported by almost circularly bent hickory bows, did not overhang front or rear. Although the wheels were iron-tired and there was iron reinforcement in the construction, metal was kept to the minimum for lightness. In spite of the fact that different well-seasoned woods (maple, Osage orange, poplar, hickory, oak, etc.) were used judiciously by the wagon-wrights for parts of the running gear, wagon-tongues and axles were common casualties. Wheels shrank in the dry-ness of the desert, but they could be swollen with water and tightened with wedges.

On most wagons, the front wheels were smaller than the rear. The choice of size had to be made, balancing maneuverability against the ease of pull, which was decreased by a smaller size of wheels. The Schooner had brakes, which were absent from the smaller vehicle; downhill, wheels could be chain-locked or the wagon half-anchored by a heavy log (*Mor-mon brake*). On a dangerous down-grade, a wagon could be eased down by a rope dallied around a tree (see *dally*)—if there was a tree handy. If a man couldn't tolerate the screech of dry axles any longer, he went to the bucket hanging from the rear axle containing tar and tallow, or some other lubricant, and greased the axles.

None of these vehicles was a comfortable ride. In fact, the big freight-ers were not ridden by the drivers: they were a sight too smart for that—they walked. The emigrants had driver's seats, and the less hardy (or more sensible) had simple springs to cushion the shock to their spines. The Prairie Schooner had a seat to the right side of the front of the wagon-box, from which the driver could reach the hand-brake.

The Mexicans, though still retaining the two-wheeled *carreta,* also adopted the gringo Prairie Schooner in modified form. Instead of a box with sideboards, they used upright stakes with connected rails at the top, as they did with their carts. (Vestal 1939; Stewart 1964; Foster-Harris 1955; Rossi and Hunt 1971)

wagon teams

The makeup of a wagon team depended on the weight of the wagon (or number of wagons) to be pulled, the length of journey, and the nature of the terrain. On the Santa Fe Trail, the merchants mostly preferred the draft ox or bull: these were the grass-trains (see *bull-train*). The cattle were less easy for the Indians to lift and could subsist well on the grass along the trail —and the country was suitable for their feet. Their drawback was their slowness—but they survived: they were strong, and they got you there. They pulled in spans (pairs) and, on a single wagon, there could be from four to eight of them (eight to sixteen animals). When it was found advanta-geous to use two or three wagons in tandem, up to twelve span of animals could be employed. The mule was a good bet for strong pulling in hard country, where the use of the *jerk-line* team was popular—particularly in mining country. Four to six span of mules were common—animals which were also used by many cow-outfits to pull their wagons, particularly on long hauls, such as a trail-drive. Some cattlemen, however, preferred a span of two good steers that could double as lead steers for the herd if necessary. One span of mules was usually enough for a light cattle-trail wagon. On the choice of a jerk-line team, I can do no better than quote Rossi and Hunt 1971: "In selecting a good team of mules, the largest pair . . . was picked . . . as the wheelers [see **wheeler**]. Next to the wagon tongue, these controlled the wagon's direction and provided the necessary holding-power when going down steep inclines. The smaller 'smarter' span was placed in the leading position. It was they who passed on signals received from the driver to the entire team. The 'nigh,' or left, leader usually was the best trained and the one who received directional orders via the jerkline in the hands of the driver astride the nigh wheeler." For long hauls horses were a risky investment, for they were far more subject to disease than oxen or mules. (Stewart 1964; Rossi and Hunt 1971; Gregg 1844)

wakiup
See *wickiup*.

walkaheap
See *heap-walk-man*.

walk-down
This is usually accepted as meaning a method of catching mustangs in which a relay of riders kept a band of wild horses on the move, not allowing them time to rest or graze; the rider stayed at a sufficient distance so as not to alarm the band into a stampede. The term has also been used to denote the walking down of mustangs by men on foot. (Ramon Adams 1944; Dobie 1952)

Walker
Also **Walker Colt**. When Sam Colt, the originator of the Colt revolver, was in financial trouble, Captain Samuel Walker of the Texas Rangers persuaded President Polk to order 1,000 revolvers. This allowed Colt to go

into partnership with Eli Whitney, Jr., and produce the famous Walker-Whitneyville Dragoon. This six-shot, percussion, single-action .44 gun, weighing four pounds nine ounces, was later replaced by a lighter gun which is now a valuable collector's item. Variations on this design were used by Colt until 1864, though the new streamlined design appeared in 1860. Sam Walker, John C. Hays, and other Rangers employed Walker Colts in the first fight with Indians in which revolvers were used: the Battle of Pedernales in 1844. (Webb 1931; Peterson 1963). See also *Colt (2); Dragoon*.

walking beaming
A pitching movement of a horse in which the animal continuously had first

its front and then its hind feet in the air. (Weseen 1934; Ramon Adams 1944)

wallet
(Texas). A saddle sack. Dobie 1964, writing of 1866: "I was the only boy on the cow-hunt. We had no wagon. Every man carried his grub in a wallet tied behind his saddle. A wallet is a sack with both ends sewed up and a hole in the middle to put things in, half on one side of the hole and half on the other."

wallow stone
A small stone you wallow around in your mouth when it's dry. (Rossi 1975)

wangler
See *wrangler.*

wapiti
See *elk.*

warbag
Dobie 1930: "A sack for personal belongings." (Weseen 1934; Ramon Adams 1944)

war bonnet
Also **head-dress.** With reference to most tribes, this has been presumed by present-day writers for the popular media to be a full-feathered head-dress worn by Indians from Canada to the Mexican border. For the sake of tourists, present-day Indians sensibly play the game and wear the things, even though their ancestors never saw them, except possibly on the heads of their enemies. Head-dresses of the Indians were varied, but they usually took the form of a skin cap or feathers worn in a variety of ways. Some Indians, such as the Shawnees, wore something like a turban. In reality, a number of Plains Indian tribes did sport the full head-dress of feathers, notably the Sioux and Cheyenne, also the Shoshoni of the uplands. But it would be wrong to call it a war bonnet, for it was brought out of its protective covering for all high ceremonials. Many were works of great beauty, with the feathers mainly of the eagle, dyed and decorated skillfully by the women. The use of feathers was full of subtle meaning and in some cases was of spiritual significance.

war dance
In various forms, a dance performed by Indians before going into battle —mainly, we are led to believe, to gain the support of spirits in the ap-

proaching ordeal, so that glory might be attained for the individual and the tribe.

war paint
(1) The cosmetics used by Indians and assumed by observers to be war paint; but an Indian might paint himself for other reasons than war, even for quite everyday reasons. Before battle, however, he might use a design on his face and body which was of symbolic significance to the coming fight.
(2) The mixture of soot and grease applied by range-riders to their faces to protect their eyes against snow-glare. (Weseen 1934)

war party
Either a group of Indians chosen by their chiefs to carry out an act of war or a small group of self-chosen warriors making an attack on whites or raiding an enemy village for scalps (as opposed to a horse-stealing party). By extension, any group of men, white or red, bent on aggression.

war path
A word that went direct from Fenimore Cooper into the pulp-fiction of the second half of the nineteenth century, and so into common speech. Not only were fictional Indians always on the war path, but the vernacular had it that anybody loaded for bear (see *bear [2]*) and on the *prod* was on the war path. See also *war trail*.

war trail
Much the same as *war path,* but used in a wider sense: it implied that a people were in a state of war.

war-whoop
An Indian war-cry. Like *war path,* another expression straight from the Fenimore Cooper period which found its way into later literature on the West. It is to be found as early as the beginning of the eighteenth century.

wash
The channel of a seasonal watercourse. (Weseen 1934)

washerwoman loop
A large, flat loop of a thrown lasso. (Ramon Adams 1944)

waste a loop
To miss a throw. (Ramon Adams 1944)

watering
Nobody with an interest in the Old West needs to be told of the importance

of water, or that, without water, there was nothing. The life of man and animal formed itself and was regulated by the presence and abundance of water. The ranging of mustang was shaped by the location of it; Longhorns would walk from their customary graze untold miles to get to it; cattledrivers, wherever possible, arranged the length of the day's drive according to the presence of water. Wild animals knew every available source of the life-sustaining liquid, and a lost man knew that if he found tracks of game he would eventually follow them to it. In arid country, Indians planned their long-distance raids over a pattern of water-holes, and tribes on the move marched from one watering place to another. Whitemen and redmen alike made up songs about it.

Man's domesticated and semi-wild animals reacted to water in ways that varied according to their natures. A mule had an admirable nicety about the way it drank and seldom over-indulged; horses were less sensible, and their drinking had to be controlled to prevent them from becoming loggy. The watering of driven cattle was an art learned only through experience. It was no easy task to water 500 or 1,000 head of Longhorns. They were avid to drink after a long day's walk, and it was some chore to drift them, once they had the smell of the stuff, bunch by bunch to water and then move one bunch on to make room for the next without the water being muddied and fouled. Such times always threatened trouble for the drover. Watering at river-crossings, for example, could bring about a stampede through the sudden flight of wild birds, the riffle of water in a light breeze, or the glitter of the sun on the river surface. Good watering was more important to Longhorns than good feed —well-watered herds always bedded down better and were always easier to handle. Charlie Goodnight recorded that, after driving a herd across the 90-mile desert between the Pecos and the Concho rivers non-stop night and day, the cattle had become so senseless that when they reached the river they swam right across and back before they stopped to drink. (Newton and Gambrell 1949; Dobie 1941; Andy Adams 1909)

water wally
See *batamote*.

wattle
An identification mark cut in the side of the neck or jaw of cattle so that a small strip of hide hung down like a fringe-tang. (Ramon Adams 1944; Forbis 1973)

way bill
Dobie 1941: "A trail boss for the Matadors named John Smith, driving a herd from their Texas ranch to Montana in 1891, was required to keep a 'way bill' or journal."

weaner
▶ (1) A newly weaned calf. (Osgood 1929; Weseen 1934; Ramon Adams 1944)
(2) A human child. (Weseen 1934; Ramon Adams 1944)

wear the blanket
See *blanket Indians.*

wear the bustle wrong
Dry cowland humor at its best in this term for a lady's pregnancy. (Weseen 1934)

well
This simple English word, prefix to many a Western sentence, appears in Western literature in a number of forms, among which we find **waal, wa-al,** and **whawl.**

well heeled
(1) In possession of plenty of money.
(2) Well-armed. (Weseen 1934). See also *heeled.*

wet diggings
An area of land that was dug for gold and that lay adjacent to water, in which the dirt was washed for the ore (contrary to *dry diggings*). (Buffum 1850)

wet stock
Cattle and horses brought into the United States illegally across the Rio Grande from Mexico. (Dobie 1930; Berrey and van den Bark 1942; Ramon Adams 1944)

wet stuff
Cows in milk. (Weseen 1934; Berrey and van den Bark 1942). Compare *dry stuff.*

we uns
Also **we'ns, us uns,** etc., meaning "us ones" and standing for *we* and *us.* It reached Texas from the old Eastern dialects.

whale line
A rope, a lariat. (Berrey and van den Bark 1942; Ramon Adams 1944; Rossi 1975)

whang
Also **whang-leather.** Words much beloved of the Western fiction writers

of the 1950s and 1960s, used in such phrases as **tough as whang-leather.**
Ramon Adams 1944 states that **whang strings** were strings attached to a
saddle for tying on things. A whang originally was a short string of any
kind so long as it was made of hide. The strings which made up the fringe
of a hunting shirt were also whangs. The Shorter Oxford English Dictionary 1973 records *whang* in the early sixteenth century.

wheat grass
See *alkali grass; grasses.*

wheeler
The animal in a wagon team nearest a wagon wheel. When the team was
hitched in spans, you had a nigh-wheeler (on the left) and an off-wheeler
(on the right). (See also *near-horse; off-horse.*)

whey-belly
A pot-bellied and therefore inferior horse. (Weseen 1934; Berrey and van
den Bark 1942; Ramon Adams 1944)

whiteman
(1) An Anglo, a Caucasian. Almost anybody who spoke English and who
was not an Italian, Mexican, Negro, Indian, or a few hundred other colors
and shades.
(2) A decent, straight man—which speaks clearly for the racial and social
differences developed in the second half of the nineteenth century.

white sage
Also **white sagebrush.** Any of a variety of sages with a whitish leaf; such
as *Artemisia mexicana.* Mathews 1951 records it in 1870.

whoop it up
To have a good time; to raise a little cheerful
hell, usually when in drink.

wickiup
(1) Also **wakiup.** In fiction, usually an Apache
dwelling place, a crudely constructed hut. The
word originated with the Sauk and Fox Indians.
(2) A quickly constructed shelter, probably of
brush or saplings or both. In the literature of
the nineteenth century, it was used in various forms to describe a variety
of Indian shelters in a variety of areas, including Colorado and California.
(Mathews 1951; Berrey and van den Bark 1942 say "improvised

shelter" and plainly refer to cowboys; Ramon Adams 1944 adds that cowmen used it in reference to their own homes)

wide loop
See *big loop.*

wide place in the road
A small town or settlement.

wigwam
The settlers' term to describe the *teepee;* actually *wigwam* comes from the Abnaki and Massachuset word *wikam,* meaning "dwelling" and referring to any hut with a frame of poles covered with bark, hides, or rush mats.

wild bunch
"An untamed bunch of horses, men, or women"—succinct quote from Rossi 1975.

wild cattle
In old Texas these were the **black cattle** or **Spanish cattle,** not to be confused with the ordinary run of Longhorn. (Dobie 1941)

wild hog
The peccary. A native of the United States, and quite distinct from the often near-wild *razorbacks.* The collared peccary sometimes congregated in herds of several hundred and, though usually shy creatures, could sometimes be extremely dangerous. (Mathews 1951)

wild Indians
Indians who retained their independence or who opposed the whiteman's wish to take their land. See also *tame Indian.*

wild stuff
Wild cattle. (Weseen 1934; Berrey and van den Bark 1942)

Winchester
Like the name Colt, Winchester immediately turns men's thoughts to the West. Though there were a number of repeating saddle-guns in use, none came up to the Winchester 1866 (known as *yellow belly*), developed from the Henry 1860. The only difference between them, actually, was that the latter was front-loaded. Competing with Winchester was Spencer, so Oliver Winchester bought the company out, then produced the most famous rifle of all time: the Winchester '73, commonly called the .44-40 —.44 caliber with a cartridge containing 40 grains of powder. The first really satisfactory center-fire repeating rifle. Westerners approved of the

fact that it could be chambered to take revolver shells, an asset that needs no underlining. If the '73 was good, the '86 was superlative and stayed in production till 1935, over 160,000 being manufactured. It offered a great variety of calibers, with choice of solid frame or take-down, rifle or light shot-gun butt, with carbine butt for the carbine model. Winchester gave the customers what they wanted—.38–56, .38–70, .40–65, .40–82, .45–70, .45–90, etc. The carbine model, a favorite in the West, had full magazine, solid frame, and lever action. The famous '94 did not differ greatly from the earlier models except in locking, and its carbine model is still being manufactured, which does not mean that the designers lack inventiveness but that the '94 is hard to improve on. It came in .32–40, .38–40, and .44–40. Being flat and light, the Winchester was the ideal saddle-gun.

carbine, 1873 model

wind-devil
A dust-devil, a whirlwind column. (Weseen 1934)

windy
(1) A tall tale (plural: **windies**), the highly artistic product of a lying yarn-spinner. (Andy Adams 1909)
(2) A teller of windies. Also called a **windjammer.**
(3) A cow driven out of canyons during round-up. The driving of windies was no easy task. (Weseen 1934; Berrey and van den Bark 1942; Ramon Adams 1944)

winged chaps
Also **Texas wing chaps.** Rather a latter-day production of the Western ranges that became universally popular in the 1890s. So called for the large flap or wing on the outer edge. Formerly they were buckled down the thigh to the calf, but unbuckled at the knee for greater freedom. Later they were usually loose from the knee downward. (Mora 1950; Foster-Harris 1955)

wing fence
Flared fencing at a corral gate that made it easier to drive cattle or horses into a corral. (Ramon Adams 1944; Berrey and van den Bark 1942)

winter
(1) As applied to man: to take shelter in a secure place during bad winter weather. In the mountains, men would build themselves cabins and stock up with supplies to cover the period when they were snowed in, or they retreated to the encampment of friendly Indians. Cattlemen would shelter

in the home ranch-house, prospectors might retire to a town or seek refuge near their diggings.

(2) As applied to cattle and horses: If cattle were on high range they would be kept in sheltered valleys; in later years, they were brought near supplies of hay for winter feed. Horse-herds might be allowed to run loose in bad weather and left to rustle for themselves, in which case they might feed on the bark of trees or paw through the snow to the grass beneath. Some might die, but in most winters the majority would survive to fatten on the spring grass. Only after this would the stock of the whiteman be strong enough for round-up (unless they had been kept in the home corral) or would the Indian horses be fit for hunts and raids. (Osgood 1929; Dykstra 1971)

wire
Usually barbwire or barbed wire.

wish book
The mail-order catalog, which was standard reading-matter in the bunk-house. Often it showed a cowboy a world beyond his financial reach and created a good few "if onlys." One of those marvelously simple yet expressive terms that the cowman produced naturally. (Mencken 1948; Weseen 1934; Ramon Adams 1944; Berrey and van den Bark 1942)

wo-ha
The cry of the ox-teamsters. It is said that, on hearing this, the Indians called the whiteman's oxen by the sound. (Ruxton 1849). Dobie 1941 gives the version **wohaw**. (Ramon Adams 1944)

wolf
Canis lupus, of which there were many local varieties. The term almost

always refers to the true timber wolf, never to the little wolf, which was the *coyote.* On the whole, a rather shy animal which, contrary to common belief, did not usually hunt in large packs; a family animal given to solitariness. Its bravery and savagery cannot be questioned, however, for wolves would, if necessary, hunt and kill anything on four feet—except for the puma, which was too formidable an adversary.

In times of hunger, in certain localities, they were a great menace to cattle, especially calves, and a professional *wolfer* was often called in to clear a range of them. The male could be five feet or more in length.

wolfer
A professional hunter of wolves who usually employed poison or dogs. He could be hired by a rancher to clear his range of wolves or would do so for the bounty placed on the animals. (Stegner 1963)

wolfing
The hunting of wolves giving trouble on a range. Carried out by a professional *wolfer* or by the cow-outfit itself.

wood-pussy
A skunk.

woolies
Sheep. (Ramon Adams 1944; Clark 1959). See also *angoras.*

woolsey
An inferior hat, not a Stetson. (Weseen 1934; Ramon Adams 1944)

work cattle
To round up cattle; to do any kind of task with cattle. (Weseen 1934; North 1942; Ramon Adams 1944)

working ground
The location of cattle during round-up—where the cattle were "worked": where brands were separated into their own herds and where mavericks and calves were branded. (North 1942)

worm-fence
Also **snake-fence, Virginia fence.** A zigzag rail fence. See also *pole fence.*

wrangle
To herd and drive horses. (Dobie 1930; Weseen 1934; Ramon Adams 1944)

wrangler

(Mex-Sp *caballerango,* corrupted by the Anglos first to **caverango** and thence to the present *wrangler*). Also **horse pestler** (Berrey and van den Bark 1942), **wangler** (Weseen 1934), **horse rustler, horse-wrangler, remudero, wrango.** The hand who, either on the ranch or the trail-drive, looked out for the horse-herd. The position, usually occupied by a young and inexperienced hand, was considered a junior position on the crew. The wrangler was expected to know every horse in the remuda and to which rider it belonged. (Dobie 1952; Ramon Adams 1944; Weseen 1934). Wentworth 1944 adds an interesting meaning with "a horse kept to catch others" and cites its use in 1928, in north-central Nebraska.

wrangling

Herding, guarding, or caring for a horse-herd or remuda. See also *wrangler.*

wrango

(1) A small enclosure for horses. Possibly this word derives from *wrangler* or from its original Spanish base. (Weseen 1934; Berrey and van den Bark 1942)

(2) A short form of *wrangler.* (Weseen 1934; Berrey and van den Bark 1942; Ramon Adams 1944)

▶ **wreck tub**

The tub carried on the trail-drive and round-up chuck wagon in which the cowboy cast his dirty cup, plate, and irons. (Mora 1950; Ramon Adams 1944)

wring tail

A horse that twitched its tail (usually as it ran), from exhaustion, pain, or discomfort. (Berrey and van den Bark 1942; Ramon Adams 1944; Rossi 1975)

xerga
See *gerga*.

XIT
One of the most famous cattle brands of all time, belonging to one of the
greatest of the Texas Panhandle ranches. Founded by the Capitol Syndi-
cate and owned by the brothers John and Charles Farwell, it covered all
or part of ten counties—hence the brand which stands for Ten In Texas.
The great Ab Blocker first burned the brand on a cow's hide. The XIT bred
cattle in Texas and fattened them in Wyoming and Montana. An XIT herd,
bossed by John McCanles in 1896, was said to have been the last up the
Western Trail.

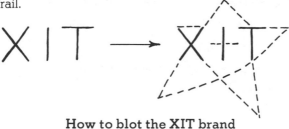

How to blot the XIT brand

yack
A stupid person. (Weseen 1934; Ramon Adams 1944)

yakima
An Indian pony. (McCarthy 1936; Ramon Adams 1944). Named for an Indian tribe of Oregon (later Washington state), in the same way as *cayuse.*

yamp
To steal. (Allen 1933; Weseen 1934; Ramon Adams 1944)

yannigan bag
A bag for personal gear. (Ramon Adams 1944; Berrey and van den Bark 1942)

yarb-woman
(from Sp *hierba:* herb; SW). A woman skilled in the use of medicinal herbs. (Dobie 1965)

yeah
Also **yeh.** This is not a Westernism, but I include it for those parents who forbid their children to use it, supposing it to be a corruption of *yes,* which it is not. It is merely another example of an old form becoming vulgar and forbidden simply because it is old. *Yeh* is the affirmative used in the East Anglia dialect of England. Similarly, in Scotland and Ireland, we find school-children being forbidden to use the old and beautiful *aye* for *yes.*

yearling
Exactly what it says—a creature of a year old or thereabouts. Usually

applied to cattle and horses. Under one year, it was a short-aged yearling, between one and two, it was long-aged. Not a Westernism.

Yellow Belly
(1) The *Winchester* Model 1866, a redesign of the old Henry rifle, so called because of its bright brass receiver or frame. Also **Yellow Boy.**
As **yellow belly:**
(2) (SW). A Mexican, in contemptuous terms. (Mencken 1948)
(3) A coward, though this definition was not confined to the West.

Yellow Leg
A U.S. cavalryman, for the yellow stripes down the seam of the pants.

yerba buena
(Sp: *good herb*; SW). Used in reference to a number of plants, even to grass at times. (Mathews 1951)

yeso
(Sp). Gypsum. Used inside buildings both as whitewash and plaster. (Gregg 1844).

yieldy
Said of land yielding good crops. In cattle-country, it referred to a hayfield. (Weseen 1934; Berrey and van den Bark 1942)

you-all
Used by the Southerners who went into the West. Similarly, we find **you-uns.** The exact replica of you-all as a collective second person is not to be found, I think, in the old English dialects, but in East Anglia one still occasionally hears **you-together.**

younker
A youngster, child. (Berrey and van den Bark 1942)

yourn
The old form of the possessive *yours,* which is still to be found in Eastern dialect. From *your own* or *your one.*

yucca
A general term for a variety of cacti of the genus *Liliaceae.* The yucca palm is the Joshua

tree (*Yucca brevifolia*), sometimes simply called the Joshua. Yucca cactus fiber was originally used by the Hopi Indians for weaving. Later its place was taken by cotton, followed by wool. (Waters 1950)

yucca country
The Southwest. (Weseen 1934; Ramon Adams 1944)

zaguan
(Mex-Sp *zaguán;* SW). An entrance or entrance hall to a building. (Mathews 1951)

zanjero
(Mex-Sp; SW). A digger of ditches, a ditcher. (Bartlett 1877). **Zanja** was an irrigation ditch, or *acequia.*

zapato
(Mex-Sp; SW). An article of footwear. (Weseen 1934)

zebra dun
A *dun* horse with stripes that reminded one of those of a zebra. (Dobie 1952; Ramon Adams 1944). See also *bayo.*

zebu cattle
See *Brahma cattle.*

zequia
A variant of *acequia.*

zerga
See *gerga.*

zorrillas
Line-backed Longhorns, which were often sprockled with white spots on the flanks and belly. (Dobie 1941; Ramon Adams 1944). See also *black cattle.*

Bibliography

Works Cited

Abbott, Edward C., and Smith, Helena Huntington 1939
We Pointed Them North: Recollections of a Cowpuncher. New York and Toronto: Farrar and Rinehart. Norman: University of Oklahoma Press, 1966.

Adams, Andy 1909
The Log of a Cowboy: A Narrative of the Old Trail Days. London: Constable and Co. Boston and New York: Houghton Mifflin Co., 1903.

Adams, Ramon F. 1944
Western Words: A Dictionary of the Range, Cow-Camp and Trail. Norman: University of Oklahoma Press.

Adams, Ramon F. 1952
Come and Get It: The Story of the Old Cowboy Cook. Norman: University of Oklahoma Press.

Adams, Ramon F. 1957
"Cookie." In *This Is the West,* edited by Robert West Howard. New York: New American Library of World Literature, Signet Books. New York: Rand McNally, 1957.

Aldridge, Reginald 1884
Life on a Ranch. London: Longmans, Green and Co.; published as *Ranch Notes in Kansas, Colorado, the Indian Territory and Northern Texas.* Published for University Microfilms by Argonaut Press, 1966.

Allen, Jules Verne 1933
Cowboy Lore. San Antonio: Naylor Printing Co.

Amber, John T., ed. 1956
Gun Digest Treasury. Chicago: The Gun Digest Co.

Askins, Charles 1956
"Gunfighters in Texas: Past and Present." In *Gun Digest Treasury,* edited by John T. Amber.

Audubon, John Woodhouse 1906
Audubon's Western Journal: 1849–1850. Cleveland: n.p.

Ball, Eve 1970
In the Days of Victorio: Recollections of a Warm Springs Apache. Tucson: University of Arizona Press.

Barrère, Albert, and Leland, Charles G. 1897
A Dictionary of Slang, Jargon and Cant. London: George Bell and Sons. Edinburgh: The Ballantyne Press, 1889–90. Reprint of 1889 ed., 2 vols., Detroit: Gale Research Co., 1967.

Barsotti, John 1956
"Mountain Men and Mountain Rifles." In *Gun Digest Treasury,* edited by John T. Amber.

Bartlett, John Russell 1877
Dictionary of Americanisms: A Glossary of Words and Phrases Usually Regarded as Peculiar to the United States. 4th ed. Boston: Little, Brown and Co. New York: Bartlett and Welford, 1848.

Beadle, John H. 1870
Life in Utah. Philadelphia: National Publishing Co.

Beadle, John H. 1878
Western Wilds, and the Men Who Redeem Them. Philadelphia: n.p.

Beal, Merrill D. 1963
I Will Fight No More Forever: Chief Joseph and the Nez Percé War. Seattle: University of Washington Press.

Berrey, Lester V., and van den Bark, Melvin 1942
The American Thesaurus of Slang: A Complete Reference Book of Colloquial Speech. New York: Thomas Y. Crowell. London: George G. Harrap and Co., 1954.

Billington, Ray Allen 1956
The Far Western Frontier (1830–1860). New York: Harper & Row.

Bowman, Hank Wieand 1953
Antique Guns. Edited by Lucian Cary. Greenwich, Conn.: Fawcett Publications.

Bradley, Glenn D. 1913
The Story of the Pony Express. Chicago: A. C. McClurg and Co. Reprint, Detroit: Gale Research Co., 1973.

Branch, Edward Douglas 1926
The Cowboy and His Interpreters. New York and London: D. Appleton and Co. New York: Cooper Square Publishers, 1961.

Brown, Richard Maxwell 1969
"The American Vigilante Tradition." In *Violence in America: Historical and Comparative Perspectives: Staff Report to the National Commission on the Causes and Prevention of Violence.* Washington, D.C.: U.S. Government Printing Office.

Brown, Will C. 1960
Sam Bass and Company. New York: New American Library of World Literature, Signet Books.

Buffum, E. Gould   1850
An Account of Six Months in the Gold Mines. Philadelphia: Lee and Blanchard.
Published as *The Gold Rush: An Account of Six Months in the California Diggings.*
London: The Folio Society, 1959.

Castetter, Edward F., and Bell, Willis H.   1942
Pima and Papago Indian Agriculture. Albuquerque: University of New Mexico
Press.

Catlin, George   1851
Illustrations of the Manners, Customs and Condition of the North American Indians.
London: n.p. New York: Dover Publications, 1973.

Chase, Joseph Smeaton   1919
California Desert Trails. Boston: Houghton Mifflin Co. London: H. G. Bohn, 1851.
2 vols.

Chilton, Charles   1961
*The Book of the West: The Epic of America's Wild Frontier, and the Men Who
Created Its Legends.* London: Odhams Press.

Chisholm, Matt   1966
Indians. London: Odhams Press.

Chisholm, Matt   1973
McAllister Gambles. New York: Ballantine Books, Beagle Books.

Clark, Thomas D.   1959
Frontier America: The Story of the Westward Movement. New York: Charles
Scribner's Sons.

Clinton, Bruce   1967
"Buckin' Horses." In *Horse and Horseman,* edited by Peter Vischer.

Colton, Walter   1850
Three Years in California. New York: A. S. Barnes and Co.

Cooke, Gen. Philip St. George   1878
The Conquest of New Mexico and California: An Historical and Personal Narrative.
New York: G. P. Putnam's Sons.

Croy, Homer   1956
Last of the Great Outlaws: The Story of Cole Younger. New York: New American
Library of World Literature, Signet Books. New York: Duell, Sloan and Pearce,
1956.

Cunningham, Eugene   1934
Triggernometry. New York: Press of the Pioneers.

Cunningham Graham, R. B.   1900
Thirteen Stories. London: William Heinemann.

Custer, George A. 1874
My Life on the Plains: Or Personal Experiences with Indians. New York: Sheldon
& Co. Reprint, Norman: University of Oklahoma Press, 1962.

Davis, W. W. H. 1857
El Gringo: Or New Mexico and Her People. New York: Harper & Brothers. Reprint,
Santa Fe: The Rydal Press, 1938.

Dayton, William A. 1931
Important Western Browse Plants. Washington, D.C.: U.S. Government Printing
Office.

Denhardt, Robert Moorman 1949
The Horse of the Americas. Norman: University of Oklahoma Press.

de Quille, Dan [pseudonym of William Wright] 1876
History of the Big Bonanza. Hartford, Conn.: American Publishing Co. Published
as *The Big Bonanza.* New York: Alfred A. Knopf, 1947.

Dimsdale, Thomas Josiah 1953
Vigilantes of Montana. Norman: University of Oklahoma Press. Virginia City,
Mont.: Montana Post Press, D. W. Tilton and Co., 1866.

Dobie, J. Frank 1929
A Vaquero of the Brush Country. Dallas: The Southwest Press.

Dobie, J. Frank 1930
Coronado's Children: Tales of Lost Mines and Buried Treasures of the Southwest.
Dallas: The Southwest Press. Published in Great Britain as *Lost Mines of the Old
West.* London: Hammond Hammond and Co., 1960.

Dobie, J. Frank 1941
The Longhorns. Boston: Little, Brown and Co.

Dobie, J. Frank 1950
The Voice of the Coyote. London: Hammond Hammond and Co. Boston: Little,
Brown and Co., 1949.

Dobie, J. Frank 1952
The Mustangs. Boston: Little, Brown and Co.

Dobie, J. Frank 1955
Tales of Old-Time Texas. Boston: Little, Brown and Co. London: Hammond Hammond and Co., 1959.

Dobie, J. Frank 1956
Apache Gold and Yaqui Silver. London: Hammond Hammond and Co. Boston:
Little, Brown and Co., 1939.

Dobie, J. Frank 1958
"Road Runner in Fact and Folklore." *Arizona Highways,* vol. 34 (May), pp. 2–11.

Dobie, J. Frank 1964
Cow People. Boston: Little, Brown and Co.

Dobie, J. Frank 1965
Rattlesnakes. London: Hammond Hammond and Co. Boston: Little, Brown and Co.

Doddridge, Joseph 1912
Notes on the Settlement and Indian Wars. Pittsburgh: J. S. Ritenour.

Dodge, Col. Richard Irving 1877
The Plains of the Great West. New York: G. P. Putnam's Sons.

Duffield, John 1924
Driving Cattle from Texas to Iowa, 1866. Annals of Iowa (Iowa City), vol. 14, no. 4 (April).

Dunn, J. P. 1886
Massacres of the Mountains: A History of the Indian Wars of the Far West. New York: Harper & Brothers. London: S. Low, Marston, Searle and Rivington. Reprint, London: Eyre and Spottiswoode, 1963.

Dykstra, Robert R. 1971
The Cattle Towns. New York: Alfred A. Knopf.

Eaton, Frank 1953
Pistol Pete: Veteran of the Old West. London: Arco Publishers.

Ellis, G. E. 1882
The Red Man and the White Man in North America. Boston: Little, Brown and Co.

Emrich, Duncan 1951
It's an Old Wild West Custom. Kingswood, Surrey, England: The World's Work (1913) Ltd. New York: Vanguard Press, 1949.

Evans, Max 1959
Long John Dunn of Taos. Los Angeles: Westernlore Press.

Farmer, John S. 1889
Americanisms: Old and New. London: privately printed by T. Poulter and Sons. Reprint, Detroit: Gale Research Co., 1971.

Farmer, John S., and Henley, W. E. 1890–1904
Slang and Its Analogues Past and Present. 9 vols. London: privately printed by Harrison & Sons. Reprint, Millwood, New York: Kraus Reprint Co., 1965.

Farrow, Edward S. 1881
Mountain Scouting. New York: printed by the author.

Fergusson, Erna 1940
Our Southwest. New York: Alfred A. Knopf.

Finerty, John F. 1961
War-Path and Bivouac: Or the Conquest of the Sioux. Norman: University of Oklahoma Press. Chicago: Donohue Bros., 1890.

Fitter, Richard, and Leigh-Pemberton, John 1968
Vanishing Wild Animals of the World. London: Midland Bank, in association with Kaye and Ward. New York: Franklin Watts, 1969.

Fletcher, Baylis John 1968
Up the Trail in '79. Norman: University of Oklahoma Press.

Forbis, William H. 1973
The Cowboys. New York: Time-Life Books.

Foster-Harris, William 1955
The Look of the Old West. New York: Crown Publishers, Bonanza Books. New York: Viking Press, 1955.

Francis, Francis 1887
Saddle and Mocassin. London: n.p.

Frantz, Joe B. 1969
"The Frontier Tradition: An Invitation to Violence." In *Violence in America: Historical and Comparative Perspectives: Staff Report to the National Commission on the Causes and Prevention of Violence.* Washington, D.C.: U.S. Government Printing Office.

Frantz, Joe B., and Choate, Julian E. 1955
The American Cowboy: The Myth and the Reality. Norman: University of Oklahoma Press.

Gard, Wayne 1949
Frontier Justice. Norman: University of Oklahoma Press.

Gard, Wayne 1954
The Chisholm Trail. Norman: University of Oklahoma Press.

Glover Jack 1972
The "Bobbed Wire" III Bible: An Illustrated Guide to Identification and Classification of Barbed Wire. Centennial Edition. Sunset, Texas: Cow Puddle Press (Sunset Trading Post, Sunset, Texas 76270).

Glyn, Richard 1971
The World's Finest Horses and Ponies. London: George G. Harrap and Co. Garden City, N.Y.: Doubleday and Co.

Gregg, Josiah 1844
Commerce of the Prairies. 2 vols. New York: Henry G. Langley. Norman: University of Oklahoma Press, 1954.

Gressley, Gene M. 1966
Bankers and Cattlemen. New York: Alfred A. Knopf.

Grzimek, Bernard, ed. 1974
Animal Encyclopedia. London and New York: Van Nostrand Reinhold Co.

Haley, J. Evetts 1936
Charles Goodnight: Cowman and Plainsman. Boston: Houghton Mifflin Co. Reprint, Norman: University of Oklahoma Press, 1970.

Hamlin, William Lee 1959
The True Story of Billy the Kid. Caldwell, Idaho: The Caxton Printers.

Harby, Lee C. 1890
"Texas Types and Contrasts." *Harper's Monthly Magazine,* vol. 81, no. 482 (June–November), pp. 229–246.

Harger, Charles N. 1892
"Cattle Trails of the Prairies." *Scribner's,* vol. 11 (June), pp. 732–742.

Harper's Monthly Magazine 1856
No. 594 (October).

Harper's Monthly Magazine 1875
Vol. 51, no. 305 (November), pp. 828–35.

Harper's Monthly Magazine 1888
No. 235 (July).

Harte, Bret 1884
On the Frontier. Boston: Houghton Mifflin Co. London: Longmans, Green and Co.

Havighurst, Walter 1957
"The Sodbusters." In *This Is the West,* edited by Robert West Howard.

Hawgood, John A. 1967
The American West. London: Eyre and Spottiswoode. Published simultaneously as *America's Western Frontiers.* New York: Alfred A. Knopf.

Haycox, Ernest 1942
No Law and Order. London: Hodder and Stoughton.

Hodge, F. W. 1907–10
Handbook of the American Indians North of Mexico. Washington, D.C.: U.S. Government Printing Office, American Bureau of Ethnology, Bulletin 30.

Hoig, Stan 1960
The Humor of the American Cowboy. New York: New American Library of World Literature, Signet Books. Caldwell, Idaho: The Caxton Printers, 1958.

Horan, James D., and Sann, Paul 1954
Pictorial History of the Wild West. London: Spring Books. New York: Crown Publishers.

Horgan, Paul 1954
Great River: The Rio Grande in North American History. New York: Rinehart and Co.

Hornady, William T. 1908
Campfires on Desert and Lava. New York: n.p.

Hough, Emerson 1897
The Story of the Cowboy. New York: Appleton.

Howard, Robert West, ed. 1957
This Is the West. New York: New American Library of World Literature, Signet Books. New York: Rand, McNally, 1957.

Howard, Robert West, and others 1960
Hoofbeats of Destiny. New York: New American Library of World Literature, Signet Books.

Inman, Henry 1897
The Old Santa Fe Trail: The Story of a Great Highway. New York: The Macmillan Co.

Jahns, Pat 1961
The Frontier World of Doc Holliday. London: Hamilton & Co. (Stafford), Panther Books. New York: Hastings House, 1957.

Jennings, William Dale 1971
The Cowboys. New York: Stein and Day.

Karr, Charles Lee, Jr., and Karr, Caroll Robbins 1960
Remington Handguns. New York: Crown Publishers, Bonanza Books. Harrisburg, Pa.: The Military Service Publishing Co., 1947.

Klose, Nelson 1964
A Concise Study Guide to the American Frontier. Lincoln: University of Nebraska Press.

La Farge, Oliver 1956
A Pictorial History of the American Indian. London: Spring Books. New York: Crown Publishers.

Lake, Stuart N. 1931
He Carried a Six-Shooter. New York: Houghton Mifflin Co.

Lamar, Howard Roberts 1966
The Far Southwest 1846–1912: A Territorial History. New Haven: Yale University Press.

Lavender, David   1969
The Penguin Book of the American West. London: Penguin Books. Originally published in somewhat different form as *The American Heritage History of the Great West.* New York: McGraw-Hill Book Co., 1965.

Lord, Walter   1961
A Time to Stand. New York: Harper & Row.

MacEwan, Grant   1969
Tatanga Mani. Edmonton, Alta.: M. G. Hurtig, Booksellers and Publishers.

MacLeod, William Christie   1928
The American Indian Frontier. New York: Alfred A. Knopf. London: Kegan Paul, Trench, Trubner and Co.

MacLeod, William Christie   1937–38
"Police and Punishment among the Native Americans of the Plains." *Journal of Criminal Law and Criminology,* vol. 28, pp. 181–201.

Majors, Alexander   1893
Seventy Years on the Frontier. Chicago: Rand, McNally.

Manly, William L.   1927
Death Valley in '49. Edited by Milo Milton Quaife. Chicago: The Lakeside Press. San Jose, Calif.: Pacific Tree and Vine Co., 1894.

Marcy, Randolph R.   1853
Exploration of the Red River of Louisiana in the Year 1852. Washington, D.C.: Engineer Bureau (R. Armstrong).

Mathews, Mitford M., ed.   1951
A Dictionary of Americanisms on Historical Principles. Chicago: University of Chicago Press.

McCarthy, Don, ed.   1936
The Language of the Mosshorn. Billings, Mont.: The Gazette Printing Co.

McCoy, Joseph G.   1874
Historic Sketches of the Cattle Trade of the West and Southwest. Kansas City, Mo.: Ramsey, Millett and Hudson.

McHugh, Tom   1972
The Time of the Buffalo. New York: Alfred A. Knopf.

McMechen, Edgar C.   1967
"Wild Horses of the Sandwashes." In *Horse and Horseman,* edited by Peter Vischer.

McNickle, D'Arcy   1962
The Indian Tribes of the United States: Ethnic and Cultural Survival. London and New York: Oxford University Press.

Mencken, H. L. 1948
The American Language III: Supplement II. New York: Alfred A. Knopf.

Moor, Edward 1823
Suffolk Words and Phrases. Woodbridge, England: J. Loder for R. Hunter. Reprinted, Newton Abbott, England: David and Charles (Publishers), 1970.

Mora, Jo 1950
Trail Dust and Saddle Leather. Charles Scribner's Sons.

Myers, John Myers 1957
Dead Warrior. London: Hutchinson and Co.; Arrow Books.

National Livestock Historical Association 1904
Prose and Poetry of the Live Stock Industry of the United States. Kansas City: Antiquarian Press.

Newton, Lewis W., and Gambrell, Herbert P. 1949
Texas Yesterday and Today. Dallas: Turner Co.

North, Escott 1942
The Saga of the Cowboy. London: Jarrolds Publishers.

Ober, Frederick A. 1885
Travels in Mexico and Life Among the Mexicans. Boston: Estes and Lauriat.

O'Connor, Richard 1957
Bat Masterson. London: Alvin Redman. Garden City, N.Y.: Doubleday.

Olmsted, Frederick Law 1857
A Journey Through Texas. n.p. Reprint of an 1859 edition, with subtitle *Or a Saddle Trip on the Southwestern Frontier,* New York: Burt Franklin, 1969.

O'Rourke, Frank 1958
The Last Ride. New York: William Morrow and Co.

Osgood, Ernest Staples 1929
The Day of the Cattleman. Minneapolis: University of Minnesota Press.

Parkman, Francis 1872
The Oregon Trail. 4th rev. ed. Boston: Little, Brown and Co. Originally published in 1849 as *The California and Oregon Trail.*

Peterson, Harold L. 1963
The Book of the Gun. London: Hamlyn Publishing Group.

Phares, Ross 1954
Texas Tradition. New York: Henry Holt and Co.

Prebble, John 1959
The Buffalo Soldiers. New York: Harcourt, Brace & World.

Richter, Conrad 1937
Sea of Grass. New York: Alfred A. Knopf.

Rifkin, Shepard, ed. 1967
The Savage Years. Greenwich, Conn.: Fawcett Publications.

Roberts, Morley 1924
The Western Avernus. New York: E. P. Dutton and Co. Westminster, England: A. Constable and Co., 1896.

Rollins, Philip A. 1922
The Cowboy: His Characteristics, His Equipment, and His Part in the Development of the West. New York: Charles Scribner's Sons.

Roosevelt, Theodore 1964
The Winning of the West. New York: Fawcett Publications, Premier Americana. New York: G. P. Putnam's Sons, 1889–96 (4 vols.).

Rossi, Paul A. 1975
Correspondence with the author.

Rossi, Paul A., and Hunt, David C. 1971
The Art of the Old West. New York: Alfred A. Knopf.

Ruede, Howard 1937
Sod-house Days. Letters from a Kansas Homesteader 1877–78. Edited by John Ise. New York: Columbia University Press.

Russell, Carl P. 1967
Firearms, Traps and Tools of the Mountain Men. New York: Alfred A. Knopf.

Russell, Charles M. 1927
Trails Plowed Under. Garden City, N.Y.: Doubleday, Page and Co.

Ruxton, George Frederick 1847
Adventures in Mexico. London: John Murray.

Ruxton, George Frederick 1849
Life in the Far West. Edinburgh: William Blackwood & Sons. New York: Harper & Brothers. Reprinted, Glorieta, N. Mex.: Rio Grande Press, 1972.

Sabin, Edwin L. 1914
Kit Carson Days (1809–1868). Chicago: A. C. McClurg and Co.

Safford, W. E. 1916
Narcotic Plants and Stimulants of the Ancient Americans. The Smithsonian Report for 1916. Reprinted in *Earth and Life,* vol. 2 of the Smithsonian Treasury of Science, edited by Webster P. True. New York: Simon and Schuster, 1960.

Sandoz, Mari 1954
The Buffalo Hunters: The Story of the Hide Men. New York: Hastings House.

Sandoz, Mari 1958
The Cattlemen. New York: Hastings House. London: Eyre and Spottiswoode, 1961.

Sawyer, Charles W. 1920
Our Rifles. Boston: Cornhill Publishing Co.

Schultz, J. W. 1935
My Life as an Indian. New York: Literary Classics. Garden City, N.Y.: Doubleday, Page and Co., 1907.

Shepherd, William 1884
Prairie Experiences in Handling Cattle and Sheep. London: Chapman and Hall. Reprint of 1885 ed., Plainview, New York: Books for Libraries, Select Bibliographies Reprint Service, n.d.

Shirreffs, Gordon D. 1965
Now He Is Legend. Greenwich, Conn.: Fawcett Publications.

Siberts, Bruce 1954
Nothing But Prairie and Sky. Edited by Walker D. Wyman. Norman: University of Oklahoma Press.

Simmons, Leo W., ed. 1942
Sun Chief: The Autobiography of a Hopi Indian. New Haven: Yale University Press. London: H. Milford, Oxford University Press.

Smith, Henry Nash 1950
Virgin Land: The American West as Symbol and Myth. Cambridge, Mass.: Harvard University Press.

Stansbury, Howard 1852
An Expedition to the Valley of the Great Salt Lake of Utah. Philadelphia: Lippincott, Grambo and Co.

Stegner, Wallace 1963
Wolf Willow. London: William Heinemann. New York: Viking Press, 1962.

Stewart, George R. 1964
The California Trail. London: Eyre and Spottiswoode. New York: McGraw-Hill Book Co., 1962.

Stuart, Granville 1925
Forty Years on the Frontier. 2 vols. Edited by Paul C. Philips. Cleveland: Arthur H. Clark Co.

Stuart, Reginald R. 1957
"The Mountain Men." In *This Is the West,* edited by Robert West Howard.

Tilden, Freeman   1964
Following the Frontier with F. Jay Haynes. Published simultaneously as *Pioneer Photographer of the Old West.* New York: Alfred A. Knopf.

Towne, Charles W.   1957
"Cowboys and Herdsmen." In *This Is the West,* edited by Robert West Howard.

Towne, Charles W., and Wentworth, Edward Norris   1955
Cattle and Men. Norman: University of Oklahoma Press.

Underhill, Ruth M.   1956
The Navahos. Norman: University of Oklahoma Press.

United States Department of Agriculture   1948
Grass: The Yearbook of Agriculture. Washington, D.C.: U. S. Government Printing Office.

Utley, Robert M.   1963
The Last Days of the Sioux Nation. New Haven: Yale University Press.

Vestal, Stanley   1939
The Old Santa Fe Trail. Boston: Houghton Mifflin Co.

Vischer, Peter, ed.   1967
Horse and Horseman. London: J. A. Allen and Co. Princeton, N.J.: Van Nostrand.

Waters, Frank   1950
Masked Gods. Albuquerque: University of New Mexico Press.

Waters, Frank   1962
The Earp Brothers of Tombstone. London: Neville Spearman. New York: Clarkson N. Potter, 1961.

Watson, Frederick   n.d.
The American Gunman. London: Withy Grove Press, Baytree Books.

Webb, Walter Prescott   1931
The Great Plains. Boston: Ginn and Co.

Webb, Walter Prescott   1935
The Texas Rangers. Boston: Houghton Mifflin Co.

Wellman, Paul I.   1939
The Trampling Herd. Philadelphia: J. B. Lippincott and Co. New York: Carrick & Evans.

Wellman, Paul I.   1956
Death in the Desert. London: W. Foulsham & Co., for the Fireside Press. New York: The Macmillan Co., 1935.

Wentworth, Harold 1944
American Dialect Dictionary. London: Constable and Co. New York: Thomas Y. Crowell.

Wentworth, Harold, and Flexner, Stuart Berg 1960
Dictionary of American Slang. London: Constable and Co. New York: Thomas Y. Crowell.

Weseen, Maurice H. 1934
A Dictionary of American Slang. London: George G. Harrap and Co. New York: Thomas Y. Crowell.

Whipple, Amiel W. 1855
Report upon the Indian Tribes. Washington, D.C.: U.S. Government Printing Office.

White, Owen P. 1945
Texas: An Informal Biography. New York: G. P. Putnam's Sons.

White, Stewart Edward 1933
Ranchero. Garden City, N.Y.: Doubleday and Co.

Willison, George F. 1952
Here They Dug the Gold. London: Eyre and Spottiswoode. New York: Brentano's, 1931.

Winslow, Kathryn 1952
Big Pan-out: The Klondike Story. London: Phoenix House.

Wister, Owen 1902
The Virginian. New York: Macmillan.

Works Consulted

Adams, James Truslow, ed. 1943
Atlas of American History. New York: Charles Scribner's Sons.

Arnold, Oren 1957
"The Honkeytonkers." In *This Is the West,* edited by Robert West Howard. New York: New American Library of World Literature, Signet Books. New York: Rand, McNally, 1957.

Arnold, Oren, and Hale, John P. 1940
Hot Irons: Heraldry of the Range. New York: The Macmillan Co.

Athearn, Robert G. 1953
Westward the Briton. New York: Charles Scribner's Sons.

Atherton, Lewis Eldon 1961
The Cattle Kings. Bloomington: Indiana University Press.

Bancroft, Hubert Howe 1889
History of Arizona and New Mexico 1530–1888. Vol. 12 of *History of the Pacific States of North America 1530–1888.* San Francisco: The History Co. Reprint, facsimile ed., Albuquerque: Horn and Wallace, 1962.

Beckwourth, James P. 1856
Life and Adventures of James P. Beckwourth. Edited by T. D. Bonner. New York: Harper & Brothers. New York: Alfred A. Knopf, 1931.

Berton, Pierre 1960
The Klondike Fever: The Life and Death of the Last Great Gold Rush. London: W. H. Allen. & Co. London: Hamilton & Co. (Stafford), Panther Books, 1962. New York: Alfred A. Knopf, 1958.

Bonser, K. J. 1972
The Drovers. Newton Abbot, England: The Country Book Club.

Botkin, B. A., ed. 1944
A Treasury of American Folklore: Stories, Ballads, and Traditions of the People. New York: Crown Publishers.

Brandon, William   1961
The American Heritage Book of Indians. Edited by Alvin M. Josephy, Jr. New York: Simon and Schuster.

Brown, Dee   1973
The Gentle Tamers: Women of the Old Wild West. London: Barrie and Jenkins. New York: G. P. Putnam's Sons, 1958.

Brown, Joseph Epes, ed.   1953
The Sacred Pipe: Black Elk's Account of the Seven Rites of the Oglala Sioux. Norman: University of Oklahoma Press.

Bruner, Helen, and Francis, Francis   1912
A Short Word List from Wyoming. University, Alabama: University of Alabama Press, American Dialect Society, Dialect Notes.

Bryson, Artemisia B.   1934
Homely Words in Texas. New York: Columbia University Press, American Speech.

Buckner, Mary Dale   1933
Ranch Dictionary of the Texas Panhandle. New York: Columbia University Press, American Speech.

Burns, Walter Noble   1938
The Saga of Billy the Kid. Toronto: S. J. Reginald Saunders and Co. Garden City, N.Y.: Doubleday, Page and Co., 1926.

Clark, Badger   1957
"Preachers and Teachers." In *This Is the West,* edited by Robert West Howard. New York: New American Library of World Literature, Signet Books. New York: Rand, McNally, 1957.

Collier, John   1947
The Indians of the Americas. New York: New American Library of World Literature, Mentor Books. New York: W. W. Norton, 1947.

Croft-Cooke, Rupert, and Meadmore, W. S.   1952
Buffalo Bill: The Legend, the Man of Action, the Showman. London: Sidgwick and Jackson.

Culley, John H.   1940
Cattle, Horses and Men of the Western Range. Los Angeles: The Ward Ritchie Press.

Curtin, Leonora S. M.   1947
Healing Herbs of the Upper Rio Grande. Santa Fe: Laboratory of Anthropology.

Dale, Edward E.   1930
The Range Cattle Industry. Norman: University of Oklahoma Press.

Davidson, L. J. 1942
Westernisms. New York: Columbia University Press, American Speech.

Deloria, Vine, Jr., ed. 1972
Of Utmost Good Faith. New York: Bantam Books.

Deloria, Vine, Jr. 1973
"The New Activism." *Dialogue,* vol. 6, no. 2. Washington, D.C.: U.S. Information Agency.

Dobie, J. Frank 1952
The Ben Lilly Legend. London: Hammond Hammond and Co. Boston: Little, Brown and Co., 1950.

Drago, Harry Sinclair 1965
Great American Cattle Trails. New York: Dodd, Mead and Co.

Driver, Harold E. 1961
Indians of North America. Chicago: University of Chicago Press.

Dunlop, Richard 1957
"Saddlebag Docs." In *This Is the West,* edited by Robert West Howard. New York: New American Library of World Literature, Signet Books. New York: Rand, McNally, 1957.

Evans, Richard L., and Bennion, Kenneth S. 1957
"The Mormons." In *This Is the West,* edited by Robert West Howard. New York: New American Library of World Literature, Signet Books. New York: Rand, McNally, 1957.

Forrest, Earle R. 1953
Arizona's Dark and Bloody Ground. London: Andrew Melrose. Caldwell, Idaho: The Caxton Printers, 1936.

Gard, Wayne 1957
"The Lawmakers." In *This Is the West,* edited by Robert West Howard. New York: New American Library of World Literature, Signet Books. New York: Rand, McNally, 1957.

Gard, Wayne 1959
The Great Buffalo Hunt. New York: Alfred A. Knopf.

Garrett, Robert Max 1919–20
A Word List from the Northwest. University, Alabama: University of Alabama Press, American Dialect Society, Dialect Notes.

Gillmor, Frances, and Wetherill, Louisa Wade 1952
Traders to the Navajos. Albuquerque: University of New Mexico Press. Boston and New York: Houghton Mifflin Co., 1934.

Grinnell, George Bird 1956
The Fighting Cheyennes. Norman: University of Oklahoma Press. New York: Charles Scribner's Sons, 1915.

Hayden, Marie G. 1915
A Word List from Montana. University, Alabama: University of Alabama Press, American Dialect Society, Dialect Notes.

Hayes, Capt. M. H. 1896
Illustrated Horse Breaking. London: W. Thacker. London: n. p., 1889. London: Hurst and Blackett, 1924.

Horan, James D. 1957
"The Gunmen." In *This Is the West,* edited by Robert West Howard. New York: New American Library of World Literature, Signet Books. New York: Rand, McNally, 1957.

James, Will S. 1893
Cowboy Life in Texas: Or, 27 Years a Mavrick. Chicago: n.p. Republished, with subtitle *27 Years a Mavrick: Or, Life on a Texas Range,* Austin: Steck-Vaughn, 1968.

Josephy, Alvin M. 1961
The Patriot Chiefs: A Chronicle of American Indian Leadership. New York: Viking Press.

Josephy, Alvin M. 1968
The Indian Heritage of America. New York: Alfred A. Knopf.

Karolevitz, Robert F. 1965
Newspapering in the Old West. New York: Crown Publishers, Bonanza Books.

Kelly, Robin A. 1955
The Sky Was Their Roof. London: Andrew Melrose.

Kluckhohn, Clyde, and Leighton, Dorothea C. 1946
The Navaho. Cambridge, Mass.: Harvard University Press.

Kneale, Albert H. 1950
Indian Agent. Caldwell, Idaho: The Caxton Printers.

Lavender, David 1959
Bent's Fort. London: Transworld Publishers, Corgi Books. Garden City, N.Y.: Doubleday, 1954.

Leighton, Alexander H., and Leighton, Dorothea C. 1944
The Navaho Door. Cambridge, Mass.: Harvard University Press.

Lockwood, Frank C. 1932
Pioneer Days in Arizona, from the Spanish Occupation to Statehood. New York: The Macmillan Co.

Longstreet, Stephen 1970
War Cries on Horseback. London: W. H. Allen & Co. Garden City, N.Y.: Doubleday.

Loomis, Noel M. 1958
The Texan–Santa Fe Pioneers. Norman: University of Oklahoma Press.

Mardle, Jonathan 1973
Broad Norfolk. Norwich, England: Wensum Books (Norwich).

Marriott, Alice 1957
"The Ladies." In *This Is the West,* edited by Robert West Howard. New York: New American Library of World Literature, Signet Books. New York: Rand, McNally, 1957.

Mathers, James 1955
From Gun to Gavel. Recorded by Marshall Houts. London: Souvenir Press. New York: Morrow, 1954.

Mathews, Mitford M., ed. 1931
The Beginnings of American English. Chicago: University of Chicago Press.

McLuhan, T. C. 1973
Touch the Earth. London: Abacus, Sphere Books. London: Garstone Press, 1972. New York: E. P. Dutton, 1971.

Mullen, Kate 1925
Westernisms. New York: Columbia University Press, American Speech.

Neider, Charles, ed. 1958
The Great West. New York: Crown Publishers, Bonanza Books. New York: Coward-McCann, 1958.

O'Connor, Richard 1960
Wild Bill Hickok. London: Alvin Redman. Garden City, N.Y.: Doubleday, 1959.

Peithmann, Irvin M. 1964
Broken Peace Pipes. Springfield, Ill.: Southern Illinois University Press.

Pyles, Thomas 1954
Words and Ways of American English. London: Andrew Melrose. New York: Random House, 1952.

Richardson, Rupert 1933
The Comanche Barrier to South Plains Settlement. Glendale, Calif.: The Arthur H. Clark Co.

Ridge, Martin, and Billington, Ray Allen, eds. 1969
America's Frontier Story: A Documentary History of Western Expansion. New York: Holt, Rinehart and Winston.

Roland, Albert 1973
"The First Americans." *Dialogue,* vol. 6, no. 2. Washington, D.C.: U.S. Information Agency.

Rollins, Hyder E. 1915
A West Texas Word List. University, Alabama: University of Alabama Press, American Dialect Society, Dialect Notes.

Russell, Don 1957
"The Scouts." In *This Is the West,* edited by Robert West Howard. New York: New American Library of World Literature, Signet Books. New York: Rand McNally, 1957.

Sandoz, Mari 1938
Old Jules. London: The Book Club. Boston: Little, Brown and Co., 1935.

Schmitt, Martin F., and Brown, Dee 1948
Fighting Indians of the West. New York: Crown Publishers, Bonanza Books. New York: Charles Scribner's Sons, 1948.

Sell, Henry Blackman, and Weybright, Victor 1959
Buffalo Bill and the Wild West. New York: New American Library of World Literature, Signet Books. New York: Oxford University Press, 1955.

Stocker, Joseph 1957
"The Prospectors." In *This Is the West,* edited by Robert West Howard. New York: New American Library of World Literature, Signet Books. New York: Rand, McNally, 1957.

Thorp, Raymond W. 1959
Crow Killer. Bloomington: Indiana University Press.

Turner, F. J. 1921
The Frontier in American History. New York: Henry Holt and Co.

Unland, Rudolph 1942
Nebraska Cowboy Talk. New York: Columbia University Press, American Speech.

Unrau, William E. 1971
The Kansa Indians: A History of the Wind People, 1673–1873. Norman: University of Oklahoma Press

Wellman, Paul I. 1934
Death on the Prairie. New York: The Macmillan Co.

Wellman, Paul I. 1959
Glory, God and Gold. London: W. Foulsham and Co. Garden City, N.Y.: Double-day, 1954.

White, Owen P. 1925
Them Was the Days. New York: Minton, Balch and Co.

Wyman, Walker D., ed. 1946
The Wild Horse of the West. Caldwell, Idaho: The Caxton Printers.

Illustration Credits

Grateful acknowledgment is made to the following for permission to reprint illustrations found on the pages indicated:

Caxton Printers, Ltd., Caldwell, Idaho for pages 128 (bottom), 270, 287, from *Triggernometry: A Gallery of Gun Fighters* by Eugene Cunningham.

E. P. Dutton & Co., Inc., for pages 105, 181 (bottom), 214, 216, 219, and 253, from *Palmer's Field Book of Mammals* by E. Laurence Palmer. Copyright © 1957 by E. Laurence Palmer.

The Thomas Gilcrease Institute of American History and Art, Tulsa, Oklahoma, for pages 164 ("Slaughtered for Hide") and 240 ("The Pipe," detail).

Jack Glover, Sunset Trading Post, Sunset, Texas, for page 22 (bottom), from *The "Bobbed Wire" III Bible* (Centennial Edition). Copyright © 1972 by Jack Glover.

Hastings House, Publishers, Inc., for pages 88 and 135, from *The Cowboy at Work*. Copyright © 1958 by Fay E. Ward.

Jefferson National Expansion Memorial, St. Louis, for the William Macy drawings on pages 290 and 341 and the Mulcahy drawing on page 348.

Alfred A. Knopf, Inc., for pages 149 and 159 (bottom), from *Firearms, Traps, and Tools of the Mountain Men* by Carl P. Russell. Copyright © 1967 by Betty W. Russell; page 307, from *The Sun Dance People: The Plains Indians, Their Past and Present* by Richard Erdoes. Copyright © 1972 by Richard Erdoes; pages 303 and 309, from *The Big Bonanza* by Dan de Quille.

The New York Historical Society for page 178 ("Pawnees capturing and breaking wild ponies" by George Catlin).

The Swallow Press, Inc., Chicago, for pages 166 (top), 188, and 235, from *Horses, Hitches, and Rocky Trails* by Joe Back. Copyright © 1959 by Joe Back.

University of California Press for page 360, from *Guns on the Early Frontier: A History of Firearms From Colonial Times Through the Years of the Western Fur Trade* by Carl P. Russell. Copyright © 1957 by The Regents of the University of California.

The illustrations on the following pages are by Virginia Tan: 110 (bottom), 123, 124, 181 (top), 247, 365, and 366.

The illustrations on the following pages are by Peter Watts: 9, 45, 49 (brands at top), 79, 125, 184, 192, 200, 232, 251 (top), and 375.

A Note About the Author

To readers in a dozen countries including the United States, Peter Watts is better known as Matt Chisholm (the McAllister and Storm series) or Cy James (the Spur series), pseudonyms under which he has authored over one hundred Westerns. He has also written a number of novels and numerous novelettes and short stories. Born in 1919 in London—where he still lives, with his wife and two sons—he has been a government servant since 1946.

A Note on the Type

The text of this book was set, via computer-driven cathode ray tube, in various weights of Stymie, originally a linotype face designed by M. F. Benton for American Type Founders in 1931. Its even weight and round, open letters make it a particularly readable face.
The type faces used on the title page and for the display letters are examples of American wood types of the period 1850–1900.

Composed by CompuComp Corporation, Hoboken, New Jersey.
Printed and bound by The Haddon Craftsmen, Scranton, Pennsylvania.

Typography and binding design by Virginia Tan